The Sunshine Economy

UNIVERSITY PRESS OF FLORIDA

Florida A&M University, Tallahassee
Florida Atlantic University, Boca Raton
Florida Gulf Coast University, Ft. Myers
Florida International University, Miami
Florida State University, Tallahassee
New College of Florida, Sarasota
University of Central Florida, Orlando
University of Florida, Gainesville
University of North Florida, Jacksonville
University of South Florida, Tampa
University of West Florida, Pensacola

The Sunshine Economy

An Economic History of Florida since the Civil War

William B. Stronge

University Press of Florida

Gainesville · Tallahassee · Tampa · Boca Raton · Pensacola
Orlando · Miami · Jacksonville · Ft. Myers · Sarasota

12 11 10 09 08   6 5 4 3 2 1

Library of Congress Cataloging-in-Publication Data
Stronge, William B.
The sunshine economy: an economic history of Florida since the Civil War/
William B. Stronge.
p. cm.
Includes bibliographical references and index.
ISBN 978–0-8130-3201-6 (alk. paper)
1. Florida—Economic conditions. 2. Florida—History—1865– I. Title.
HC107.F6S75 2008
330.97599–dc22   2007044700

The University Press of Florida is the scholarly publishing agency for the State
University System of Florida, comprising Florida A&M University, Florida Atlantic
University, Florida Gulf Coast University, Florida International University, Florida
State University, New College of Florida, University of Central Florida, University
of Florida, University of North Florida, University of South Florida,
and University of West Florida.

University Press of Florida
15 Northwest 15th Street
Gainesville, FL 32611–2079
http://www.upf.com

For Joyce,
my partner and best friend for more than forty years.

Contents

Maps

U.S. Maps

Charts

Table

Charts

Preface

Even at the beginning of the twenty-first century, Florida remains an exotic place to millions of people. For Americans, Florida is the southernmost part of the continental United States—in the same latitude as Egypt. The state straddles the boundary between North and South America, at least culturally, if not quite geographically. Millions of Americans drink Florida orange juice, eat Florida grapefruit, and rely on Florida for fresh vegetables during long cold winters "up north." More people from outside the state than from inside it are found on Florida's beaches, especially during the winter months. Millions of people from around the world come to the state each year to visit Disney World and the other theme parks in Central Florida or to take cruises from Miami or Fort Lauderdale.

Yet less than 150 years ago, Florida was one of the least populated states in the Union. After the Civil War, Florida's population was fewer than 200,000 persons, compared to a national population of close to 40 million. East of the Mississippi, Florida had the fifth largest area but by far the lowest density, with only three persons per square mile. The relatively slow economic development of the state was reversed with a vengeance in the last half of the twentieth century. Indeed, one modern historian has likened the explosion of growth in this period to the "Big Bang" which many believe created our universe![1] Between 1950 and 2000, the state's population rose from under 3 million to about 16 million. By the end of the century the state was the fourth most populated state and on its way to achieving a third-place ranking.

I moved to the state in 1971 when I joined the faculty of economics at Florida Atlantic University. I was one of the millions who came from "up north," moving from Iowa, where I had completed my graduate studies in economics. Before that, I had spent the first twenty years of my life in Ireland. The exploding population of Florida was a sharp contrast to my previous experience, since neither Iowa nor Ireland had experienced much population growth in recent decades.

My training as an economist told me that economic factors must have played an important role in stimulating the population growth so characteristic of my new situation. Although many excellent books had been written about the history of Florida, there was no book that undertook a comprehensive analysis of the economic factors that had stimulated the growth of the state. Historians tended to emphasize other factors, and economic studies tended to be narrow in focus.

As a young economist, I joined my colleagues in undertaking a variety of narrowly focused studies of the Florida economy. But I retained a sense of awe at the development of the state and continued to wonder where the remarkable economy had come from. It was not until more than a decade ago that I was able to devote considerable time to developing an understanding of the big picture. This book is the result.

I do not claim that economic factors alone led to the development of twentieth-century Florida. But I believe there is room for a book that concentrates on these factors in order to round out our understanding of the state's history. Other books fill in other parts of the picture and they have been written by scholars with a different set of skills than mine.

An economy develops because of the efforts of a large number of people and a wide range of industries. Every day, many people make improvements in production techniques, time management, and the development of new markets and processes. These improvements raise labor productivity and move the aggregate economy forward. In telling the story of the economic development of Florida, I limit my attention to the subset of industries that sold goods and services outside the state during the late nineteenth and twentieth centuries. These industries, especially those in what I called the sunshine sector, are relatively unique to Florida and explain why the state developed differently than many other parts of the country. The industries that supported the growth of these basic industries had a less distinctive development and receive much less attention in this book. However, I do not argue that these industries are less important than the export-oriented industries, and, indeed, I believe that they will be more important in the century ahead.

This book is aimed at the general reader, avoiding complex economic analyses that belong more properly in scholarly journals. In one respect, however, my background as an economist still shows through. This book is "data-driven," relying on the U.S. census and a multiplicity of other, primarily official, data sources that were developed during the past century. Economists believe that actions rather than words contain the most information about the activities of the population and that the best guide to actions is to be found in the available data. The data are presented using maps and charts, rather than tables, in an effort to retain the attention of the reader. Just as a picture is said to be worth a thousand words, a map or chart can be worth a hundred numbers. I prepared the charts myself in a standard spreadsheet computer program. With one exception, I prepared the maps myself using standard mapping software. The two sketch maps were drawn in a word-processing program. The charts and maps use data from the data sources cited in the bibliography.

Many people have helped me to write this book. First and foremost are the legion of Florida historians and others who have provided insight into Florida economic history for more than a century. Additionally, like other writers of history, I have benefited from the assistance of librarians. I have received my greatest assistance from librarians in charge of government documents and especially the dedicated government documents librarians at Florida Atlantic University. A number of economists have read some or all of the manuscript. Chief among these has been David Denslow of the University of Florida, who provided many insights and a great deal of encouragement. I also benefited from the comments of James Cato at the University of Florida and Phyllis Isley of Georgia Southern University, as well as an anonymous referee during the review process at the University Press of Florida. Ralph Sexton, cattle rancher, hotel and restaurant operator, and brother of a citrus grower and packer personally lived through much of the ups and downs of the sunshine economy over the last fifty years and gave me many insights. Family and friends, including my wife Joyce and brother Paddy as well as Sol Bloomenkranz and Jack Latona, improved the manuscript and tolerated my obsession for more than ten years. Of course, errors in the manuscript are my responsibility and mine alone.

Florida Map Front-1. Florida's Counties, 2007

Table 1. Counties, Regions, and Important Cities

County	Region[1]	Major City/Town[2]	County	Region[1]	Major City/Town[2]
Alachua	N. Peninsula	Gainesville*	Lake	C. Peninsula	Leesburg
Baker	N. Peninsula	Macclenny*	Lee	S. Peninsula	Fort Myers*
Bay	W. Panhandle	Panama City*	Leon	E. Panhandle	Tallahassee*
Bradford	N. Peninsula	Starke*	Levy	N. Peninsula	Cedar Key
Brevard	C. Peninsula	Melbourne	Liberty	E. Panhandle	Bristol*
Broward	S. Peninsula	Fort Lauderdale*	Madison	N. Peninsula	Madison*
Calhoun	E. Panhandle	Blountstown*	Manatee	C. Peninsula	Bradenton*
Charlotte	S. Peninsula	Punta Gorda*	Marion	N. Peninsula	Ocala*
Citrus	C. Peninsula	Inverness*	Martin	S. Peninsula	Stuart*
Clay	N. Peninsula	Orange Park	Miami-Dade	S. Peninsula	Miami*
Collier	S. Peninsula	Naples*	Monroe	S. Peninsula	Key West*
Columbia	N. Peninsula	Lake City*	Nassau	N. Peninsula	Fernandina Beach*
Dade	S. Peninsula	See Miami-Dade	Okaloosa	W. Panhandle	Fort Walton
DeSoto	S. Peninsula	Arcadia*	Okeechobee	S. Peninsula	Okeechobee*
Dixie	N. Peninsula	Cross City*	Orange	C. Peninsula	Orlando*
Duval	N. Peninsula	Jacksonville*	Osceola	C. Peninsula	Kissimmee*
Escambia	W. Panhandle	Pensacola*	Palm Beach	S. Peninsula	West Palm Beach*
Flagler	N. Peninsula	Palm Coast	Pasco	C. Peninsula	Zephyrhills
Franklin	E. Panhandle	Apalachicola*	Pinellas	C. Peninsula	St. Petersburg
Gadsden	E. Panhandle	Quincy*	Polk	C. Peninsula	Lakeland
Gilchrist	N. Peninsula	Trenton*	Putnam	N. Peninsula	Palatka*
Glades	S. Peninsula	Moore Haven*	St. Johns	N. Peninsula	St. Augustine*
Gulf	E. Panhandle	Port St. Joe*	St. Lucie	S. Peninsula	Fort Pierce*
Hamilton	N. Peninsula	Jasper*	Santa Rosa	W. Panhandle	Milton*
Hardee	C. Peninsula	Wauchula*	Sarasota	S. Peninsula	Sarasota*
Hendry	S. Peninsula	Clewiston	Seminole	C. Peninsula	Sanford*
Hernando	C. Peninsula	Brooksville*	Sumter	C. Peninsula	Wildwood
Highlands	S. Peninsula	Sebring*	Suwannee	N. Peninsula	Live Oak*
Hillsborough	C. Peninsula	Tampa*	Taylor	N. Peninsula	Perry*
Holmes	W. Panhandle	Bonifay*	Union	N. Peninsula	Lake Butler*
Indian River	C. Peninsula	Vero Beach*	Volusia	C. Peninsula	Daytona Beach
Jackson	E. Panhandle	Marianna*	Wakulla	E. Panhandle	St. Marks
Jefferson	E. Panhandle	Monticello*	Walton	W. Panhandle	DeFuniak Springs*
Lafayette	N. Peninsula	Mayo*	Washington	W. Panhandle	Chipley*

Notes. 1. For the purposes of this table, the state of Florida has been divided into: the *western panhandle* (northwest) along the western boundaries of Gulf, Calhoun, and Jackson counties; the eastern boundary of the *eastern panhandle* is the eastern boundary of Jefferson County. The northern boundary of the *central peninsula* is the northern boundaries of Levy, Marion, and Volusia counties. The northern boundary of the *south peninsula* is the northern boundaries of Sarasota, DeSoto, Highlands, Okeechobee, and St. Lucie counties.

2. The places in the third column are generally the most populous towns or cities or are economic hubs because of their location. The names of county seats bear an asterisk. The purpose of including column 3 is to assist the reader in finding the counties on Map Front-1.

Chapter 1

1900

A Western Economy in a Southern Setting

The 1900 U.S. census reported a population of more than half a million for the state of Florida. This was a very small number compared to the 16 million that would be counted in the state in 2000. Indeed, it was not much more than the estimated as population of 350,000 of the modern territory of Florida at the time Ponce de Leon had made his first landing almost 400 years earlier.[1] Only four of the twenty-six states east of the Mississippi had smaller populations than Florida—Vermont, New Hampshire, Rhode Island, and Delaware. The population of Georgia was more than four times that of Florida, and the population of Alabama was more than three times as large. To the south, the population of Cuba was more than 1.5 million, and the population of the island of Hispaniola was even larger. The population of Puerto Rico was almost 1 million, and Jamaica had more than 700,000 persons.

There are several reasons for the small size of Florida's population in 1900. When Florida became part of the United States in 1821, it had a population of about 10,000 that was relatively evenly divided between Seminoles and European Americans, with a small number of African Americans, most of whom were enslaved. Florida was not a magnet for European settlement in the centuries before 1800. Spanish immigrants to the New World were attracted to the densely populated areas in Latin America and the Caribbean. Although St. Augustine in Florida was founded as a colony in 1565, by the end of the sixteenth century, it had shrunk to a military outpost designed to deter settlement by other European powers and serve as a haven for shipwrecked Spanish sailors. In the seventeenth century, Spain established a relatively successful system of missions among the Native Americans in the northeastern part of Florida. However, depopulation due to infectious diseases, war, and abuse forced the missions westward from St. Augustine, The mission system was finally destroyed at the beginning of the eighteenth century by an English military invasion from

South Carolina. Spain did not succeed in developing a replacement economy over the following century.

After Florida was organized as a territory of the United States in 1822, the process of surveying the new land and making it available to settlers was delayed by the existence of land grants the Spanish had made and some the English had made during their 20-year period of rule from 1763 to 1783; the United States had agreed to honor land grants dated prior to the signing of the treaty that handed Florida to the United States in 1819. After the territory was organized, legal proceedings were required to establish the validity of the grants. In the last half of the 1820s, cotton plantations were established in the eastern part of the state's panhandle, and sugar plantations were established along the banks of the St. Johns River in the northeast.

War with the Seminoles broke out in 1836 and lasted until 1842. Many northeastern plantations were destroyed, and the war discouraged migration into the state as well as investment in the war-torn area. In the course of the war, most Seminoles were forcibly removed to Oklahoma. The end of the Seminole War opened up most of peninsular Florida to development by whites, and higher cotton prices in the 1850s led to an expansion of the state's cotton economy south to the north-central part of the state near Gainesville and Ocala. This expansion was interrupted by the Civil War in 1861 and postwar readjustments, and significant growth in the state was delayed until the 1880s.

Nineteenth-century Florida developed primarily as an extension of the antebellum southern cotton economy, and the state's population in 1900 still reflected this origin. Most of the most densely populated counties were lo-

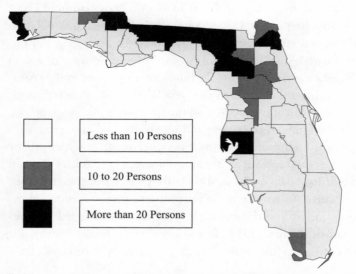

Florida Map 1–1. Population per Square Mile in Florida's Counties, 1900

cated on or near the state's borders with Georgia and Alabama. To the south of Orlando only Hillsborough County, whose county seat was Tampa, had more than twenty persons per square mile. Monroe County was the only other county with at least ten persons per square mile, and the majority of these lived in the city of Key West.

Those who traveled down the Florida peninsula in 1900 went by rail. Most traffic entered the state at Jacksonville, whose population of 28,429 made it the state's largest city. From Jacksonville, the traveler could continue southwest to the Tampa tri-city complex, which had a population of 19,561 and included the cities of West Tampa and Port Tampa. Alternatively, the traveler could travel west to Pensacola, which had a population of 17,747. Key West, whose population of 17,114 could be reached only by sea, was the only other city that had more than 5,000 persons in 1900. The traveler could also take the Florida East Coast Railroad south from Jacksonville to the new cities of West Palm Beach (population 564) and Miami (population 1,681) in the southeastern part of the state.

Much of the southern half of the peninsula was not even divided into a significant number of counties in 1900. Dade County stretched from Homestead to Stuart, Lee County stretched from Naples to Fort Myers and included the modern Hendry County, Manatee County included Sarasota and immediately to the east was DeSoto county, which would later be split into several counties.

The small size of the state's towns in 1900 reflected a population that was overwhelmingly rural. About one in six Floridians lived in an urban area, which the census defined as a place with a population of at least 4,000 persons. (Nationally, more than one person in three lived in an urban setting.) Florida's low urban population was characteristic of the other southern states and reflected the importance of agriculture as a source of employment. In 1900, almost 60 percent of the labor force in the southern states, defined to

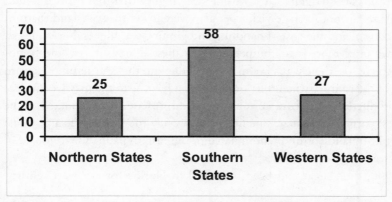

Chart 1–1. Percent of U.S. Labor Force in Agricultural Pursuits (by Region)

include the South Atlantic and South Central census divisions, was employed in agricultural pursuits. This contrasted with the other broad regions of the country. In the northern and western regions, a little over 25 percent of the working population was employed in agriculture; in Florida, 44 percent were employed in agriculture.

In 1900, cotton and tobacco, the crops that southern agriculture had developed worldwide markets for before the Civil War, were still important. The region also produced small amounts of two other unique crops: sugarcane and rice. Although most of the production took place on slave-based plantations in the antebellum period, the plantations were divided into small farms after the war. Many of these farms were operated by former slaves on a sharecropping basis.

The four "southern" crops accounted for 40 percent of the value of all crops produced in the southern states in 1899. The percentage was lower in Florida, although even there the southern crops accounted for more than 25 percent of the value of all crop production. Cotton accounted for more than 80 percent of the total value of the southern crops in the south as a whole. In Florida, cotton accounted for more than 70 percent.

Florida produced two types of cotton, the upland, or short-staple, and the sea-island, or long-staple, varieties. Of the thirteen states that each produced more than 1 million pounds in 1899, only three produced sea-island cotton—Georgia, Florida, and South Carolina. This variety was relatively more important in Florida than in the other two states. Sea-island cotton produced a fiber that was longer, silkier, and stronger than upland cotton. It required a hot and humid climate and was originally most successfully produced on the Sea Islands off the coast of South Carolina.[2] The original sea-island variety was crossed with upland cotton and several intermediate varieties were also obtained. The closer a variety was to the "classic" sea-island cotton, the higher the price. The 1900 census classified all cotton with a price higher than ten cents a pound as sea-island cotton. Average yields per acre were lower for sea-island than for upland cotton, and the cost of handling and ginning was higher. Nevertheless, the higher price more than compensated for these disadvantages, and beginning in the 1850s, there was a boom in its production that was resumed toward the end of the century when the price of cotton fell due to the massive increase in the production of upland cotton. Sea-island varieties predominated in the northwest corner of the state's peninsula, especially the Gainesville and Ocala areas, while upland cotton predominated in the eastern panhandle centered in Tallahassee.

By 1900, cane sugar had been produced in Florida for almost a century, since it had begun under Spanish rule before Florida became part of the United States in 1821.[3] The initial center of the industry was in the northeast coast of the state, but this industry was destroyed during the Second Seminole War, fought between 1836 and 1842. There were also sporadic efforts to develop sugar production in Florida's cotton belt, but competition from Cuban and West Indian producers prevented the establishment of a large-scale industry. Most plantations and large farms produced a small amount of sugarcane for their own use.

There was renewed interest in sugar in the early 1840s as cotton prices fell substantially. Two notable cotton-belt planters, Robert Gamble and Joseph Braden, moved to the Manatee River and established sugar plantations. These plantations survived until the financial panic of 1857. Once the economy returned to a sense of normalcy after the Civil War, sugarcane production expanded. Acreage in sugarcane in Florida increased by more than 50 percent from 1879 to 1899.

Louisiana accounted for more than 70 percent of the sugarcane produced in the continental United States in 1899. Georgia and Alabama tied for a distant second place, and Texas, Mississippi, and Florida rounded out the top six producers. Louisiana and Texas sold almost 25 percent of their cane to sugar factories. The remainder of the top six producing states, including Florida, sold no more than 5 percent of their cane to factories, instead processing the cane as syrup on producing farms or plantations. The largest Florida acreages in sugarcane were in the state's traditional cotton belt, where plantations had existed prior to the Civil War. Jackson and Gadsden counties, which straddled the Apalachicola River just south of Florida's border with Georgia and Alabama, had the largest acreages in cane sugar in the state.

Although a little tobacco had been grown around St. Augustine soon after Florida became part of the United States in 1821, its production expanded rapidly after the territorial governor, William P. Duval, introduced Cuban tobacco seed about 1828.[4] Shortly afterward, immigrants from Virginia began producing it east of the Apalachicola River in Gadsden County, the next county west of Tallahassee. These Virginians were familiar with tobacco culture in their home state. Initially, the tobacco was manufactured into cigars that were much criticized for being insipid and flavorless.

After the national financial panic of 1837, much of Gadsden's production sat in New York warehouses. In 1842, a shipment of Gadsden tobacco leaf was sent to Bremen in Germany, where it was quickly recognized as excellent for wrapping cigars. The warehouse inventory was quickly sold, and Gadsden farmers greatly expanded their production. This was one of the many examples of a "fever," a rush to produce a crop newly seen to be highly profitable. Such fevers, or booms or bubbles, arise periodically in free-enterprise economies. Several will be encountered during the story of Florida's economic development, and they remained a feature of the state's economy at the beginning of the twenty-first century.

In 1845, there was a huge glut of tobacco production when the county's farmers produced more than 1 million pounds, an amount more than ten times the amount produced in 1843. The average price decreased by half, and annual production stabilized around 600,000 pounds shortly thereafter. During the latter part of the 1850s, production expanded again and was close to 1 million pounds annually when the Civil War broke out. The war, however, disrupted the state's tobacco industry, and tobacco from Sumatra in the East Indies overtook Florida's export markets. Production dropped sharply and continued to fall during the 1870s as the overseas market for Florida wrapper tobacco was not regained.

In 1887, the tobacco industry revived in Gadsden County. This was a result of the introduction of Sumatra wrapper seed by a New York firm that had begun growing tobacco near Bainbridge in southwest Georgia, just north of Gadsden County. The firm's operations spread quickly across the border into Florida. A second boom ensued in the county, but it collapsed after the national financial panic of 1893.

Shortly after the panic ended, two Gadsden planters were visiting a tobacco plantation in Cuba and noticed that tobacco growing in the shade of orange trees had a thinner leaf and finer texture than plants growing in the open fields. They returned to Gadsden and began growing filler tobacco in the shade. After some experimentation, they successfully grew a high-quality product, and the practice of growing tobacco in the shade spread rapidly throughout the county and in the neighboring area of southwest Georgia. Another tobacco boom ensued that was still in progress as the nineteenth century drew to a close.

Florida's southern setting ensured that a high percentage of its population was black in 1900. Blacks did not move outside the South in large numbers until World War I opened up job opportunities in northern cities in 1917. In 1900, the black population of Florida amounted to 44 percent of the total. This was the sixth highest percentage among the 48 states and territories.

Blacks constituted a majority of the population in most of the counties in Florida's historic plantation belt, a legacy of the slavery of the antebellum period. These included Marion County (61.7 percent black population) and Alachua (58.8 percent) in the northern part of the peninsula, and Madison (57.6 percent), Jefferson (77.9 percent), Leon (80.4 percent), Gadsden (64.4 percent), and Jackson (52.5 percent) in the eastern panhandle of the state. Out-

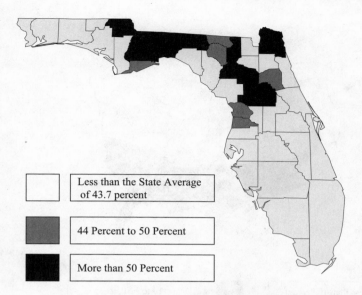

Florida Map 1–2. Black Population in Florida's Counties as a Percent of Population, 1900

side this general region, only Duval and Nassau counties in the northeastern corner of the state had majority black populations in 1900.

Florida had a high rate of illiteracy compared to most of the rest of the country. In 1900, more than one in five Floridians aged 10 years and over was illiterate. The state shared this characteristic, another legacy of slavery, with the other southern states. In 1870, 84 percent of black Floridians were illiterate. This was similar to the 85 percent rate in the southern states as a whole, and it contrasted with the rate of 44 percent for blacks outside the South. The illiteracy rate among the nonblack population in Florida was 28 percent, compared to rates of 23 percent in the South as a whole and 8 percent in the rest of the country. Many parents of black children in Florida and elsewhere in the South were unable to provide educational opportunities for their children.

It is remarkable how quickly the illiteracy rate fell among freed slaves in Florida and elsewhere in the South. Although largely illiterate, freed slaves recognized the importance of basic education, and one of the long-lasting benefits of Reconstruction was improved educational opportunity. The rate of illiteracy among Florida nonwhites (almost all of whom were black), fell from 84 percent in 1970 to 44 percent in 1900; elsewhere in the South, the rate was 48 percent. The gap between black illiteracy and white illiteracy had not closed since 1870, however, since only around 10 percent of white Floridians were illiterate in 1900.

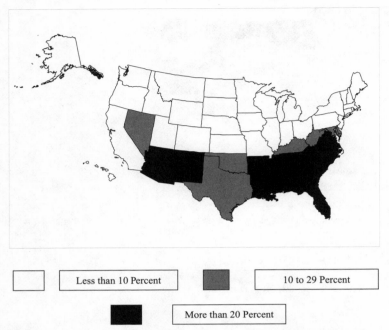

| | Less than 10 Percent | | 10 to 29 Percent |
| | More than 20 Percent |

U.S. Map 1–1. Illiterate Population as Percent of Total by State, United States, 1900

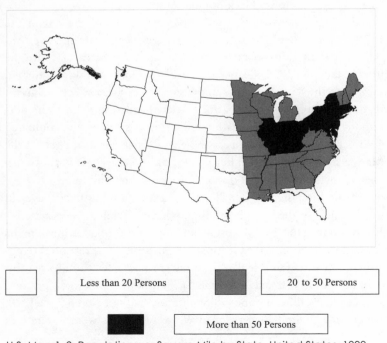

| | Less than 20 Persons | | 20 to 50 Persons |
| | More than 50 Persons |

U.S. Map 1–2. Population per Square Mile by State, United States, 1900

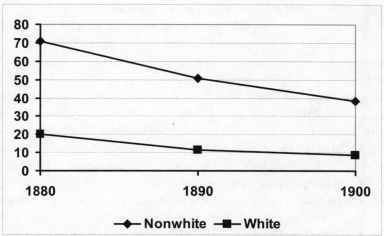

Chart 1–2. Illiteracy in Florida by Color, 1880, 1890, and 1900 (by Percent of Population)

Although Florida's population shared many of the characteristics of the populations of other southern states in 1900, its small size gave the state's economy many of the characteristics of the economies west of the Mississippi. These states, which had been regarded as the frontier in the last half of the nineteenth century, had relatively small populations, especially in relation to their land areas. Florida, with the lowest population density east of the Mississippi, was more similar to the western states than to its eastern neighbors. For example, Florida's population density was similar to that of California and Texas.

The abundant natural resources of western states initially attracted people from the East. These included minerals (gold in California and silver in Colorado, for example), extensive forests, and grasslands suitable for open-range cattle-herding. Florida's natural resources also attracted ambitious entrepreneurs, and in 1900, the mining, forestry, and cattle industries were present in the state.

Florida had relatively little in the way of mineral resources in 1900. An exception was phosphate mining, which was developed beginning in 1888. Phosphate was originally formed from the bones and shells of seafish, and Florida was discovered to have large and rich deposits, particularly in the "Bone Valley" areas of Hillsborough and Polk and (what would later become) Hardee counties. Phosphate is used to make phosphorous, a valuable component of agricultural fertilizer by the late nineteenth century.

Phosphate comes in the form of river pebble or hard rock or land pebble. River pebble was the first source to be mined, specifically along the Peace River

near Arcadia.[5] Hard-rock mining developed a couple of years later at Dun-
nellon in Marion County. In 1900, production from hard rocks accounted
for about 75 percent of the phosphate production in the state. Ten years later,
production from river pebble ended and land pebble became the main source
of production.

Florida's phosphate industry followed the familiar pattern of an initial period of great enthusiasm followed by a shakeout and a settling down of the
industry by the end of the century. The price per long ton of phosphate fell
from about $4.00 in 1892 to about $2.00 in 1898. Although there was a general
decline in prices during the 1890s due to the recession that began in 1893, the
decline in phosphate prices was much greater and was a sign of the maturing
of the industry. By 1900, Florida accounted for about 50 percent of phosphate
production in the United States, and this share increased in the years that followed. The United States, in turn, accounted for more than 50 percent of the
world's production.

Florida had a large cattle industry in 1900. Although most of the state's land
was forested, Florida's pine trees were spaced relatively far apart and the forest
was frequently broken up by prairie openings.[6] Additionally, there was acreage

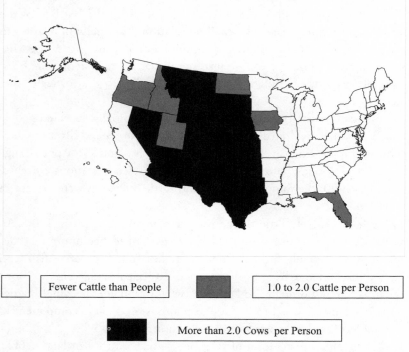

| | Fewer Cattle than People | | 1.0 to 2.0 Cattle per Person |

| | More than 2.0 Cows per Person |

U.S. Map 1–3. Number of Neat Cattle per Person by State, United States, 1900

where the timber had been cut and only stumps remained. Florida's cattlemen turned their animals loose to range across the landscape, feeding on native grasses and obtaining water from the abundant small lakes and streams. There were 750,000 cattle in Florida in 1900, a number considerably higher than the number of human beings in the state.

Most Florida cattle were descended from stocks owned by the Spanish before Florida became part of the United States in 1821. These cattle were small and scrawny, averaging about 750 pounds when shipped. The meat was tender and well flavored, according to the 1880 U.S. census report, although the beef served in Florida's winter resorts was shipped in from other states.

Florida's main export market for its cattle was Cuba. Captain James McKay of Tampa had discovered this market toward the end of the 1850s. The trade was interrupted during the Civil War, when Florida's cattle became a major food asset of the Confederacy after the Battle of Vicksburg cut the South off from western cattle. Florida's cattle were moved southward deep into the peninsula. After the war, trade with Cuba resumed and the business expanded. During Cuba's Ten Years' War to free itself from Spain (1868–1878), Havana was cut off from Cuba's cattle areas, and Florida's cattle exports mushroomed. Initially, the cattle were shipped from Tampa and then from Manatee and even Cedar Key, but the main exporting port eventually became Punta Rassa at the mouth of the Caloosahatchee River in Fort Myers, where the Sanibel Causeway joined the mainland a century later.

There were more cattle than people in Florida in each census year from 1840

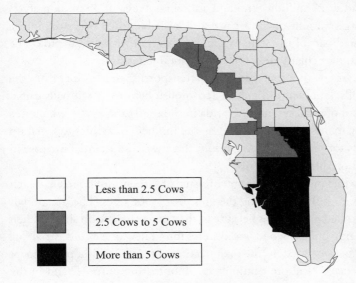

Less than 2.5 Cows

2.5 Cows to 5 Cows

More than 5 Cows

Florida Map 1–3. Number of Cattle per Person in Florida's Counties, 1900

to 1900. The largest numbers of cattle relative to the population were found in the regions north and west of Lake Okeechobee and in Osceola County, where there were more than twenty animals per person; Desoto County, where there were ten animals per person; and Lee County, where there were seven animals per person. These counties were the source of the shipments of cattle from Punta Rassa. The most urbanized counties had the fewest cattle per capita, although the large but sparsely populated Dade County on the southeast coast also had no cattle.

Lumbering was a feature of the U.S. frontier because it was necessary to clear the forests for farming and the forests had been substantially reduced in the more mature parts of the country. Forest products were used to construct houses and other buildings and as fuel. Originally, lumber was obtained from the local region for these purposes, but as virgin timber stands were cut, it became necessary to import lumber products from other regions of the country. By the middle of the nineteenth century, the more developed northeastern states had begun to import lumber products from the Great Lakes area, and in 1899, Wisconsin, Michigan, and Minnesota were the leading lumber states in the nation.[7]

In 1900, Florida produced 800,000 board feet of lumber. Most of this was yellow pine, with a small amount of cypress. Remaining species accounted for less than 1 percent of the value of production. Because cypress brought a higher price per board foot, it accounted for a smaller share of board feet sawed (11 percent). An estimated 24 million acres of Florida was forested, compared to an original stand of 28 million acres and a total land area of 35 million acres. Obviously, a large amount of timber was still available to be harvested in the state. The forested part of the state was mainly covered with yellow pine. The swampy regions, particularly near the coast, contained cypress.

A major task lumber producers faced was transporting the product from the forest to the mills. This was difficult to accomplish before the railroads came. The development of a rail system in Florida in the 1880s and 1890s, which was characterized by many small roads built by the lumber companies, opened up the state's forests for production. As a result, there was a substantial increase in Florida production during the 1890s.

A second product of Florida's forests consisted of turpentine and rosin, which was obtained as a result of distilling the gum from pine trees. These materials were originally called naval stores because of their extensive use on ships. When ships stopped being built of wood, naval stores found new uses as industrial raw materials. They became used in "the manufacture of paint, varnish, paper, soap, lubricants, pharmaceutical preparations, for illuminating purposes and in the rubber industry."[8]

The industry was concentrated in the Carolinas in 1850, which accounted for 95 percent of production in the United States. Production gradually shifted southward and westward. By 1900, Georgia was the largest producer, accounting for 40 percent of the nation's production, followed by Florida, which accounted for 32 percent, and Alabama, the Carolinas, and Mississippi, each accounting for around 10 percent. Like the lumber industry, Florida's naval stores production expanded rapidly in the 1890s. These increases in production resulted from the rapid expansion of the state's railroads that will be chronicled in Chapter 3.

We call lumber and naval stores manufacturing, phosphate mining, and open-range cattle-herding Florida's "frontier" industries, since they were present to some degree along the nation's frontier at the end of the twentieth century. Lumber manufacturing, mining, and cattle-herding were major industries west of the Mississippi at the time. The lumber industry dominated the frontier sector of the Florida economy, accounting for about 70 percent of the production.[9] Gum naval stores accounted for 15 percent of the sector's production. Phosphate mining and cattle were each in the range of 5 percent.

Economies grow as a result of larger and more highly skilled labor forces and because of improvements in production technology. Regions within economies share in the growth of the labor force and its increasing skill level, and they benefit from improvements in technology. Additionally, they grow as a result of the development of industries that sell goods and services to national and even international markets. The industries that make substantial sales to national markets are often called the economic base of the region. So far in this chapter we have seen two parts of Florida's economic base in 1900: traditional southern export agriculture, which emphasized cotton and tobacco, and frontier indus-

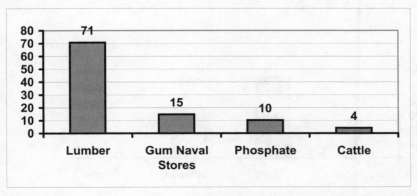

Chart 1–3. Share of Lumber, Gum Naval Stores, Phosphate, and Cattle Industries in Value of Production of Florida's Frontier Sector 1899 (by Percent)

tries, which included phosphate mining, cattle-herding, lumber products, and naval stores.

Florida's economic base had two other components—a group of maritime industries centered at the state's seaports and a group of "sunshine" industries based on the state's warm winters. The state's maritime sector consisted of fishing, sponge-fishing, cigar production, and the state's defense payroll. The cigar industry was included as a maritime industry because of its locations in the port cities of Tampa and Key West. It imported tobacco by sea from Cuba and sent cigars by rail and by sea to its markets in the northern states and Western Europe.

Cigar manufacturing accounted for more than 50 percent of the total production of the maritime sector in 1900, and fisheries accounted for more than 33 percent. The contributions of the other two industries were relatively small.[10] Cigar manufacturing became important in Florida after the Civil War. Two factors led to the development of the industry: a series of tariff acts in the 1860s that raised taxes on imported (primarily Cuban) cigars and the immigration of cigar manufacturers and their workers to Key West during Cuba's Ten Years' War that began in 1868.[11] The strong national economic growth of the 1880s facilitated an increase in domestic cigar production and the new high level was given added protection in tariff legislation in the 1890s. By 1906, Florida "manufactured more Havana cigars than Cuba."[12]

By 1900, the center of the state's cigar industry had shifted to Tampa in order to take advantage of the rail connection to northern markets that arrived in the mid-1880s as well as to get around other constraints at the Key West location, such as a shortage of space and fresh water. There were also labor problems in the Key West cigar industry. By 1900, the cigar industry in Tampa was about twice the size of the industry in Key West, judged by the gross output in both cities in the 1900 census of manufactures. Smaller

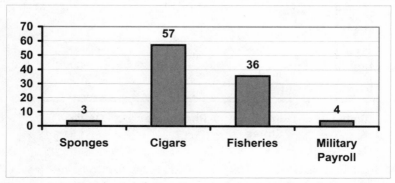

Chart 1–4. Share of Sponges, Cigars, Fisheries, and Military Payroll in Value of Production of Florida's Maritime Industries 1899 (by Percent)

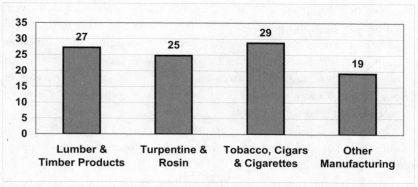

Chart 1–5. Share of Florida's Major Industries in Value of Production of Manufacturing Industries, 1899 (by Percent)

locations elsewhere in Florida, including the cities of West Tampa and Ocala, also produced cigars. In 1900, cigar manufacturing had become the largest of the state's manufacturing industries, accounting for 29 percent of the value of total production.

The fishing catch along the northeast coast of the United States had the largest value in the nation around 1900, and the southeast coast had the second most valuable catch.[13] Although the Gulf coast had the smallest fisheries in terms of value, Florida was unique in having fisheries in both the southeast and Gulf coast regions.

Even judged against the South Atlantic region as a whole, Florida had a relatively large fishing industry. The state accounted for about 15 percent of the value of the region's ocean catch in 1901–1902, compared to 5.1 percent of the region's population. Florida's share of the region's catch had expanded rapidly in the last two decades of the century as faster transportation became available.

Florida was the only state to have a sponge fishery in 1900, when there were 228 boats in the fishery. A fleet of turtle-fishing boats discovered the sponge beds off Key West in 1853, but the industry did not take off until the 1880s, when it replaced imported sponges on domestic markets. In the 1890s, it became evident that there were sponge beds near Tampa Bay and even farther north. The industry expanded northward toward the end of the decade, when concerns for their safety during the Spanish American War induced some Key West sponge fishermen to move to Tarpon Springs, just north of Tampa Bay. In the first decade of the twentieth century, Greek immigrants at Tarpon Springs introduced diving equipment to replace the hook-fishing methods of the Key West spongers and Tarpon Springs became the capital of the industry.

Sponge-fishing was just one of several unique industries in Key West, many of which had originated in the Bahamas. Another was "wrecking," the salvaging of cargo from ships that ran aground along the Florida Keys. This industry had been of major importance before the Civil War, when sailing ships were the dominant form of shipping and before lighthouses and other navigational aids had been constructed and developed. Even though lighthouses and other navigation aids were available by 1900, in the first decade of the twentieth century, more than $200,000 was awarded to wreckers by court decree and an additional $100,000 was paid for claims settled out of court.[14] Key West also had a turtle-fishing industry in 1900.

Finally, some indication of the importance of federal military installations in the state, at the ports and elsewhere, is given by the number of people occupied as soldiers, sailors, and marines in 1900. Florida was like a western state in this respect; it had a large number of soldiers, sailors, and marines relative to its population, almost three times as many relative to its population as the South Atlantic states as a whole.

The newest sector of the state's economic base in 1900 was the sunshine sector, the collection of industries in Florida that depended on its warm winter climate. These industries became identified with the state's economy in the twentieth century as they grew to dominate its economic base. The sunshine sector consisted of the production of semitropical agricultural products, winter and early spring vegetables and strawberries, and winter tourism. Citrus products, especially oranges and grapefruit, held a dominant place in semitropical agriculture, although there was a significant pineapple industry early in the century and a small avocado industry survived throughout the century. Florida's advantage in the production of vegetables stemmed from its ability to bring them to market earlier in the year than other parts of the country. Finally, most tourists who came to Florida arrived in winter to escape the harsh weather farther north, and they purchased lodging, food, and a variety of services that provided employment and incomes to thousands of Floridians.

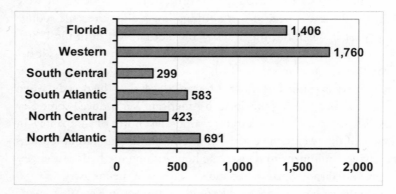

Chart 1–6. U.S. Military per Million Population, Florida and U.S. Regions, 1900

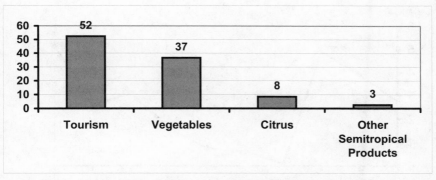

Chart 1–7. Share of Tourism, Vegetables, Citrus, and Other Semitropical Products in Value of Production of Florida's Sunshine Sector 1899 (by Percent)

In 1900, tourism was the largest sunshine industry, accounting for more than 50 percent of the state's total production.[15] Vegetable production was the second largest industry, accounting for more than 33 percent of total production. Citrus and other semitropical agricultural products accounted for about 10 percent. (Citrus products were a relatively small part of the sector due to the catastrophic freezes of 1894 and 1895.)

The main products of Florida's semitropical agriculture in 1899 were citrus products and pineapples, which together accounted for virtually all of the production of this sector.[16] Small amounts of avocados, guavas, and bananas were also produced. The pineapple industry, which accounted for 23 percent of semitropical production, was centered in Brevard and Dade counties; both of these counties were much larger in geographic extent than they would be a century later. The industry ran south along the west bank of what would become the Intracoastal Waterway from the Sebastian Inlet to the southern end of what would become Palm Beach County.

The bulk of the state's citrus industry was destroyed by back-to-back freezes in December 1894 and February 1895. The first freeze destroyed the crop, but the second freeze destroyed the trees that had begun to sprout new leaves in the intervening period. Although many farmers replanted, another severe freeze in 1899 further negatively impacted the industry. Not until 1907 did the value of Florida's citrus production reach the pre-freeze level of 1893.[17] Yet even in 1899, the freeze-ravaged citrus industry accounted for over 75 percent of the state's semitropical agricultural production. Florida's citrus industry was almost entirely composed of oranges at the turn of the century. Grapefruit and limes were the other main components.

Florida vegetable production expanded by 50 percent in the 1890s until the

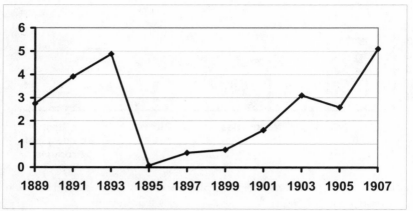

Chart 1–8. Gross Output of Florida Citrus, 1889–1907, in Millions of Current Dollars (Unadjusted for Inflation, Biennial Data)

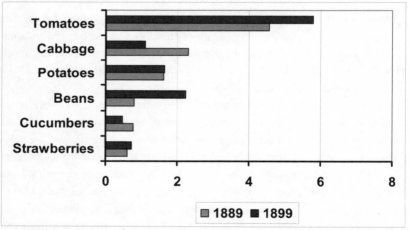

Chart 1–9. Acreage in Selected Vegetables and Strawberries, Florida, 1889 and 1899 (in Thousands of Acres)

temporary setback due to the freeze of 1899. Freezes are much less devastating to vegetables than to citrus products because a new crop can be produced the following year and sometimes even in the year of the freeze itself. After the 1894–1895 winter season, many farmers expanded their summer watermelon production in an effort to obtain some income. Of course, the result was a glut and low prices.[18] The winter vegetable with the largest acreage was the tomato, which was grown on almost 6,000 acres by the end of the decade. The second largest acreage was in beans (more than 2,000 acres), whose production had expanded rapidly. Acreage in cabbage had declined.

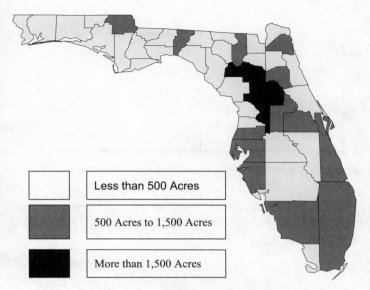

Florida Map 1–4. Acreage in Vegetables in Florida's Counties, 1899

There were two centers of vegetable production in 1899: the Gainesville-Ocala region in the northern peninsula and Miami-Dade County (which ran south from Stuart to Homestead at the time).[19] Leon County (Tallahassee) was the only county outside these areas with more than 1,000 acres in vegetables in 1899.

Vegetable production per acre was particularly high in the southern two-thirds of the Florida peninsula, which enjoyed an economic advantage from earlier marketing in the year. Clay County on the southwest border of Jacksonville also had valuable vegetable production, perhaps because of the tourist market in Jacksonville and St. Augustine.

The frontier industries of lumber, manufacturing, turpentine and rosin production, phosphate mining, and cattle-ranching (primarily on the open range) accounted for more than 60 percent of Florida's economic base in 1900. This was due to the frontier nature of the state, which was characterized by sparse population and a resource-based economy. The large size of the frontier industries is the basis of the statement that Florida had a western economy in a southern setting in 1900.

Florida's new sunshine industries were a relatively small part of the state's economic base in 1900 in part because of the citrus freezes of 1894–1895 and also because of the vegetable freezes in 1899. As Florida proceeded through the twentieth century, however, the frontier industries declined in importance and the sunshine industries grew to dominate the state's economy.

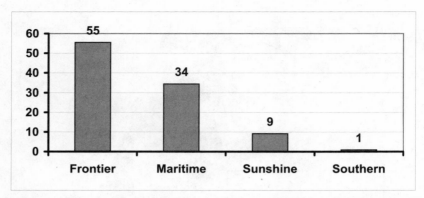

Chart 1–10. Share of Frontier, Maritime, Sunshine, and Southern Industries in Value of Production of Florida's Economic Base 1899 (by Percent)

The state's large cigar manufacturing industry, which had been transplanted to Key West and Tampa from Cuba, was the basis for the importance of the state's maritime industries. This segment of the state's economic base was still important later in the twentieth century, although cigar manufacturing would almost disappear. At the century's end, national defense expenditures dominated the state's maritime sector. The southern industries of cotton, tobacco, sugar, and rice production, which had been such an important part of the state's economy in the antebellum period, accounted for the smallest part of its economic base in 1900. This would remain true throughout the twentieth century.

Chapter 2

The Transfer of Public Lands

At the end of the Second Seminole War in 1842, the federal government owned close to 25 million acres of Florida's total of 35 million acres. Although federal legislation enacted in 1850 set a process in motion that would transfer the bulk of this land to the state, it was not until the last two decades of the nineteenth century that ownership of most of the federal land was transferred to the private sector. Florida's economic development could not proceed until the massive transfer of land was largely completed. This chapter traces the process by which the land was transferred and discusses the implications for the economy. Florida emerged from the process with a large supply of underutilized land—cheap land that shaped the economic development that emerged in the late nineteenth century and most of the twentieth century.

The legislation that transferred the extensive federal lands to the state was the Swamp Lands Act of 1850. The federal government had granted all swamp and overflowed lands to Louisiana for the purpose of aiding in their reclamation in 1849, and in 1850 the provisions of the act were extended to the twelve other public-domain states, including Florida. As of June 30, 1954, Florida had received more than 20 million acres, which was more than twice the amount granted to Louisiana, the second largest grantee, and accounted for more than 30 percent of all lands granted under the various swamp acts.[1] The wording of the Swamp Lands Act of 1850 committed the U.S. government to transfer to Florida all sections of federally owned land, "the greater part of which were wet and unfit for cultivation."[2] The land could be disposed of by the state "provided . . . that the proceeds of said lands . . . shall be applied, exclusively, as far as necessary, to the purpose of reclaiming said lands by means of levees and drains." Florida interpreted the phrase "as far as necessary" liberally to permit the use of the lands for internal improvements. These included some drainage or canal projects, but primarily, the internal improvements financed by the disposition of the lands consisted of the rail network whose development will be described in the next chapter.

It took time for the Florida legislature to pass laws that provided a mechanism for transferring the lands it received from the federal government to the private sector. A system of railroads could be developed only by corporations, since no other form of business organization could raise the large sums of capital for such risky ventures while protecting the personal assets of the owners from seizure in the case of bankruptcy. But Florida Democrats had a strong aversion to the chartering of corporations.[3] In his 1858 message to the assembly, Democratic governor Madison Starke Perry wrote that "how far corporate powers may in safety be granted is problematical. Corporate powers and privileges are sometimes essential to the successful prosecution of enterprises, both of a public and private nature, and when feasible and founded on public utility should be granted as necessary evils. The tendency of all corporate powers is to centralize and concentrate power and influence, as do all monopolies, and grind out tribute from the people for the benefit of a privileged few, which is at war with the spirit and genius of our government and people, although extensively practiced."[4]

Anti-corporate sentiment was exacerbated by the state's recent experience with the charters that had established banks as corporations in the 1830s. It was regarded as an outrage, for example, that the new stock issued by the banks was almost exclusively issued to existing stockholders even as it was advertised for sale to the public at large. Many believed that the banks had been captured by a clique of wealthy cotton planters who were seen as setting the policies of the banks for their own interest rather than the general interest of the public—the ostensible reason for chartering the banks as corporations in the first place.[5] After the Panic of 1837, the banks encountered economic difficulties that continued during the period of low cotton prices that characterized the 1840s. As the decade began, the banks defaulted on bonds that the territorial legislature had guaranteed. There was a huge public controversy, and the newly elected state legislature refused to honor the guarantee. Ultimately the banks failed.

Opposition to corporations began to diminish soon after 1850 as the pressure to develop a state transportation network grew.[6] In 1848 the legislature began to charter railroads as corporations, and in 1850 it signaled its willingness to provide assistance to a corporation for railroad construction when it granted a charter to the Florida Atlantic and Gulf Central Railroad Company. In 1854, the newly elected Democratic governor of Florida, James E. Broome, indicated his strong support for the use of internal improvement lands to aid in the construction of a statewide rail system in his first message to the legislature. He was concerned that the available resources would be used on local projects of interest to powerful politicians instead of for the development of a comprehensive statewide network. Broome argued for rail lines that would connect Fernandina or some other point on the northeast coast with Tampa in the southwest and Pensacola in the northwest to Jacksonville in the northeast.

The Internal Improvement Board that had been set up in 1850 established a committee to prepare recommendations for the legislature. The members of the committee contained several railroad promoters, including, notably, David Yulee, who would develop the Fernandina–Cedar Key railroad, and A. E. Baldwin, president of the company that would develop the Jacksonville–Lake City railroad. The committee presented both a report and draft legislation to the legislature, which adopted the legislation with minor revisions.

The Internal Improvement Fund Act created the Internal Improvement Fund (IIF), a state agency charged with receiving swamp lands and administering them to promote internal improvements. It created a Board of Trustees to oversee the IIF that consisted of the governor and cabinet. This was designed to ensure that the people would control the disposition of the lands through their elected representatives and that projects would have a statewide perspective. The legislation enumerated the specific projects to be included in the statewide network.[7]

The IIF was authorized to assist the projects by providing land grants to the corporations undertaking the construction, by guaranteeing interest on construction bonds issued by the companies, by accepting equity in the corporations when making interest payments on the bonds, and by being permitted to invest its surplus in the guaranteed construction bonds. The legislation contained numerous provisions relating to the timing of the assistance and ensuring that performance standards were met. On completion of the railroad, the corporation was required to pay 1.5 percent of the value of the construction bonds, whose interest payments were guaranteed by the IIF, into a sinking fund account every six months. The IIF could use this fund to meet any shortfalls in the companies' interest payments. The IIF was authorized to seize the assets of any corporation that failed to make the sinking-fund payments and sell them at public auction to the highest bidder. The Internal Improvement Fund Act also authorized local governments that benefited from the railroads to issue general obligation bonds (backed by property taxes) in order to purchase stock in the railroad companies. The federal government also enacted legislation that promised federal land grants for the IIF projects.

By 1861, much of the progress on the projects that had been contemplated in the Internal Improvement Fund Act had been completed. David Yulee's railroad company had completed the line between Fernandina and Cedar Key, and two companies had completed the line that connected Jacksonville to Tallahassee, one building west from Jacksonville to Lake City and the other building east from Tallahassee to Lake City. The previously constructed railroad from Tallahassee to St. Marks had been upgraded. Two other railroads had been built, one north from Pensacola to the Alabama state line and one from a port on the St. Johns River to St. Augustine. The lines connecting Tallahassee to Pensacola had not been constructed, nor had the extensions to St. Andrew's Bay or Tampa. The canal linking the St. Johns and Indian rivers also had not been constructed. Finally, the IIF had guaranteed the interest on $3.6 million in construction bonds and had purchased $160,600 in guaranteed interest bonds from the railroads. In addition, the IIF had granted 531,166 acres to the railroads. But disaster was around the corner.

During the Civil War, the Union naval blockade drastically reduced commerce through Fernandina, Cedar Key, Jacksonville, and St. Marks. As a result, the Fernandina–Cedar Key railroad was unable to provide an alternative to ship traffic around the dangerous southern end of the peninsula. Indeed, the railroad was unable to benefit from a substantial mail contract awarded by the U.S. Post Office just as the war began.[8] The blockade also prevented cotton exports through St. Marks and lumber exports through any of the railhead ports.

Although the railroads gained some revenue from troop movements, their overall revenue was substantially reduced. As a result, they had limited resources

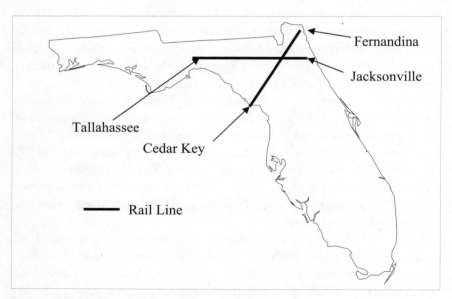

Florida Map 2–1. Florida's Railroads in 1861

to maintain their tracks and equipment.[9] Equipment maintenance also suffered because the blockade cut off sources of spare parts and replacements. Additionally, military operations inflicted considerable damage on facilities owned by the railroads. The terminals at each end of the Fernandina–Cedar Key railroad were destroyed, as were facilities in Jacksonville and Baldwin, where the Fernandina–Cedar Key and Jacksonville-Tallahassee roads intersected. The biggest loss, however, occurred when twenty-five miles of the Fernandina–Cedar Key railroad track was torn up at the order of the Confederacy and used to build a link northward from the Tallahassee-Jacksonville line into Georgia.

The plan to link the Tallahassee-Jacksonville to a line in Georgia that terminated at the port of Savannah had been proposed before the war started, but it had been opposed by northeast Florida interests who wanted the cotton exports of the Tallahassee region to be exported through Fernandina.[10] The Georgia section of the connector was graded by the end of 1861, and the Georgia line had the rails needed to complete the line. But the company that owned the Tallahassee–Live Oak portion of the Tallahassee-Jacksonville line lacked enough rails to complete the Florida link.

In 1862, the Florida Executive Council authorized Governor John Milton to remove the tracks west of Fernandina to safety in the face of an expected invasion by Union troops. A period of protracted negotiations followed between Milton and David Yulee, president of the railroad. When the Union Army entered Georgia in early 1864, the Confederate government became determined to complete the connector. After a delay resulting from a state court injunction, the tracks were eventually removed, but the connector was not completed until 1865. By this time, the connector was of little use to the Confederacy, and it was some time after the war before the rails were returned to the Fernandina–Cedar Key railroad.

After the war, Florida railroads were in default on their interest payments and had failed to make the required payments into the sinking fund. One by one the state seized them and sold them to the highest bidder. The Jacksonville-Fernandina line was sold in 1866 to an investment group headed by E. N. Dickerson, who had also headed the main antebellum group that had invested in the line. The proceeds of the sale were sufficient to redeem the bonds at twenty cents on the dollar. Although this offer was made, many bondholders rejected it.[11] It took the new management sixteen years to restore the railroad to a healthy condition.

Although the IIF ordered the company that owned the eastern portion of the Jacksonville-Tallahassee line to be sold in 1867, legal maneuvering delayed the sale until 1868.[12] Once again, the proceeds of the sale were sufficient to redeem the outstanding bonds at twenty cents on the dollar, and this time 90 percent of the bonds were redeemed. The company that owned the westward portion of the Jacksonville-Tallahassee railroad, which had been extended west to Quincy in Gadsden County during the war, was sold in 1869, and it emerged from the war without having suffered damage. It was successful in obtaining capital to replace the tracks on the Georgia link and even earned a small operating profit in 1865–1868, but its failure to pay interest on its bonds and to make the required sinking-fund payments led to its sale.

The Internal Improvement Fund resumed its policy of making land grants to assist internal improvement construction projects after the war.[13] Only one project was actually carried out—the 1878 dredging of the Ocklawaha River, for which Hubbell Hart received a grant of 33,000 acres of land. Hart was able to expand his steamboat service up the river to Silver Springs, which might be regarded as Florida's first tourist attraction. Most of the postwar contracts were conditional, providing assistance only as substantial completion occurred, and most projects foundered because of inadequate financing. In many cases, however, failure led to proposals of even more grandiose projects.

The activities of the IIF were halted in 1871 when Francis Vose, a bondholder of the prewar Fernandina–Cedar Key railroad, secured an injunction in federal court that prohibited the IIF from disposing of any additional state lands unless it was for U.S. currency.[14] In 1872, the court appointed a receiver for the IIF, and grants for internal improvements were effectively halted.

The IIF had received almost $300,000 from land sales from 1869 to 1880, most of which was consumed by legal expenses.[15] It was clearly impossible for the fund to sell land piecemeal and accumulate enough revenue to pay off its debts. It sought a large cash buyer that would provide enough revenue to pay off its debt, which was almost $1 million by 1880. Additionally, there was urgency because the debtors of the IIF had applied to the federal court for an order requiring that all the IIF lands be sold, or enough to satisfy the fund's debts. After several attempts to sell 3 million acres at thirty cents an acre failed, the new governor of Florida sold 4 million acres at twenty-five cents an acre to Hamilton Disston of Philadelphia in 1881.

Hamilton Disston was the son of an English immigrant, Henry Disston, who had been apprenticed to a saw manufacturer in Philadelphia.[16] Henry opened his own saw manufacturing firm in 1840, and in 1855 he built his own steel mill, gaining an advantage over the competition by his independence from British steel. During the war he expanded into the manufacture of steel plates and files, whose foreign supply had been interrupted by Confederate raiders. His son Hamilton joined the firm after he returned from the war and was made a partner in the business newly named Henry Disston and Son. Hamilton Disston became interested in Republican politics, and it may have been with colleagues from the Philadelphia Republican Party that he made his first visit to Florida in 1877. He also met Henry Sanford, who may have interested him in the potential of investments in Florida. Sanford believed that emerging markets were the best places for investments and was already heavily invested in the state. At the end of the 1870s, Sanford was in negotiations with the IIF to make investments in the Ocklawaha River area that would help the IIF deal with its liquidity crisis.

With the death of his father in 1878, Hamilton Disston became head of the family firm. He clearly had considerable resources available for investment. Shortly after William D. Bloxham assumed the office of governor in January 1881, Disston entered negotiations with the IIF to undertake drainage in the Kissimmee River Valley area. A contract was signed in March whereby Disston and a group of associates agreed to drain up to 12 million acres of IIF swamp land located south of where the modern town of Kissimmee is situated, south to Lake Okeechobee, and west to the Peace River. He would receive half the lands he drained, with the first grants to be obtained after he drained 200,000 acres. Presumably, some or all of the 200,000 acres could be sold to pay off the Francis Vose claim and lift the injunction. But because other bondholders of the prewar Fernandina–Cedar Key railroad had applied in federal court to have enough IIF lands sold at public auction, it was not possible for Disston to obtain clear title to the drained lands.[17]

The drainage contract could not be implemented without paying off the bondholders, and Governor Bloxham, chairman of the IIF, offered 4 million acres of IIF lands to Disston in return for $1 million. Disston agreed, and a land purchase contract was signed on June 1, 1881. Disston was allowed to select 10,000-acre tracts of land up to 3.5 million acres and to select the last 500,000 acres he would buy from the state in 640-acre tracts. Disston was to make an initial payment of $200,000 that could be used to pay off the Francis Vose debt and get the injunction lifted and make regular payments thereafter. By September 1881, Disston had paid $500,000, almost all of it in cash with only about $15,000 in (discounted) coupons on state debt.

Two sticking points had to be solved in regard to the transaction. One was the fate of squatters. Squatters on federal land were entitled to buy their land for $1.25 an acre, and Disston agreed that squatters on his lands would receive the same option. Of course, $1.25 an acre represented a fivefold profit on Disston's purchase. The second was the concern of some railroad companies that Disston not select lands that they hoped to receive as grants for the construction of new lines. Disston agreed to be sensitive to the issue in his choice of lands. Of course, rail projects near Disston's holdings would add value to his lands.

In December 1881, Sir Edward Reed of England, who headed an Anglo-Dutch investment group, agreed to take over responsibility for the $500,000 balance of Disston's payment in return for 2 million of Disston's acres. Reed, a distinguished British ship designer, Member of Parliament, and fellow of the Royal Society, was interested in investment opportunities in Florida.[18] He had just purchased the Fernandina–Cedar Key railroad and merged it with an extension to Ocala and a rail line from Jacksonville to Fernandina.[19] Reed completed the payment of the additional $500,000 to take care of Disston's balance in December 1882. The lands Disston purchased ranged throughout the peninsula, including the northeast and along the west coast of the state, running from the south end of the Pinellas Peninsula northward to Lafayette County. They included much of modern Sarasota County and more than 100,000 acres in eastern Polk County.[20]

Disston also pursued lands under the drainage contract. He incorporated the Atlantic and Gulf Coast Canal and Okeechobee Land Company in 1881 and began two canal projects.[21] The first connected Lake Okeechobee to the Caloosahatchee River, which enters the gulf at Fort Myers.[22] Disston's second project consisted of a series of canals based around Lake Tohopekaliga. He established his headquarters at a settlement on the northern edge of the lake that would become the town of Kissimmee, south of Orlando. He provided land grants to the South Florida Railroad to construct a rail line between Orlando and Kissimmee, and he and the railroad jointly developed the town of Kissimmee. From Orlando, the line went to Sanford on the St. Johns, which had river connections to Jacksonville and points farther north.

The first canal Disston completed ran from Southport at the southern end of Lake Tohopekaliga to Lake Cypress in 1883. Soon after, samples from twenty acres of sugarcane that had been grown on reclaimed land took first prize at the Cotton Centennial Exposition in New Orleans.[23] This success led to Disston's St. Cloud Sugar Plantation (discussed below). An additional canal from Lake Cypress gave access to Lake Kissimmee, from which the Kissimmee River provided access to Lake Okeechobee and, through Disston's Caloosahatchee canal project, access to the gulf. In 1882, a company vessel made the first steamboat trip from Kissimmee to the Gulf of Mexico.[24] Disston completed a canal that connected Lake Tohopekaliga to its eastern sister, East Lake Tohopekaliga, in 1885. This led to new settlements at Runnymede and Narcoossee on reclaimed land and, some years later, to the town of St. Cloud.

At the end of 1885, Richard Rose bought 420 acres of Disston's land grant under the drainage contract and grew sugarcane. Disston bought a half-interest in this business, now called the St. Cloud Sugar Plantation, and furnished capital to expand the acreage and build a sugar mill in 1887. Soon after, it became evident that the federal government would pay a bounty to sugar producers in order to lessen the nation's dependence on imports. Disston wanted to undertake further expansion, and Rose sold him his half-interest. In the early 1890s, more than 1 million pounds of sugar were produced on 1,000 acres at the plantation. The Panic of 1893 and the loss of the sugar bounty in 1894 led to difficulties for the plantation that had not been resolved when Disston died. By 1897, production at the plantation had come to a standstill, and the sugar mill machinery was sold in 1900.

Hamilton Disston also took an active interest in the development of his lands in the Pinellas Peninsula. In 1882, Disston and a party of friends visited the upper Pinellas Peninsula near the Anclote River.[25] As a result of this visit, Disston laid out the town of Tarpon Springs. Wealthy northerners were soon attracted to the natural beauty of Tarpon Springs and built exquisite Victorian homes on the bayous in the late 1880s and 1890s.[26] Disston also began development in the lower part of the peninsula. He established a settlement called Disston City in 1884 in the midst of a large tract of land that he owned.[27] Although the community had some initial success, Disston realized that further success required rail connections. In 1886, he approached Peter Demens, who had completed the construction of a railroad from the St. Johns River near Sanford southwest to Oakland. Demens was seeking an opportunity to extend the railroad to the gulf, and Disston offered him land grants to bring the railroad to the Pinellas Peninsula. After many vicissitudes, Demens brought the railroad to St. Petersburg in 1888. Although Disston's settlement at Tarpon Springs benefited from a stop on the railroad, Disston City went into a decline because it did not become the railroad's Pinellas terminus.

Hamilton Disston is not as well remembered a century later as are his contemporaries Henry Flagler and Henry Plant, in part because of his early death. Recently, historian Joe Knetsch has updated our knowledge about Disston and debunked the myth that he committed suicide in 1896.[28] It also seems likely that Hamilton Disston on the whole made considerable profits from his Florida investments, contrary to the traditional reporting of the story, even though he may have had liquidity problems at the time of his death. He sold much of his purchase of 2 million acres for considerably more than twenty-five cents an acre. Even though his heirs sold what remained of his land holdings after his death at a very low price, the mortgage company that provided a $2 million mortgage placed a high value on his holdings, and a decade later the new owners of the land were making substantial profits from land sales. Finally, the widespread view that the Disston family was never interested in Hamilton's Florida ventures is not consistent with the involvement of his brother Jacob in the Pinellas Peninsula and in the Sugar Belt Railroad.[29] It is ironic that the remaining estate of Henry Sanford, who may have inspired Disston, was also sold for a pittance after Sanford's death. The impact of the catastrophic freezes in 1894–1895 on Florida land values may have led to excessive pessimism on the part of both men's heirs.

The Disston purchase permitted the IIF to resume land grants for railroad and canal projects. By 1904, 17 million of the 20 million acres in lands that the state had received from the federal government had been disposed of.[30] Of this, about 50 percent went to railroad companies and more than 5 million acres went to Hamilton Disston (the 4-million-acre purchase plus about 1.2 million under the drainage contract). Canal companies received over 2 million acres.

Most of the remaining land that had not been transferred at the beginning of the twentieth century was in the Everglades area of south Florida. Although it was known that the land was composed of muck soil that was believed to have high agricultural potential, it was normally inundated under from one to eighteen inches of water.[31] It was clear that drainage would be required to bring the land into agricultural production. A report submitted as early as 1848 had suggested that cutting the "rock rim" of the everglades at the heads of rivers that received their waters at low places on the rim would lower the level of water in the everglades by several feet. The land immediately south of the lake was twenty-one feet above sea level, and there was a gradual decline in elevation, which caused the water to drain slowly southward from below the lake. The canals would lower the water level in the lake, reducing overflow during wet periods, and they would also drain water from the everglades land itself.

The question remained of how to secure enough capital to undertake the canal-building projects. The first problem was the fact that existing commitments of lands to railroad companies more than exhausted the anticipated everglades lands that were expected to be received under the Swamp Lands Act.[32] In order to make these lands available to finance the drainage projects, the claims of the railroad companies would have to be adjusted.

The controversy over the railroad claims on the impending federal transfer of everglades lands came to a head as a new governor, W. S. Jennings, assumed office in 1901. Jennings, a cousin of unsuccessful Democratic presidential candidate William Jennings Bryan, was a populist and was elected at a time when many U.S. voters were angry about what was considered the abuse of power by trusts and large corporations with monopoly powers. At the national level, this had led to the establishment of the Interstate Commerce Commission in 1887 to regulate the interstate practices of railroads as well as the first national antitrust legislation in 1890. Florida had responded by creating a railroad commission in 1887. Although this commission was abolished in 1891 for fear it would be captured by railroad interests, a new commission was reestablished in 1897.[33]

Jennings argued that the railroad claims to IIF lands were not valid because the intent of the Swamp Lands Act was to transfer the land to the state so it could be drained and reclaimed.[34] As a result of this position, no land was transferred to the railroad companies during the Jennings administration, although the state received 2.9 million acres of everglades land from the federal government in 1903. Jennings left office with a series of pending lawsuits against the state by the railroad companies and other claimants.

Jennings was succeeded by Napoleon Bonaparte Broward, who was committed to the Jennings position but who also believed that the state should undertake the drainage program. His proposed program would have drained not only lands owned by the IIF but also lands owned by private property owners. He requested that the legislature provide a mechanism for assessing private property owners for the benefits they would receive from the state drainage program. The legislature approved a constitutional amendment that required voter approval, creating a State Board of Drainage Commissioners that would have the power to undertake the drainage program, establish drainage districts, and levy an annual tax not to exceed ten cents per acre.[35] The members of the board would be the same state officials who made up the Board of Trustees of the IIF.

The drainage board initiated the drainage program using the accumulated surplus in the IIF and proposed levying a tax of five cents per acre on a large drainage district that included five counties both north and south of Lake Okeechobee. More than 95 percent of the private land in the drainage taxing district was owned by railroad, canal, or land development companies. However, the constitutional amendment establishing the program was decisively rejected by the voters in the midterm election of 1906.

In 1907, the federal district court issued a series of rulings in connection with the railroad and other claims on the IIF lands. The judge rejected the railroads' claims and sustained the IIF's right to sell or dispose of land for the purpose of drainage and reclamation. At the same time, the judge ruled that land claims that IIF trustees had certified had to be provided to the certified owner or compensation had to be paid. Further, the judge granted an injunction that prevented the IIF from selling or disposing of land, except in small amounts as authorized by the court, pending the settlement of the claims. Soon after, the IIF began to settle the claims, primarily in relation to certified lands, and by the end of 1907 it had settled all claims but the Florida East Coast railroad claim, which was not be settled until the Key West Extension was completed in 1912. In the process, the IIF managed to hold on to about 2 million acres.

The legislature passed legislation creating the Everglades Drainage District in 1907. The district, lying south and east of Lake Okeechobee, was smaller than the one that would have been created under the failed constitutional amendment. However, litigation once again prevented the district from collecting the tax. The failure to find a source of tax revenue as well as an underestimation of construction costs jeopardized the future of the drainage projects. Broward switched tactics and sought buyers of large tracts of land to raise the funds to keep the project going. In the fall of 1908, he sold 500,000 acres to Richard J. Bolles at $2 per acre to be paid in eight annual installments. With these funds he was able to start the construction of drainage canals. In addition to the New River Canal, canals were also started between Lake Okeechobee and the Hillsborough and Miami Rivers.

Broward was succeeded by Albert Gilchrist in 1909, who continued the drainage efforts. Construction was turned over to private companies under the management of James O. Wright, an engineer who had produced an optimistic report on everglades drainage for the U.S. Department of Agriculture in 1909. Wright proposed that additional canals be built southeast from the lake, most of which were eventually built later in the century. The privatization of the drainage effort satisfied the major landowners, who agreed to pay back drainage taxes and support the project in 1910. But revenues from taxes remained low.

Although the purpose of building the large canals from Lake Okeechobee was to drain excess water from the lake, the canals also drained the land just west of the coastal ridge in Dade, Broward, and Palm Beach counties. The initial impact was on Broward County, because the New River Canal was the first to be constructed. About seven-eighths of the county's land was in the Everglades.[36] Construction began at Fort Lauderdale, affecting drainage in that area first. The first development west of the coastal ridge occurred in southwest Broward County in 1908. The Davie tract, immediately south of the New River Canal, was drained by R. P. Davie, and the tract immediately south was developed by the Everglades Sugar and Land Company. Davie used the state canal as the northern boundary and built a dike around the other borders. These dikes were natural roadbeds for roads. Inside the development, a network of canals and ditches drained the excess water during the rainy season into the state canal and provided irrigation during periods of drought. By 1914, 200 people were growing vegetables in the development.

The modest progress made on the New River canal, the optimistic report from the United States Department of Agriculture (USDA), and the support of the local landowners set off a speculative boom in land that was to be drained under the program. By October 1911, the trustees of the drainage district were offering ten-acre tracts on the unfinished canals at $35 per acre, and the Bolles Company had sold 10,000 of its ten-acre farms at from $20 to $24 an acre.[37]

Richard Bolles had previous experience selling farm land in Oregon. As part of his deal to purchase the 500,000 acres from the state, he secured an agreement that half the proceeds of the sale would be spent on drainage. Bolles created the Florida Fruit Lands Company to sell 180,000 acres of his land. He created 8,000 ten-acre tracts and 4,000 larger tracts that varied in size up to 640 acres. He also created a subdivision in Fort Lauderdale called Progresso, which featured 12,000 lots for homes that would be included with the purchase of one of the agricultural tracts. Purchasers paid twenty-four installments of $10 to secure a contract on a Bolles tract and a Progresso lot. The size and location of the tract was to be determined by a lottery, although each tract was guaranteed to be a minimum of ten acres. Bolles sent salespeople around the rural communities of the Midwest seeking purchasers of the tracts. Other land companies imitated Bolles's techniques, and many land sales occurred in 1910–1911.

In March 1911, the first Bolles lottery was held before several thousand people who had traveled to Fort Lauderdale for the event. Contract-holders elected trustees to receive the lands from the company. The trustees accused the company of assigning the tracts instead of by lottery, and they sued. Since most of the contract-holders could not travel to Fort Lauderdale for the lottery, there was a storm of protest in the Midwest and the federal government began to investigate. The fact that the lands were still under water added to the scandal. A judge froze the collection of payments by Bolles in 1913, but no money was refunded. At about the same time, Bolles was indicted on charges of mail fraud in Kansas City, but he died in 1917 before being forced to face the charges outside the state. Although he was the target of out-of-state prosecutors, Bolles had widespread support in Florida, especially in Fort Lauderdale.

Many people who held Bolles contracts stayed in Fort Lauderdale to await the successful drainage of the Everglades, which was still widely expected to be accomplished. Some purchased land on the coastal ridge. The growing population in the Fort Lauderdale area secured its own county (Broward) in 1915; the area's population had grown from an estimated 1,471 in 1910 to 5,135 in 1915.[38]

The controversies about the land promotion schemes dried up land sales, which had virtually ceased by the summer of 1912. The new governor, Park

Trammel, persuaded the legislature to enact new legislation that reorganized the Everglades Drainage District. Drainage "taxes," more properly called assessments, were to be levied in proportion to anticipated benefits; taxes would be highest close to Lake Okeechobee and the main canals. The taxes were to increase gradually as the drainage works were completed. The district was given the authority to issue bonds backed by the taxes instead of relying on land sales as a financing technique.

The new legislation also provided for local drainage tax districts to be established by a petition of a majority of property owners in the proposed district or the owners of a majority of the land. The districts could be administered by the local county or by an elected board. Special taxing districts, of which the drainage districts were an early prototype, became widely used in the state during the twentieth century. They permitted benefit-based taxation and the issuance of bonds to finance internal improvements backed by special assessments.

An example of a local special taxing drainage district is the Lake Worth Drainage District, established at the request of landowners in 1915 to drain the lands west of Lake Worth in Palm Beach County for agricultural purposes. By the end of the twentieth century, this district was managing over 500 miles of canals (drainage ditches) in an area that was largely urban. Another example is the Disneyworld complex near Orlando which was initially constructed on land in the Reedy Creek Drainage District a half century later. This district was created at the request of the landowners, all of whom were subsidiaries of the Disney Corporation. This drainage district was later transformed into an improvement district that obtained powers similar to local governments in the state.

Although benefit-based taxation and bonds based on district revenues seemed to resolve the financing problems of the Everglades Drainage District, bond markets proved unwilling to purchase the bonds because of the previous failures to complete the drainage project and the Bolles scandal. A commission of prestigious engineers was established to study the drainage problem, and its 1913 report reaffirmed that the drainage of the Everglades was practicable. It proposed the construction of a new canal linking Lake Okeechobee to the St. Lucie River that would enable surplus waters entering the lake from the north to be diverted away from the agricultural lands to the south. The new canal would relieve the burden of draining Lake Okeechobee on the canals to the south, which could be enlarged and deepened to provide drainage to the agricultural area.

The district drainage bonds were finally sold in 1917, and construction resumed. Progress was slow, however. Most of the funds were used to deepen and expand the existing system, and the St. Lucie Canal was not completed until 1926. Subsidence, or sinking, of the organic soils south of Lake Okeechobee increased their susceptibility to overflows, and a new dike had to be constructed along the lake's southern rim.

Vegetable farming was the main economic activity around the lake in the 1920s. Yields were initially disappointing, but it was soon discovered that the lakeside soils were deficient in fertilizer trace elements, especially copper. In the early 1920s, a period of relative drought came to an end and it became evident that the area south and west of the lake was subject to overflow. In 1921–1922, almost 6,000 acres were planted in vegetables around the lake, but flooding reduced this almost to 4,000 in 1923–1924. In 1926–1927, more than 9,000 acres grew vegetables, in spite of a hurricane. A more severe hurricane in 1928 reduced acreage slightly in 1928–1929. Tomatoes were an important crop in the lake region throughout the 1920s, but they were overshadowed by string beans in the last half of the decade. Irish potatoes were an important crop in the beginning of the decade, but potato acreage declined by two-thirds as string beans emerged as the crop of choice.

A hurricane in 1926 caused Lake Okeechobee to overflow its southwestern banks. The town of Moore Haven was destroyed, and between 300 and 400 people were killed. This was only the preview, however. In 1928, a second hur-

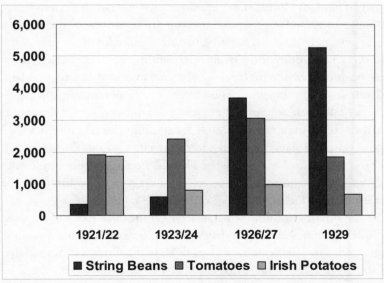

Chart 2–1. Acreage in String Beans, Tomatoes, and Irish Potatoes in Counties Bordering Lake Okeechobee in Florida, 1921–1922 to 1929 (Selected Years)

ricane struck and the lake again overflowed its banks, this time to the south and southeast. An exact count of the dead was not possible because many bodies were never recovered, but relief workers estimated the count at 2,400.[39] This was probably the second-largest number of deaths from floods up to that point in U.S. history; only the Galveston hurricane of 1900 had a higher death toll. Many of those killed were black farm workers.

The 1928 hurricane brought an end to the state's leadership in everglades drainage. The scale of the disaster convinced the federal government to act. An earthen dike was built around the lake and additional canals and spillways were constructed. Although these actions have prevented a recurrence of the 1928 disaster, numerous additional projects later in the century attempted to balance the needs of agriculture for flood control and irrigation, of the urban population for a backup water supply, and of recreational users of Lake Okeechobee and impacted rivers for clean water and healthy fisheries and other environmental resources.

Most of the public lands that were transferred beginning in 1880 did not become farmland. Some land was sold to settlers for farming, but it was a relatively small amount. Between 1880 and 1920, the acreage in Florida farmland rose from a little more than 3 million to about 6 million. This increase of about 3 million is dwarfed by the more than 20 million acres of public lands that were transferred.

The share of farms in Florida's land was similar to the share in western states. Between 1880 and 1920, land area in farms rose from less than 5 percent to a little over 20 percent in the western states. Farmland exceeded 40 percent of the total in all the other regions of the country except for the south-central region at the very beginning of the period. The share of farmland in the total land area of Florida rose over the same period from 11 to 17 percent. At the beginning of the period, Florida's farmland rate exceeded the rate in the West, but it was lower than the western rate by 1920. Clearly, farms did not absorb a large percentage of the public land transferred to the private sector in the 1880–1920 period. This was presumably because the Florida's new agricultural industries (fruit and vegetables) required small acreage and open range continued to be available for the cattle industry.

Some of the public land that was transferred from 1880 to 1920 was used for urban development. New urban developments were created at stops along the railroads and at new settlements such as those in the Pinellas Peninsula that were built in advance of the railroads. Florida's urban population increased by about 300,000 persons from 1880 to 1920.[40] If each of these persons absorbed three acres on average, the urban growth absorbed just about 1 million acres, compared to the total transfer of 20 million acres.

The conclusion is that most of the land transferred was not absorbed as farmland or as urban land. Most of the land was used for harvesting lumber, extracting turpentine, and herding cattle. As we saw in Chapter 1, these industries grew in Florida during the last decade of the nineteenth century. In the twentieth century, this surplus of relatively cheap land facilitated the rapid development of the state once uses for land emerged.

Chapter 3

Developing the Rail Network

The period 1880 to 1900 was characterized by the construction of the main parts of Florida's rail network. This network became linked to the extensive national network and transported Florida's exports to northern markets and brought tourists to the state. Railroad mileage in the state increased from about 500 miles in 1880 to more than 3,000 miles by 1900. The rail lines built by 1880 served the northern part of the peninsula and the eastern panhandle region. Much of the new mileage constructed after 1880 was in the southern two-thirds of the peninsula, south of Gainesville, although the rail link between Pensacola in the far northwest and the Apalachicola River was also completed at this time.

The building of the railroad down Florida's east coast from Jacksonville helped to open up a vast but sparsely populated part of the state. The southeast coast, in particular, had few people; its population was only 257 in the 1880 census. Fifty years later, this region had more than 200,000 persons and Miami-Dade County, which accounted for less than half the southeast coastal area, was the third most populated county in the state.

The northern rail lines were designed to replace sea voyages. At that time, cotton and other southern exports were shipped from Gulf of Mexico ports around the peninsula of Florida and up the Atlantic coast to New York and other northeastern ports and across the Atlantic to Liverpool and other British ports. The passage around the southern end of the Florida peninsula was hazardous because of storms, and the two major Florida railroads hoped to replace this ship traffic by bringing the goods on land to the northeastern Florida ports of Jacksonville and Fernandina.

The eastern panhandle of Florida, where Tallahassee was located, was the major cotton production region of the state, and Quincy immediately to its west was a center of tobacco production. The promoters of the Quincy-Jacksonville railroad hoped to ship cotton and tobacco from Florida's eastern panhandle and from southwest Georgia and southeastern Alabama. The promoters of the Cedar Key–Gainesville–Fernandina railroad hoped to receive goods shipped from Gulf of Mexico ports, such as New Orleans, Mobile, and Apalachicola, at Cedar Key, transport them by rail to Fernandina, and ship them from that point. Bypassing south Florida would speed up delivery and avoid the vulnerability to storms in the Florida Keys area. The Cedar Key–Fernandina railroad also traversed a major cotton-producing region in the state, centered at Gainesville in Alachua County.

Florida's railroad mileage, except for the 20-mile Tallahassee–St. Marks section, had all been constructed in the 1850s, and much of the mileage had been barely completed before the Civil War began in 1861. During the war, the railroads suffered from damage to terminals and bridges as well as a lack of maintenance. Additionally, the Cedar Key–Fernandina railroad lost a portion of its rails that the Confederacy commandeered to connect the Jacksonville-Tallahassee-Quincy line northward from Live Oak to Lawton in Georgia. The damage to the railroads was estimated at $1 million, about one-seventh of the value of the entire rail system.[1] At the end of the war, amid general destruction and economic dislocation, the state's railroads attempted to repair their tracks and equipment. Most of the lines passed through several hands before emerging once again in a healthy condition by the beginning of the 1880s.

The difficulties of the railroads had a direct impact on the finances of the state of Florida. Not until 1880, when Hamilton Disston bought millions of acres, was it possible once again to use the public lands given to the state under the 1850 Swamp Lands Act to provide inducements to the private sector to complete the rail network in the state. The widespread publicity of Disston's sensational purchase generated interest in Florida, not only from elsewhere in the United States, but also from England. Other wealthy northerners began to make investments in Florida at this time. Two residents of New York, Henry Plant and Henry Flagler, also invested in the state, and their investments went a long way toward completing the railroad system in the Florida peninsula.

Henry Bradley Plant owned the largest share of Florida's rail lines at the time of his death in 1899. Although he was often called a railroad builder, the number of miles he constructed was actually relatively small. He was an investor rather than a builder, and much of his rail mileage was purchased after the Panic of 1893 created difficulties for the independently owned Florida roads.

Plant was born in Branford, Connecticut, in 1819. His father died when he was six years old, and Henry completed the equivalent of an eighth grade education.[2] At the age of 18, he became a deck hand on the New York–New Haven steamboat run. At that time, the need for express delivery of small packages was growing. The captain of the steamboat on which Plant served saw a need to organize this business. He assigned a stateroom where all the packages would be stored and made a single crew member responsible for their care. He chose Henry Plant for this task. After Plant was married in 1842, he obtained a position for a time in a store that supplied items for the West India traffic; this may have been a source of his interest in establishing shipping services between Tampa, Cuba, and Jamaica later in his life. Within a short time, Plant went to work in the express business, first in New Haven, Connecticut, and soon after in New York City.

In the late 1830s, the express business began to meet the need for the transportation of small packages between cities. Ship and railroad companies handled bulk freight and the U.S. postal system handled the mails.[3] Express companies were developed to handle the reliable and speedy transportation of small packages. Much of the early demand came from bankers. After the charter of the U.S. central bank (the second Bank of the United States) was not renewed in 1836, banks had to hire couriers to deliver bank drafts at a cost of 10 percent of the value of the draft. Express companies lowered costs by achieving economies of scale. Although point-to-point express service over relatively limited distances had been created earlier, it gradually became evident that a more widespread network was needed. Additionally, by expanding the number of packages shipped on a trip, the fixed cost of hiring an accompanying messenger could be spread over a larger number of items.

One of the earliest express companies was founded by Alvin Adams to transport packages between New York and Boston after his business collapsed during the Panic of 1837. Adams enjoyed considerable success and secured an effective monopoly on the business along the eastern seaboard and throughout the south. Adams & Company purchased the express company that employed Henry Plant and transferred its sea-based routes to railroads. Plant soon rose in the ranks of the larger company.

During the period 1853–1854, Adams & Company reorganized as Adams Express Company and decided to expand to the South. Henry Plant was appointed a superintendent of the Company "in charge of all the interests controlled by [the] company and all that might be acquired by the company in the South through his management or through his efforts."[4] Plant's wife had become ill in 1853 with congestion of the lungs, and her doctors had suggested a trip to Florida. When the Plants visited Florida, his wife's health improved. Henry Plant felt that a southern location would benefit his wife's health, and they moved to Augusta, Georgia, in 1854. Plant expanded the southern business of Adams Express throughout the South, culminating in the acquisition of the Texas and New Orleans Express Company in 1858.

When the Civil War began, it was clear that the southern division of the Adams Express Company would be vital to the Confederacy. But the company was owned by northerners and subject to seizure by the Confederate government. Plant approached the top management in New York and suggested that they spin off the southern division to him and to shareholders with southern addresses. This was done, and Plant gave $500,000 in personal notes in return for 90 percent of the shares in the new Southern Express Company. He also received a guarantee of his personal safety from President Jefferson Davis of the Confederacy.

During the Civil War, the Southern Express Company carried out many services for the Confederate government, including carrying military pay. It is likely that the business was very profitable for Henry Plant, although it was also very demanding. In 1862, his wife died, and shortly thereafter Plant's own health deteriorated. His doctor recommended a change of climate, and Plant decided to leave the South until the war ended. He secured a passport from the Confederate government and in the fall of 1863 he traveled to the neutral territory of Europe.

At the end of the war, Plant returned to Augusta and resumed management of the Southern Express Company. Once the South recovered, the business of the Southern Express Company presumably regained its profitability. Plant paid off his $500,000 in debt to the Adams Express Company in 1868 and 1869 and moved to New York City.

As in Florida, the railroads of Georgia and South Carolina emerged from the war in financial distress. Many limped along for a number of years, but the Panic of 1873 plunged the nation into an economic recession that lasted until 1878.[5] The lengthy recession forced a number of southern railroads into bankruptcy. Plant was presented with an opportunity to use his considerable capital to purchase a number of these railroads, and although he was approaching sixty years of age, he decided to obtain control of the rail network on which he was most dependent and to extend it southward into Florida. It is clear from his actions that Plant was not interested in railroads per se but rather that he saw them as parts of a general multimodal transportation network. Rail was one mode of travel and travel by sea was another. Plant was especially interested in speeding up the movement of freight and people across the network by developing faster links and extending the network at the periphery.

In 1879, Plant purchased the Atlantic and Gulf Railroad at a bankruptcy sale.[6] This railroad ran from Bainbridge in southwest Georgia across the southern end of Georgia to the Atlantic seaport of Savannah. The railroad carried cotton from southwestern Georgia to Savannah for shipment to the northeast or Liverpool in England. There was also steamboat service from Bainbridge down the Flint River to the Florida port of Apalachicola on the Gulf of Mexico, and Plant may have believed that goods from elsewhere in the Gulf could be brought up the river to Bainbridge and shipped across to the Georgia port of

Savannah on the Atlantic, thereby avoiding the long and dangerous trip around the southern end of the Florida peninsula. In 1883, Plant extended the railroad west to the Apalachicola River, opening up the possibility of shipping cotton from southeast Alabama and linking to a proposed railroad from Pensacola to the river. Plant bought a second bankrupt line that linked Savannah with the South Carolina port of Charleston in 1880, providing access to a second and larger Atlantic port for his rail line. The combined rail lines were reorganized as the Savannah, Florida and Western Railroad.

Plant turned his attention to Florida. He already owned the only rail link into the state that ran south from the Savannah, Florida and Western Railroad to Live Oak, which was on the Jacksonville-Tallahassee-Quincy line. The trip to Jacksonville, however, which was the gateway city into the state for northern visitors, was roundabout and the rail line was shared with the Florida Railway & Navigation Company, which was not subject to his control. Plant's first project was to construct the Waycross Short Line, a direct and faster link from the Savannah, Florida and Western to Jacksonville. This was completed in 1881 and absorbed into the parent line. Soon after, Plant put steamboat service south from the St. Johns River to Sanford, the river gateway to central Florida.

Next, Plant began to push south into the peninsula. In 1882, he completed a line from Live Oak to a point on the Suwannee River near the modern town of Branford, which was named after his birthplace in Connecticut. The river was navigable from there to its mouth on the Gulf of Mexico and provided boat access to Cedar Key, at that time the biggest Gulf of Mexico port on the west coast of the Florida peninsula. Cedar Key was the west coast terminus of the cross-state railroad from Fernandina in the northeast corner. Plant met a chilly reception in his efforts to link his railroad with Cedar Key and determined to push southward to Tampa Bay and Charlotte Harbor, both of which could be developed into significant Gulf ports. The more ambitious plan down the western side of the peninsula required an estimated $5 million, and Plant, needing access to capital, formed the Plant Investment Company, a holding company that had access to several wealthy northerners willing to provide capital to finance his projects in Florida. Among the investors was Henry Morrison Flagler, a wealthy executive of the Standard Oil Company, of whom more will be said shortly.

Plant commenced construction from Branford toward Gainesville but discovered that another railroad, the Florida Southern, was building north from that city to Lake City, about twenty-five miles east of Live Oak. This would have resulted in two parallel lines running north from Gainesville, and Plant agreed not to build south from Gainesville provided Florida Southern did not build northward.

At this time another railroad, the South Florida Railroad, entered the picture. Incorporated in 1879, the South Florida had constructed a line from Sanford to Orlando in 1880 and had reached Kissimmee by 1882. Soon afterward, James C. Ingraham became president of the railroad. Ingraham had been the Florida agent of Henry Sanford, another wealthy northerner who had invested in Florida and was pioneering the development of the citrus industry. Ingraham ultimately became one of Henry Flagler's chief lieutenants, managing his real estate holdings. The South Florida Railroad needed to complete a line from Kissimmee to Tampa in a very short time to satisfy the terms of a large land grant from the state. Sanford introduced Ingraham to Plant, who knew about the South Florida Railroad's problem. The Plant Investment Company took a three-fifths stake in the railroad, began construction of the line from both Tampa and Kissimmee, and finished the project in January 1884, two days before the deadline. Plant also helped the South Florida push south to Bartow to connect to the southern division of the Florida Southern coming up from Charlotte Harbor.

As Plant was constructing the line from Kissimmee to Tampa, another railroad company, the Jacksonville, Tampa, Key West Railroad, was constructing a line down the west bank of the St. Johns to Sanford. This line, which was completed in 1885, provided through service from New York and other northern cities to Tampa. In 1886, when standard gauge became the norm, Pullman car service was available from New York to Tampa. In the 1890s, after the financial

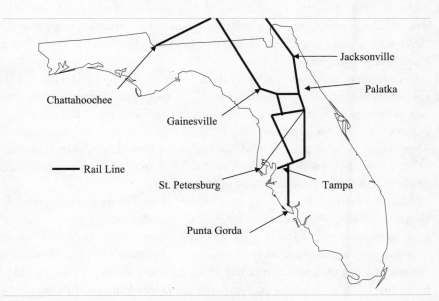

Florida Map 3–1. Sketch of Plant Railroads in 1899

panic in 1893, Plant gained full control of all of these railroads and merged them into the Plant System. After his death, the Plant System of railroads was purchased by the Atlantic Coast Railroad line, a major company with rail lines along the East Coast of the country.

Tampa was the port on Florida's west coast that Plant had wanted so he could participate in the West Indies traffic since he had begun to push his railroads down the state. He extended his railroad southwest of the town to a place on Tampa Bay where there was relatively deep water; he named it Port Tampa. He constructed a large terminal· and two immense piers there, each nearly a mile long.[7]

In 1885, Plant ordered construction of the *Mascotte*, a steamship to provide passenger and cargo service between Port Tampa, Key West, and Havana. This was so successful that he ordered the larger *Olivette* a year later. Because business declined in the summer season in Florida, he placed the *Olivette* in service between Boston and Bar Harbor in Maine. During the winter months, the *Olivette* also provided weekly service to Mobile, Alabama, as well as to Key West and Havana. Plant built the Port Tampa Inn as a place for his passengers to stay while waiting for sea or rail connections. He also built the Tampa Bay Hotel, a large luxury hotel, for affluent winter tourists.

By 1891, the *Mascotte* and *Olivette* were providing thrice-weekly service between Tampa, Key West, and Havana during the winter season. A third ship, the *William G. Hewes*, provided weekly service between Tampa, Santiago de Cuba, and Port Antonio, Jamaica. Finally, he placed the steamboat *Margaret* in daily local service to the Manatee River (Bradenton) south of Tampa Bay. By 1896, service had been extended to the Caloosahatchee River (serving Punta Rassa and Fort Myers).

As a result of his development of the rail system to Tampa and its port, Cuban cigar manufacturers moved from Key West to Tampa, making it one of the largest centers of cigar manufacturing in the state. Tampa was also the closest major port to the phosphate-mining industry that had developed in the 1890s. These became major items of trade in Tampa. In 1901, Tampa shipped a total of $8.4 million of goods by sea and rail.[8] Of this total, $5.2 million consisted of cigars and $1.8 million consisted of phosphate.

During the Spanish American War in 1898, Port Tampa was designated as the principal port of embarkation for military expeditions to Cuba. The initial expedition consisted of 16,286 men and 2,295 horses. The fleet of thirty-two transport vessels and five tenders included several of Plant's ships. Additionally, the government used the Tampa Bay Hotel to house the expedition's leaders, including Colonel Teddy Roosevelt. Although Henry Plant did not found the city of Tampa, the transportation links he built put the city on the map. Not long after his death, Tampa became the second most populated city in the state.

The second wealthy northerner who began to invest in Florida railroads in the 1880s was Henry Morrison Flagler. Although he came to Florida to create a winter version of Newport, Rhode Island, an exclusive resort for the wealthy, he also built the Florida East Coast Railway more than 400 miles down the east side of the peninsula, founding the city of Miami in the process. Henry was born to Isaac and Elizabeth Flagler on January 2, 1830.[9] Henry's father was a Presbyterian minister with a limited income. When Henry's half-brother Dan Harkness was fourteen, he went to live with his deceased father's family near Bellevue in western Ohio. The family had prospered in the area by establishing a network of country stores along a new railroad that linked Bellevue to the port of Sandusky on Lake Erie. The stores served as shipping points for the region's grain and as sources of manufactured goods for the region's farmers. Dan was quickly absorbed into the growing family enterprise and rose through the ranks. In 1839, he brought his half-brother Stephen to Ohio to run a family-owned harness shop, and in 1844, fourteen-year-old Henry joined him in managing a family store in Republic, Ohio.

In 1848, Flagler moved to the Harkness store in Bellevue. This business was reorganized as D. Harkness and Company in 1852, headed by Henry's half-brother Dan with Henry as a partner. In 1853, Flagler married Mary Harkness, who was his mother's niece but was not his blood relative. The marriage brought Henry fully and formally into the Harkness family with its considerable financial resources.

The Bellevue business prospered in the 1850s. The Harknesses and Flagler shipped grain, the major export of the community, to Cleveland. One of the Cleveland commission merchants they used was John D. Rockefeller, who had begun working in the business for Hewitt & Tuttle in 1857 before forming his own firm with Maurice B. Clark in 1859. D. Harkness and Company also used grain to distill whiskey, which contributed greatly to the prosperity of the firm. Stephen Harkness, half-brother to Dan, made even more from the distillery business by stockpiling whiskey in advance of a tax that was imposed during the Civil War and selling the stockpile at the higher price.

Henry Flagler decided to move into a new business in 1863. With Barney York, who had just married his wife's sister, he moved to Saginaw, Michigan, in 1863 to start a salt-producing business. The demand for salt had increased substantially due to the Civil War, and production had skyrocketed in Michigan, rising from less than 5,000 bushels in 1860 to more than 100,000 in 1861 and more than 200,000 in 1862. By the time Flagler arrived in 1863, a classic speculative bubble was under way. Although he did well in 1863 and 1864, the end of the war reduced the demand for salt substantially and a condition of oversupply prevailed. By 1866, Flagler's salt enterprise was bankrupt.

Flagler did not return to Bellevue after the war. He moved to Cleveland and entered the grain commission firm that John D. Rockefeller and Maurice B. Clark had established in 1859. Although Rockefeller had moved into the oil business in 1863, he retained an office in the building where the grain business was housed, and he and Flagler developed their friendship.[10] In 1867, when Rockefeller needed capital to expand his refining business, he asked Flagler to become a partner. The firm was reorganized as Rockefeller, Andrews and Flagler (RAF). Stephen Harkness, half-brother of Flagler's half-brother Dan, was a silent partner, and the Harknesses provided Flagler with funds to buy his way into the firm.[11]

Flagler was responsible for shipping crude oil to Cleveland and refined oil to New York, from where it was shipped to Europe, the main market in the 1860s and 1870s. Cleveland, which was west of the oil fields, was vulnerable to competition from oil refiners in Pennsylvania and New York. It was essential that RAF secure advantageous transportation rates to counter the location advantage of the competition. RAF could get favorable rates if it signed a contract that committed the company to ship a large minimum amount of oil along the railroad's line. These contract negotiations occupied much of Flagler's time with RAF. By 1870, favorable transportation rates had been negotiated.

Economy of scale was the key to the success of RAF; greater volume in shipping would lower the cost of transportation. But expansion required capital. According to Rockefeller, it was Flagler who proposed the solution to this problem, namely, the restructuring of RAF as a joint stock company (corporation) that could issue shares and use them to buy other refiners.[12] The Standard Oil Company was formed in January 1870 with John D. Rockefeller as president, his brother William as vice president, and Henry Flagler as secretary-treasurer. The new company set about taking over the other oil refineries in Cleveland, putting it in a position to get ever-lower transportation rates. The new low rates enabled Standard Oil to acquire parts of the petroleum industry outside Ohio and to gradually become the dominant player in the national industry.

The expansion of Standard Oil outside Ohio and Pennsylvania prompted Rockefeller and Flagler to move the company's headquarters east. In 1878, they moved the headquarters of Standard Oil to New York City.[13] At the same time, however, Mary Harkness Flagler's health deteriorated. She was diagnosed with tuberculosis and was advised to spend the winter in Florida. The Flaglers planned to spend the months of February, March, and most of April in Florida, but they did not arrive until the end of February in 1878, and when Flagler decided he must return to New York on March 17, his wife accompanied him.[14] This was the time when Flagler was preoccupied with what one of his biographers called the Great Pipeline Battle. Standard Oil was dealing with a threat occasioned by proposals from potential competitors to ship refined oil by pipe to East Coast ports without using the railroads on which the company had an advantage. Flagler was in the front line, negotiating lower rail rates to discourage new pipelines and attempting to influence state legislatures interested in granting charters to pipeline companies.

After returning to New York, Mrs. Flagler's health continued to deteriorate and Flagler urged her to spend the following winter in Florida on her own, but she did not wish to make the long trip on her own and be away from her family for such a long period.[15] In the winter of 1880–1881, Flagler became alarmed at his wife's deteriorated condition and thought of going back to Florida. But the doctor vetoed a Florida trip, and Mary died in March 1881, leaving Flagler with an adult daughter and an eleven-year-old son.

The death of his wife was a shock to Flagler that caused him to reassess his life. He decided to reduce his involvement with Standard Oil in order to spend more time with his family and devote more of his energy to activities he enjoyed. A few years later, when Flagler was asked why he was building a hotel in Florida, he replied, "There once was a good old church member who had always lived a correct life until well advanced in years. One day when very old he went on a drunken spree. While in this state he met his good pastor, to whom, being soundly upbraided for his condition, he replied, 'I've been giving all my days to the Lord hitherto, and now I'm taking one for myself.' This is somewhat my case. For about fourteen or fifteen years, I have devoted my time exclusively to business, and now I am pleasing myself."[16]

There may have been other reasons why Flagler reduced his involvement with Standard Oil. The 1870s was a period of rapid expansion for the company, and Flagler may have enjoyed the excitement as Standard Oil rose to dominance in the industry. The 1880s, however, were dominated by defensive activity, particularly lawsuits and critical government investigations. Although Flagler assumed the roles of company lawyer and governmental affairs officer, he lacked formal legal training and found testifying before adversarial legislative committees unpleasant. Flagler found a knowledgeable attorney who had successfully sued Standard Oil and gradually turned much of the company's legal affairs over to him.

After the death of his wife, Flagler leased an estate at Mamaroneck, New

York, on Long Island. He spent the summer of 1881 there with his half-sister Carrie and his son. His daughter Jennie was also a frequent visitor. The family enjoyed the experience so much that Flagler decided to buy the estate, which he did at the beginning of the summer of 1882. The purchase of the estate was a harbinger of things to come. Flagler completely renovated the property both inside and out. He purchased new furniture and even designed his own chandeliers. He constructed a seawall and breakwater and brought in sand from the New Jersey shore to build a private beach.

On June 5, 1883, Flagler married Ida Alice Shourds, who had been one of Mary Harkness Flagler's nurses during her final illness. Business commitments prevented Flagler from going on a honeymoon until the following winter, and he decided to return to Florida. On his first Florida visit in 1878, he must have observed the absence of first-class resort hotels and the poor quality of transportation in the state. In 1882, he invested in the Plant Investment Company, showing an interest in the state and a belief in its future development. Henry Plant was a prominent resident of New York City, and he may have known other wealthy New Yorkers who were investing in Florida. One was William Astor, who had purchased 80,000 acres along the Upper St. Johns River in 1874 and often spent a portion of his winters in Florida. Much of his time was spent aboard his yacht *The Ambassadress*, reputed to be the largest yacht in the world.[17] Flagler bought two railroads from William Astor shortly after completing his hotel developments in St. Augustine.

The Flaglers set out on the 90-hour rail trip to Jacksonville in December 1883. The trip was so long because of frequent changes of carriages necessitated by the different gauges the railroads used and the roundabout trip between Savannah and Jacksonville. The Flaglers spent a few days in Jacksonville and then moved on to St. Augustine. They took a boat trip down the St. Johns River to Tocoi, a landing area fifteen miles west of St. Augustine. From there they took a small narrow-gauge train on the St. Johns River Railroad to St. Augustine. It is not known where they stayed, since the city lacked an upscale hotel. However, they were charmed with St. Augustine and delighted to be away from a severe northern winter. They stayed through the month of February and determined to return the following winter.

When the Flaglers returned in February 1885, they took the new Jacksonville, St. Augustine and Halifax River Railroad from South Jacksonville directly to the city. On this second trip, Flagler decided to build a resort hotel in St. Augustine to serve the needs of wealthy northerners for a mild location during the winter months. His massive Ponce de Leon Hotel was opened for the winter season in January 1888. During construction of the hotel, Flagler became concerned about the quality of the Jacksonville, St. Augustine and Halifax River Railroad. The narrow-gauge road with 30-pound rails was slow and subject to breakdowns under the pressure of the materials being carried to St. Augustine for the hotel's construction. Flagler urged the railroad's owners to make improvements, but when this did not occur he purchased it and improved it himself at the end of 1885.[18] Flagler was joined in his purchase of the Jacksonville, St. Augustine and Halifax River Railroad by investors who owned and managed the Jacksonville, Tampa and Key West Railroad that had been constructed along the west bank of the St. Johns River from Jacksonville south to Sanford. Flagler joined forces with these investors because he "did not wish to bother with the administration of the road."[19]

Flagler's interest in railroads did not stop there. He wanted to make sure that his hotel guests could reach St. Augustine quickly and safely. He bridged the St. Johns River at Jacksonville in January 1890 and built a passenger depot in South Jacksonville.[20] In 1888, he purchased the two railroads owned by William Astor: the fifteen-mile line between Tocoi and St. Augustine and a branch from this line southeast to Palatka on the St. Johns. The Tocoi–St. Augustine connection facilitated passenger travel between Jacksonville and St. Augustine. There may also have been considerable travel by his hotel guests to Palatka in order to take cruises up the Ocklawaha River to Silver Springs or up the St. Johns River to Sanford; winter river cruises had been popular on these rivers since the 1870s.

Late in 1888, Flagler purchased and improved the Palatka-Ormond-Daytona railroad owned by S. V. White that had developed from the four-mile road built by a Hastings vegetable farming pioneer. This provided his hotel guests with an opportunity to go farther down the east coast. Flagler provided for their needs by purchasing the Hotel Ormond near Daytona.

About forty miles south of Daytona, the Indian River began—the 200-mile lagoon between Cape Canaveral and the Jupiter inlet that would later become part of the Atlantic Intra-Coastal Waterway. The communities along the west bank of the Indian River were major producers of oranges and pineapples and provided Flagler with a potential market if he could extend his rail line farther south. Additionally, the Celestial Railroad, which had been built in 1889, linked the Jupiter inlet to the town of Juno at the north end of Lake Worth.[21]

Before Flagler could extend his railroad south of Daytona, he needed to terminate his partnership with the owners of the Jacksonville, Tampa and Key West Railroad; he had promised that he would not compete with their Indian River Steamship Company. This he accomplished in May 1892, but in the process he hired some personnel connected to the railroad, including Joseph

R. Parrott, who became general manager of his railroads. Flagler ordered the construction of a new fifteen-mile line south from Daytona to New Smyrna. This was completed by December 1892. Henry Flagler had finally become a railroad builder.

In 1893, the Florida legislature increased land grants from 3,840 acres (six square miles) to 8,000 acres (12.5 square miles) for each new mile of rail line constructed. Flagler unified his railroad companies into the Jacksonville, St. Augustine and Indian River Railway and built the 175-mile New Smyrna–Lake Worth extension. His railroad reached the future site of West Palm Beach in March 1894. He thought that his Florida project was finished when he arrived at Lake Worth. He had constructed more than 200 miles of rail line, had developed a winter resort in St. Augustine, and was in the process of developing another resort in Palm Beach. He had a railroad company and a hotel company and knew that he would soon be entering the land development business. For these reasons he rejected the proposal of Julia Tuttle, who owned land at the mouth of the Miami River, to extend this rail line to the Miami area.

Julia Tuttle was the daughter of Edward Stuyvesant, who had moved to the mouth of the Miami River with the Brickell family in 1871. They homesteaded on the south side of the river. Their daughter Julia was married to Frederick Tuttle of Cleveland, the son of one of the founders of the Hewitt & Tuttle trading company, the grain merchants who had hired John D. Rockefeller when he finished his education. Mrs. Tuttle was also a member of Rockefeller's church in Cleveland. During the 1870s, Julia Tuttle had visited her father and liked the Miami area well enough that she purchased 640 acres on the north side of the Miami River. By the end of the 1880s, she had become a widow and had moved permanently to the Miami area, where she built the Miami Hotel.

Flagler's interest in extending his railroad to the south was stimulated by the disastrous back-to-back freezes in the winter of 1894–1895. His land development manager, J. C. Ingraham, also had an interest in the Miami area. Ingraham had effectively become an employee of Henry Plant when Plant took a controlling interest in the South Florida Railroad in 1883. Julia Tuttle had tried to persuade Henry Plant to extend his railroad from Fort Myers to Miami, but this required crossing the Everglades. Plant sent Ingraham on an expedition across the Everglades in 1892 to search for a potential rail route, but the results discouraged him from proceeding with the project. The trip took more than two weeks.[22] During the trip, Ingraham became convinced that much of the Everglades could be drained and he knew that such land might become available for railroad and drainage projects in the region.

In the fall of 1892, Flagler hired Ingraham to manage the land grants that he was receiving because of the construction of the new rail line south of Daytona. After the disastrous freezes in 1894–1895, Flagler sent Ingraham to look at the potential of the Miami area. At the same time, J. R. Parrott, the general manager of his railroad, secured a promise of private land grants in return for extending the railroad south. The Florida East Coast Canal and Transportation Company was engaged in the development of what would become the Atlantic Intra-Coastal Waterway south of Lake Worth. The company lacked funds and was struggling to complete the project. Failure to complete the project would jeopardize its land grants, and Flagler provided capital to help complete the project in return for 1,500 acres for each mile of railroad constructed.[23] The railroad, of course, would increase the value of the remaining land belonging to the canal company.

The Boston and Florida Atlantic Coast Land Company was affiliated with the Florida East Coast Canal and Transportation Company, which had been established in 1892 to exploit some of the land grants that the company was receiving as a result of its canal construction. The investors in the land company had provided $100,000 to be used to purchase 100,000 acres of the land grants the canal company would receive as a result of its canal construction.[24] The land company agreed to provide 10,000 of their acres if the railroad was completed to Miami. Finally, Julia Tuttle and the Brickells agreed to share their one-square-mile sections on either side of the mouth of the Miami River. These lands would become the heart of the city of Miami.

Flagler completed the railroad to Miami in 1896 and laid out the new city. As had become his practice, one of his first acts was to build a luxury hotel for affluent winter tourists, the Royal Palm Hotel. The hotel opened in 1897, the same year he moved his Nassau steamship service from Palm Beach to Miami, creating a shorter journey with a departure pier that was less exposed to Atlantic storms. He purchased a new ship, the *Miami*, to make the journey. Flagler also provided shipping service between Miami and Key West. In 1898, the Spanish American War boosted his business. Indeed, the *Miami* was the lead ship in the convoy that delivered the initial military expeditionary force from Tampa to Cuba.[25] After the war, he initiated regular service between Miami and Havana.

In 1903, Flagler resumed the southward movement of his railroad, building the twelve-mile Cutler Extension to collect the fruits and vegetables being produced in that area. In 1904, he extended the line twenty-eight miles farther south to what would become the town of Homestead. Flagler's most expensive railroad project was the Key West Extension. The excitement generated by the construction of the Panama Canal in 1902 made him anxious to develop a port at Key West. Finally, after much planning, Flagler announced his decision to construct the railroad to Key West in 1905.[26] Although construction began on the mainland in April of that year and in Key West in November, the 127-mile project from Homestead to Key West was not completed until January 1912.[27]

The construction of the overseas railroad was one of the great engineering feats of the era, like the completion of the channel tunnel linking England and France was a century later. There were logistical problems of providing accommodations and food and water to a 4,000-member work force scattered across an archipelago of small islands. A special program to provide health care to the work force had to be developed. Hurricanes hit the project in three years, causing more than 100 deaths.[28]

Because of the small size of the local population, the work force for the project had to be brought in from outside the state. Many were immigrants recruited in northern cities. The workers were brought on contract and were totally dependent on the company while working offshore. The company was accused of the crime of peonage—overcharging workers and encouraging them to accumulate large debts that required them to continue renew their contracts. Charges against the railroad's engineers, William J. Krome and Joseph C. Meredith, were dropped as their case came to trial in November 1908.[29]

The railroads Plant and Flagler owned at the end of the nineteenth century provided a network for taking goods and passengers up and down the Florida peninsula. The 150-mile gap across the western panhandle of the state between the Apalachicola River and Pensacola was closed as a result of the efforts of William D. Chipley, a Confederate war veteran who had become general manager of the Pensacola Railroad in 1872.[30] The Pensacola Railroad was the successor company to the Alabama and Florida Railroad, another of Florida's railroads that had had the misfortune to be completed on the eve of the outbreak of the Civil War.[31] The Alabama and Florida ran south from a railroad at Flomaton, Alabama, to Pensacola. Chipley arranged for the sale of the Pensacola Railroad to the Louisville and Nashville in 1880 and became a division superintendent of that railroad.

In March 1881, the Louisville and Nashville incorporated the Pensacola and Atlantic Railroad to build a line from Pensacola to the Apalachicola River. The railroad expected a grant of more than 3 million acres from the state of Florida and more than 500,000 acres from the federal government. Bonds were issued to finance the new road that the Louisville and Nashville guaranteed. Construction began in the summer. Several large bridges were constructed, especially one across Escambia Bay.

Sir Edward Reed combined the rest of the major prewar Florida railroads into the Florida Railway and Navigation Company in 1884. By this time, parts of the old railroad were no longer viable, such as the line to the obsolete port of St. Marks. The port at Cedar Key lost out to Tampa during the rest of the 1880s, and Fernandina lost out to Jacksonville. The railroad was reorganized as the Florida Central and Peninsular Railroad in 1888, and the new company took on a more north-south orientation. The Waldo extension of the railroad was extended to Plant City and from there a line was completed west to Tampa in 1890.[32] It also connected to Orlando in 1891.

In 1893, the Florida Central and Peninsular Railroad turned its attention to the north. It completed a line north from Yulee to Savannah in 1894, and in 1895 it purchased a rail line from Savannah to Columbia, South Carolina. At this time, however, the finances of the company began to deteriorate, partly because of the depression after the Panic of 1893 and also because of the collapse of the Florida citrus industry after the freezes of 1894 and 1895. In 1898, the company was purchased by the investor group that was putting together the Seaboard Airline, a 2,475 rail network extending from Montgomery, Alabama, to Richmond, Virginia, and Tampa.

As the twentieth century began, Florida developed a railroad grid and was linked into the national network through the Atlantic Coast Line, which had purchased the Plant System and the Louisville and Nashville at Pensacola. Several decades later, the Atlantic Coast Line and the Seaboard Airline merged and eventually became CSX. The Florida East Coast Railway remained independent of the big systems, and this would be true even a century later.

The role of railroads in the development of the U.S. economy in the last half of the nineteenth century has been a matter of controversy among economic historians.[33] There is agreement that the economy was transformed during the period and that there was a big expansion in railroad mileage during the transformation. The question is whether the state's economic transformation could have occurred without the expansion of the rail network.

We have seen that the expansion of the rail network in Florida, which occurred much later than in most of the rest of the country, occurred at a time when the state economy underwent a significant expansion. It is noticeable, however, that much of Florida's expansion took place along the coasts of the southern half of the peninsula—in exactly those places that could have been served by alternative (sea) transportation. There would have been economic development in southern Florida even if the railroads were not there. Northern capitalists had become interested in Florida by 1880, as is demonstrated by the investments of Hamilton Disston, which were largely unrelated to railroads.

On the other hand, the expansion of the rail network facilitated and contributed to the geographic expansion of the economy, especially by opening up the state's forests to exploitation.

Florida's new rail network and, even more important, the linking of state to the national network reduced the cost of transporting Florida products to northern markets and transporting northern customers (tourists) to Florida. The railroads were important to the development of the fresh fruit and vegetable industry in the state. In the early years, techniques for preserving the freshness of these products were undeveloped, and speed to market at an economically feasible cost was a dominant consideration. Over time, technologies for preserving freshness reduced the premium on speed. These technologies included picking products before they were ripe, altering the appearance of products that were not yet ripe, pre-icing before shipment, shipping in refrigerated or well-ventilated cars, and so on. By the end of the twentieth century, it was possible to transport fruit and vegetables over enormous distances to northern U.S. markets. For example, Chile exported fresh fruit and vegetables to the United States, and New Zealand was an important source of apples.

Speed of transportation is more important to passengers because their travel cost includes the cost of their time as well as their out-of-pocket costs. The travel cost includes the income or alternative consumption a passenger forgoes while he or she is traveling. We will see that one of the achievements of the cruise industry later in the twentieth century was its transformation of the travel experience into a consumption item, but with that one exception, most passengers have repeatedly chosen faster speeds, other things being equal. For example, the introduction of transoceanic air travel in the 1950s led to the drastic shrinkage of travel to Europe by ocean liner. On the other hand, automobile tourism to Florida remains important a century later because it has a lower per-person cost for families with children and for other groups. The automobile is also important to winter residents who do not want to rent a car in Florida or pay to transport their car from their place of origin.

Railroad development was a key part of the transfer of the state's enormous public domain into private hands. This process turned many railroad companies into land development companies. As a result, the railroads did more than merely facilitate the development of the economy; they became important direct participants in that development.

Chapter 4

Sunshine Agriculture before 1900

As the twentieth century began, a number of preconditions were in place that facilitated the rapid growth of Florida's economy. These included national and local transportation networks that enabled Florida to export goods and services from its position on the nation's periphery to the developed center of the economy, an endowment of cheap undeveloped land that accommodated the state's economic expansion, and new industries whose competitive advantage stemmed from the state's geographic position. This chapter traces the historical development of two of these new industries, semitropical agriculture and fresh winter vegetables. Collectively, these are called sunshine agriculture, industries that thrived because of the state's warm winter.

The state's semitropical products were chiefly citrus, which is grown in the summer and fall and harvested in the winter and spring, pineapples, and avocados. Most citrus species are thought to have originated on the warm southern slopes of the Himalayas in northeastern India and what is now Myanamar.[1] The citron, a type of citrus, was introduced to Palestine by Greek colonists about 200 BC. Citron production had reached southern Italy by the first century AD. The sweet orange developed in southwestern China before the middle of the first millennium BC, but it was not grown in Europe until several hundred years later. When it spread to India, it obtained the Sanskrit name of *nagarunga* and later *naranj* in Persian and *naranja* in Spanish, from which the English word orange is derived. The frescoes at Pompeii in southern Italy suggest that sweet orange trees were growing in southern Italy in the first century AD. By the fourth century, there were elaborate orangeries there to protect them from the cold. When the Roman empire collapsed about the middle of the first millennium AD, Italian citrus culture apparently died out.

Citrus culture reappeared in Europe before AD 900, after the Moors invaded Spain. Southern Spain became identified with a type of sour orange, the Seville. It is likely that sweet oranges were also introduced around the same time because of their ready availability in Egypt and Iraq, from which the Spanish Moors imported products for their gardens.

Christopher Columbus took orange, lemon, and citron seeds from the Canary Islands with him on his second voyage in 1493.[2] They were planted on the island of Hispaniola and spread rapidly over the next two or three decades. Soon after Pedro Menéndez d'Avilés founded the Spanish colony of La Florida in 1565, the second governor of the colony, his nephew Pedro Menéndez Marqués, wrote that oranges were beginning to be available "in great quantity" around St. Augustine.[3]

During Florida's period as a Spanish colony, oranges were not cultivated for export, perhaps because Spain grew her own oranges and because oranges were widely grown elsewhere in Spain's American empire. During a brief occupation by the English prior to the American Revolution, colonists sent oranges and orange juice to England, but this trade ended when the Spanish returned in 1783.[4]

When Florida became part of the United States in 1821, there was considerable interest in citrus. A freeze in 1822 destroyed sweet orange trees in Pensacola, but replacements were reported as bearing by 1827.[5] Count Odette Phillippi, former chief surgeon in Napoleon's navy, introduced the grapefruit to Florida at Safety Harbor near Tampa in 1823.[6] This citrus fruit, named because it grows in bunches on the tree, apparently arose in the West Indies in the eighteenth century as a mutant of the shaddock, a large fruit of little commercial importance named after the English sea captain who introduced the seeds from the Orient. Zephaniah Kingsley used profits from his slave-trading operations on Fort George Island near Jacksonville to purchase land for orange groves on the Upper St. Johns River in 1824.[7] Both the Safety Harbor and Kingsley groves became sources of seed for the expansion of the citrus industry after the Civil War.

Two other groves that were established in the early 1830s were an important supply of stock in the later citrus expansion. The groves were sheltered enough to withstand a devastating freeze in 1835. In 1830, Douglas Dummitt established an orange plantation on the northern end of Merritt Island.[8] Trees from this plantation survived into the twentieth century, when they were photographed and shown to have consisted of sweet orange scions that were budded onto a sour orange rootstock. This is the earliest evidence of the budding (a type of grafting normally employed in Florida's citrus industry) of Florida orange trees. The other grove was originally established a little farther north in Turnbull Hammock. John D. Shelton transplanted some of its orange trees to a site near the Hillsborough River north of Tampa in 1842.

In 1827, more than a million oranges were shipped from the St. Augustine area and investments had been made in new groves and in nurseries.[9] These trees began to bear in the early 1830s, and several million oranges were shipped both in 1833 and in 1834. But in February 1835, Florida experienced what was called at the end of the twentieth century "the most severe freeze [recorded] in the history of the state."[10] February freezes have often been the most severe in their impact on citrus because the trees are not dormant and new growth is particularly vulnerable to damage. The year 1835 had historically low temperatures—the 7 AM temperatures in St. Augustine and Tampa were 10 degrees and 20 degrees, respectively. Temperatures in the northern part of the peninsula remained below freezing for fifty-six hours, and temperatures in the lower part of the peninsula remained below freezing for thirty hours. Most of the trees in the state were destroyed.

The citrus industry did not regain its pre-1835 production levels until after the Civil War. First, the outbreak of the six-year Second Seminole War in 1836 was accompanied by the destruction of the plantations along the St. Johns River. This was followed by economic difficulties after the Panic of 1837. As renewed plantings began in 1838, the trees were attacked by a pest, later called the purple scale. By the early 1850s, all the groves around St. Augustine and most of those as far up the St. John's River as Lake George (east of Ocala) had been destroyed. Further damage resulted from a severe freeze in 1857.[11]

As the Civil War ended, it became evident that there was a large and growing market for oranges in the United States and that Florida was in a position to capture most, if not all, of these sales. The result was "orange fever," a rapid expansion of investments in orange groves in the state. At the time, the demand for oranges was largely met by imports, especially from the Mediterranean area. In 1855, the first year for which the value of orange imports was separately published, their value amounted to almost half a million dollars, and this value increased by more than 50 percent in the following four years.[12] In 1883, when separate data for orange imports were again reported, their value had quadrupled to over $3 million.[13]

Investments in orange groves took years to pay off, particularly if trees were grown from seedlings. Even budded trees took three years to begin bearing. Additionally, it took time to learn where oranges would grow successfully, and the choice of location was constrained by the need to be close to water transportation and the small amount of railroad mileage available in the state in the mid-nineteenth century.

The most famous of the early post–Civil War groves was established by Henry Shelton Sanford, whose experience illustrates the difficulties in developing the industry at that time. Sanford, a wealthy Connecticut investor who had spent the war years in diplomatic posts in Europe, made an offer for an

orange grove in St. Augustine in 1867.[14] Soon afterward, in 1870, Sanford purchased 12,547 acres on Lake Monroe where the modern city of Sanford now
stands. The lake was part of the St. Johns River, the main north-south traffic
artery in Florida until the railroad boom of the 1880s and 1890s. There were
several orange groves along the banks of the river and their production was
sent on steamboats that regularly traveled between Lake Monroe and Jacksonville. Sanford's idea was to sell the land in small parcels and use the proceeds
to finance a model grove. On finishing high school, Sanford had spent a year
at Washington College (now Trinity College) in Hartford, Connecticut.[15] The
college had been founded on a philosophy that stressed practicality in education, and its curriculum included courses in the natural sciences. The college
maintained a greenhouse and arboretum. Sanford's desire to establish a model
citrus grove was presumably influenced by his experience at Trinity.

Sanford's first problem was in obtaining an adequate labor force to clear
his land, plant a grove, build a road, lay out a town, and build a wharf on the
lake. He also built a general store, a hotel, a sawmill, a slaughterhouse, and a
real estate office. The local labor force was inadequate and Sanford began by
bringing in black workers from north Florida. Resentment by the local white
population forced Sanford to hire guards to protect his workers, but eventually
the imported workers were driven out of the city. He next imported Swedish
laborers as the equivalent of indentured servants under the contract labor law.
Although he had some occasional difficulties with his new labor force, many
of these immigrants remained with him for many years and founded a Swedish
immigrant colony in the vicinity of the town.

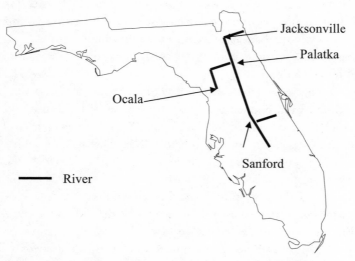

Florida Map 4–1. Sketch of the St. Johns River System 1870-90

Sanford originally laid out two groves on his property, one called St. Gertrude and the other Belair. Because the St. Gertrude Grove sat on top of hard pan, it suffered from flooding, and after two years the trees were transferred to Belair.[16] The Belair grove contained 145 acres, of which ninety-five were in oranges and fifty were in lemons. Ten acres were devoted to nursery stock. Sanford imported stock from all over the world and is credited with the first importation of blood oranges and other varieties that included the Jaffa and Valencia.[17] He also introduced lemon varieties, including the Villafranca, and varieties of pineapples. He rigorously tested varieties and became a source of stock for many other orange growers in the state. Although, as will be shown below, Sanford's attempt to establish a citrus grove was ultimately unsuccessful, his research into citrus varieties and production methods was a key part of the development of the state industry. Sanford planted seedlings at Belair rather than budding his trees. As a result, he had to wait ten years before the grove began to produce significant amounts of fruit. Although it appeared likely that a good crop of oranges would be harvested in 1882, exceptionally dry weather caused much of the fruit to drop while still unacceptably small.[18] Lemons, harvested in the summer, were successful in 1882 and 1883. In 1883, exceptionally wet winter weather delayed the orange harvest because oranges rotted if they were picked and shipped while wet. Nevertheless, Belair finally had some success in the following two years.

In January 1886, a freeze struck Florida that was the most severe since 1835. The freeze lasted for four days and destroyed most of the orange crop north of Tampa.[19] Damage to the trees reduced Belair production in the following year. Irrigation was introduced into the grove in 1887. In the summer of 1888, Sanford was unable to ship his fine crop of lemons because of a yellow fever scare. There was an outbreak of yellow fever in Florida and goods from state were refused entry to northern cities because of fear that they carried the source of the fever. Maryland health authorities ordered a cargo of Florida lemons dumped into the sea, and Orlando's City Council banned incoming trains. Sanford shipped fruit to London, where they were sold at low prices.[20] In 1888–1889, wet winter weather delayed orange picking, but it was the most successful production that had been recorded at Belair. A hard freeze in March 1889 severely damaged lemon trees but left orange trees unscathed. Lemon production was abandoned—the lemon trees were budded with oranges. In 1889–1890, dry weather led to fruit drop, but there was less damage at Belair because of its irrigation system. Most of the crop was purchased by Chase and Company, which covered the picking, processing, and packing expenses.[21] Henry Sanford died in 1891, and Belair was sold to Chase shortly after the devastating freezes of 1894–1895.

Most other early citrus growers after the Civil War used budded trees, a strategy that brought production and revenues more quickly than in Sanford's case. There were groves of wild orange trees in most woodlands and forests south of St. Augustine.[22] Many of these groves were located next to lakes or rivers, where there had been Indian communities in earlier centuries. By the middle of the nineteenth century, these wild groves were composed of sour orange trees—the variety most tolerant of wetlands and cold weather. Transplants from these groves became the base from which the new citrus industry expanded.

The availability of water transportation was a critical ingredient in determining the location of Florida's new citrus industry. Florida Map 4–2 shows the distribution of orange production by county in Florida in 1881, measured in units of boxes of 150 oranges.[23] Putnam County, where the Ocklawaha River joins the St. Johns River, had the largest production in the state, followed by Marion County to the southwest. Orange County (which contained Sanford at that time) and Volusia County, both south and southeast of Putnam, were also important production centers. Hillsborough County was the most important orange production center on the west coast of the state.

Toward the end of the 1860s, a number of settlers began to cultivate the wild orange groves around Orange Lake, sixteen miles north of Ocala, in Marion County. It was said to have the largest number of wild orange trees anywhere in the state.[24] Transplanting the wild trees was a demanding job. Many of the

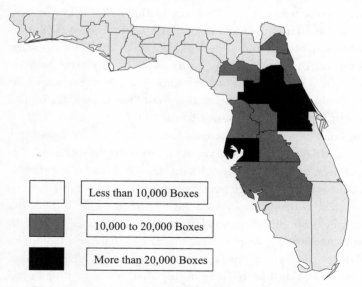

Florida Map 4–2. Orange Production in Florida Counties, 1881

trees were very large; some had been full-grown trees before the 1835 freeze. Some had thrown up three or four large trunks as they recovered. The roots of the trees were intertwined. The orange trees often grew below tall pine trees, many of which also had to be removed. Transplanters cut off the sour orange trees about two to three feet above the ground and budded sweet oranges on to them. Budwood was in short supply and it was necessary to travel quite far to find enough. Considerable distances also had to be traveled to the nearest store and post office, and the fruit had to be hauled to the Ocklawaha River eight miles away. Malaria was also a hazard.

Significant production at Orange Lake began about 1877. Initially, the orange stems were cut with pocket knives, during harvesting, but it was too easy to accidentally puncture the rind using this method. A circular pair of shears was invented, but even these could damage the rind. Finally, orange growers began to use clippers with curved blades. Fruit was cured by placing the field boxes in rooms for several days to allow excess moisture to evaporate. Once cured, the fruit was graded and sized. Initially, fruit was sized by eye, but H. B. Stevens, an employee of P. P. Bishop, invented the first patented sizer about 1880.

Fruit was graded by color into two classes: brights and russets. Brights had a relatively smooth skin free of defects; russets had a rust-colored peel due to being punctured by the rust mite. Fruit was also graded by quality into Fancy No. 1 and Fancy No. 2. But standards for these grades were not uniform.

Eban B. Bean, brother-in-law to P. P Bishop, invented the 90-pound box for packing oranges in 1876 at Bishop's packing house in San Mateo, near Palatka, and by 1880, much of the industry had adopted it.[25] The box was 12" × 12" × 27", divided into two compartments, each with a capacity of one cubic foot. Although the box was originally made from Florida cypress, the wood was too heavy and rough, and Bean imported birch veneer sidings and solid birch heads for construction. The number of oranges depended upon the size packed in the box.

Fruit was normally sent by steamboat from Palatka or Jacksonville and from there to Savannah, Georgia, or Charleston, South Carolina, where it was transferred to larger steamboats for transport to northeastern cities. Rail shipments were not widely used until the Waycross Short Line was opened in 1881. The adoption of the standard railroad gauge in 1886 and the growing use of refrigerated rail cars boosted rail shipments in the late 1880s.

Orange production expanded greatly during the 1880s. Between 1881 and 1889, production of Florida oranges increased almost ninefold. The development of the state's railroads was an important stimulus to production. Production moved southward into the central peninsula, following the new railroads.

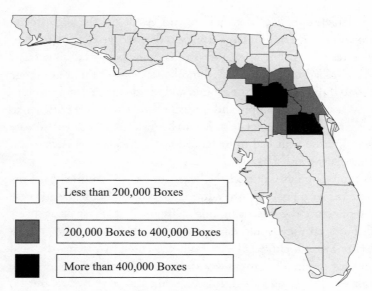

Florida Map 4–3. Orange Production in Florida Counties, 1889

Orange County became the largest producer in the state, producing 50 percent more than Marion County, the second-ranked county.

However, production outstripped demand, as can be seen from the 50 percent reduction in prices from $2.09 per box in 1881 to $1.00 in 1889.[26] As it became evident that markets had a tendency to glut, growers began to ship their oranges earlier, often while the fruit was still green. This damaged the reputation of Florida oranges, depressing prices further. The 1884–1885 season became a legendary disaster when early shipping and panic selling resulted in a collapse of prices.[27] The golden era of high prices had come to an end.

Efforts were made to solve the problems of market gluts after the disaster of 1885. The Florida Fruit Exchange cooperative was founded in 1885 to "receive, prepare, distribute, and provide for the transportation and sale of oranges, lemons, and other fruits and perishable products."[28] The exchange had bonded agents located in the principal distribution centers who reported daily on market conditions, including the number of oranges on hand, the number of unsold oranges, and prices. However, the exchange never accounted for more than 10 percent of production, presumably because most growers believed that they could do better on their own.[29] It was about this time that buying on the tree began, and the exchange promoted this new method of marketing. A lack of storage or holding facilities that forced the exchange to ship production on receipt may have been partly to blame for the relatively low level of support.[30]

The exchange folded after the freezes of 1894–1895, although it was revived and expanded almost twenty years later.

The increased difficulty of growing oranges profitably forced improvements in production and packing. To promote the use of commercial fertilizers, the state created the office of state chemist, which began sending inspectors to examine products on the market in 1889.[31] In 1891, the federal government began sending scientists to study pests and diseases of orange trees; E. F. Smith and W. T. Swingle went to Florida in that year to study orange blight. In 1893, the U.S. Department of Agriculture established the Sub-Tropical Laboratory at Lake Eustis, where scientists studied the properties of different rootstocks. They found that the rootstocks of sour or bittersweet orange were immune to foot-rot and that rough lemon rootstock was most appropriate for pinelands. Beginning in 1890, many orange growers began to use irrigation systems. Growers were urged to handle fruit "as though it were made of china," to grade the fruit carefully, then wash it and pack it in attractive wrapping paper.[32] Machines for washing and packing paper were in use by 1894.

Much of the progress being made in the industry was interrupted by the devastating freezes in 1894–1895. The first freeze began on December 27th, when the temperature fell to 14 degrees. The cold temperatures continued through December 29th in most parts of the northern and central parts of the peninsula and were accompanied by strong winds. About 3 million oranges were still on the trees, and the bulk of these were frozen solid. Most of the larger trees were not seriously damaged by the freeze, although they lost their leaves a couple of weeks later. The *Yearbook of the United States Department of Agriculture* described how growers sold the frozen fruit: "The frozen oranges and pomeloes [grapefruit] remained firm and solid for fully a month after the freeze and were eaten in great numbers and also shipped to northern markets. It is safe to say that there has never been a time in the history of Florida or America when so many oranges were eaten in so short a time. The cautions of physicians were unheeded, but the result was not disastrous, as so many feared. Indeed such sickness as occurred from eating frozen oranges was unquestionably due to excessive indulgence. Many of the frozen oranges were sent to Northern markets and placed on sale while still juicy and palatable. In some cities their sale was forbidden by the health authorities, who claimed that they were injurious, but this claim has been thoroughly disproved by their extensive use, as above described."[33]

About the middle of January, numerous sprouts began to grow vigorously on the trees. Fine weather persisted into early February, with highs around 80 degrees and night temperatures above 50 degrees. This encouraged the new growth. But on February 7th through the 9th, Florida experienced a second freeze of a similar magnitude to the freeze six weeks before. The trees, with their young growth and no leaf cover, were particularly hard hit by this freeze. In many cases, it was some months before the full extent of the damage became apparent. Some large trees resprouted some distance above the ground, but later the new sprouts died because the trunk below had been killed in the freeze. Tree destruction was fairly complete north of Lake Okeechobee, except for trees protected by bodies of warm water, such as on the south banks of Lake Harris and Lake Eustis, and trees bordering on Tampa Bay.

The destruction of the trees reduced Florida orange production in 1895 and 1896 to a little more than 40,000 boxes, mostly from Dade and Lee counties, two enormous counties that accounted for the entire southeastern and southwestern areas of Florida at that time. This was a major blow to Florida's most glamorous agricultural industry and the most important new industry in the state's economy at that time.

The negative impact of the major freezes affected population growth, a key indicator of the health of the state's economy. The rate of population growth rose from about 15 percent in the late 1880s to almost 20 percent in the first half of the 1890s, before the impact of the freeze.[34] In the post-freeze late 1890s, the rate of population growth fell below 15 percent and remained at a relatively low level in the first five years of the twentieth century.

Another indicator of the negative impact of the freeze was the effect on the value of farms in the state. Between 1890 and 1900, the value of Florida farms, including land and buildings but excluding equipment and livestock, fell by more than 40 percent. Elsewhere in the South Atlantic states, farm values increased by 10 percent. The special distress Florida farmers experienced as a re-

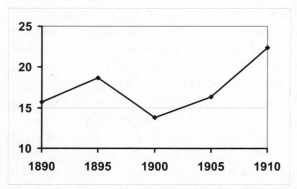

Chart 4–1. Population Growth Rate in Five-Year Intervals, Florida, 1890–1910 (by Percent)

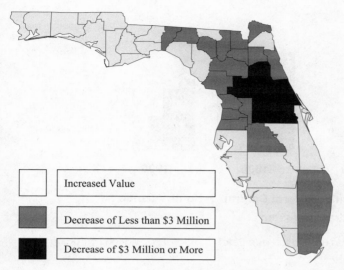

Florida Map 4–4. Change in Farm Values in Florida Counties, 1890 to 1900

sult of the freezes in 1894–1895, compounded by the additional severe freeze in 1899, is also illustrated in the census estimates of the average income of farmers and other farm workers in 1899.[35] The average annual labor income in Florida was $119.72, the lowest for any state or territory. Florida's average labor income was less than half the level in the country as a whole and just over 70 percent of the level in the other South Atlantic States. The low Florida level reflected the capital losses farmers suffered when the value of their farms declined. The largest losses were in the north-central part of the peninsula—Putnam, Marion, Orange, Lake, and Volusia counties, the northern part of the Orange Belt. These counties together experienced a loss of $30 million in farm values between 1890 and 1900.[36]

Fresh winter vegetables constituted the other sunshine agricultural industry developed in Florida in the closing decades of the nineteenth century. Florida gradually developed the capacity to supply northern markets with vegetables earlier in the year than any other production region in the nation. Commercial vegetable production developed as the United States became more urbanized. By 1880, the first census which reported the nation's urban population, almost 50 percent of the population of the North Atlantic states lived in urban places with populations of at least 4,000 persons. Urban dwellers accounted for about 25 percent of the population in both the North Central and Western regions.

All urban centers imported fresh vegetables from the countryside. The

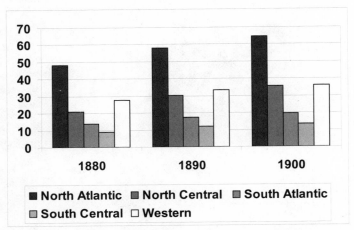

Chart 4–2. U.S. Urban Population as a Percent of Total Population by Region, 1880, 1890, and 1910

market demands of smaller cities could be met by the farmers just outside the city limits. Larger cities, however, imported vegetables from farther afield, particularly if a fast enough means of transportation was available. Until the 1880s, such transportation tended to be water based. Production for nearby urban centers was called market gardening, while production for more distant markets was called truck farming. The census category "production of market gardens" included both market gardening and truck farming.

In 1870, eight counties in the United States produced over $400,000 worth of vegetables for sale. The largest production was in Queens County, adjacent to New York City, and the second largest was in Middlesex County, adjacent to Boston. Both of these counties produced about $1 million in vegetables. The fourth largest production was in Philadelphia County, and the sixth was in Hamilton County, Ohio, home to the city of Cincinnati. The seventh and eighth counties with the largest production both were on the outskirts of Baltimore, Maryland. Two of the top eight counties were on the east side of the Delaware River in New Jersey—Burlington, ranked third in production, and Camden, ranked fifth in production. These counties, the first large truck farming centers, sent their production by boat to New York City or Philadelphia, the cities ranked first and second in population size in 1870. New York City had more than 900,000 persons within its borders and Philadelphia had more than 650,000.

The climatic conditions in the New Jersey counties made it possible for them to produce vegetables earlier in the season than was possible in the counties closer to the two large cities.[37] The earliest vegetables commanded the high-

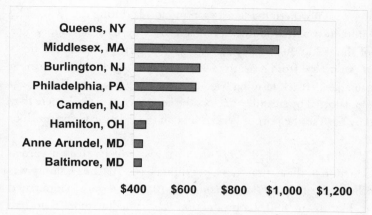

Chart 4–3. U.S. Counties with Vegetable Production Valued at More than $400,000 in 1870 (in Thousands of Current Dollars)

est prices, and a greater distance from the cities made land cheaper, resulting in strong economic incentives to engage in truck farming there. New Jersey was ranked second among the states in the value of its vegetable production, after New York and before Massachusetts and Pennsylvania. On a per capita basis, New Jersey was ranked first in the country. It had already earned the nickname of Garden State.

The climatic advantage that enabled New Jersey to bring vegetables to market earlier than other northeastern counties was present to an even stronger degree in the regions farther south, and by 1870 truck farming had begun in the South Atlantic states. Among the 100 largest vegetable-producing counties in the nation, three coastal South Atlantic counties—Norfolk County in Virginia, Beaufort County in South Carolina, and Chatham County in Georgia—were ranked in the top thirty in terms of the value of their vegetable production per capita. (A high value of production per capita indicated that local farmers produced more vegetables than the local population needed, thus producing surplus for export.)

Norfolk County in Virginia, home to the port of the same name, produced the seventeenth largest amount of vegetables among the more than 2,200 counties in the nation, and it was ranked fifteenth on a per capita basis among the 100 largest producing counties. The first shipment of vegetables from Norfolk to New York was brought on the steamship *Roanoke* in 1854.[38] The long time needed to make the trip (thirty-six hours) made it difficult to maintain the quality of the vegetables, but improvements in steamships had cut the trip time in half by the end of the century.

Truck farming for northern markets began in Florida during the 1870s. The industry was initially centered southeast of Gainesville in Alachua County on a flat lowland of about 20,000 acres known as Payne's Prairie. A stream that flows into a sink in the prairie from a nearby lake became clogged in 1871, turning the prairie into a lake. Truck farming began south of the new lake.[39] The vegetables were transported by steamboat across the lake to Gainesville, where they were shipped by train to the port of Fernandina on the Atlantic Coast north of Jacksonville.

By 1880, Alachua was ranked fifty-fifth in the size of its market garden vegetable production in the nation. On a per capita basis, Alachua County was ranked twelfth among the 100 largest counties. Alachua County dominated production in Florida in 1880. Its production was valued at more than half the value of the state total. Three other counties had significant production; Duval County with its port of Jacksonville; Putnam County, which was located up the St. Johns River from Jacksonville; and Levy County, located southwest of Gainesville. Both Levy and Alachua counties were on the railroad that ran between the Gulf Coast port of Cedar Key and the Atlantic port of Fernandina in the northeast corner of the state. Vegetables were shipped from these ports by sea to northern markets.

The data are very limited on vegetable production in the old Middle Florida region centered at Tallahassee between the Apalachicola and Suwannee rivers, but it had become a center of production by the 1870s and 1880s. The 1900 census noted that the Irish potato in the southern states in the last decades of the nineteenth century was "purely a garden truck crop" because locals preferred sweet potatoes. The production of Irish potatoes can thus be taken as an index of the development of the trucking industry there.[40] The distribution of production of potatoes from the 1880 census shows that Irish potatoes were relatively important in the Middle Florida region. This is not surprising; the region had rail connections to northern markets. Vegetables were transported some 80 miles east to Live Oak before turning north to join a railroad in Georgia. The vegetables were sent by express, and transportation expenses accounted for a large part of the total expenses farmers incurred.[41]

The value of vegetable production increased in Florida during the 1880s as the state's rail network was completed. By 1890, the state's production had more than tripled in value. Alachua County was still the dominant producer, although it now accounted for only one-third of the state's total. Vegetable production was beginning to move south as the new railroads opened up new sources of supply. The second largest producing area consisted of Marion, Orange, Sumter and Lake counties, located in central Florida southeast of Gainesville.[42]

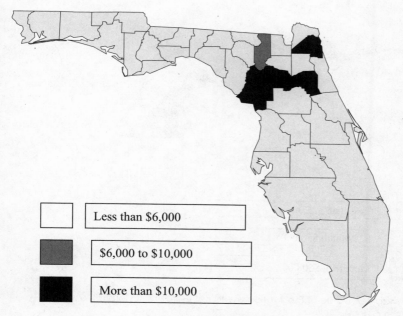

Less than $6,000

$6,000 to $10,000

More than $10,000

Florida Map 4–5. Value of Production of Market Gardens in Florida Counties, 1879, in 1879 Dollars

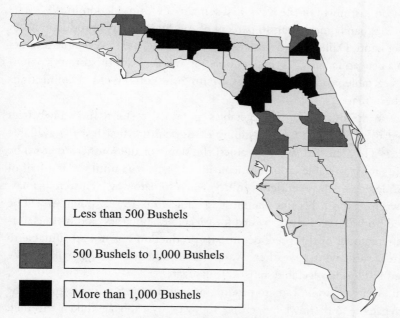

Less than 500 Bushels

500 Bushels to 1,000 Bushels

More than 1,000 Bushels

Florida Map 4–6. Production of Irish Potatoes in Florida Counties, 1879, in Bushels

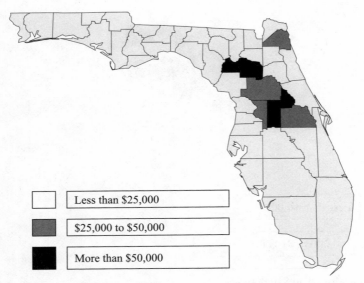

Florida Map 4–7. Value of Production of Market Gardens in Florida Counties, 1889, 1889 Dollars

Even Dade County, which had no rail connections until the 1890s and which at the time extended from Stuart in modern Martin County south to Homestead just north of the Keys, had some modest production in 1890. The amount was barely more than 10 percent of Alachua County's production. On the other hand, Dade County was ranked first in the state in vegetable production on a per capita basis. Its small population was aware of the county's potential for vegetable production and was awaiting the coming of rail connections to northern markets.

Data on the production of vegetables, potatoes, melons, and strawberries collected by the Florida Commissioner of Agriculture first became available in 1889.[43] They showed sweet potatoes, the staple of the southern diet, to be the state's most valuable crop. This continued to be true until the last half of the first decade of the twentieth century, when tomatoes, which were primarily grown for export, became the most valuable crop. (Sweet potatoes will be excluded from the statistics provided for vegetables, potatoes, and melons during the remainder of this book because its production was not attributable to the state's warm winter weather. Watermelons and strawberries will also be included in Florida vegetable statistical aggregates.)

Even as early as 1889, tomato production was the most valuable among the other vegetable and strawberry crops, followed by cabbage. Taken together, these two crops accounted for 55 percent of the vegetables exported to northern markets. Alachua County was the largest producer of both crops. Strawberries were the third most valuable crop in the state.[44] In the words of a 1902 observer, "Since the introduction of the improved system of refrigeration the strawberry industry has been largely developed, especially on the western slope of the peninsula. A long chain of stations, each cultivating from 24 to 150 acres, extends down this side of the peninsula from Clay to Hillsborough County, and at the height of the shipping season a special service is established by the railroads traversing this section for the rapid dispatch of the fruit, putting it in New York in 72 hours and in Cincinnati and Chicago in less time. One peculiarity of the cultivation of the strawberry in Florida is that the work is performed almost entirely by hand, with light gardening instruments. The reason is that the profits on two or three acres managed under the intensive system are greater per acre than they would be on twice that area under less careful methods."[45]

The city of Lawtey in Bradford County became a center of strawberry production in the late 1880s through the efforts of Stephen Powers, editor of *Florida Farmer and Fruit Grower* magazine.[46] Lawtey was a stop on the Cedar Key–Gainesville–Fernandina railroad. In 1889, Bradford County accounted for a little over half of the value of the state's strawberries. This was more than three times the level in Alachua County, the second largest producer. After the 1894–1895 freezes, production expanded greatly in Hillsborough, Polk, and Pasco counties. Production in this area was introduced by in-migrants from Mississippi, where strawberries had long been an important crop.[47] The rail junction at Plant City in eastern Hillsborough County became an important shipping center.

The fourth most valuable vegetable crop consisted of watermelons.[48] The largest production of this crop was in the state's panhandle in Jefferson County, immediately east of Tallahassee. The 1900 U.S. census lists Jefferson as part of an important watermelon belt around Thomasville, Georgia, just across the state line.[49] The historian of Jefferson County notes that W. M. Girardeau "was already making Jefferson County the watermelon seed supplier for the nation in 1884. . . . By 1892 he was acknowledged as the 'melon king.'"[50]

On a per-acre basis, strawberries were by far the most valuable of the state's export and vegetable crops and watermelons were among the least valuable. Watermelons, of course, need a relatively large input of land per unit produced.

As the 1890s progressed, the railroad reached southeast Florida, arriving in West Palm Beach in 1894 and in Miami in 1896, and vegetable production expanded into this region of the state. Data in the annual report of Florida's commissioner of agriculture for 1901 showed an increase in production value that was almost two and a half times greater than the 1889 figure. The report

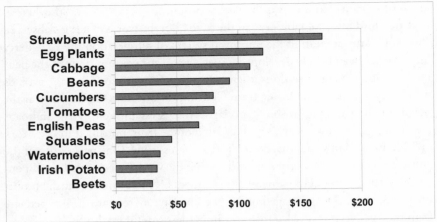

Chart 4–4. Value of Vegetable Production per Acre, Florida, Current Dollars, 1889

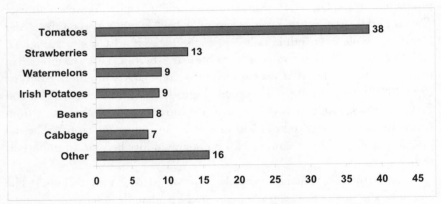

Chart 4–5. Value of Vegetable Production in Florida as a Percent of Total Production, 1901

showed that tomatoes were the most valuable crop, accounting for 38 percent of production value, excluding sweet potatoes but including melons and strawberries. Strawberries were second at 13 percent, and watermelons and potatoes each accounted for 9 percent. Beans accounted for 8 percent and cabbage for 7 percent. Relatively smaller amounts of miscellaneous vegetables, including beets, cantaloupes, celery, eggplant, lettuce, peas, peppers, and squashes, accounted for 16 percent of production value. The 1901 data show a greater diversity of vegetables being produced in the state than in 1889 and a decline in the importance of cabbage.

By 1901, Dade County, which was still enormous in size, had displaced Alachua County as the largest vegetable producer. The value of its production was

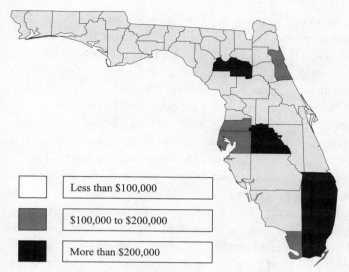

Florida Map 4–8. Value of Vegetable Production in Florida Counties, 1901, in 1901 Dollaras

more than two and a half times the Alachua County level. Alachua was ranked third, behind Polk County, the first county east of Tampa. Hillsborough County was ranked fourth, and Pasco County was ranked fifth.

The bulk of Dade County's vegetable production was accounted for by tomatoes. Alachua and Pasco counties were relatively diversified across a variety of vegetables, but both Polk and Hillsborough counties had important strawberry production. By 1901, the area around Plant City had displaced Lawtey in Bradford County as the center of strawberry production in Florida.

Two other counties ranked in the top ten in production value. St. Johns (ranked sixth) and Orange (ranked ninth) were in the process of developing the production of a signature vegetable with which each county would be associated for decades into the future. In the case of St. Johns it was the potato, and in the case of Orange County it was celery. The area of Orange County where celery was becoming important (the area around Sanford) was split off and became the new county of Seminole in 1913.

The center of potato production in St. Johns County was the town of Hastings, about nineteen miles southwest of St. Augustine. After state land grants became available for railroad construction once again in the 1880s, a lumberman, U. J. White, received a land grant in the Hastings area in return for building a logging railroad south from East Palatka on the St. Johns River four miles to San Mateo. Although many companies abandoned lands that had been logged at that time, White noticed there was a "surface of rich black soil from eighteen inches to two feet deep below which was a subsoil of clay. Deep Creek, a considerable stream that empties into the St. Johns River, skirts the tract and there is quite a fall to the creek. . . . He took his [railroad laborers] . . . and set them at work digging a canal through the tract. He also sank an artesian well and with an ox team broke up forty acres of land. . . . [He] dug several lateral ditches not connected with each other but leading to the canal. [These] performed the duty of sub-irrigation."[51] Although White initially grew cabbage on the tract, it was discovered soon afterward that the soil in the area was particularly adapted to potato growing. In 1901, potatoes accounted for 97 percent of the county's vegetable production and the county accounted for 54 percent of the total value of potatoes produced in the entire state.

Celery production in the Sanford area of Central Florida began when orange growers turned to vegetables after the catastrophic freezes in 1894 and 1895. Even if they had budded or planted new citrus trees, it would be several years before those trees would produce a marketable crop, and farmers needed a cash crop in the meantime. The celery industry encountered problems with water management, disease, and frost in the early years, which inhibited its development.[52] Celery acreage in Florida rose from 92 acres in 1902 to 932 acres in 1912 and 1,661 acres in 1918. By 1927, this land had grown to 4,929 acres, with 4,322 acres in Seminole County, whose county seat was Sanford. Sanford became known as "the Celery City." Farmers there used a subirrigation system that flowed across tiles using artesian wells as the water source. They also planted banana plants as windbreaks.[53] The celery was "boarded up" by placing long cypress planks along the rows to shield the plants from direct sunlight. This "bleaching" produced a white and tender celery that was more desirable in northern markets.

California dominated early celery production, and California shippers threatened to blacklist Florida distributors in northern markets. Chase and Company broke market resistance to Sanford celery by sending free samples to distributors and following up with personal contacts.[54] Prior to shipment, the celery was cooled and sent in railroad cars packed with ice at each end. As a result, Sanford became home to one of the largest ice plants in the country.

The tendency toward specialization in a single vegetable crop, as is evident with tomatoes in Dade County, potatoes in St. Johns County, and celery in Seminole County, had several advantages.[55] First, farmers in the area gained experience, which reduced uncertainty about the suitability of land and its likely yield. Second, specialization led to the development of grower associations that could improve marketing practices by developing appropriate packing facilities and attracting wholesale buyers. Third, the produce could also be shipped in relatively large car lots at a reduced rate. Finally, specialization enabled the growers to brand their production as coming from a location that was well known as a high-quality source of supply.

Much of the state's production of vegetables took place on muck lands. These lands were analyzed in a publication of the Florida Agricultural Experiment Station in 1897, which noted that they contained a rich soil that would need to be drained and supplemented with certain chemical elements. Once this was accomplished, they would make "excellent garden lands."[56] By 1900, many muck areas were contributing to the state's vegetable industry, and the muck area south of Lake Okeechobee became the largest source of vegetable production in the state as the twentieth century progressed.

Chapter 5

Tourism before 1930

Tourism was the third of Florida's sunshine industries that had begun to develop by the end of the nineteenth century. This industry, like sunshine agriculture, obtained the bulk of its revenues by selling to customers who were residents of northern states. In contrast to agriculture, however, the products of the state's tourism industry were not shipped north. Instead, the industry's customers traveled to Florida to make their purchases.

The beginnings of modern tourism in Western Europe can be found in travel to holy sites in the late middle ages. One of the first works in English literature, *The Canterbury Tales* by Geoffrey Chaucer, was a fictionalized account of stories told by a group of pilgrims traveling to the shrine of Thomas à Becket in England. Pilgrims who journeyed to holy sites linked travel with spiritual and physical health. Popular pilgrimage destinations often had holy wells that were assumed to have medicinal properties, perhaps as a result of the divine intervention of holy figures associated with them.[1]

After the Protestant Reformation in the sixteenth century, pilgrimages diminished, particularly in northern Europe, but the cult of watering places lived on. In seventeenth-century England, people traveled to mineral springs to imbibe or bathe in their waters in search of health and the amelioration of pain. By the beginning of the eighteenth century, English mineral springs had developed into major resorts. Midway during the century, a medical treatise extolling the virtues of seawater for the treatment of diseases of the glands provided a health justification for travel to the seaside. In 1783, this practice was sanctioned by royalty when the Prince of Wales made his first visit to Brighton seeking relief from swollen glands.

By the nineteenth century, well-to-do Americans were also traveling for their health to mineral springs and seaside locations. Saratoga Springs in New York and Cape May in New Jersey had become established resorts that provided both health benefits to invalids and entertainment and opportunities for social interaction for their attending relatives. They also provided refuges for those fleeing an unhealthy summer climate, such as the Low Country of South Carolina or Georgia or the larger cities of the North, where cholera was a hazard.

The northern winter climate was also regarded as hazardous to health, particularly to those suffering from consumption (tuberculosis), and doctors began to recommend that patients at risk from tuberculosis travel to the warmer climate in the South. As a result, invalids, particularly those suffering from tuberculosis, were the largest group of winter visitors to Florida before the Civil War. One of the first was the poet Ralph Waldo Emerson, who came in the winter of 1826–1827, barely five years after Florida became a U.S. territory. Forced to drop out of Harvard Divinity School because of an inflammation of the eye related to the beginnings of tuberculosis, Emerson traveled south to Charleston but moved to St. Augustine as the winter grew colder.[2] His trip successfully prevented the onset of tuberculosis, but a few years later, the disease claimed his first wife and two of his brothers. Another prewar visitor was Henry Bradley Plant, who brought his sick wife to Jacksonville in the winter of 1854. She ultimately succumbed to the disease during the Civil War years.

After the Civil War, invalids continued to come to Florida. Doctors frequently recommended a change of climate to their patients, especially those suffering from consumption or other lung diseases. In 1978 Henry Flagler brought his sick wife to the state on the advice of her doctor. These were the days before the wonder drugs of the twentieth century removed this much-feared disease from its prominent place in life.

One of the first guidebooks published about Florida after the Civil War was written by Daniel Garrison Brinton, a medical doctor, and published in 1869.[3] He noted that "the advantages to health of a change of climate should be considered by everyone. . . . Consumption is cureable if taken in its early stages. And in its cure, change of climate is an essential element." Brinton argued that the best climate for a consumptive should have an equable temperature, moderate moisture, moderate and regular winds, and freedom from local disease. While he believed that a warm winter climate might not be suitable for all patients who suffered from diseases of the throat and lungs, he argued that the seacoast of southeast Florida was the best location in the country for those who could benefit from such a climate.

The importance of Florida to invalids is attested by the inclusion of advice to invalids in numerous books about Florida published in the 1870s and 1880s. One of the earliest, published in 1873, claimed that invalids accounted for 25 percent of the state's winter visitors.[4] The prevailing view was that the mild climate promoted health because it furnished the "opportunity for interesting, comfortable and healthful exercise, [and] thoroughly ventilated sleeping rooms

. . . [with] the least necessity for burdensome clothing."[5] The noted author of *Uncle Tom's Cabin*, Harriet Beecher Stowe, a winter resident of Florida during most of these years, noted that "merely to come to Florida, and idle away time at the St. James or the St. Augustine [hotels], taking no regular exercise, and having no employment for mind or body, is no way to improve by being here. It is because the climate gives opportunity of open-air exercise that it is so favorable; but if one neglects all these opportunities, he may gain very little."[6]

After the Civil War, northerners began to come to Florida to escape the harsh winter. Some purchased or constructed private residences that they occupied during their time in the state. Others stayed at hotels and boarding houses.[7] Northerners entered Florida at Jacksonville. Prior to the 1880s, the most comfortable travel to Jacksonville consisted of a steamship from New York or Philadelphia to Charleston, South Carolina, or Savannah, Georgia. From there, travelers transferred to a smaller steamship that took them to Jacksonville or even as far up the St. Johns River as Palatka. There were rail connections between Charleston, Savannah, and Jacksonville that cost about the same as the steamship route and were a little bit faster, but they were a lot more uncomfortable; this was before railroads adopted the standard gauge.[8]

Most of the winter visitors to Florida after the Civil War would have been classified as winter residents rather than tourists a century later. A relatively short stay, involving weeks, characterizes a tourist; seasonal residents stay longer, usually for months. The longer the distance a tourist travels to a destination, the longer he or she tends to stay.[9] In the years just after the Civil War, travel to Florida would have been viewed as a very long trip (not only in distance but in time spent traveling), and visitors to the state would have stayed a relatively long time.

Harriet Beecher Stowe was among the most famous of the state's winter residents. She initially came to the state in 1867 to check on an investment she had made in a cotton plantation on behalf of her son.[10] Although the investment was a failure, she bought a cottage at Mandarin, just south of Jacksonville on the St. Johns River, and returned to Florida every winter thereafter until 1883. Stowe wrote a series of articles for the *Christian Union*, a magazine her brother Henry Ward Beecher edited. These articles about winter life on the St. Johns River were published as a book entitled *Palmetto Leaves* in 1873, adding to the books and articles published about Florida in the period after the Civil War that helped attract northerners to the state as tourists, settlers, and investors.

Another winter resident was Frederick DeBary, who had a winter home on the upper St. Johns across Lake Monroe from Sanford, where there is a town named after him a century later. He started steamboat service between Jacksonville and the lake; his steamship line eventually became the largest on the St.

Johns.[11] William Astor of New York was another winter resident of the state.[12] He purchased 80,000 acres along the upper St. Johns River in 1874 and spent a portion of his winters at his estate just south of Lake George. A small community in the area still bears his name more than a century later.

In the early 1870s, there were about 14,000 winter visitors to Jacksonville, a figure that had increased to about 40,000 a decade later.[13] Since Jacksonville was probably the largest tourist destination in the state in the 1870s, it is clear that the industry was not large at that time, although it was important in cushioning the state from the general business downturn that occurred after the Panic of 1873.

Northern visitors enjoyed touring the various parts of the state. Touring was a newly fashionable activity of the well-to-do that had roots in the Grand Tour of Europe that the English aristocracy initiated in the eighteenth century. Touring became popular in the United States in the 1820s after the Erie Canal was opened, when "tour-ists" began traveling from New York City up the Hudson River to Albany and Saratoga Springs.[14] From Albany, they took the Erie Canal west to Niagara Falls. Many continued into Canada, visiting Montreal and Quebec, before returning to the state via New England, where they frequently visited the White Mountains in New Hampshire.

Prior to the 1880s, winter visitors traveled on the state's rivers, particularly on the St. Johns River. Harriet Beecher Stowe referred to it as the "Grand Tour Up River." It combined unusual scenery and "the mysteries and wonders of unbroken tropical forests" with the natural wonder at Silver Springs and the "ancient" city of St. Augustine with its seventeenth-century Spanish fort.[15] Silver Springs, on the Silver River near Ocala, can lay claim to being Florida's first tourist attraction. The Silver River was a tributary of the Ocklawaha River, which joined the St. Johns River near Palatka. Large artesian springs yielded clear waters up to eighty feet deep through which many fish could be seen.[16] The development of Silver Springs as a tourist attraction was the special project of Hubbard Hart, a transplanted Vermonter who had begun steamboat service to the natural attraction before the Civil War. After the war, he secured assistance from the Internal Improvement Fund to clear the entrance to the Ocklawaha. He put a fleet of steamboats on the river, built a hotel in Palatka, and opened an advertising office in Boston.[17]

The St. Johns River tour could also include a trip to the historic city of St. Augustine. William Astor improved a rail link to Tocoi, a landing place on the river, in the 1870s, and a major hotel was opened in 1869.[18] The layout and architecture of the colonial-style city was a novelty to visitors, and the seventeenth-century Castillo de San Marco was considered a fine specimen of military architecture.[19]

Other tours of Florida before the 1880s were limited by the need to use two railroads, the Fernandina–Cedar Key and Jacksonville-Tallahassee lines, or the steamboats on the rivers or along the coast. In 1885, Henry Lee published *The Tourist's Guide of Florida* shortly after the railroads began to move south into the peninsula. He described a number of tours, including one from Jacksonville to Tallahassee with a side trip to White Sulphur Springs near Lake City. A second tour was a trip from Jacksonville to Cedar Key on the Gulf of Mexico. The Waldo and Gainesville areas were reputed to have air that was particularly favorable to invalids suffering from lung diseases.[20] Lee noted the availability of steamboat service from Cedar Key north to the Suwannee River or south along the coast to Manatee, Charlotte Harbor, and the Florida Keys. A third tour, highlighting Florida's lake country, began by steamer from Jacksonville to Astor on the St. Johns River south of Lake George. The traveler transferred to the new St. Johns–Lake Eustis railroad, "touching Lakes Eustis, Dora, Harris, Yale and Griffin, and connecting with Lake Apopka and Leesburg."[21] Lee also outlined a tour of the Indian River. The traveler could take a steamboat up the St. Johns to Sanford and a smaller boat farther up river to Lake Poinsett. From there it was three miles to Rockledge on the Indian River.

As Florida's tourist industry grew, the lodging industry expanded as well. The hotel company associated with Henry Flagler's railroad produced a listing of eighty-two lodging places located close to the railroad for the 1901–1902 winter season.[22] The median charge for room and full board was $2 per day. If we assume that the average length of stay in the state was 90 days, the meals and lodging portion of a tourist's visit to Florida would have amounted to

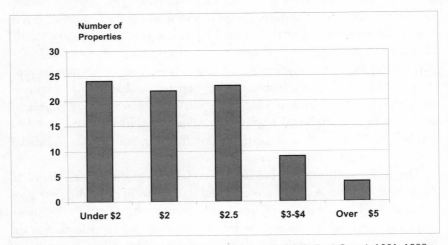

Chart 5–1. Average Daily Room and Board Rates, Florida's East Coast, 1901–1902 Season

$180. This compared with average annual wage earnings in manufacturing and construction of $526, as reported in the 1900 census.[23] The meals and lodging portion of a 90-day trip to Florida would have cost 34.2 percent of average annual manufacturing wage earnings. Most manufacturing workers could not take time away from employment for a winter trip to Florida in 1900. Such a trip was possible only for the relatively wealthy, and many of those who came to Florida were sick.

Properties that charged the median cost or below were typically small—some were boarding or rooming houses. In the last thirty years of the nineteenth century, however, there was a considerable expansion of first-class hotels in the state. In this, Florida was part of a national trend. The Grand Union Hotel at Saratoga Springs had opened its doors in 1874 after its owner had spent more than $1 million on remodeling. "The hotel . . . had over 1 mile of piazzas overlooking street and garden, 2 miles of corridors, 12 acres of flowered Brussels carpets, and 1 acre of marble in floors and table tops. The dining room could seat 1,400. The 824 spacious guest rooms were furnished with elaborately carved walnut pieces and thick lace curtains. Crystal chandeliers sparkled overhead in the public rooms. A steam-powered Otis elevator carried guests from floor to floor, thus making the previously hard-to-reach and undesirable top floor rooms equal in price with those on lower floors."[24]

In many respects, the luxury hotels of the late nineteenth century resembled the cruise ships of the late twentieth century. They catered to large numbers of visitors, providing large public spaces. Bedrooms were small, and guests spent most of their time in public spaces. Meals were eaten at sittings, and a daily program of entertainment and excursions was available.

The luxury hotels also provided an opportunity for male-female interaction away from the watchful eyes of family, friends, neighbors, and pastors. Women seemed to be more available to men, and "naughty" behavior became commonplace.[25] Sexual behavior was greatly stimulated when men and women began to bathe together at the beach and women discarded the layers of clothing that normally concealed their bodies from the watchful eyes of the other sex. Risqué behavior would later become associated with Florida's winter beach resorts, especially Miami Beach.

The first luxury hotel built for winter tourists in Florida was probably the St. James Hotel, which opened in Jacksonville in 1869. During the following decade, accommodations for winter tourists expanded in the city and other sites on the St. Johns River became tourist destinations.[26]

As noted in Chapter 3, Henry Flagler's primary interest in coming to Florida was to build a winter resort destination for the wealthy. It is likely that he was thinking of duplicating his Long Island summer residence with a winter residence in Florida. In 1884, Flagler was impressed with a new first-class hotel that had finally been built in St. Augustine. He also observed the construction of Franklin Smith's Villa Zorayda, which was built in Moorish architectural style using a mixture of cement, coquina shells, and water. During his 1884 visit, Flagler decided to build a first-class resort hotel in the city. He purchased the land and returned with a New York architect and construction expert. Construction on the Ponce de Leon began in December 1885. He hired the builders of St. Augustine's existing first-class hotel to construct his Ponce de Leon hotel. It was a massive undertaking. "The building was one of the first large structures in the country to be made of poured concrete. St. Augustine offered no natural building stone other than coquina which in many instances was too soft. Ton upon ton of coquina gravel was brought over from Anastasia Island across the bay and mixed with cement. Twelve hundred Negroes were engaged to tramp this mixture as it was poured into forms. Hundreds of other laborers, both black and white, were employed to do the many duties connected with construction."[27] The hotel opened for business in the 1887–1888 winter season. A few months later, Flagler bought Franklin Smith's nearby hotel, which he renamed the Cordova. He opened the Alcazar, a more modest hotel, in time for the 1889 season.

As Flagler expanded his rail line to the south, initially by purchasing and improving existing lines and then by new construction, he continued to expand his hotel interests. In 1890, he purchased control of the hotel in Ormond, his first beachfront hotel. Although it was built on the bay side of the island, guests could easily reach the ocean beach. Flagler built a railroad bridge across the Halifax River that gave hotel guests exclusive access to the barrier island. Although a bridge for motor vehicles was later constructed, the community remained relatively inaccessible from the mainland, and this may have been a reason why John D. Rockefeller made it the site of his winter residence in 1918.[28] The Ormond hotel also featured a golf course, another first for a Flagler hotel.

Daytona Beach was Florida's first community based on beach tourism. As would be true of so many beachfront communities later, the development of the beach area meant that bridges had to be built to the mainland. The first of these was built in 1887, the second in 1899, and the third in 1902.[29] All three were originally privately financed toll bridges that came under the control of the city in 1926.

It was quickly discovered that the hard beach sand (a mixture of coquina shell and sand) could be used for bicycle races, a fashionable sport of the time. In 1902, guests began to race their automobiles on the beach, and in 1903 the American Automobile Association sanctioned official speed runs on the beach between Daytona and Ormond. Thus began the association of Daytona Beach with automobile racing.

It is interesting that in the early twentieth century, the Daytona Beach tourist season was during the winter, in contrast to the summer season that began toward the end of the century. Around 1925, an observer estimated the Daytona winter tourist population at 126,500 and the summer tourist population at 25,000. This was presumably because Daytona had developed the winter beach activities of bicycling, auto racing, and walking. Over time, those in search of surf swimming and sunbathing migrated farther south during the winter months.

In the early 1890s, Flagler was already giving up on his idea to make St. Augustine the "Newport of the South." He purchased 100 acres on Palm Beach Island in April 1893 in order to construct a resort hotel there. Construction of the Royal Poinciana began in May; it opened for the 1895–1896 winter season. Flagler built a railroad spur across the lake for the convenience of the guests, some of whom brought private railroad cars with them to Florida. The Royal Poinciana was reputedly "one of the largest wooden buildings in the world used exclusively for hotel purposes."[30] Flagler constructed a beachfront hotel for the following season. Initially called the Palm Beach Inn, its name was changed to the Breakers. It continued to function as a beachfront resort hotel in the possession of Flagler's heirs a century later.

Flagler decided to terminate his railroad on the west side of Lake Worth across from his hotel at Palm Beach. He purchased several hundred acres of land and laid out the town site for West Palm Beach. This was Flagler's first town site, and he placed it in the charge of James E. Ingraham, his lieutenant for land development.

At Palm Beach, Flagler built a large pier out into the Atlantic and began steamship service to Nassau in the Bahamas, where he built the Colonial, a luxury hotel. After he moved to Miami in 1896, he moved his Nassau steamship service to the new city. He began construction of the Royal Palm Hotel in Miami in 1896 and opened it in January 1897. The last Flagler hotel, the Casa Marina in Key West, was constructed by Flagler's hotel company in 1920.

Florida's other railway magnate, Henry Plant, also entered the hotel business. In 1888, he opened a "modest and utilitarian" inn at Port Tampa as part of his development of the port.[31] He wanted the inn to provide a stopover point for transit passengers between his trains and his steamships. Perhaps stimulated by the publicity Flagler's Ponce de Leon in St. Augustine was receiving and recognizing the potential for resort hotels to serve the needs of wealthy tourists using his rail network, Plant began to develop a hotel network at the end of the 1880s. Following his typical business practice, he purchased more hotels than he built. In 1889, he purchased the Hotel Seminole at Winter Park, a stop on his railroad north of Orlando.[32] The Seminole was a resort that had been constructed in 1885 by the same company that had built the Ponce de Leon. It was situated between two lakes with paved bicycle paths and walking trails. In 1890, Plant bought the Hotel Kissimmee, "beautifully situated on the shore of Lake Tohopekaliga . . . [which was] particularly attractive to those who enjoy fishing, hunting and outdoor sports."[33]

In 1888, seeing the success of the Ponce de Leon Hotel, Henry Plant decided to build the Tampa Bay Hotel on the undeveloped west side of the Hillsborough River; he wanted a property that would rival Flagler's hotel in opulence and splendor.[34] The city of Tampa and Hillsborough County built a bridge across the river to provide access to the hotel. The cornerstone of the hotel was laid in July. The bricks were made locally with local sand and cement. Old narrow-gauge rail tracks from one of Henry Plant's railroads were used to reinforce the concrete walls and ceilings, and old submarine steel cable from the telegraph station at Punta Rassa was used for a similar purpose. Plant's wife bought forty-one carloads of furniture and art in France and England to decorate the hotel's public rooms. The hotel was also surrounded with beautifully landscaped gardens. The hotel opened in 1891 at a cost similar to what Flagler spent for the Ponce de Leon. Plant added a large theater and an exhibition building for the 1896–1897 season. He added a race track and a golf course a year later. Plant was making Tampa the Saratoga Springs of the South.

The sinking of the battleship *Maine* and the loss of over 400 lives in Havana Harbor in February 1898 led the United States to declare war on Cuba in April after a naval inquiry reported that the sinking was caused by an external explosion, probably a mine. Tampa became a staging area for the military expedition to Cuba and dozens of journalists stayed at the Tampa Bay Hotel, making it, for a short time, "the best known hotel in the world."[35]

After the Panic of 1893, Plant purchased or built first-class hotels along the routes of the Florida railroads he acquired. He purchased the Hotel Punta Gorda in 1894 and the Ocala House in 1895. The Hotel Punta Gorda was another hotel oriented toward the sportsman and angler, and the Ocala House letterhead advertised its five-mile bicycle path to the "world-renowned Silver Springs."[36]

In 1897, after acquiring the Orange Belt Railroad in the Pinellas Peninsula, Plant built the Hotel Belleview in Clearwater on a high bluff with a view of the Gulf of Mexico across Sand Key. This is the only one of Plant's hotels still in existence a century later. A spur from the railroad took guests directly to the hotel and could accommodate fifteen private railroad cars. In addition to access to the beach by boat across to the barrier island, the guests enjoyed a championship golf course. In 1897, Henry Plant also built the Hotel Fort Myers near the southern terminus of his railroad at Punta Gorda.

The first two decades of the twentieth century were the heyday of railroad tourism in Florida. Revenues from passengers traveling on the state's railroads, adjusted for inflation, increased by more than 150 percent from 1901 to 1913.[37] Tourism expenditures, calculated by using rail passenger revenues as a proxy, displayed some sensitivity to the business cycle. They declined slightly in 1902–1903 as the national economy entered recession, although they recovered quickly in the following year. Florida's tourism remained flat in 1907–1908 as the national economy entered another recession. The industry seemed untouched, however, by the two-year recession that began in January 1910. This was the period of excitement when many lots in eastern Broward County were sold after Richard Bolles's marketing campaign in the Midwest.[38]

Florida rail passenger revenues were flat in 1913–1914 as the national economy went into recession, but they continued to decline after the recession ended in December 1914. The decline continued until a modest recovery in 1919. The extent to which this decline was due to a decline in tourism is open to question because of the negative impact on Florida's economy of the outbreak of World War I in Europe in August 1914. Travel by European tourists to Florida was presumably substantially reduced by the war, although some Americans may have chosen to travel to Florida rather than going to Europe during the war

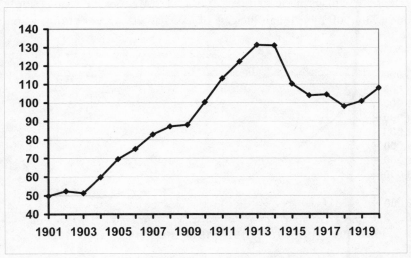

Chart 5–2. Rail Passenger Revenues in Florida, 1901–1919, Selected Years (in Millions of 2000 Dollars)

years. But the state was a major exporter of raw materials to Western Europe, and travel in connection with this trade was also reduced.

In the second decade of the twentieth century, a new development occurred in transportation that transformed Florida tourism, particularly in the years after the war ended in November 1918. This was the invention of the mass-produced automobile by Henry Ford. The Model T automobile was introduced in 1908 using assembly-line production techniques that significantly reduced its price. By 1914, the price had fallen by about 50 percent relative to the general level of prices.[39] By 1921, it had fallen another 50 percent. This brought the automobile into the price range of the middle class. The price of a Model T in 1921 amounted to 35 percent of the average annual wage of a manufacturing worker.[40] (When the car was first introduced, its price exceeded the annual income of a manufacturing wage earner by a substantial amount.)

The decline in automobile prices created a large group of automobile owners, many of whom were in a position to drive to Florida during the winter season, provided roads were available and lodging, food, and gasoline could be obtained along the way. In 1913, the number of registered automobiles in the nation exceeded 1 million for the first time.[41] By 1918, the number of registered vehicles exceeded 5 million, and by 1922 the number exceeded 10 million. In the following five years, the number of registrations grew to over 20 million.

Construction of surfaced roads lagged behind car ownership. At the end of 1914, there were a little over 250,000 miles of surfaced roads in the United States (including gravel and shell roads); surfaced roads accounted for just over 10 percent of the roads in the country.[42] Surfaced road mileage increased slowly to almost 300,000 by 1918, an increase of less than 20 percent during a time

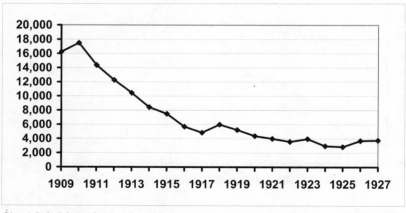

Chart 5–3. Price of a Touring Model T in the United States, 1909–1927, Selected Years (in 2000 Dollars)

when car production more than tripled. Road production was initially a local government function, and some proposals were made to have the automobile industry finance the surfacing of the major interstate highways.[43] But states gradually developed road-building programs, and the federal government initiated a national program in 1916. By 1928, more than 20 percent of the nation's roads had been surfaced.

One major interstate road project was initiated in the years before World War I that had a major impact on the state—the Dixie Highway. This was the brainchild of Carl Graham Fisher, the primary developer of Miami Beach. Fisher had opened a bicycle shop in Indianapolis in 1891 at the height of the bicycle craze.[44] He expanded into automobiles around the turn of the century, and in 1903 he founded the Presto-O-Lite Company, which manufactured the first headlights for cars.

In 1905, Fisher was a member of an American automobile team that was badly defeated in a race in Europe, and he became convinced that America needed a speedway to test cars and promote their technical improvement. He constructed the Indianapolis Speedway and inaugurated the first Indianapolis 500 race in 1910. In 1912, Fisher became involved in the first of his two transcontinental road projects, the Lincoln Highway between New York City and San Francisco. In a September letter to Henry Ford, he proposed that members of the automobile industry commit one-third of 1 percent of their revenues over three years or one-fifth of 1 percent of their revenues over five years to purchase the materials necessary to build a transcontinental highway.[45] In Fisher's plan, state and local authorities would do the actual construction to specifications prepared by government engineers and the route would be selected by a national committee. Automobile owners would make a contribution by buying memberships. Henry Ford turned Fisher down on the grounds that public roads should not be built by private subscription.

In spite of Ford's refusal to back the project, it generated widespread public enthusiasm. The Lincoln Road Association was formed and a route was selected with a spur south to Denver, Colorado. The route later became U.S. Highway 30; Interstate 80 follows a path similar to its route a century later. But cash contributions remained small, and gradually the Lincoln Road Association devoted its attention to encouraging the marking of the highway, the use of the name Lincoln Way on those parts of the highway that were complete, and the construction of several small demonstration projects. In 1918, the federal government greatly increased its support for highway construction, and by 1925 the name Lincoln Highway was dropped for the new federal highway numbering system.

Carl Fisher's other project built a highway that connected the northern part

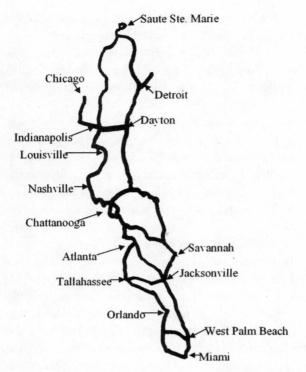

U.S. Map 5–1. Schematic Drawing of Dixie Highway System

of the country to the South, the so-called Dixie Highway. This time, Fisher proposed that the highway be constructed with public funds. On April 3, 1915, the governors of Indiana and Tennessee called a meeting to discuss the project in Chattanooga, Tennessee. Although the governors could not agree on a route, they formed the Dixie Highway Association and agreed to form a commission with two delegates per state to receive submissions from local communities who wished to be part of the highway. Carl Fisher was appointed an Indiana delegate.

The commission selected two routes in 1915, an eastern route through Detroit, Cincinnati, and Knoxville, and a western route linking Chicago, Louisville, and Nashville. The southern half of the highway was eventually split into a western route through Atlanta, Tallahassee, Orlando, and Naples and an eastern route through Ashville, Savannah, and Jacksonville and down the east coast of Florida. The Dixie Highway system was constructed during the period 1915 to 1927.[46]

The gradually developing system of roads enabled many members of the American middle class to drive their newly affordable automobiles to Florida for a winter vacation, especially after the end of World War I. Many of these were referred to as tin-can tourists because they drove their automobiles into the state, stayed in campgrounds, and ate food from tin cans.[47] They formed an organization called Tin Can Tourists of the World in 1922 and held annual conventions in Tampa's De Soto Park. Initially, the tourists stayed by the side of the road, but gradually both the public and private sectors began to provide modern campgrounds with running water, electric lights, toilets, showers, laundry facilities, and meeting rooms. Children could be enrolled in the local public schools for free in St. Petersburg and Broward County and for a charge of 50 cents a week in Tampa.

Tin-can tourism is an example of home-produced vacation services. Instead of making purchases in the marketplace, the traveling group provided their own transportation in the family car. They provided their own lodging in tents that they owned and set up themselves, albeit at leased sites. They cooked their own food from tin cans on campfires. The home production of vacations seemed to have a particular appeal to rural Americans, who were accustomed to growing and cooking their own food and relying on home production for most of their consumption. Many tin-can tourists came from the Midwest and vacationed on the southwest coast of Florida. Tourists from the northeast were often more urban, seemed more likely to travel by train, and seemed to prefer the southeast coast of the state. As the century progressed, the home production of vacations was gradually supplanted by vacations in paid lodging with food consumed at commercial establishments. By the last decades of the century, even winter residents, who stayed in their own homes, ate in restaurants on a daily basis.

Florida's winter tourist boom was stimulated by a vigorous marketing campaign. Jacksonville led the way in the 1880s. In the winter of 1886–1887, California secured attractive transcontinental passenger fares from the railroads, and tourist organizations sent representatives to Jacksonville to publicize California as an attractive winter tourist destination.[48] Jacksonville responded to the threat by organizing a winter exposition of subtropical and tropical products in 1888 that was a considerable success.

Twenty years later, communities in the southern half of the peninsula followed suit. The Miami Board of Trade merged with the Merchant's Association to form the Miami Chamber of Commerce in 1913 and began developing the city's tourist industry in earnest.[49] It started an advertising campaign in northern newspapers and magazines with the unofficial slogan "It is always June in Miami." The campaign was initially financed with private funds, but later both private and public funds paid for it. By the middle of the 1920s, the Chamber of Commerce was advertising in fifty-two newspapers and fourteen major periodicals. The chamber organized state societies and provided social events. It organized pageants, parades, festivals, tournaments, and regattas. In an effort to lengthen the winter season, the chamber sponsored some special events before the traditional start of the season in January and after the traditional end of the season in early April.

Perhaps the most creative publicist was John Lodwick, who was hired by St. Petersburg in 1918.[50] He interviewed tourists and wrote articles for their hometown newspapers complete with photographs showing them dressed in beachwear or holding tarpons caught in the Gulf of Mexico. Lodwick staged publicity events such as world horseshoe and shuffleboard championships, and he sent the mayor of St. Petersburg to New York to stroll down Broadway in a white suit attended by several beauty queens. Lodwick also persuaded the mayor to pretend to do battle with the fictional St. Petersburg Purity League, which was supposedly backed by the respectable women of the city to protect their husbands from the wiles of scantily clad "sea vamps."

St. Petersburg was also one of the pioneers in bringing baseball spring train-ing to the state. Although Jacksonville had enticed the Washington Capitals for a four-day camp in 1888, the team did not return the following year and spring training did not really begin in the state for another twenty years.[51] In the intervening period, spring training became routine for most baseball teams at locations outside Florida. One of the early boosters of spring training wrote to an owner that "the games you play in the South mean nothing, but the score of even a five-inning practice game will be greedily scanned by enthusiasts . . . and will boom your team for the coming season."[52] In 1912, Tampa brought the Chicago Cubs and signed a five-year contract with them a year later. At about this time St. Petersburg mayor Al Lang attempted to obtain a spring training team for his city. A one-year stay by the St. Louis Browns in 1914 was followed by a four-year stay by the Philadelphia Phillies. Two other teams made short-term spring training visits to the state prior to 1920. The Brooklyn Dodgers came to Daytona Beach in 1916 as a result of the efforts of Michael Sholtz, a resident of Brooklyn who built a baseball field to accommodate the team.[53] When funds for a new auditorium and gymnasium ran out at the University of Florida in 1919, Gainesville boosters agreed to provide funds to complete construction if the university made its facilities available to the New York Gi-ants.[54] After a hiatus caused by World War I and postwar readjustment, spring training expanded in Florida. By the mid-1920s, seven teams were training in Florida, including at Lakeland (Cleveland Indians) and at Sarasota (New York Giants).[55]

While the growth of tin-can tourism was the most dramatic development in the tourism industry in the early decades of the twentieth century, especially in the early 1920s, not all middle-income winter visitors stayed in tents. In

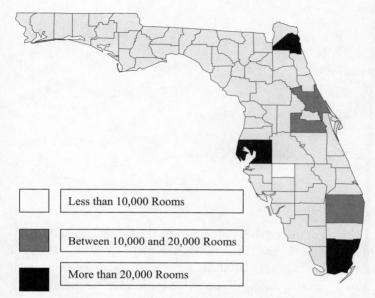

Florida Map 5–1. Hotel and Rooming House Rooms in Florida Counties, 1928

fact, the number of rooms in hotels and lodging places more than quintupled between 1919 and 1928.[56] Four counties had more than 20,000 hotel and rooming house rooms in 1928: Miami-Dade (73,557 rooms), Pinellas (29,204 rooms), Hillsborough (25,230 rooms), and Duval (22,638 rooms). Three other counties had more than 10,000 rooms: Palm Beach (16,412 rooms), Volusia (13,096 rooms), and Orange (10,280 rooms). Most of the growth in the counties with the largest number of rooms occurred in the 1920s. The exceptions were Volusia (Daytona Beach) and Orange (Orlando), whose capacity grew by less than 10,000 rooms.

The expansion of the state's tourism industry created many new jobs in the 1920s. Tourism accounted for an estimated 4.6 percent of total employment in 1920.[57] By the Depression year of 1930, this share had increased to 7.4 percent. This was an increased share of a much larger state economy, of course. Overall employment in Florida had increased by more than 55 percent from 1920 to 1930, compared to a 17 percent increase nationally. The number of jobs in the Florida tourist industry more than doubled during this decade.

Chapter 6

The 1920s

Urbanization, Boom, and Collapse

The image of Florida in the 1920s is dominated by the land boom and its collapse in the middle of the decade. Although these events were the most vivid of the decade to those who lived through them, a major change in the structure of the state's economy occurred during the decade that continued in the late 1930s and culminated in the huge expansion after World War II.

The boom was actually another example of a fever, a period of intense investment after the discovery of a new way of making money, as had occurred in the state's orange, tobacco, and phosphate markets toward the end of the nineteenth century. Fevers inevitably led to overinvestment, followed by a collapse of prices and a retrenchment in the industry. The land boom was notable because of the many people who participated compared to the other fevers and because of the severity of the impact of the price collapse, not only on the real estate industry and construction but also on other parts of the economy, such as the state's banks and local governments. This was not the first real estate fever in the United States; indeed, a contemporary observer noted that the land boom in Florida was similar to a land boom in southern California in the 1880s and an earlier land boom in Chicago in the 1830s.[1]

The most visible manifestation of the structural change in Florida during the 1920s was the increased urbanization of the state. By 1930, Florida's urban population had become became larger than its rural population for the first time.[2] The state passed this milestone ten years after the nation as a whole. At the beginning of the decade, 37 percent of Floridians lived in urban areas, compared to 51 percent nationally. By 1930, 52 percent of Floridians lived in urban areas, compared to 56 percent nationally.

The increased urbanization was the result of the development of job opportunities in the state's urban areas. In the 1920s, workers who migrated to Florida were seeking jobs in urban areas rather than in the agricultural sectors that had attracted in-migrants previously. A key reason was the rapid growth

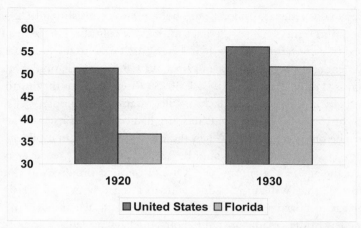

Chart 6–1. Urban Population as a Percent of Total Population, United States and Florida, 1920 and 1930

of the tourist industry (broadly defined to include seasonal winter residents). The construction and development industry expanded on the boundaries of the state's tourist-oriented urban areas, creating more job opportunities and attracting additional workers. Jobs were also created in trade and services to meet the needs of the growing urban population.

The automobile (and the bus) also encouraged the expansion of the state's urban areas. In the 1920s, the expansion of the tourist industry in Miami Beach was made possible by the bridges that were built from the mainland, where many of the workers lived. A similar bridge project integrated St. Petersburg into the Tampa area and resulted in major urban expansion in Pinellas County.

Almost 25 percent of the increase in the urban population occurred in Miami-Dade County, the major center of growth in the tourism industry.[3] During the 1920s, the urban population of Miami-Dade increased by almost 100,000. The state's other two relatively large urban counties, Duval (Jacksonville) and Hillsborough (Tampa), had the second and third largest increases, but the growth in both these counties combined was less than the growth in Miami-Dade. Pinellas County (St. Petersburg), another tourist center, had the fourth largest increase, and Palm Beach County ranked sixth.

Many of the state's future large cities experienced relatively large population increases in the 1920s. Among the state's ten largest cities in 1930, the populations of Miami, Orlando, Daytona Beach and West Palm Beach tripled and the populations of Tampa, St. Petersburg, and Lakeland doubled during the 1920s.[4] The population of Jacksonville increased by a more modest 40 percent, the population of Pensacola experienced no growth, and the population of Key West actually declined by about 30 percent.

As the state's major cities expanded, metropolitan areas consisting of clusters of cities began to form. This was perhaps most evident in the Tampa area, where improved transportation links with St. Petersburg began to integrate the urban development of the region. Between 1915 and 1930, the population of St. Petersburg increased more than fivefold. By 1930, St. Petersburg was the fourth most populated city in the state, after Jacksonville, Miami, and Tampa.

As noted in the previous chapter, St. Petersburg had committed itself to the tourist industry before World War I. When the war ended, it became evident that a network of roads and bridges would be needed to continue to develop this industry in the age of the automobile. One of the first projects was the Pass-a-Grille Bridge that William McAdoo built to Long Key in 1919.[5] This was the first bridge to a barrier island from the Pinellas Peninsula, and over the following years new bridges made most of the offshore keys available for development. In 1924, the Gandy Bridge linking Tampa to St. Petersburg across the bay was completed. The bridge, which was two and a half miles long, reduced the distance between Tampa and St. Petersburg from forty-three to nineteen miles. The bridge stimulated development between the bridge and downtown St. Petersburg, but soon the city's eastern shore was developing as well.

The Miami metropolitan area also began to form during the 1920s. Two adjacent cities in particular gave an impetus to this development: Miami Beach and Coral Gables. In the 1880s, coconut farming was the first venture on the narrow peninsula across the bay from Miami that would become Miami Beach.[6] Although the project failed, one of its backers, New Jersey vegetable farmer John Stiles Collins, returned some years later to the area and planted 2,495 avocado trees. His agricultural success was also meager, but it gradually became evident that the narrow sandy peninsula might be developed into a beachfront community similar to those that had been developed along the New Jersey shore. With his sons, Collins established the Miami Beach Improvement Company with the objective of constructing a canal from the Collins farm to the bay and a bridge from there to the mainland.

By 1912, the Collins family had run out of money and the bridge was still incomplete. Carl Fisher, the Indianapolis automobile headlights manufacturer, loaned enough money to the Collins Company to enable the bridge to be completed. Fisher had purchased a house on the bay in Miami in 1910 and had begun to spend much of his time during the winter in the city. The loan Fisher made was just a small part of the proceeds he had received when he sold the Prest-O-Lite Company to Union Carbide in 1911.

As part of the deal to secure the bridge funds, the Collins family gave Fisher title to 200 acres in the beach area—"a mile long strip 1,800 feet wide from ocean to bay."[7] Fisher added to these holdings when he loaned another sizeable sum to the Lummus brothers, who had established a development company to develop the southern part of the peninsula. They gave him 150 acres and he added 60 acres more by purchase. Carl Fisher, the Collins family, and the Lummus brothers were the developers of Miami Beach.

The beach was the attraction of the offshore peninsula, but the developers realized that the bayside also held much potential. In the words of the historian of Miami Beach: "Carl [Fisher]'s love of boating told him that the bay shore could be valuable as well. Yachts can't be kept on ocean beaches; protected shorelines are needed for docks, yacht clubs, and the kind of vacation homes . . . on the Great Lakes . . . Carl had seen . . . on his summer cruises. To him it was obvious that filling in the mangroves would in one operation give him a basin deep enough for boating, and triple his usable land area, besides getting rid of the sand flies and mosquitoes that bred in the swamps."[8] Fisher and the Lummus brothers combined to finance Florida's first large-scale dredge-and-fill project.[9] They destroyed mangroves and built up the land with sand dredged from the near shore. They barged in topsoil from the Everglades to cover the new sand, made roadbeds with crushed limestone from the mainland, and laid water mains.

Large-scale waterfront land development based on dredging and filling spread throughout Florida. D. P. Davis brought the technique to Tampa, where he began construction of Davis Islands at the mouth of the Hillsborough River in 1924.[10] John Ringling used it to develop the keys across the bay from Sarasota, and William McAdoo used dredge and fill on the eastern shore of St. Petersburg.[11] Charles Rodes further developed the dredge-and-fill technique in Fort Lauderdale.[12] There was no source of sand to fill the mangrove swamp that he owned north of the New River in Fort Lauderdale. To solve the problem, he dredged a parallel series of canals perpendicular to the river and placed the fill on the peninsulas between each pair of canals. This technique, which he called "finger-islanding," spread throughout south Florida.

By 1914, all three Miami Beach developers had lots for sale in new subdivisions, but sales were slow. Miami Beach seemed a long way from Miami. It was reachable only by a wooden toll bridge and did not have much retail development. It was a nice place to visit, but few wanted to live there. In 1916, developers began dredging to deepen a ship channel in Biscayne Bay. As the sand from the dredging piled along the north side of the channel, it became "clear that a little more dredging could enlarge this bank into a wide, firm roadbed from the south end of the Beach to Miami."[13] The county commission was persuaded to authorize the sale of bonds to construct a causeway to the south end of Miami Beach. The project was delayed by lawsuits and then by the entry of the United States into World War I. Its postwar construction would be one of the factors that enabled Miami Beach to finally experience the development its three founders had envisaged.[14]

The causeway was only one of the factors that enabled Miami Beach to grow, however. Another was the construction of the Flamingo, Miami Beach's first luxury hotel, and a third was Fisher's introduction of polo. These factors attracted the type of clientele who would buy Fisher's lots and build winter homes on the beach. Fisher also announced that he would raise the prices of his lots 10 percent per year in an effort to convince buyers that their value would increase in the future.

But Fisher's most dramatic sales technique was his genius for obtaining free media coverage. "Fisher's publicity office bombarded the tabloids with photos of comely young women in daring one-piece bathing suits and rolled stockings (or even—gasp!—no stockings) or such typical sights in wonderland as children using an elephant as a diving board."[15] In 1921, Fisher persuaded president-elect Warren Harding to visit Miami Beach. While Harding played golf during his visit, Fisher supplied an elephant to carry the clubs, and a photo of the event appeared in newspapers around the country.

From 644 year-round residents in 1920, the population of Miami Beach rose to 2,342 in the state census of 1925 and to 6,494 in the national census of 1930. While the 1930 population seems tiny for a city now, it gave Miami Beach a ranking of twenty-third out of 288 incorporated places in Florida in 1930.[16] The population figure did not include the city's many part-time winter residents.

Coral Gables was the brainchild of George Merrick, whose father had purchased a homestead in Miami in 1899. After his father's death in 1911, George took over the family farm, and by 1922 he had amassed 3,000 acres, almost five square miles.[17] He decided to use this acreage to create Coral Gables, a new city six miles from Miami.

Merrick created Florida's first land development company to plan his development, undertake its construction, and market its products. Merrick hired an artist, an architect, and a landscape architect to plan a unique suburb of Miami, "a project that would be an unrivaled beauty, constructed in the Mediterranean Revival style, featuring all the elements of the City Beautiful Movement right down to the finest details, like city lamp posts." Merrick subdivided his land holdings with clear zoning and usage specifications. The city planners who oversaw Merrick's subdivision included residential and country club areas; business, industrial, and craft subdivisions; and "bridle paths, parks, tennis courts and golf courses."[18]

The city beautiful movement emphasized beautification and monumental architecture to promote harmony in a community.[19] Merrick built a striking entrance to the city, the Douglas Entrance, a rock portal with arches and gates, and the Biltmore Hotel, which cost $10 million to build, five times the cost of Carl Fisher's Flamingo on Miami Beach. He pushed his development to Biscayne Bay, built the Coral Gables Canal and a network of smaller canals to produce desirable waterfront property, converted a rock quarry into the Venetian Pool, and founded the University of Miami.[20]

Merrick did not neglect the marketing side of his project. He sent a fleet of more than eighty buses all around the nation to collect potential buyers of his lots. The buses had Coral Gables signs painted on them, advertising his development in all the towns they passed through on their way to south Florida. Merrick also hired William Jennings Bryan, the gifted orator and three-time Democratic candidate for president, to address prospective purchasers from a platform in the city's Venetian Pool.[21]

The first lots were not sold in Coral Gables until after 1920. The city reported a population of 901 in the state census of 1925, and it had reached 5,697 by 1930. Like Miami Beach, the population of Coral Gables placed it in the top 10 percent of the 228 incorporated places in Florida in the 1930 U.S. census.

The major national publicity campaigns that promoted new real estate developments and those that promoted the state as a tourist destination also attracted in-migrants seeking the job opportunities created by the expansion of these two industries. Between 1920 and 1925, Florida's population grew by 30 percent, compared to the 5 percent growth that had occurred between 1915 and 1920, when many Floridians had moved north in search of jobs created by the war. After the collapse of the land boom, the rate of population growth fell back to 16 percent.

Florida real estate could be purchased with a down payment of 25 percent with the balance financed with one-, two-, or three-year notes. Because of the increasing demand for properties, it became possible to sell a property for a profit before one or more of the notes became due, and the market gradually attracted speculators who "bought for a turn" instead of buyers who wished to occupy the properties. As the boom gathered steam in 1924, speculators accounted for an ever-larger portion of the market and properties turned over very rapidly. One contemporary observer noted that "around Miami, subdivisions, except the very large ones, are often sold out the first day of sale."[22]

Buyers purchased a binder which held the lot for the buyer for thirty days, when the down payment of 25 percent of the purchase price would become due. Binders were used because of delays in recording title transfers; county recording offices were overwhelmed at the height of the boom. The binder could be sold before the down payment became due. One observer described the speculation process: "Practically all lots immediately go on resale, marked up by the new owner at a new figure. They may be listed at a dozen or more sales offices. The promoter announces 'Sold Out' and individual trading begins. Ordinarily they turn fast. A lot, or the binder for it, may change hands several times before the first payment is due."[23]

The rise of speculation in the real estate market in 1924 was accommodated by the Federal Reserve's easy monetary policy, a response to the national recession that began in 1923. The Federal Reserve Bank of New York, for example, cut its discount rate from 4.5 percent in the fourth quarter of 1922 to 3 percent in the second quarter of 1923. Although the discount rate was raised in the fourth quarter to 3.5 percent, it remained at this relatively low level for a year.

The 1923 national recession was relatively mild; the decline in per capita income, adjusted for inflation, was 1.4 percent.[24] In 1925, per capita income regained almost all of the 1924 loss, and it jumped by 4.8 percent in 1926. The combination of low interest rates and growing income stimulated the construction industry across the nation and facilitated growth in Florida's construction and real estate development industries. The value of new buildings authorized for construction in 272 large cities across the country rose by 19 percent in

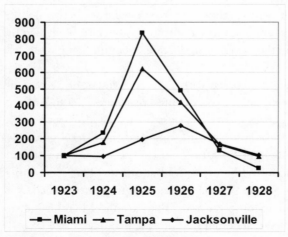

Chart 6–2. Value of Building Permits in Miami, Tampa, and Jacksonville, Florida, 1922–1928 (Index 1923=100)

1925.[25] Construction in Florida's cities grew even more rapidly. In 1925, the proposed cost of new buildings increased by 250 percent in Miami and Tampa, and it increased by 100 percent in Jacksonville.[26]

Florida's banks provided much of the financing for the boom. They increased their loans by over 75 percent in 1925, and in 1926, their loans were twice the 1924 level.[27] The state's banks were only one source of financing. Banks and financial institutions elsewhere in the country provided much of the financing. There was also direct finance: "The relatively low yield on high grade investments made it possible to tempt investors into purchasing real estate bonds (paying 8%) which were secured by new structures located in the boom territory."[28]

The extent of speculative activity in Florida real estate can be gauged from income tax statistics during the boom period. Because income taxes are paid with a one-year lag, the boom period in the income tax statistics refers to the tax years of 1926 and 1927. Floridians accounted for about half of 1 percent of personal income tax collections in the nation in 1925.[29] This share more than tripled in 1926 and 1927, but it fell back to its 1925 level at the end of the decade. A major part of the sharp increase in income during the boom consisted of capital gains, presumably realized on the sale of real estate. Capital gains income rose from less than $1 million in 1923 to $279 million in the peak year of 1925 before falling back to $40 million in 1927.

The boom was largely confined to the latter half of the peninsula, especially in Miami-Dade, Broward, and Palm Beach counties on the southeast coast and

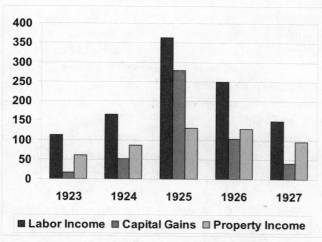

Chart 6–3. Labor Income, Capital Gains Income, and Property Income in Florida, 1923–1927 (in Millions of Current Dollars)

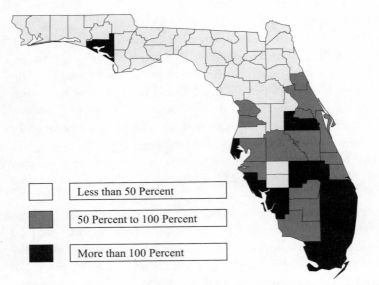

Florida Map 6–1. Increases in Assessed Property Values in Florida Counties during the 1924-1926 Boom, (by Percent)

Pinellas, Sarasota, Charlotte, and Lee counties on the southwest coast. Total assessed values increased in these counties by over 100 percent from 1924–1925 to 1926–1927.[30]

Florida's real estate boom began to collapse in 1926—the crowd clamoring to purchase real estate suddenly switched direction and sought to sell rather than buy. Building-permit activity slowed down nationally in 1926 as the Federal Reserve raised interest rates. The national decline of 5 percent, however, was extremely small relative to the declines of more than 40 percent in Miami and more than 30 percent in Tampa. By 1927, the value of building permits in Miami was 15 percent of the 1925 peak and the value in Tampa was 27 percent of the peak. Why the sentiments of a crowd suddenly change is never clear, either to members of the crowd or to observers. Many explanations have been advanced in the case of the Florida boom.

Because of the large speculative element in the boom, it was inevitable that when sentiment changed, the reversal in activity would be dramatic. Problems unique to the local industry played a major role in turning sentiment around. One of these was the inability of the local infrastructure to provide the support services necessary to keep up with the demands of the boom. In June 1925, the *Miami Herald* reported a shortage of low-cost housing for construction workers.[31] Tent cities were built to accommodate laborers, but the general rise in the cost of living put upward pressure on construction wages and slowed the pace of construction. The increase in construction wages attracted laborers from the rest of the economy, limiting the ability of sectors that supported the industry to develop an adequate level of service.

The railroad transportation sector also was unable to keep up with construction demand, so much so that Florida's rail system faced a crisis in the summer of 1925. In August, the Florida East Coast Railway declared an embargo on all carload freight except fuel, petroleum, livestock, and perishable material. The primary difficulty was the slow pace with which freight cars were unloaded. In addition to a shortage of labor, there were not enough trucks to drive the unloaded freight to its destination and a shortage of warehouse space for storage. On August 22, 1925, 820 freight cars were sitting in Miami rail yards and an additional 1,300 were parked on sidings just north of the city. On that day, 145 cars were unloaded but 133 new cars arrived. The high demands placed on the railroads in the summer interfered with the company's ongoing program of double tracking (building a second track along the line) and construction of new facilities.

A number of actions were taken locally to ease the crisis, including using city workers and prisoners and constructing warehouse space on city property. A statewide system of permits was instituted to determine priorities for freight transportation, and the Interstate Commerce Commission issued an order governing the routes of freight to Florida for all railroads operating south of the Ohio and east of the Mississippi rivers. Finally, in February 1926, the commission declared that normal service had been restored.

Problems also arose in shipping, the other major mode for transporting freight to Miami. The port suffered from the same shortage of laborers, trucks, and storage space as the railroads. In addition, the port itself was congested. In December 1925, the *New York Times* reported that thirty-one ships lay off Miami Beach waiting to enter the harbor for unloading. The wait was between ten days and three weeks, and about sixty ships were already in the harbor. In January, the *Prinz Valdemar*, a ship being renovated to become a floating cabaret, capsized and blocked the channel. A makeshift channel had to be dredged around the wreck until it was salvaged toward the end of February.

The problems with delivering freight to Miami were widely reported, adding to other negative publicity about the Florida boom in northern news media. The Ohio legislature passed a "blue sky" law preventing Florida real estate firms from obtaining licenses to sell in the state. The law prevented buyers from purchasing Florida real estate sight unseen. Northern financial institutions, which claimed they were losing deposits to Florida, welcomed the negative publicity. About 100,000 Massachusetts savings bank accounts were reported as having been drawn upon for Florida investment. But Floridians responded that many transactions were made between northern banks, making the transfer of funds to Florida unnecessary.

More serious were charges of unethical practices among Florida real estate promoters. The general manager of the National Better Business Bureau called for the creation of a local chapter in Florida, and one was organized in September 1925. But the bureau's announcement of the results of complaints it had investigated exacerbated the situation.[32] This drumbeat of criticism eventually caused a delegation of Florida businessmen, led by the state's governor, to call a meeting of the northern press for a "Truth about Florida" meeting. The ineffectiveness of this mission was underscored when one of its most prominent members, Senator Coleman du Pont, resigned in October 1925 as chair of Addison Mizner's Boca Raton Development Corporation because of a concern about false advertising and the criminal record of Wilson Mizner, the developer's brother and treasurer of the company.[33]

The final blow was the hurricane of September 1926. Most residents of southeast Florida had not experienced a major hurricane. The initial reaction to news that a storm was coming was doubt.[34] Even after the storm had hit, Floridians who were out of the state discounted the newspaper reports as "more bad publicity."[35] Yet the storm was deadly. In Miami, 107 were killed, and in Broward County, 49 were killed.[36] Thousands more were injured.

The collapse led to bankruptcy for some development projects, including Hollywood and Floranada in Broward County, Mizner's Boca Raton in Palm Beach County, and the Davis Island Project in Tampa. Some projects limped along; these included Merrick's Coral Gables and the Ringling Estates in Sarasota.

The collapse of the boom brought the state's economy back to earth from the heady heights to which it had risen in 1925. There was a lasting impact, however. Real per capita income in Florida in 1929 was no higher than it had been in 1920.[37] This contrasted with the increase in national per capita income, adjusted for inflation, of more than 20 percent. Florida, whose per capita income was already lower than that of the nation as a whole in 1920, ended the decade with a per capita income even farther below the national level.

Chart 6–4 is the first of many charts in this book that compares per capita income adjusted for inflation in Florida and the United States. Many other charts will express other economic measures, especially components of per capita income, adjusted for inflation. Per capita income is the most commonly used measure of economic development. It is expressed per capita in order to highlight the impact of changes in the economy on the average individual. Economic growth occurs naturally as the population grows; growth beyond the rate of population growth represents an improvement in the economic situation of

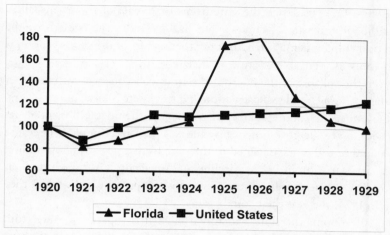

Chart 6–4 Per Capita Income in Florida and the United States, 1920–1929, Adjusted for Inflation (Index 1920=100)

the average individual. Per capita income is adjusted for inflation because if per capita income rises at the same rate as the rate of inflation, the average individual will not be able to purchase any additional goods and services—his or her material standard of living will not have increased. Frequently economists use the terms "real prices," "constant prices," or "constant dollars" instead of the term "adjusted for inflation."

Per capita income is expressed as an index with a base year (1920 in the case of Chart 6–4). An index enables the reader to see the percentage of change in a measure relative to the base year. Chart 6–4, for example, shows that in 1925 and 1926, real per capita income in Florida was about 80 percent higher than its 1920 level and that by 1929, it had fallen back to its 1920 level. In Chart 6–4, 1920 is used as the base year in order to give a sense of developments during the decade relative to the beginning of the decade. Using an index has the additional advantage of not drawing the reader's attention to underlying numbers that may seem extraordinarily low relative to corresponding values that refer to decades later.

It is not true that because of the end of the boom, Florida entered into depression four or five years earlier than the rest of the country and that Florida thus escaped the worst of the massive downturn in the early 1930s. As we will see in Chapter 8, Florida's economy contracted even further in the early 1930s. The economic weakness in Florida at the end of the 1920s was a result of local factors, and the further decline in the early 1930s was a result of national factors. Indeed, the strength of the national economy (even with a mild recession in 1926–1927) cushioned the state from the impact of the severe fall in construction and real estate. Many workers in those industries could leave the state and find employment.[38] In addition, other sectors of the state's economy, especially tourism, were able to grow in the late 1920s.[39]

However, the collapse of the boom had serious consequences for two other parts of the economy besides construction and real estate—local and state government revenue and banking. Banks encountered difficulties as borrowers defaulted. Local and state government revenue was negatively impacted because assessed values of real estate declined in the state from a peak of $800 million in 1926 to $600 million in 1929, a decline of 25 percent.[40] Although this was a sharp decline, property values were still almost 50 percent higher than they had been in 1924, the year the boom began.

During the boom, the state had rolled back its property tax rate from about 10 mills to 7.5 mills. Most of this decline was in the millage for general revenue. The state was also able to build up balances. When the boom ended, the state drew down the balances and restored the property tax rate to its level before the boom. The state also raised gasoline taxes after the boom ended and drastically reduced expenditures on roads. In 1926–1927, total state spending was $44 million. By 1929–1930, it had fallen to $30 million.[41]

Local government finances also deteriorated sharply after the boom ended. The decline in assessed values lowered property tax revenues, the most important tax source for local governments. An important difference between the state government and local governments was the latter's debt burden. The state constitution prohibited the state from issuing bonds, so it emerged from the

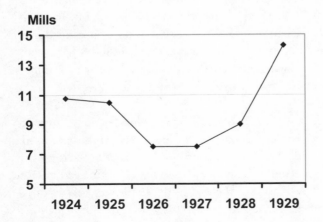

Chart 6–5. State Property Tax Rate in Florida, 1924–1929 (in Mills)

boom period without a significant debt burden. Local governments, on the other hand, were allowed to issue bonds, and many counties and cities emerged from the boom period with substantial debt burdens.

Data on local government debt did not become available until the census of governments produced figures for 1931. The numbers at that time reflected the onset of the Great Depression and the economic impact of a hurricane that hit the Lake Okeechobee area in 1928. The data show the impact of the boom-time borrowing, however, because the highest debt burdens are in the lower half of the peninsula, where the boom had its greatest impact. Outstanding debt exceeded 200 percent of the assessed values of property in Broward and Palm Beach counties in southeast Florida; it also exceeded 200 percent in Sarasota County in the southwest.

Data are available for the state's three largest cities—Jacksonville, Miami, and Tampa—beginning in 1926.[42] Per capita debt doubled in Miami between 1926 and 1928 and there was another increase by 1930. There was a modest increase in Jacksonville and no increase in Tampa. Cities reacted to the revenue squeeze by sharply reducing their capital outlay budgets. Jacksonville reduced its capital budget by 40 percent, Miami by 75 percent, and Tampa by 90 percent from 1926 to 1929.

The collapse of the boom also had a serious impact on the banks in the

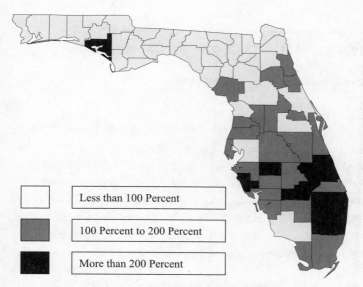

Less than 100 Percent

100 Percent to 200 Percent

More than 200 Percent

Florida Map 6–2. Local Government Debt in Florida Counties Relative to Property Values, 1931

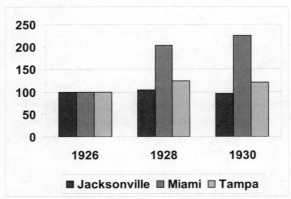

Chart 6–6. Per Capita Net Debt in Jacksonville, Miami, and Tampa, Florida, 1926, 1928, and 1930 (Index 1926=100)

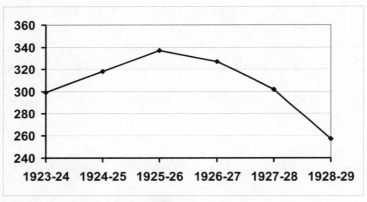

Chart 6–7. Number of Banks in Florida, 1923–1924 to 1928–1929

state. Florida had about 300 banks just before the boom began.[43] There were five times as many state-chartered as nationally chartered banks, but the national banks were larger so that deposits in state banks were less than five times as great as deposits in national banks. Bank deposits in Florida doubled in 1924–1925 during the frenzy of the initial boom period, and they rose again in 1925–1926. They declined sharply (25 percent) in 1926–1927 and again in 1927–1928. In 1928–1929, deposits were still 25 percent above their 1923–1924 level, although loans had returned to the level of five years earlier.

The number of banks in the state peaked at 337 in 1925–1926. The decline was slow initially—the number fell by only 3 percent in 1926–1927—but there was a sharp decline of 10 percent in 1927–1928. The decline in 1928–1929, the last year before the onset of the Great Depression, was 15 percent.

The trauma of the boom and its reversal overshadowed Florida's economy in the 1920s. While the national economy roared ahead, the state ended with the same per capita income that it had in the beginning of the decade. In spite of this disappointment, Florida was transformed from a rural state that was dominated by agriculture and industries that processed natural resources into an urban state with a service-oriented economy.

Chapter 7

1930

A Frontier Economy with a Sunshine Sector

In spite of the large in-migration of population in the 1920s, the population of Florida remained small in 1930, about 1.5 million. The population had tripled since 1900, and the 3 percent average annual rate of growth in the intervening thirty years was more than twice the national rate of population growth. Yet Florida's population ranking had risen from thirty-third to only thirty-first among the forty-eight states. Georgia's population was almost twice the size of Florida's, and Alabama's population was more than 70 percent larger. Nearby in the Caribbean, Cuba's population was more 3 million and Haiti had a population of more than 2 million.[1]

Florida's population growth slowed two times during the 30-year period between 1900 and 1930. One period was in the last half of the 1920s after the land boom ended, when the five-year growth rate was 15 percent, a rate similar to the rate in the decade after the freezes of 1894–1895 and the 1893 national economic recession. This was much lower than the 30 percent rate the state achieved in the first half of the 1920s.

The other period of slow population growth occurred from 1915 to 1920, when the five-year growth rate of 5 percent was barely more than the half the growth rate in the Great Depression period (1930–1935). This is the lowest five-year growth rate ever recorded in Florida.[2] The low rate of population growth during 1915–1920 is not attributable to economic difficulty as much as it is to economic opportunity. Labor markets tightened with the outbreak of World War I, particularly in the northern industrial cities. This was partly in response to the mobilization of workers into the armed forces; the size of the U.S. Army increased from 190,000 troops in March 1917 to 3.665 million in November 1918. It was also partly due to the sharp decline in immigration after Europe entered the war in 1914; immigration from Europe declined from more than 1 million in 1914 to less than 200,000 in each of the following years until 1920.[3] The tight northern labor markets attracted workers from the South, including from Florida. Many of the workers who moved north were black, and Florida's black population decreased from 360,394 in 1915 to 329,487 in 1920, a decline of almost 10 percent.[4] The state also lost white workers; the white population of the state increased by only about 13 percent between 1915 and 1920, half the rate of the previous five years. The slowdown in the growth of the white population may have reflected diminished in-migration to the state as well as out-migration.

The largest declines in the black population were in the old plantation belts centered on Tallahassee in the eastern panhandle and Gainesville in the northern peninsula. There were also sizeable declines in the lumber/naval stores areas in the western panhandle and in Hillsborough and Polk counties, where the phosphate industry was concentrated.[5] The black population grew in Dade and Palm Beach counties and along the northeast coast.

In spite of the fact that Florida's population tripled from 1900 to 1930, the state remained a relatively empty place. Florida's population density of twenty-seven persons per square mile in 1930 was lower than the national average of thirty-five persons per square mile.[6] The state's population density was lower than every state east of the Mississippi except Maine. Florida's density was similar to the density of the western states except California, whose density was thirty-six persons per square mile.

Between 1900 and 1930, the southern half of the Florida peninsula acquired an extensive population for the first time. Growth was particularly strong in

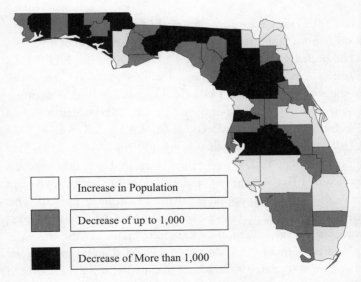

Florida Map 7–1. Change in Black Population in Florida's Counties, 1915–1920

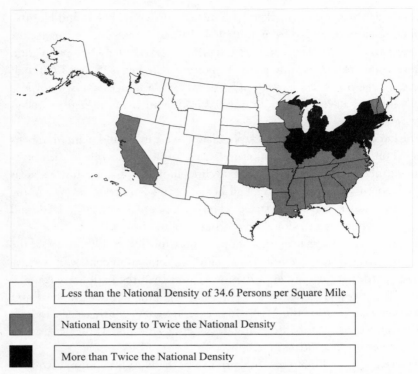

☐	Less than the National Density of 34.6 Persons per Square Mile
▨	National Density to Twice the National Density
■	More than Twice the National Density

U.S. Map 7–1. Population Density per Square Mile by State Compared to National Level, United States, 1930

the southeast. In 1900, Dade County, which stretched along the southeast coast for almost 150 miles from Homestead to Stuart, had a population of 4,955. By 1930, this area had been split into four counties—Dade, Broward, Palm Beach, and Martin counties—and had a population of 219,941, a 44-fold increase.[7] The portion of the area still known as Dade County was the third most populated county in the state. Manatee County and Lee counties, which stretched almost 150 miles from Tampa Bay to Marco Island, had a population of 7,734 in 1900. By 1930, these two counties had been split into five counties that together had a population of 58,221, a sevenfold increase. The southwest coast of Florida below Tampa Bay was more populated than the southeast coast in 1900, but it was considerably less populated than the southeast in 1930. This part of the state had poor transportation connections: rail transportation was relatively slow to come to the area south of Charlotte Harbor in the late nineteenth century, and the Tamiami Trail, which linked Miami and Fort Myers, was not completed until the late 1920s. Much of the interior of the southern half of Florida's peninsula was relatively empty of people in 1930. The coastal

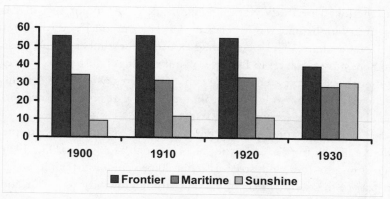

Chart 7–1 Changes in Florida's Frontier, Maritime, and Sunshine Industries as a Percent of the Value of the Production of the State's Economic Base by Decade, 1900–1930

counties north of Tampa and south of Tallahassee were also devoid of people. These sparsely populated areas would continue to host Florida's forestry and cattle industries, key parts of the state's frontier economy.

The relatively sparse population of Florida meant that the state's frontier industries remained the most important part of the state's economic base in 1930, accounting for 40 percent of the production of the basic sector. The sunshine and maritime economies each accounted for 24 percent. The antebellum southern agricultural industries accounted for only 1 percent of the base. The most striking development in the state's economic base from 1900 to 1930 was the growth of the sunshine sector. Although there was some growth in the sector prior to 1920, particularly as the citrus industry recovered from the effects of the 1894–1895 freezes, the big growth in the size of the sector occurred during the 1920s as middle-income tourists came to the state.

The lumber industry dominated the state's frontier sector in 1930, as it had in 1900. In fact, lumber increased its share of sector output from 79 percent to 86 percent in the 30-year period. The shares of both the gum naval stores and cattle industries shrank drastically over that period. Gum naval stores fell from 10 percent to 7 percent and cattle production fell from 4 percent to 1 percent. Lumber was the largest of the state's manufacturing industries, accounting for 20 percent of manufacturing output and 25 percent of manufacturing employment. Another forest-based industry, gum naval stores, was the second largest manufacturing employer, although it was ranked only fifth in production.

Florida was ranked ninth in lumber production among the states in 1930.[8] Production in the state reached 1 billion board feet in 1909, and, apart from a jump before the United States joined World War I, it remained close to this level over the following thirty years. The downside to the importance of the lumber industry in the state was its relatively low labor productivity, which resulted in low wage rates.[9] The average wage earned in the lumber industry was about 86 percent of the level in Florida's manufacturing industry as a whole. Average annual wages were even lower in gum naval stores. We will see that the low wage levels in these two important industries are part of the explanation for the level of per capita income in the state in 1929.

The decline in production of naval stores occurred not only relative to the size of the totality of frontier industries but also in absolute terms. The 1930 level of gross output of the industry was about 20 percent lower than it was in the early part of the twentieth century.[10] The strong growth of output in the last half of the first decade came to an end when war broke out in Europe in August 1914 and the state lost its export markets. There was a second dramatic decrease in output after the United States entered the war in 1917 and workers became scarce. Production increased slowly in the 1920s but never returned the industry to its 1916 size (the same size it had been in 1905–1906), let alone to its peak levels before 1914.

Florida's mining production was still dominated by phosphate mining in 1929, although the state had developed some limestone mining in the 1920s and some clay, sand, and gravel mining in the 1910s. Phosphate mining accounted for 66 percent of the state's mining production in 1929. Florida phosphate production accounted for about 75 percent of national production in 1929; the bulk of the remainder was produced in Tennessee. Indeed, Florida accounted for a significant part of global production.[11]

The outbreak of the war in Europe in 1914 disrupted the industry's exports.[12] One consequence may have been considerable consolidation of the industry. In 1929, there were less than one-third as many operators as had existed twenty years earlier.[13] Phosphate production gradually recovered during the 1920s, but the state never regained some of the markets that it lost at the outbreak of the war in Europe.

Cattle-herding was another of Florida's industries that had developed in its frontier areas, but its contribution to the output of the frontier sector was very low in 1930. The industry was in transition from open-range cattle-herding with descendents of cattle that had roamed the state in Spanish times to modern breeds fed by sown grasses behind fences. Cattle numbers fell by 50 percent from 1900 to 1930.[14] A primary cause of the decline was the loss of the Cuban export market around the time of World War I, when Cuba replaced imports from Florida with imports from other Caribbean nations, especially Venezuela.[15] The quality of the beef produced by the cattle that were native to Florida had limited acceptability elsewhere in the country, and it became clear

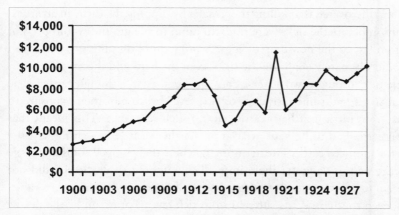

Chart 7–2. Gross Output of Naval Stores in Florida, 1906–1930, in Constant Prices (Selected Years; Index 1906=100)

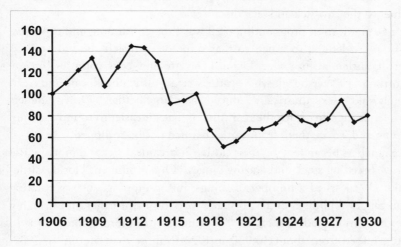

Chart 7–3. Value of Phosphate Production in Florida, 1900–1927 (Selected Years; Thousands of 1895 Dollars)

that the industry needed to upgrade its breeds to increase sales in northern markets. Efforts to bring in thoroughbred bulls had previously failed because most of the bulls died of cattle tick fever within a year.[16] Successful introduction of new breeds required the elimination of the cattle tick, the source of the fever. In 1923, the Florida legislature introduced a mandatory tick eradication program.

The young ticks were born on the ground and jumped on to the cattle as soon as they could. On reaching maturity, the ticks mated, and between eighteen and twenty-one days later the female dropped on the ground to lay her eggs. It was discovered that killing the females by dipping the cattle in an arsenical solution before the ticks were ready to jump to the ground would prevent them from laying the new crop of eggs. A program of dipping every fourteen days would ultimately eradicate the ticks from the herd and the range.

Cattle ticks brought two adverse consequences. First, although cattle in the southern states had some resistance to tick fever because of their exposure to the ticks from birth, northern cattle had no such resistance. This meant that southern cattle had to be kept away from northern cattle, which limited the market for southern cattle. Furthermore, ranchers that shipped southern cattle to Chicago had to slaughter them immediately upon arrival; the city did not allow them to pen their herds near the city until prices became more favorable. Second, even southern cattle suffered from tick fever. For example, the deaths of 3 percent of Florida cattle each year were attributed to "exposure," but the Florida Commissioner of Agriculture's report claimed that these deaths were really due to "the cow tick and lack of care."[17]

The tick eradication program imposed was time-consuming and expensive for Florida's cattlemen, so much so that some of them left the industry. "A number of cattlemen in Taylor, Dixie, Lafayette and Levy counties [on the coast north of St. Petersburg], where cattle were so difficult to locate and treat, completely sold out or drastically reduced their large herds."[18] Other ranchers began to fence their herds for the first time to make it easier to round them up for dipping and isolate them from cattle that had not been dipped.

Once ranchers began fencing their cattle, "it became easier and more logical to improve breeding stock and grazing ranges." One prominent Florida cattleman said, "We learned a number of things during dipping, such as rotating cattle on ranges, building chutes to make working them easier and bringing in better bulls to upgrade our cattle."[19] The number of thoroughbred cattle in the state climbed from about 30,000 in 1924 to more than 50,000 by 1932; during the same period, the number of native cattle fell from 580,000 to less than 500,000. By 1932, thoroughbreds accounted for more than 10 percent of the cattle in the state.[20] The improvement to the state's herds raised the value of stock cattle in the state. A modest increase from 1924 to 1927 was followed by a substantial increase by 1932.

As noted previously, Florida's sunshine sector had risen to be the second largest component of the economic base by 1930. Within the sector, tourism was the largest industry, accounting for more than 70 percent of the total.[21] Vegetables were in second place, and semitropical agriculture was third.

The state's semitropical agriculture was dominated by citrus. A small but significant pineapple industry that was present in 1900 was lost before World War I. The number of crates of pineapples produced in 1909 was 778,644; by

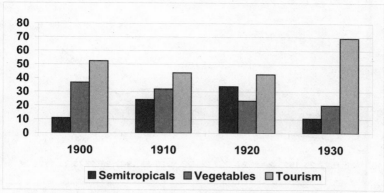

Chart 7–4. Share of Semitropicals, Vegetables, and Tourism in Value of Production of Florida's Sunshine Industries, 1900–1930 (by Percent)

1919, the number of creates had fallen to 26,016.[22] The primary reason cited for the collapse of pineapple production was the U.S. acquisition of the Hawaiian Islands.[23] U.S. pineapple canners switched their source of supply from Cuba to Hawaii, causing the Cubans to increase their shipments of fresh pineapples to the U.S. market, especially after the Key West–Havana car ferry was begun after the railroad arrived in 1912. One reason for the better competitiveness of the Cuban industry was lower labor costs. Cuban pineapple shippers also had lower rates on the Florida East Coast Railway than Florida shippers did. At the same time, Florida production was hit by a disease that may have been exacerbated by poor soil management practices induced by the reduction in margins due to the increased Cuban competition. The loss of the pineapple industry was partly compensated by the growth of the production of alternative noncitrus semitropical fruits, especially the avocado. Avocado production grew strongly in Miami-Dade County in the first half of the 1920s.[24]

Citrus production was dominated by oranges in 1930, as it had been since its earliest establishment in the state. Oranges accounted for over 70 percent of the total, and grapefruit accounted for almost all of the rest.[25] Production of lemons, limes, and other citrus products was negligible. A new market for grapefruit opened when it was discovered in Puerto Rico that grapefruit could be canned. In the overly excited words of a contemporary, "Seldom has a food product of any kind been introduced to the consuming and the investing public that has met with such immediate and universal approval; and in the realm of canned fruits grapefruit is unique. Not only is it more like the natural fresh fruit than any of its competitors, but good authorities state that it is the only canned product which is liked by everybody at first acquaintance, and which nearly everybody likes better canned than fresh."[26] Production of canned grape-

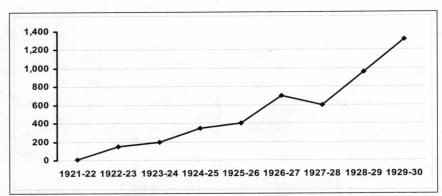

Chart 7–5. Production of Canned Grapefruit in Florida, 1921–1922 to 1929–1930 (in Thousands of Cases)

fruit hearts increased from 10,000 cases in 1921–1922 to 700,000 in 1927; by the end of the decade, it topped 1 million cases.[27]

Production of oranges expanded almost tenfold from the freeze-induced low point at the beginning of the century.[28] There was an increase in the 1920s, when much of the growth occurred on the ridge, an elevated portion of land that lies mostly in Polk County and the counties to the south, including De Soto, Hardee, and Highlands. (The latter two counties were formed from De Soto in the middle of the 1920s.)[29] Polk and the other counties added more than 2 million trees in the 1920s, about 60 percent of the total increase in the state. An important innovation that spurred production on the ridge was the substitution of "rough lemon" orange for sour orange root stocks. The "rough lemon" had the more vigorous and extensive root system needed to find the water table below the elevated land. As a result of the increase in tree plantings, the "ridge" became the dominant area of production in the state.

A shift in consumer tastes made the large expansion in Florida citrus production possible. In 1911, Americans consumed 74 pounds of apples per capita and 20 pounds of citrus products. By 1929, consumption of apples had declined and consumption of citrus products had increased such that Americans consumed 40 pounds of each.[30] Cooperative marketing helped the citrus industry increase its share of the fruit market. California took the lead; local cooperatives were organized there in the 1890s and eventually merged under the name Southern California Fruit Exchanges in 1905.[31] Florida orange growers followed with the establishment of the Florida Citrus Exchange in 1908.

Vegetable production, including potatoes, melons and strawberries, quintupled between 1900 and 1930. The most rapid expansion occurred during the 1920s.[32] Nationally, the U.S. census reported that farm acreage in vegetables

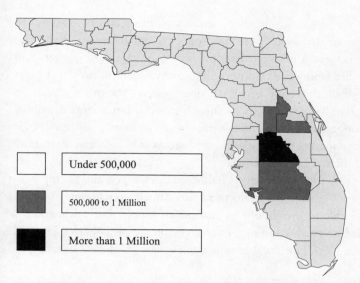

Florida Map 7–2. Increase in the Number of Orange-Bearing Trees in Florida Counties 1919-29

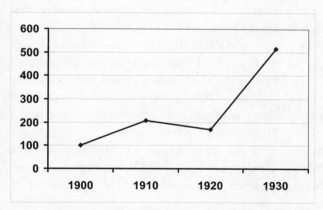

Chart 7–6. Value of Vegetable Production in Florida by Decade, 1900–1930, in Constant Prices (Index 1900=100)

raised for sale almost doubled from 1.5 million acres in 1919 to 2.8 million in 1929.[33] Acreage in Florida rose by 130 percent. The modern national vegetable industry came of age in the 1920s.

The increased production in Florida and the United States led to greatly increased competition for market share. A 1925 article described the response of growers to what it called "severe competition": "This has been expressed in a constant effort to expand the market territory for fruits and vegetables of all kinds. It has appeared also in organized and unorganized efforts to stimulate consumption, in the development of by-product manufacture, in spasmodic efforts to develop foreign markets, and, finally, in the efforts of growers and shippers to keep marketing and transportation costs to a minimum."[34] Growers standardized their products and began packing them for the market, often in packing houses that were owned by groups of growers. Once large distributing firms and cooperative sale agencies were created to handle distribution, it became possible to market the standardized products as brands and extend the markets beyond the large urban centers.

As the national market for early vegetables was developed and as improvements in transportation such as refrigerated cars came into widespread use, it became more feasible for neighboring countries to supply the U.S. market.[35] Mexico expanded its production of winter vegetables, especially tomatoes, in direct competition with Florida. Bermuda competed with Florida in early potato production.

A state census in 1926–1927 provides detailed information on the vegetable industry toward the end of the decade.[36] Potatoes and tomatoes, the largest crops by value, had similar levels of production and celery was in third place. There was also significant production of beans, sweet potatoes, strawberries, cucumbers, watermelons, and peppers.

Seminole County, north of Orlando, had the largest vegetable industry in 1926–1927, followed by Miami-Dade, St. Johns, and Hillsborough counties. Seminole County was the home of the state's celery production, producing more than 90 percent of the state total. Miami-Dade produced more than half the state's tomatoes, and St. Johns County produced more than 40 percent the state's potatoes. Plant City in Hillsborough County was the center of the state's strawberry industry, producing 57 percent of the state's total. The areas in the adjacent counties of Polk and Hardee produced an additional 30 percent. Palm Beach and Broward counties produced almost 40 percent of the state's string beans

The third sector of Florida's economic base in 1930 included the state's maritime industries. The largest of these was cigar manufacturing, which accounted for 50 percent of the production of the state's maritime industries. Fisheries and sponges accounted for 30 percent. During the period 1900–1930, the defense industry, measured by the earnings of military personnel in the state, increased its share to 20 percent of the sector's total.

Florida's cigar production in 1929 was the third highest in the nation after Pennsylvania and New Jersey.[37] Output doubled in the first decade of the century and remained relatively stable in the twenty years before 1929.[38] Most of Florida's cigars were produced by hand for the high end of the market. The high

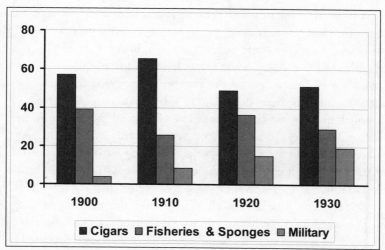

Chart 7-7. Share of Cigars, Fisheries and Sponges, and the Military in Value of Production of Florida's Maritime Industries by Decade, 1900–1930 (by Percent)

level of skill of Florida's cigar makers made average wages in the Florida industry higher than elsewhere in the country. However, by the end of the 1920s, the gap between Florida and national wages had narrowed.

When limited mechanization was gradually introduced to cigar-making, workers reacted by negotiating a detailed list of labor rates for more than 100 sizes and shapes and grades of cigars.[39] In 1919, there was a major confrontation between employers and workers in the industry as a new wage contract came up for negotiation after the sharp increase in prices due to World War I. Employers felt the need to "break free from the methods and rules of cigar production to which they had been held by the cigar and allied workers."[40] Workers sought a union shop, and when employers fired union organizers, a large number of workers went on strike. Employers retaliated with a two-month lockout, after which they re-employed only workers who agreed to the new work rules they had imposed. There was a gradual return of some of the work force amid charges that strikers were intimidating returning workers. The union finally dropped its demand for a union shop more than eighteen months after the initial strike.

By 1929, the earnings of the average cigar worker were only 6 percent more in real terms than the 1919 level, which was almost 10 percent less than the level twenty years earlier. Workers were becoming more interested in left-wing politics. It was a traditional practice for lectors to read newspapers and books to the workers while they worked, and owners felt that when "the readers read a paper like the *Daily Worker* [of the Communist Party] . . . they were influencing the cigar makers to make trouble." But one reader later said, "We were not responsible for the material we read. The cigar makers decided what we read."[41] The stage was set for another confrontation in the industry when the Depression forced cutbacks in production and wages in the industry.

The second largest component of the maritime sector was fishing.[42] This industry was substantial in size in 1929. Almost 150 million pounds were caught in virtually equal amounts on both coasts. The Gulf coast fisheries, however, had a much higher value per pound—five cents as opposed to three cents—and the Gulf fishery accounted for almost two-thirds of the value of the state's fish catch in 1929. Florida's fish production doubled between 1902 and 1918 before slipping back to finish at a 1930 level of 78 percent higher than the 1902 level.

In the 1920s, concern grew that overfishing posed a threat to the industry. In an article published in 1927, the deputy commissioner of the U.S. Bureau of Fisheries observed that the catch of the older fishes that had been exported to northern states since the end of the nineteenth century, including mullet and red snapper, had not changed since 1902. The deputy commissioner wrote, "Unfortunately, it is not safe to conclude that these older fisheries are holding their own. The investment in the fisheries and the efficiency of fishing operations have increased, and an increased number of units of fishing gear may be maintaining the catch while actually depleting the supply [stock of fish]. That this is happening is indicated by the concerns of the fishermen themselves over the future of the fisheries for mullet and red snapper."[43]

Mullet was the most valuable of the state's fisheries in 1923.[44] This fishery, based in the Cape Sable region, doubled in size around the turn of the century after netting practices were established.[45] Red snapper was the second most valuable industry, which was carried on along most of the state's Gulf coast. Shrimp fishing began off Florida's northeast coast around the turn of the century. The introduction of the otter trawl in 1912 enabled fishermen to fish in deep water and drag where the concentration of fish was heaviest. Production almost trebled between 1890 and 1918.

In 1929, about 400,000 pounds of sponges were sold at the Tarpon Springs Exchange.[46] The Tarpon Springs industry had received a major boost in 1905 when a group of Greeks arrived and replaced hooking technology with diving.[47] The gasoline engine, which fueled the boats and supplied air to the divers, greatly improved labor productivity in the fishery.[48] Production peaked in 1922, accompanied by a sharp decrease in prices. Thereafter production fell for most of the rest of the decade even though prices rose. Supply seemed unable to respond to the stimulus of higher prices. The deputy commissioner of the U.S. Bureau of Fisheries noted in a 1928 article that close supervision of the industry was needed to prevent depletion.[49]

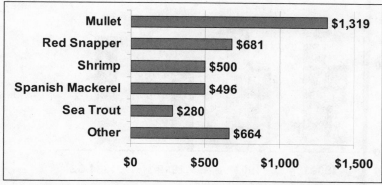

Chart 7–8. Value of Commercial Fisheries Production in Florida in 1923 (in Thousands of Current Dollars)

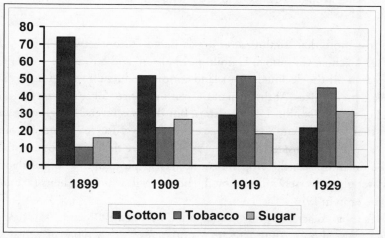

Chart 7–9. Share of Cotton, Tobacco, and Sugar in Value of Production of Florida's Southern Industries by Decade, 1899–1929 (by Percent)

The story of Florida's small southern sector in the 1900–1930 period is the sharp decline of the cotton industry and the growth of the shade-tobacco industry. Toward the end of the 1920s, sugar production expanded. Cotton accounted for about 75 percent of the sector in 1900, but this had fallen to 20 percent by 1930. Tobacco expanded its share from less than 10 percent in 1900 to more than 40 percent by 1920.[50]

In the 20-year period prior to 1930, Florida lost its sea-island cotton industry completely, although there was modest growth in the upland cotton industry.[51] Sea-island cotton was a traditional product of the northern peninsular counties, and the loss of the industry was concentrated in this part of the state. Five

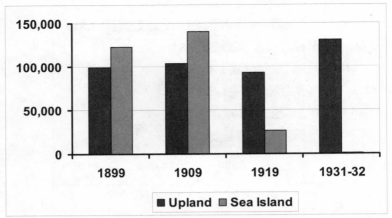

Chart 7–10. Acres in Upland Cotton and Sea-Island Cotton, Florida, 1899, 1909, 1919, and 1931–1932

counties lost more than 18,000 acres of sea-island cotton between 1909 and 1931–1932: Alachua, Columbia, Hamilton, Madison, and Suwannee.

One reason for the decline in sea-island cotton production was an unfavorable movement in prices. At the turn of the century, prices for sea-island cotton were higher than prices for upland cotton, but this was reversed beginning in 1909. In that year, although yields per acre were lower for sea-island cotton, the higher price compensated for the lower yield. Once the sea-island price fell below the upland price, the crop was no longer as profitable. The sea-island industry was also adversely affected by the boll weevil, which made its first attack on the crop in 1916.[52]

Florida's tobacco acreage grew in the period between 1905 and 1931–1932, increasing from about 2,000 acres to 7,000 acres.[53] Two types of tobacco were grown in Florida during this period, open-field tobacco and shade tobacco. The shade-tobacco industry expanded rapidly in the first decade of the twentieth century until the combination of the financial panic of 1907 and a poor-quality crop in the same year led to a collapse of the industry. The price per pound of shade tobacco fell between 1905 and 1909–1910 at the same time that the price for open-field tobacco rose.[54] A consolidation followed when the American Sumatra Tobacco Corporation merged eleven local producers in 1910. This enabled the producers to obtain working capital on Wall Street and avoid the poor quality that had damaged the reputation of the crop in 1907.[55]

The period around World War I was particularly prosperous for the shade-tobacco industry; the price per pound rose from about 40 cents to more than a dollar between 1909–1910 and 1919–1920. But disaster struck in the mid-1920s

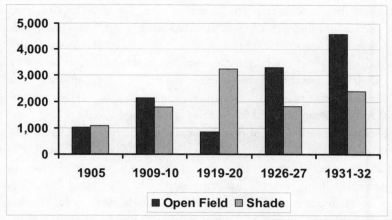

Chart 7–11. Acres in Open-Field Tobacco and Shade Tobacco, Florida, 1905–1932, Selected Years

when the blackshank fungus decimated the crop in some fields.[56] Acreage in shade tobacco declined, and although a resistant strain to the fungus was discovered in 1928, the acreage was not restored by the 1931–1932 crop year.

Hamilton Disston made an attempt to grow sugarcane for sugar rather than syrup at St. Cloud in the early 1890s, but the operations were closed down after his death in 1896. A new attempt was made at the end of World War I in response to a period of exceptionally high prices.[57] This was the result of the relaxation of wartime price controls and shortfalls in domestic production due to plant diseases.[58]

The postwar high prices lasted long enough to convince a number of large investors to invest in sugarcane-growing south of Lake Okeechobee.[59] By the time these new enterprises were operational, sugar prices had fallen sharply and many domestic producers had experienced severe losses. In 1921, Congress raised the duty on Cuban sugar, the largest foreign supplier to the U.S. market, from 1 cent to 1.6 cents per pound.[60]

In 1919, the Pennsylvania Sugar Company (Pennsuco) bought about 75,000 acres on the Miami Canal seventeen miles northwest of Miami, later the site of the city of Hialeah.[61] It also purchased a sugar mill in Texas and moved it to Florida.[62] In January 1924, the mill began grinding cane, but sugar operations ceased after a year or two. It became evident that a successful sugarcane-growing operation in southern Florida required sophisticated water management, the development of varieties of cane suitable to the muck soils, and the application of appropriate fertilizers. Pennsuco was one of several false starts in the early 1920s. By 1921, Pennsuco had planted 800 acres of cane and was planning a further expansion. The Pennsuco initiative ended in failure, however, as the development of new disease-resistant varieties of cane led to an expansion of domestic production and depressed prices beginning in 1925. In 1925, Bror G. Dahlberg, a Chicago wallboard manufacturer, purchased and leased a large acreage south and east of the lake and created the Southern Sugar Company. Dahlberg wanted to use sugar bagasse, the remains of the cane after the juice was extracted, as a raw material for manufacturing wallboard. Dahlberg purchased the mills of Pennsuco and Florida Sugar and Food Products Company and combined them with new equipment to construct a large mill near Clewiston, a new town he had developed on the west side of the lake. By 1930, Dahlberg had 25,000 acres of cane, more than half the total acreage in all crops in the Everglades. Declining prices as the Depression took hold created difficulties for his high-cost enterprise, and it was forced into receivership in July of that same year. A year later Dahlberg's company was purchased by a new company, the United States Sugar Corporation, and the everglades sugar industry was further expanded during the decade that followed.

The combination of the depressing effect of the boom's collapse and the structure of the economy gave Florida a low level of per capita income in 1929.[63] The state level of $517 was 74 percent of the national level of $698, indicating that the average Floridian had a much lower income than the average American in 1929. Indeed, this was the largest gap between Florida's per capita income and the U.S. level that was recorded in the twentieth century.

The per capita income measure used in this book is derived from the personal income estimates produced for states and counties by the Regional Economics Division of the U.S. Bureau of Economic Analysis. Personal income, as the name suggests, is the income of persons. It includes wages and other labor compensation, which, together with the income of the self-employed, are called earnings. Personal income also includes dividends, interest and rent, and net government transfer payments. Net contributions to Social Security and other federal government transfer payments such as unemployment compensation are included in net government transfer payments. Transfer payments were a very small component of personal income in 1929, since Social Security and a national system of unemployment compensation had not yet been established.

Although Florida's per capita income was much lower than the national figure, it was higher than that of any of the other states that had been members of the Confederacy. The per capita income of Texas was 8 percent below the Florida level. Per capita incomes in the neighboring states of Georgia and Alabama were more than 33 percent below the Florida level. Florida's economy was clearly shaped by different forces than the other southern states.

In the case of Florida, earnings is a better measure of the state's economy

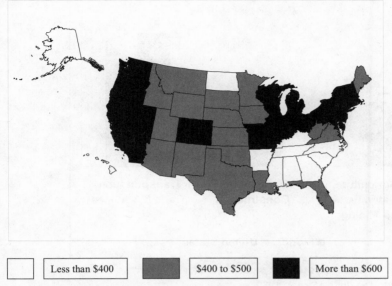

U.S. Map 7–2. Per Capita Income by State, United States, 1929

than personal income because such a large part of dividends, interest, and rent Floridians receive comes from elsewhere in the nation. This is also true of net government transfer payments. Personal income differs from gross state product (statistics for which did not become available until the second half of the twentieth century) because the latter does not include transfer payments and it includes the dividends, interest, and rent paid by Florida businesses and households, as opposed to what they received, which is what is included in personal income.

In 1929, Florida labor earnings were an even smaller percentage of the national level than personal income was.[64] It is clear that the low level of per capita income relative to the national level is the result of low earnings per worker in its industries. It did not reflect a broadly different industry structure, since the broad distribution of employment in Florida was not strikingly different from the national distribution in 1930.[65] The percentage of Floridians employed in agriculture, forestry, fishing, and mining fell from 52 percent in 1900 to 25 percent in 1930, a proportion similar to the national proportion. By 1930, employment in the state was no longer dominated by agriculture and the other extractive industries. Services, including transportation and trade, were the largest source of employment, both nationally and in the state. The primary difference between Florida and the nation was a larger manufacturing and construction share nationally and a larger share of services

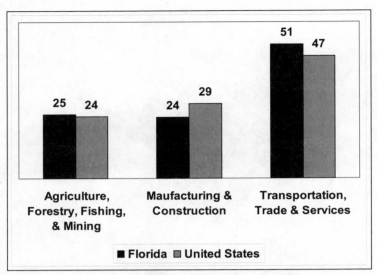

Chart 7–12. Distribution of Employment by Sector as a Percent of the Total, Florida and the United States, 1930

in Florida. The latter presumably is attributable to the tourist industry, which is characterized by lower earnings per person than is manufacturing and construction. Additionally, Florida's manufacturing employment was dominated by lumber and naval stores, two industries with low average earnings per wage earner.

Chapter 8

1930–1945

Depression, Recovery, and War

The period of the 1930s has been characterized as the Great Depression because of the severity of the economic decline compared to other national recessions in the twentieth century. Nationally, per capita income, adjusted for changes in prices, was 30 percent lower in 1932 and 1933 than it was in 1929 before the depression began. National per capita income did not return to its 1929 level until 1940.[1]

Although economists have written much about the causes of the Great Depression, there is no unanimity of opinion, even though more than seventy years have elapsed since it began.[2] There is general agreement that a national economic recession began in August 1929 partly as a result of a tight money policy the Federal Reserve instituted in 1928 in an attempt to eliminate excessive speculation in the stock market.[3] Other factors that caused the initial downturn included an oversupply in the housing market, the stock market crash, and poor agricultural harvests in parts of the United States.[4] The level of aggregate spending dropped, national output dropped, and workers were laid off from their jobs. This was not unusual—in the decade of the 1920s alone there were national economic recessions in 1920–1921, 1923–1924, and 1926–1927. There had also been three recessions in the decade of the 1910s and two in the first decade of the century.

Recessions occur after declines in aggregate spending because wages and prices in a modern economy do not fall quickly enough to restore equilibrium in the national economy. As business inventories increase, employers lay off workers. It takes time before the prices of nonperishable items are cut and it takes additional time before wage earners experience a decline in their hourly rates. The decline in the economy is also accompanied by declines in consumer and business confidence. As consumers lose confidence in the future they cut back their spending on consumption items they can postpone, and as businesses lose confidence they cut back on their spending on new plants and equipment.

The Depression was unusual in the length of its contraction (at forty-three months it was by far the longest in the twentieth century) and the severity of its impact on a population that had become urbanized and was largely dependent on money wages for its support. Although economic growth resumed in 1933, it was 1940 before national per capita income was restored to its 1929 level.

One reason for the persistence of the economic downturn in the early 1930s was that the economy experienced a series of negative economic shocks spread over a period of years. In October 1929, the stock market crashed, and this further shook confidence in the economy and deterred business investment. In 1931, monetary policy was tightened when the United Kingdom abandoned the gold standard. This monetary tightening was especially inappropriate because the banking system had begun to experience a severe lack of liquidity and a monetary easing was needed to enable the Federal Reserve to fulfill its function as a lender of last resort. As a result, the banking system experienced a major collapse that disrupted the economy and dried up the major source of credit needed to bring about economic recovery. Finally, as the recession spread across the world, countries (including the United States) adopted protectionist policies, reducing the volume of trade and adding to the downward pressures on the U.S. economy.

The data on personal income by state, the first annual regional economic series made available by government statisticians in the twentieth century, provide a convenient way to track the impact of the depression on Florida's economy and to compare this to the impact on the national economy, the aggregate of the economies of the forty-eight states and the District of Columbia.[5] In undertaking the comparison, we express per capita income as an index with the base year of 1929, the peak year before the national recession began. Florida's per capita income, adjusted for changes in the general price level, closely tracked the national level downward in 1930 and 1931, although the bottom Florida reached in 1932–1933 was not quite as severe as that experienced nationally. By 1933, national per capita income was 70 percent of the 1929 level, compared to 73 percent in Florida.

Earnings (composed of wages and other labor compensation as well as the income of the self-employed) is a better measure of the strength of a state economy than personal income because the latter includes receipts of dividends, interest, and rent as well as net government transfers, which are largely brought into the state from elsewhere in the nation. The earnings data show that Florida's economy did not decline as rapidly as the national economy and not as deeply. The state economy held up better during the economic contraction than the national economy did.[6]

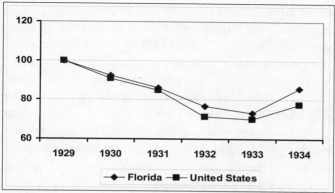

Chart 8–1. Real per Capita Income, Florida and the United States, 1929–1934 (Index 1929=100)

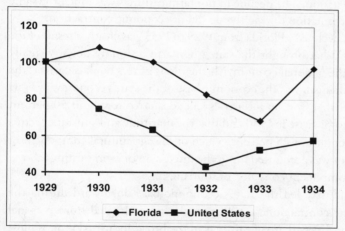

Chart 8–2. Per Capita Farm Earnings, Florida and the United States, 1929–1934 (Adjusted for Price Changes, Index 1929=100)

We can look to industrial sources of earnings by industry in the personal income data to understand the reason for the better performance of Florida earnings. The main explanation was the relative strength of the state's agricultural industry. By the bottom of the general recession in 1933, earnings on the nation's farms had dropped sharply to 53 percent of their 1929 level. Earnings in Florida's farm sector also declined, but only to 68 percent of the 1929 level. Not only was the decline in the state not as deep as the national decline, but in 1930, Florida's farm earnings actually exceeded the 1929 level and were at the 1929 level in 1931.

An infestation of the Mediterranean fruit fly was discovered in Orlando in April 1929 that resulted in restrictions on the shipment of fruits and vegetables from the state that lasted until October 1933.[7] Earnings in the state's farm sector in 1929 were presumably depressed by these restrictions, and a partial recovery from the infestation may partly account for the better performance of the state's farm sector during the economic contraction. On the other hand, there were bad harvests elsewhere in the country in 1929, so farm earnings nationally were also depressed that year. Florida's farm sector was dominated by fruit and vegetables, and these crops may have been less sensitive to the economic decline because they were benefiting from a favorable shift in consumer preferences.

The remaining part of labor-market earnings consists of the nonfarm sector, which accounted for about 75 percent of the total in the state and more than 90 percent in the nation. The decline in nonfarm earnings was much the same in the state as in the nation during the period of economic contraction.

The economic decline in Florida from 1929 to 1933 was clearly a result of the national decline. What brought the state's nonfarm economy down virtually in lockstep with the national economy? If the thesis of this book is correct, the transmission mechanism was the economic base of the state's economy. We saw in the last chapter that frontier industries still accounted for about 50 percent of the state's economic base in 1930 and that the maritime and sunshine sectors each accounted for almost 25 percent. Much of the agricultural component of the sunshine sector was accounted for in the discussion of farm earnings above. The remaining component consisted of tourism.

The tourist industry led the state's economic base downward during the national economic contraction. Tourist earnings are estimated from personal income data as the excess share of earnings in the broad industrial groups most impacted by tourists in the state relative to the nation. By 1932, this measure of tourism had declined by 60 percent from the 1929 level. Earnings in industries identified with the other basic sectors—the frontier and maritime sectors—did not begin to decline until 1931, and the decline to their low in 1933 was only 35 percent.[8]

We have observed in previous chapters, and we will observe in future chapters as well, that Florida's tourist industry is pro-cyclical—it has a tendency to decline during national economic recessions and to expand during national expansions. This is because a vacation is a postponable item of consumption. Consumers tend to reduce their vacation spending during periods of economic difficulty or uncertainty. They may shorten the length of their vacations or travel closer to home. These decisions are likely to have slowed the flow of tourists from the North to Florida at the beginning of the 1930s.

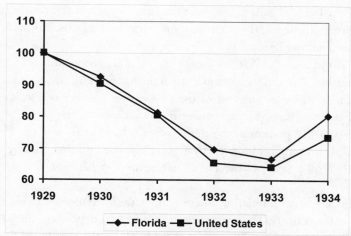

Chart 8–3. Per Capita Private Nonfarm Earnings, Florida and the United States, 1929–1934 (Adjusted for Price Changes, Index 1929=100)

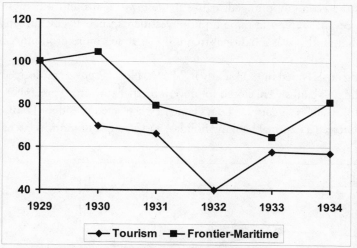

Chart 8–4. Per Capita Earnings in Florida's Tourism and Frontier-Maritime Industries, 1929–1932 (Adjusted for Price Changes, Index 1929=100)

Later in the century, when long-distance travel was much faster and cheaper, Florida experienced some benefit from the substitution of closer for more distant destinations.

We have seen that a collapse of the nation's banks was a major reason for the severity of the depression at the beginning of the 1930s. Nationally, bank deposits fell by about 30 percent from $53 billion on June 30, 1929, to a low of $36.5 billion in 1933.[9] The declines were not uniform across the country, however. The largest declines (50 percent or more) were found in the Midwest and the South, including Florida.

By a number of measures, Florida's banks experienced greater difficulties during the depression than did banks elsewhere in the nation. This was because of their weakened position at the end of the 1920s. The number of Florida banks declined more rapidly than elsewhere in the country as the recession began. By 1930–1931, 13 percent of the nation's banks had failed, whereas 25 percent had failed in Florida. However, by 1932–1933, the bottom of the recession, more than 40 percent of banks had failed, both in the state and the nation.

Bank deposits, adjusted for inflation and per capita, declined more in Florida than elsewhere in the country. The greatest decline in Florida deposits occurred in 1929–1930, the same year that 20 percent of the banks in the state failed. In an effort to help the banks, the state legislature passed a Banking Act in 1931 that placed limits on withdrawals of deposits and required some banks to call in loans.[10] As the economy plunged, banks made fewer loans and put more of their resources into safer and more liquid investments, such as government securities. Although this was a national trend, it was much more pronounced in the state.

The banking crisis ended in 1933. Early in March, Florida's governor decreed a banking holiday—banks were closed to prevent further runs from precipitating further bankruptcies. A couple of days later, newly elected president Franklin Roosevelt decreed a national banking holiday, and a couple of months later a

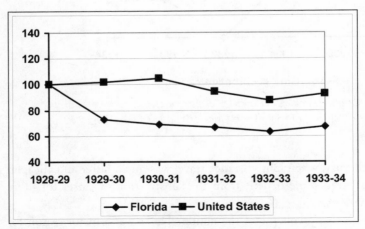

Chart 8–5. Per Capita Bank Deposits, Florida and the United States, 1928–1919 to 1933–1934 (Adjusted for Price Changes, Index 1929=100)

major banking bill (the Glass-Steagall Act) passed Congress. This act instituted federal deposit insurance, and the cycle of bank runs and bank collapses came to an end.

Another sector of the Florida economy that experienced difficulties during the economic contraction was local government. Like the banking sector, the local government sector was in a weakened condition as the depression began. The economic downturn squeezed the revenue of local governments both nationwide and in Florida.

The revenue squeeze pushed the state's local governments into a state of crisis because of their high debt levels, largely accumulated during the boom years. The debt of local governments per capita and per $1,000 of personal income was about three times higher in Florida than in the other states of the nation. The initial response of local governments was to slash capital outlays. In many cases, the reductions came on top of sharp reductions that had occurred after the boom ended in 1926. Data are available for the state's three largest cities and they show that capital spending had been virtually eliminated by the bottom of the recession in 1933.[11] The capital outlays of local governments accounted for a smaller share of total spending in Florida than in all state and local governments in the nation. In 1931, the capital outlays of Florida's local governments accounted for 5 percent of total spending; the national figure was 20 percent.[12]

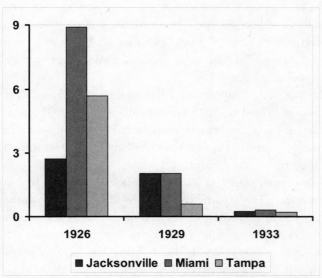

Chart 8–6. Capital Expenditures in Jacksonville, Miami, and Tampa, Florida, 1926, 1929, and 1933, in Millions of Current Dollars

During the Depression, the finances of Florida's local governments were in a state of crisis. Even though they virtually eliminated capital expenditures, cut operating expenditures sharply, and raised funds from sources other than taxes, most Florida local governments were unable to make payments on their bond issues.[13] In 1944, an economist explained the collapse of local government funding during the Depression: "The first default on a bond payment in Florida since the first World War occurred in 1926. This isolated event was soon followed by an avalanche of collapses. By 1929 bond issues throughout the state were in default. The great 1929–33 depression, following immediately upon the collapse of the Florida land boom, undermined local property tax collections, forced more than 85 percent of local public debt into default and virtually paralyzed local public debt throughout the state."[14] The state government did not experience the same crisis because it was constitutionally prohibited from issuing debt. Local governments, including counties, school districts, cities, and special taxing districts, were responsible for virtually all public debt in Florida.

Much of the local government debt was issued during the boom, and the counties with the most severe debt problems were in the areas most impacted by the boom or in nearby areas infected by the boom.[15] Local governments had issued debt to finance infrastructure, including schools, in anticipation of a population growth that did not materialize and in the expectation that the local revenue base would grow.

In Florida, 60 percent of the local revenue base was generated by taxes. The remainder came from fees and licenses, special assessments, and revenues from other branches of government. Over 90 percent of that tax base came from property taxes. As a result, over 50 percent of the local government revenue base was generated by property taxes.

Property values, the base of the property tax, fell from their peak (boom) level of almost $800 million in 1926–1927 to just over $400 million in 1932–1933, a decline of 45 percent, before beginning a slow recovery.[16] This sharp drop in property values put the debt service requirements of many local governments beyond the limits of their taxing capabilities.

Statewide, annual debt service costs for local government debt amounted to 8 percent of property values.[17] This statistic conceals a wide variation across the counties. The debt service requirements of nineteen of the state's sixty-seven counties equaled 10 percent or more of property values. In this situation, local governments in those counties would have had to bill residents for local property taxes at an amount equal to 10 percent of their homes to meet their debts, obviously not a feasible strategy during the Depression. On the other hand, nineteen counties had debt service ratios of less than 4 percent.

The counties with high debt service included the east coast counties north from Fort Lauderdale to Vero Beach: Charlotte, Sarasota, and Pinellas counties on the west coast and Bay County in the panhandle. A number of counties in the south-central region also had high debt service ratios. The counties with the state's largest cities (Miami-Dade, Tampa, and Jacksonville) did not have very high debt service ratios, except for Pinellas County.

Where annual debt service requirements were high, attempts to raise property tax rates to avoid default backfired. Taxpayers simply did not pay the taxes that were levied. The normal process for handling delinquent property taxes was to offer a tax certificate for sale to investors, who would pay the taxes in exchange for a lien against the property and a rate of interest on their investment. When the property owner paid off the taxes plus interest and costs, the tax certificate holder was reimbursed for his tax payment plus the agreed interest. The holder of the tax certificate could petition the tax collector to auction the property to the highest bidder if the taxes were not paid two years after the certificate was issued. The delinquent taxes had first claim on the proceeds of the sale. During the economic conditions of the 1930s, however, because few investors could purchase tax certificates, the state purchased them.[18] In 1937, the legislature passed the Murphy Act, which transferred the ownership of properties against which there were outstanding tax certificates older than

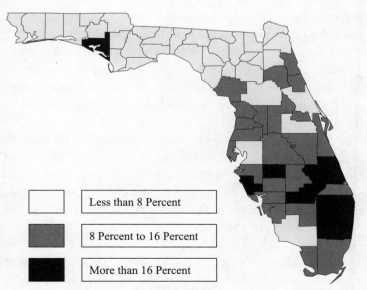

Less than 8 Percent

8 Percent to 16 Percent

More than 16 Percent

Florida Map 8–1. Debt Service as a Percent of Assessed Property Values in Florida Counties 1931

two years to the state. The properties could be purchased for the amount of the tax certificates.

Because so many local governments could not meet their debt service obligations, they petitioned the state legislature for debt relief. In 1929, the legislature voted to use the revenue from two cents of the gasoline tax to liquidate road and bridge bonds that the counties had issued. However, the Florida Supreme Court declared this action unconstitutional because it used a state tax to pay the expenses of local governments. The 1931 legislature reformulated the provision as a reimbursement for expenses incurred in constructing *state* roads and bridges that had been constructed by the counties. This passed the test of constitutionality, and ownership of county roads and bridges was transferred to the state along with their debt of more than $100 million. This sum amounted to 20 percent of the public debt of local governments.

In 1933, the legislature passed the Kanner Act, which established the State Board of Administration, comprised of elected cabinet officers who administered the gasoline tax revenues that were set aside to assist the counties with their road and bridge debt. The act permitted the Board of Administration to purchase such debt below par at the request of the local county commission. While this action removed some of the county debt at a fraction of its long-run cost, it returned the annual debt service requirement to the property tax.

Some bondholders sued counties to collect on defaulted bonds and interest payments. In successful cases, the courts ordered counties to adopt high property tax rates in order to pay the bondholders. This increased the rate of tax delinquency. Some owners were in danger of losing their homes because of the high tax rates, and in 1933 the legislature initiated a constitutional amendment that provided a homestead exemption against property taxes. The voters passed the amendment, providing relief to homeowners but exacerbating the funding crisis of local governments.

By 1939, reimbursements by the state for county construction of state roads and bridges were falling behind the debt service needs for roads and bridges of almost all the counties. The road and bridge debt problem was again threatening local property taxes. The 1941 legislature passed a constitutional amendment earmarking two cents of the gasoline tax for local roads and bridges, and voters ratified the amendment in 1942.

Two other parts of the local public debt problem were brought under control in the early 1930s. School debt, which accounted for about 10 percent of the total, was placed under the management of the state superintendent of public instruction, who pooled resources from the different districts to prevent defaults. Drainage districts accounted for another relatively small part of the debt (less than 5 percent). Many of these were able to take advantage of the Wilcox national Municipal Bankruptcy Act and solve their debt problems with assistance from the Reconstruction Finance Corporation.

As economic recovery proceeded in the last half of the 1930s, the remaining debt became more manageable, although it remained a problem for the state's local governments. By 1940, Florida's public debt in current dollars, all of which was incurred by local governments, was about half the 1931 size relative to the population and to personal income.[19]

Along with other local governments, the finances of public school districts were squeezed during the economic contraction.[20] School district revenues fell by 30 percent from 1929–1930 to 1932–1933. Districts cut expenditures

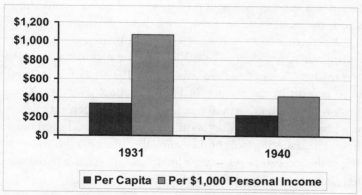

Chart 8–7. Local Government Debt per Capita and per $1,000 Personal Income, Florida, 1931 and 1940, Current Dollars

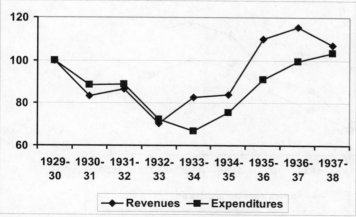

Chart 8–8. Revenues and Expenditures in Florida School Districts, 1929–1930 to 1937–1938 (Index 1929–30=100)

sharply, but the reduction was somewhat less because fund balances were drawn down.

Revenues began to recover in 1933–1934 as the economy began to recover. The growth in revenues, however, was largely a result of increased state funding. As the recession began, most state funding of public education was financed from the gasoline tax. In 1932, the state shifted gasoline tax revenues to county road and bridge funds (as noted above) and began using motor vehicle license funds to fund schools. The state provided school districts with additional local sources such as a portion of the tax on racing adopted in 1931, a share in the proceeds of beverage taxes imposed after Prohibition was repealed in 1933, and some revenue from retail licenses.[21] These new sources, however, were a small part of the funding for public education. Effective from the 1935–1936 school year, the state added a substantial portion of its general revenue and almost doubled the size of the teachers' salary fund. With these adjustments, the state accounted for 49 percent of school district revenue, up from 23 percent in 1929–1930. During the remainder of the 1930s, the state maintained its commitment to the teachers' salary fund. As a result, in 1939–1940, state funds accounted for 50 percent of the revenue of Florida's school districts. During World War II, however, the state share slipped back below 50 percent.

The recovery from the depression began in 1933 both in Florida and in the nation as a whole. The leadership role of the national economy is shown by the common timing of the recession lows and the broadly similar trends in the state and nation after the recovery began.

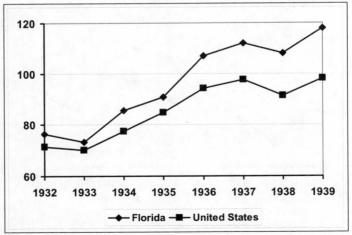

Chart 8–9. Per Capita Income, Florida and the United States, 1932–1939, Adjusted for Price Changes (Index 1929=100)

A number of actions the Roosevelt administration took played a major role in bringing about the economic recovery, including an expansive fiscal policy and devaluation of the dollar.[22] After federal insurance for bank deposits ended the threat of bank runs, the money supply ended its decline and expanded strongly in the early years of the recovery.

Roosevelt greatly increased federal spending in the state and elsewhere in the nation. Federal expenditures in Florida rose from about $20 million in 1933 to more than $60 million in 1934. The federal government maintained this high level of spending in the state for the remainder of the decade.[23] Most of the increase in federal spending was for employment relief by the Civil Works Administration (CWA), the Federal Emergency Relief Administration (FERA), and the Civilian Conservation Corps (CCC). The CWA was put into place during the winter of 1933–1934 to provide short-term public service jobs for the unemployed. At the national level, there are seasonal decreases in employment during the winter months, but the reverse is true in Florida. CWA workers in Florida were released in the spring, precisely the season when the number of available jobs falls in Florida.[24] FERA provided employment to the former CWA workers but at reduced wages. The significance of these relief programs for Florida's economy can be seen in the fact that the $38 million expended in 1934 was equal in value to 9 percent of the total earnings in the state in that year.

In 1934, federal spending also increased to maintain Florida's infrastructure. Spending for roads rose from $2.3 million to $5.3 million, and expenditures on rivers, harbors, and flood control rose from $4.3 million to $8.6 million, although these were partly offset by a decline in expenditures on federal buildings

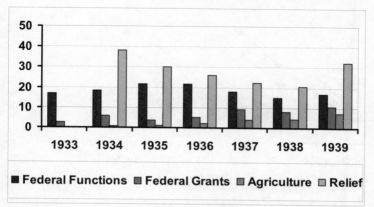

Chart 8–10. Percent Federal Spending in Florida on Federal Functions, Federal Grants, Agriculture, and Relief, 1933–1939, in Millions of Current Dollars

from $2.0 to $1.1 million and a decline in Veterans Administration spending from $10.1 million to $6.7 million.

Florida's economy enjoyed a stronger economic recovery than the nation's and actually began a new economic expansion beyond the pre-Depression 1929 level in 1936. In contrast, the national personal per capita income remained below its 1929 level for the remainder of the 1930s. The relatively strong performance of the state is attributable to the strength of the local economy rather than to the effect of inflows of property income or personal transfers from the rest of the country. There was virtually no difference between the growth of Florida earnings and personal income as a whole after the low point of the recession in 1933.

We saw above that the farm sector did not decline as much in Florida during the 1929–1933 contraction as it did in the nation. This pattern continued during the economic recovery. Per capita farm earnings had returned to the pre-Depression 1929 level by 1934, and they remained above the 1929 level for the rest of the decade with the exception of 1938. Farm earnings, however, provide only part of the explanation for the stronger economic recovery in the state. Nonfarm per capita earnings grew more rapidly in the state than in the nation after the recession low of 1933. By the end of the decade, Florida's nonfarm earnings were 17 percent higher than the pre-Depression level. Nationally, nonfarm earnings were 7 percent above the pre-Depression level.

A turnaround in tourism was a major feature of Florida's economic recovery. Earnings in tourism had declined more sharply than in the rest of the

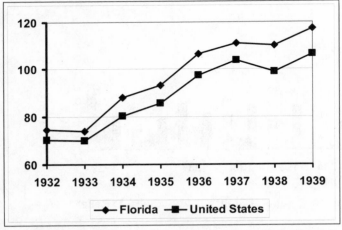

Chart 8–11. Per Capita Non-Farm Earnings in Florida and the United States, 1932–1939, Adjusted for Price Changes (Index 1929=100)

state's economic base during the economic contraction, and they recovered more strongly after the recession low of 1933. The rapid recovery of tourism may be attributable to the greater flexibility in prices, wages, and employment that characterized the industry. The industry's work force had few labor union members and it was characterized by a preponderance of small businesses. Much of its employment was seasonal, and many producers made hiring, pricing, and wage decisions on an annual basis. These decisions could be guided by advance bookings, which provided the industry with an indication of the seasonal outlook. These patterns in tourism were very different than those found in manufacturing, for example.

By 1937, the year before the 1938 national recession that will be discussed below, earnings in tourism were almost three times their depression low. Earnings in the frontier-maritime industries had fallen less sharply during the economic contraction, but they remained below the 1929 level for the remainder of the 1930s.

The strength of farm earnings and earnings in tourism during the 1930s increased the importance of the sunshine industries in the state's economic base. Indeed, the 1930s were the decade when Florida's economic base stopped being dominated by its frontier industries. The frontier share of the economic base fell from 51 percent in 1930 to 32 percent in 1940. In contrast, the share of the sunshine industries rose from 24 percent to 42 percent during the decade. In 1940, the sunshine industries were the largest component of the state's economic base, and this remained true for the rest of the century.

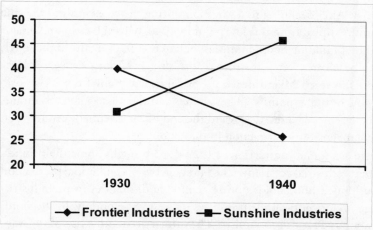

Chart 8–12. Percent Share of Frontier and Sunshine Industries in Value of Production of Florida's Economic Base, 1930 and 1940

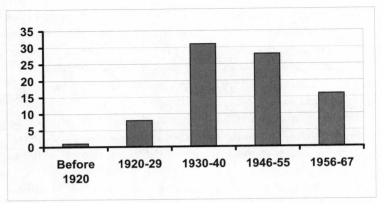

Chart 8–13. Number of New Tourist Attractions Opened in Florida, 1900–1967 (Selected Years)

Florida's tourism sector was strong because many Americans continued to go on vacation during the 1930s, particularly when the low point of the Depression had passed. Expenditures for vacation travel grew from 6 percent of total consumer expenditures in 1925 to 8 percent in 1935.[25]

The movement by tourists from one location to another within the state stimulated the development of the attraction industry. A historical study of the state's attractions showed that the largest number of roadside attractions was opened during the 1930s.[26]

The increased tourism also stimulated hotel construction. The value of permits for new hotels rose from a negligible amount in 1933 to more than $8 million in 1936.[27] After declining to $5 million during the recession in 1938, the value of permits tripled from this low point by 1940. Miami Beach was a major part of the hotel-building boom in the last half of the 1930s; many of the hotels of the South Beach area were constructed at this time.[28] Tourists traveled thirty or more hours to reach Miami Beach in special trains, many from New York, and stayed one or more months. (These hotels and their associated restaurants and night clubs enjoyed a revival toward the end of the twentieth century that made them a major tourist attraction in the state.)

The severe economic contraction of 1929–1933 brought home the riskiness of the modern industrial economy. The family networks and home production that had cushioned households during economic difficulties in preindustrial decades were no longer prominent features of the U.S. economy. In the words of a contemporary Florida economist: "The primary economic risk of the wage or salary earner is that something will happen to divorce him from his wages. Without wages or salary, the worker must turn to savings already accumulated against the 'rainy day' or face destitution and poverty. . . . That most wage earners do not have sufficient savings to carry over long periods of wage cessation is well known. . . . Insecurity—the lack of food, clothing, shelter—thus arises when wage cessation, whatever may be its cause, takes place. . . . Wage cessation has been a characteristic condition of a capitalistic economy. Of the many causes of wage cessation, the chief ones are 1, involuntary unemployment; 2, old age; and 3, illness or disease."[29]

At the initiative of President Franklin Roosevelt, the Social Security Act was passed in 1935; it came into effect in 1937. The contemporary economist described its provisions: "In general, it provides a plan for old age insurance, a means of encouraging state unemployment compensation plans, provisions for grants to old persons in need, needy blind, and dependent children, and various specialized services or grants for crippled children, child welfare services, vocational rehabilitation, maternal care and others. It does not tackle the problem of health insurance though it [does] provide for the expansion of public health services. Nor does it provide any coverage for industrial accidents and disease since all but two states had a workmen's compensation law."[30] Although the framers of the Social Security Act focused on unemployment insurance, the old age pension was a factor in the huge in-migration of retirees to the state after World War II.

Recovery from the Depression was interrupted by a recession in 1938 caused by the tightening of the federal budget deficit as a result of the passage of the Social Security tax in 1935 and by revenue acts that raised taxes in 1936 and 1937.[31] Additionally, the Federal Reserve tightened monetary policy by raising bank reserve requirements. The 1938 recession was brief but relatively deep. National personal income per capita, adjusted for inflation, fell by 6 percent— the second largest decline in the twentieth century aside from the Depression and the readjustments after the two world wars. The decline in Florida was almost 4 percent—only the 1973–1975 decline was deeper.

Because Florida's economy outperformed the national economy during the last half of the 1930s, per capita income in the state rose from 74 percent of the national level in 1930 to 89 percent in 1939. During World War II, Florida almost completely closed this gap, but only temporarily.

Although World War II exacted a huge toll in lives and human suffering, both the state and national economies boomed as war-related expenditures by the federal government stimulated production and employment. Florida's economy, adjusted for population growth, expanded more than the national economy during the war. The state's per capita income reached 95 percent of the national figure by the final year of the war.

One of the main ways Florida's economy benefited from federal war-related

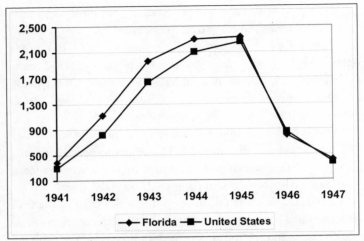

Chart 8–14. Per Capita Military Earnings, Florida and the United States, 1941–1947, Adjusted for Price Changes (Index 1940=100)

expenditures was its role as a center of military training because of its good year-round weather. In effect, defense, which had formerly been a maritime industry, became a sunshine industry. By the last year of the war, military earnings in Florida, adjusted for population growth and inflation, had expanded by more than twenty times the prewar 1940 level.

The expansion in personnel necessitated the creation of a large number of military installations.[32] Prior to the war, there were four naval air bases (at Jacksonville, Miami, Key West, and Pensacola), two army bases (McDill in Tampa and Orlando), and Camp Blanding seven miles east of Starke in Bradford County. Camp Blanding, a Florida National Guard camp, was leased to the army as an active-duty training center in 1940. In the following five years more than 800,000 troops received all or part of their training there. There was also a gunnery range near Valparaiso in Okaloosa County. By late 1943, the number of military installations had grown to 172.

As the new military installations were occupied in 1943, military earnings jumped in the state. The increased military presence impacted Florida's other industries. The state's farmers benefited from increased sales of food, not only to military installations in Florida but also to military stationed elsewhere. Citrus growers began to process concentrate for the first time, shipping it to England in dehydrated form.[33] (Frozen concentrate was not invented until the end of the war.) The state produced an average of 42 million boxes of oranges during 1936–1940, which increased to 64 million boxes during the 1941–1945 war years. Florida's vegetable and cattle industries also experienced

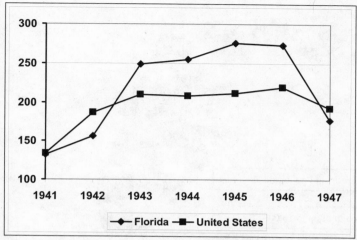

Chart 8–15. Per Capita Farm Earnings, Florida and the United States, 1940–1947, Adjusted for Price Changes (Index 1940=100)

strong growth during the war. As a result, farm earnings per capita, adjusted for inflation, more than doubled in Florida and in the nation. The increase in Florida was greater than in the nation as a whole.[34]

Florida's relatively small manufacturing sector was less impacted by defense purchases of nonagricultural products. An exception was boats and ships, which were easily manufactured using the state's abundant lumber. The Wainwright Company manufactured 108 vessels in Panama City in Bay County, and Jacksonville firms constructed 82 liberty ships as well as many wooden minesweepers and PT boats. The Pensacola Shipyard and Engineering Company employed 7,000 workers by early 1942, and the Tampa Shipbuilding Company employed 9,000 workers by the end of 1942.

The state's tourist industry shrank during World War II as military and gasoline rationing prevented tourists from making the long trip to Florida. Earnings in the state's transportation, trade, and services industries accounted for a smaller share of total earnings than the same industries did nationally. However, the military used many of the larger hotels at Florida's best-known resorts to house personnel. The families of servicemen also came to Florida to be near their loved ones. The war introduced many people to Florida who would return as tourists or residents after the war.

In spite of the massive inflow of military personnel to Florida during the war, some parts of the state experienced declines in population. This was because war-related jobs were created in the state that attracted workers from rural agricultural areas to Florida's urban manufacturing and service centers.[35] From 1940 to 1945, the population in twenty-nine of Florida's sixty-seven counties

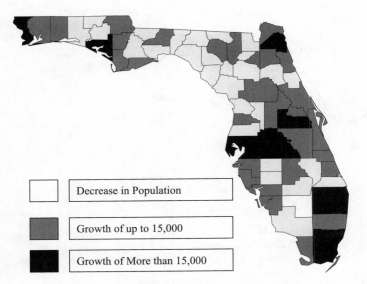

Decrease in Population

Growth of up to 15,000

Growth of More than 15,000

Florida Map 8–2. Population Change in Florida by County, 1940–1945

declined. Almost all of these counties were rural, many in the Big Bend area of North Florida, but some were in the interior of the southern part of the peninsula. The loss of labor in the rural areas precipitated a shortage of workers for Florida's agricultural industries. Ultimately the labor shortage was solved by the importation of 75,000 workers from the Bahamas and Jamaica.[36]

There was one final development during World War II that had a major impact on Florida in the postwar years: the national growth of employee benefits. During the war, the government sought to reallocate national production from civilian to military needs and to control wages and prices. The wage controls stimulated an increase in employee benefits, including pensions, medical insurance, and paid holidays and vacations.[37] In 1939, supplements to wages and salaries, including legally required benefits and private health and welfare plans, accounted for less than 4 percent of employee compensation, but by 1953, 95 percent of office workers and 95 percent of plant (production) workers who participated in a Bureau of Labor Statistics survey had paid vacations of two weeks or more and 66 percent of office workers and 52 percent of plant workers were covered by pension plans.[38] By the end of the 1950s, 80 percent of office workers and 66 percent of plant workers were covered by pension plans. Growth in vacations affected tourist destinations such as Florida in the immediate postwar period, and growth in private pension plans had a growing impact on retiree migration later in the century.

Chapter 9

1945–1960

Postwar Readjustment and Boom

The end of World War II brought about a period of readjustment. The national economy had to be reoriented from its military focus and the suppression of consumption during the war had led to a pent-up demand for consumer goods and a buildup of household assets that fueled an economic boom in the 1950s. Military earnings fell in the state and nation as the military was downsized. Earnings fell by two-thirds in Florida in 1946, eliminating the increases the state had experienced in 1942 and 1943. In 1947, military earnings declined by another 50 percent both in the state and the nation. By 1948, the military downsizing was complete. The federal civilian sector was also downsized, presumably because much of its activity had supported the military and the war effort. The cutback in this sector was also completed by 1948. Much of the military downsizing had a transitory impact on the state because it resulted in soldiers returning to their home states elsewhere in the nation. During this period of cutbacks, Florida lost both earnings and population. Indeed, Florida's population declined in 1945 and 1946—a rare event in the state's history as part of the United States.

As the federal contribution to the economy declined, earnings also declined elsewhere in the economy. Per capita earnings in the national economy, adjusted for inflation and excluding federal military and civilian earnings, declined in the aftermath of the war, reaching a low that in the recession year of 1949 was more than 10 percent below the 1945 level. The decline in the nonfederal economy in Florida, in contrast, began a year later than the decline in the national economy and was much milder. Per capita earnings in Florida, adjusted for inflation and excluding federal military and civilian earnings, actually rose in 1946 before declining to a low of 96 percent of the 1945 level in 1948.

Moreover, the decline in the Florida economy seems to have been a result

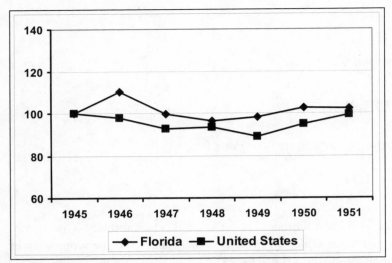

Chart 9–1. Real per Capita Nonfederal Earnings in Florida and the United States, 1945–1951 (Index 1945=100)

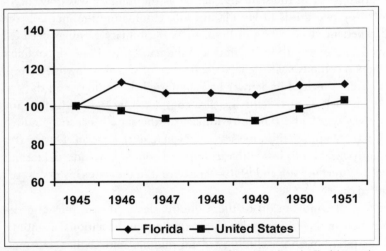

Chart 9–2. Real per Capita Nonfederal Nonfarm Earnings in Florida and the United States, 1945–1951 (Index 1945=100)

of developments in farm incomes rather than a readjustment from military to civilian production. Florida's nonfederal economy was strong enough to counterbalance the recessionary forces caused by the change in the orientation of production. Florida's nonfarm nonfederal economy remained above its 1945 level in the aftermath of the war but moved sideways after 1946.

Two hurricanes struck the southern part of the state in 1947. The first storm,

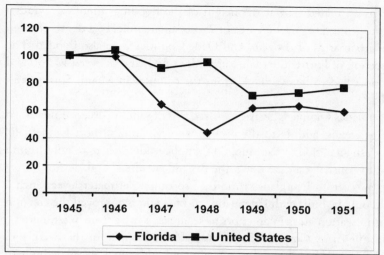

Chart 9–3. Real per Capita Farm Earnings in Florida and the United States, 1945–1951 (Index 1945=100)

a category 2, was characterized by sustained winds of 90 miles an hour in Miami and Fort Myers, 100 miles per hour at West Palm Beach, and 105 miles per hour at Naples, and the damage was extensive.[1] The storm made landfall in the state shortly after noon on September 17 between Fort Lauderdale and Lake Worth. It crossed over the extensive agricultural economy in the eleven-county Everglades Drainage District as it made its way to the west coast. Broward County, which sustained the largest losses in the district, experienced two-thirds of its losses in citrus. St. Lucie, Miami-Dade, and Palm Beach counties had losses of about half the level experienced by Broward. Miami-Dade experienced substantial losses in its dairy industry, and Palm Beach and St. Lucie counties experienced significant losses in vegetables. Although vegetable losses can be made up by replanting, a second hurricane struck the everglades area a year later, causing more losses. Areas outside the Everglades Drainage District, particularly to the west, also sustained losses. The Army Corps of Engineers estimated total losses of $59 million, a very large amount for a state that was relatively unpopulated in 1947.[2] The 1947 and 1948 hurricanes caused a substantial decline in farm earnings. Per capita farm income, adjusted for inflation, fell by 40 percent in 1947 and another 20 percent in 1948.

The 1947 hurricane caused little wind damage, but damage from flooding was extensive. Eleven counties were more than 50 percent inundated, and 5 million acres in southeast Florida were covered with water for at least a month; some for several months. Cross-state highways were closed for extended periods. It was estimated that at the height of the flooding, there was enough water on the ground to cover an area of 2,400 square miles to a depth of seven feet.[3] The urban areas of Broward and Dade Counties were also flooded. The business section of Fort Lauderdale was under water, and between 10,000 and 12,000 people had to be evacuated from their homes in Miami Springs and Opa-Locka.[4]

The Everglades Drainage District was accused of sending excess water down the drainage canals, adding to the problems in Miami and Fort Lauderdale. Eventually, after a period of recrimination, public leaders began to rally around a proposal to construct a dike down the east side of the Everglades to protect the urban areas from Everglades runoffs, a so-called perimeter levee. Such a levee could only be built with federal aid, and the voters approved the creation of three conservation areas in an effort to secure assistance from Washington.

In 1948, the Army Corps of Engineers published a plan for the Everglades that recommended that the perimeter levee and additional levees be built to store water in the conservation areas. The plan required pumping stations to move water into the conservation areas or Lake Okeechobee and additional works for the area north of Lake Okeechobee, the upper St. Johns and Kissimmee river basins, in order to reclaim prairie marshes and other wetlands for agricultural use.[5] The Army Corps predicted that ten years would be needed to finish construction and estimated the total cost of the plan at $208 million (about $1.5 billion in 2000 dollars). The plan was based on 85 percent federal financing and 15 percent local financing. Congress approved the plan in 1948 and the Florida legislature made its first contribution in 1949.

Local taxpayers paid for right-of-way and operating costs. The legislature replaced the Everglades Drainage District with a new Central and Southern Florida Flood Control District comprised of all or parts of seventeen counties. A key feature of the new flood control district was that it was financed by ad valorem taxation rather than acreage-based special assessments, as in the past. The bulk of the district's revenues came from general property taxes rather than from the great landowners who had financed the Everglades Drainage District.

Work began in 1950, but it proceeded more slowly than planned. By 1965, the district had completed the construction of the perimeter levee and had established and enclosed the three conservation areas. It was operating eleven pumping stations, more than 1,300 miles of canals and spillways, and over sixty major spillways and dams. Barriers had been installed in all canals leading to the ocean to prevent saltwater intrusion. Extensive work had also commenced to improve drainage in Central Florida.

In one respect, Florida needed to undergo a major restructuring as a result of developments during the war. At the end of the decade of the 1940s, the state reformed its government finances. The state had amassed sizeable balances in its accounts during the war in much the same way as it had during the boom of the 1920s. State government consumption and investment had been postponed while the state and national economy were oriented toward national defense. The balances represented an opportunity for the state to address some of its pressing needs, and public education was a top priority. As the war entered its final year, outgoing governor Spessard Holland appointed a Citizen's Committee on Education to assess educational needs and make recommendations to the state.[6] In 1945, the new governor, Millard Caldwell, reappointed the committee and the legislature approved its appointment.

The committee reported that Florida ranked third from the bottom among the states in terms of educational performance relative to ability to pay. The committee also noted that there was substantial variation in the quality of education among the state's school districts. Many of the counties with the largest number of children had relatively low assessed valuations and were in the worst position to pay for public education.

The Florida legislature passed a Minimum Education Foundation Program in 1947 by which the state agreed to supplement local funds in order to provide a minimum education program in all counties. The motivation for this action may have been a desire to promote the economic development of the state and provide its children with better opportunities, but there was also a concern that the relatively poor condition of the schools for black children might lead to a charge that Florida's educational system was separate but unequal.[7] The immediate result was that state funding increased for local public schools, but in the years ahead this action transferred primary responsibility for funding public education from locally elected officials to the state. Ultimately, the state assumed financial control of the local systems.

At first, the state could increase K-12 educational funding using the surpluses built up during the war years. However, there were other pressures on the state budget, both from education and elsewhere. There was a rapid increase in university enrollments as returning soldiers used the GI Bill to resume their postsecondary education. Both the University of Florida in Gainesville and the newly named Florida State University in Tallahassee were opened to (white) students of both sexes for the first time.[8] The legislature also recognized the need to build new educational buildings at the three state universities.

In addition, the legislature funded a major building program for state government in Tallahassee, including a capitol wing and a building for the Supreme

Court and government agencies. State correctional institutions and state agencies elsewhere in the state also received increased funding. There was also an increased demand for social spending. From 1945 to 1948, the number of elderly Floridians eligible for old age assistance doubled and the number of dependent children eligible for assistance increased by more than 50 percent. The governor increased the number of public health units so that there would be one in each county by the end of his term in 1948.

While many of these expenditures could initially be funded from the accumulated balances built up during the war, it soon became clear that the state could not operate at the higher level without new revenue sources. This was not the result of relatively low taxation in the state, since Florida's state taxes were higher than the national average on a per capita basis and relative to personal income. General revenues of the state per capita were about 18 percent higher in the state than in the nation.[9] After adjusting this statistic for intergovernmental transfers and excluding unemployment compensation taxes, Florida taxes per capita were almost 30 percent higher than the corresponding national figure.

The same picture emerges when Florida taxes are related to personal income. General revenues in Florida per capita were about 25 percent higher in the state than in the nation. After adjusting for intergovernmental transfers and excluding unemployment compensation taxes, Florida taxes relative to personal income were more than one-third higher than the corresponding national figure.

Even though Florida did not have a general sales tax in 1947, selective sales taxes per capita were higher in the state than in the nation. These were the most important source of state revenue.[10] Florida's selective sales taxes, which included taxes on gasoline, alcohol, and tobacco and the racing tax, collected substantial revenues from tourists.

The second most important source of state revenue both in the state and the nation consisted of license revenues, the largest share of which was borne by operators of motor vehicles.[11] In Florida, licenses for motor vehicles and their operators accounted for 62.5 percent of license revenues in 1947. Sales taxes and license revenues accounted for 93 percent of state tax revenues (excluding the unemployment tax).

The revenue shortfall came to a head in the 1949–1951 biennial budget as the wartime surpluses were finally fully expended. Requests from state agencies totaled $258.7 million, compared to anticipated revenues of $153.9 million.[12] The budget commission reduced the requests by 20 percent, but the legislature reversed two-thirds of these changes. The only tax action the legislature took in the regular session raised the tax on alcoholic beverages. The budget commission responded by withholding 25 percent of each state agency's appropria-

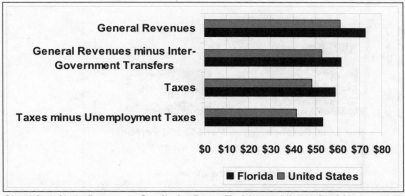

Chart 9–4. State Taxes per Capita by Type, Florida and the United States, 1947

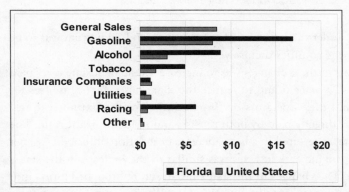

Chart 9–5. Sales Taxes per Capita by Type, Florida and the United States, 1947

tion. In response, the legislature held a special session that adopted a revenue program whose central element was a 3 percent general sales tax with exemptions that included food at the grocery and prescription drugs to eliminate its regressivity. Most services were also exempted from the tax, although lodging was taxed when the length of stay was less than six months. A state tax on retail inventories was also eliminated to help defray the collection costs imposed on merchants.

A second feature of the 1949 revenue program was authorization to cities to levy a five-cent cigarette tax to be collected by the state. Cities were required to reduce property taxes by 50 percent of the amount of tax revenues for cigarettes. Cigarette taxes collected outside municipal areas were to be used to fund tuberculosis hospitals and supplement the state's general revenues. Finally, the revenue program gave the proceeds of the seventh cent of the gas tax to the counties. Eighty percent of these revenues would be used to pay the state high-

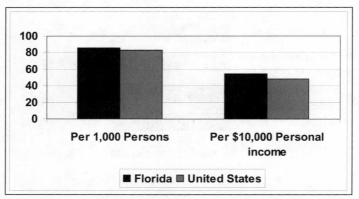

Chart 9–6. Florida and U.S. State Taxes, 1957 (Excluding Unemployment Taxes), by Population and Personal Income (Current Dollars)

way department under the direction of the counties, and 20 percent was to be spent directly by the counties themselves.

The main effect of these changes was to increase the share of state taxes paid by consumers by 25 percent and to reduce the share raised by license fees for motor vehicles and their operators by 10 percent.[13] Florida continued to rely on taxes that were directly paid by both tourists and residents of the state. The increase in state taxes resulted in a large increase in inflation-adjusted taxes per capita, although the increase in taxes was similar to the increase in the state's personal income. The changes in the state's tax structure brought Florida into line with the situation nationally. In 1957, Florida's taxes per capita and per $1,000 of personal income were much closer to the aggregate nationally than they had been in 1947.[14]

The national economy entered a period of rapid growth in the 1950s as the postwar readjustments were completed. In the five-year period 1950–1955, personal income adjusted for inflation grew at the second fastest rate in the last half of the twentieth century. Consumers played a major role in propelling the economy forward in the 1950s. Service in the armed forces had curtailed the formation of new households, and federal rationing programs had curtailed the supply of consumer durable goods during the world war. The personal savings rate jumped from 5 percent of disposable income before the United States joined the war to 25 percent of disposable income during the war before returning to 5 percent in 1947.[15] Households accumulated large savings balances that fueled a postwar boom.

The most dramatic feature of the postwar consumer boom was a sharp increase in the rate of new household formation as returning members of the armed forces got married and started families. The U.S. birth rate jumped

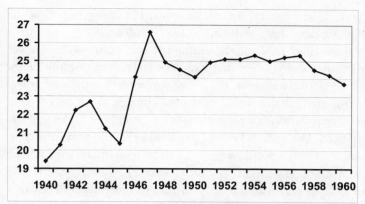

Chart 9–7. Live Births per 1,000 Population, Florida, 1940–1960, Annual Data

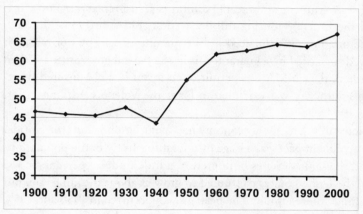

Chart 9–8. Owner-Occupied Units in Florida as a Percent of Occupied Housing Units by Decade, 1900–2000

sharply beginning in 1946, touching off a baby boom that lasted throughout the 1950s.[16] The new baby-boom generation impacted the educational system in the 1950s and 1960s, the labor force in the 1970s and 1980s, and the rate of retiree in-migration to Florida in the early decades of the twenty-first century.

New households needed new housing units, and the national construction industry boomed soon after the end of the war.[17] Construction of new homes came to a virtual standstill during World War II; the value of new construction was less than the value of homes demolished during most of the war years. As soon as the war ended, net residential investment jumped above its 1941 level, and by 1950 it was three times the level it had been in 1941. The purchase of new homes by consumers after World War II and during the 1950s caused a striking jump in homeownership during this period of the twentieth century.

Even allowing for the temporary drop in homeownership during the 1930s, the homeownership rate expanded rapidly in the 1945–1960 period.

Aside from the savings accumulated during the war, homeownership was stimulated by institutional changes that had been enacted during the 1930s. Chief among these was the creation of federal government-sponsored enterprises, private corporations that could raise funds in capital markets at very favorable interest rates because they were viewed as having the backing of the national government. The Federal Home Loan Banks (FHLB) were created in 1932 to make loans to banks in order to provide them with funds that could be used to make mortgages. The Federal National Mortgage Association (FNMA) was created in 1938 to create a secondary market in mortgages. Banks that made mortgages could sell them to the FNMA. The assets of the FHLB and FNMA increased more than fivefold between 1947 and 1955.[18]

The federal government also created a mortgage insurance program when it established the Federal Housing Administration (FHA) in 1934. Although this insurance program was financed by the premiums paid by borrowers, it was also viewed as backed by a guarantee from the federal government. When it was established, the FNMA was permitted to invest in FHA-insured mortgages, and this authority was extended to loans the Veterans Administration guaranteed in 1944.

Developments in the national economy had major implications for Florida. The most noticeable impact was a huge in-migration. In 1948, the populations of Florida and the United States both grew at a little under 2 percent. In the next 15 years, the United States continued to grow at about the same rate, but Florida grew much more rapidly. The peak growth occurred in 1956 and 1957, when the state's population grew by about 8 percent. Although the surge in population growth had begun before the 1950 census and although the growth continued beyond the 1960 census, in 1950–1960, the population grew at its most rapid pace since the first decade after Florida became part of the United States. The population grew by almost 80 percent during the 1950s.

A major component of Florida's population growth during the 1950s was an influx of retirees from elsewhere in the country. Like younger people, those who retired in the 1950s had accumulated savings during World War II. While younger people used their savings to create new households and start families, older people used their savings to retire and move to a more pleasant climate. During the 1950s, Florida's population increased by 2.2 million people.[19] Of these, about 900,000 were under the age of 20 and almost 1 million were between 20 and 65 years old. More than 300,000 were age 65 and over. Although the increase in the number of persons age 65 and over was the smallest among the three age groups, this age category had the fastest rate of growth. Between

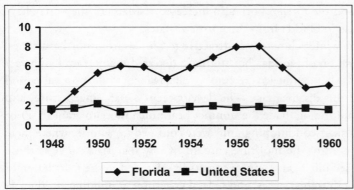

Chart 9–9. Annual Percentage Population Growth, Florida and the United States, 1948–1960

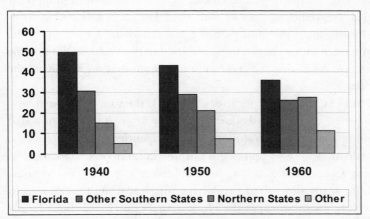

Chart 9–10. Place of Birth of Florida Population, 1940, 1950, and 1960, by Percent

1950 and 1960, the under-20 age group doubled in Florida and the 20–64 age group increased by 60 percent. But those in the group aged 65 years and older increased by more than 130 percent.

As a result of the large increase in those aged 65 and older, this age group accounted for a much larger share of the state's population than for the nation as a whole by 1960.[20] In 1940, the share of this age group was about 7 percent both in the state and in the nation. By 1950, the share had risen to about 8 percent nationally and a little more in Florida. By 1960, the share of this group had increased slightly to 9 percent nationally, but in Florida, it had increased to 11 percent. Most of the in-migrating retirees were fleeing the cold winters in the northern states. Between 1940 and 1960, the share of Florida's population that had been born in the northern states almost doubled, rising from 15 to 27 percent.[21] The share of Florida's residents who were U.S. citizens who had been born overseas and the foreign born also increased.[22] Many of these may have been in-migrants to Florida from the northern states.

Although the winter climate was attractive to retirees from northern states, the lengthy duration of Florida's hot summers deterred many from living year round in the state before the war. Technological advances in the postwar period greatly reduced this disadvantage. The development of safe, inexpensive, and efficient air conditioning made the summer heat much more tolerable.[23] Prior to the mid-1920s, air-conditioning units were confined to factories where there was a need to control the moisture content of raw materials, such as those producing textiles and cigars. Improvements in safety led to the installation of air conditioning in trains, stores, and federal government buildings in the late 1920s. In 1951, the installation of air conditioning in private homes received a big boost after safe, inexpensive, and efficient window air-conditioning units were developed. Nevertheless, only 18 percent of Florida homes had air conditioning in 1960—about the same percentage as elsewhere in the South. The big growth in residential air conditioning occurred in the 1960s, and it became particularly important during the condominium boom that began toward the end of that decade.

The development of effective pesticides also made the summer more tolerable in Florida, where standing water during the rainy summer months provided a fertile breeding ground for mosquitoes.[24] Municipalities sprayed pesticides; special taxing districts were set up for this purpose in unincorporated areas.

In-migrating retirees may also have been able to reduce their cost of housing. Presumably, many downsized their living quarters when they moved to the state. In the 1950s and most of the 1960s, retirees purchased single-family homes, many of which had two bedrooms and a carport. The homes usually had a single story without basements, attics, or porches.

Taxes may also have had an impact on retiree in-migration, although Florida was not a low tax state in the 1950s. But features of the state's tax code may have appealed to retirees. Estates paid no taxes to the state, other than the amount that could be credited against the federal tax. Additionally, there was no personal income tax, and the intangible property tax was difficult to enforce.

In-migrating retirees brought retirement incomes to the state. Such income tended to be drawn from three sources: dividends and interest earned on retirement savings, private pensions, and public pensions. Dividends and interest were the largest component of property income, and public pensions (which included Social Security receipts) were a major part of personal transfer payments. In the 1950s, in-migrating retirees led to a large increase of the share of the state's personal income accounted for by property income, but the share accounted for by personal transfer payments remained relatively

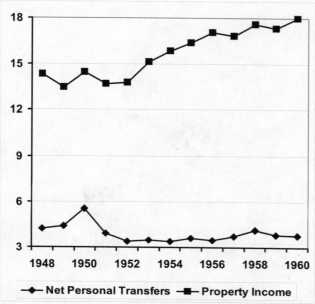

Chart 9–11. Net Transfers of Personal Property and Property Income as a Percent of Personal Income, Florida, 1948–1960

stable.[25] Little data are available on how many new residents brought private pensions to the state. Taken together, the growth in the importance of property income and the stability of net personal transfers suggest that retirees who moved to Florida in the 1950s were a relatively affluent segment of the retired population. Retirement savings and private pensions fueled the movement to Florida.

The growth in the percent of population aged 65 and over was not evenly distributed throughout the state. If it had been, the increase in the population of this age group would have been about 4,711 in every county.[26] In fact, the population aged 65 and over grew by more than 4,711 in only thirteen of Florida's sixty-seven counties. The largest increases were in Pinellas County (which grew by 63,226), followed by Miami-Dade County (56,199) and Broward County (31,864). Both Hillsborough and Palm Beach counties grew by more than 18,000, and Volusia County grew by 15,519. The map shows that the growth in the population aged 65 and over was concentrated in a belt along a line from Daytona Beach to Sarasota, south of Tampa Bay, and in the southeastern corner of the state. Most of the elderly moved to coastal counties in the southern half of the peninsula, consistent with the desire of retirees for warm winter weather. In 1950, Broward County had the ninth largest population in

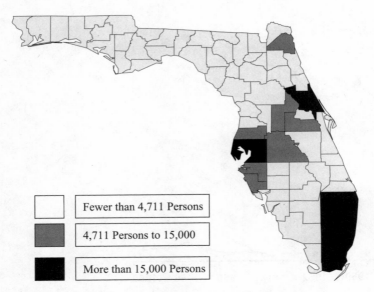

Florida Map 9–1. Growth in Population Aged 65 and Older by
County, Florida, 1950–1960

the state, in 1960 it was ranked fifth, and by 1970 it was ranked second, a ranking it retained into the twenty-first century.

The incoming retirees needed housing, and the local commercial sector and
infrastructure needed to be expanded to meet their needs. The result was an
increase in construction, although this sector developed unevenly. In the early
1950s, per capita earnings in Florida construction adjusted for inflation did
not grow as rapidly as they did nationally. The state's construction sector experienced sharper slowdowns by this measure during the national recessions of
1949 and 1954. Earnings expanded much more rapidly in the middle years of
the decade, rising by more than 25 percent between the 1954 recession low and
the cyclical peak in 1957.

Tourism also expanded during the consumption-led boom of the 1950s.
Earnings in Florida's transportation, trade, and services (adjusted for inflation and measured relative to national earnings in these industries) expanded
strongly during the 1950s. The 80 percent increase in earnings in these industries in the state was twice the rate of growth in U.S. consumption expenditures
as a whole.

The growth in these earnings is attributable to the growth of retirement and
tourism. Hotel and motel revenues are a more targeted indicator of tourism,
although hotels serve residents as well as tourists. Additionally, not all tourists
stay in hotels; some rent apartments and some stay with friends or relatives.

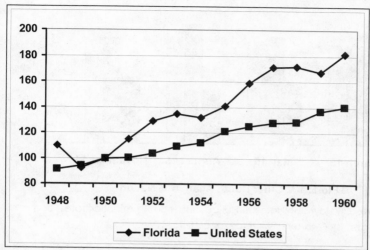

Chart 9–12. Tourism-Retirement Earnings in Florida and Personal Consumption Expenditures in the United States, 1948–1960, (Index 1950=100)

In 1948, Florida accounted for 4.6 percent of the nation's hotel revenues, although it accounted for only 1.8 percent of the nation's population.[27] During the next fifteen years, Florida hotel revenues increased by 150 percent, growing far more rapidly than in the nation as a whole. In 1963, the state accounted for 3.0 percent of the national population, but its share of hotel revenues was 7.6 percent.

The tourist boom was driven by the same motivation that led to the inflow of the retirees—a desire to escape the harshness of northern winters. This is seen from the growth in hotel revenues by county, which primarily occurred in the southern half of the peninsula, especially Miami-Dade, Broward, and Palm Beach counties, as well Lee County, Sarasota County, and the Tampa–St. Petersburg area. There was also some growth in the Daytona Beach area.

Florida's peak tourist season was the first quarter of the year. This was a marked contrast to the rest of the South Atlantic states and the nation as a whole, where the peak season was in the summer months. The August weekly payroll in Florida's hotels was less than 60 percent of the weekly payroll in March. In the other South Atlantic states, the August payroll was 11 percent higher than the March level, and in the nation as a whole it was 15 percent higher.

The first comprehensive survey of Florida's tourists was undertaken in 1958.[28] More than 60 percent of the respondents indicated that their visit to Florida that year was a repeat visit, indicating that the state was a relatively

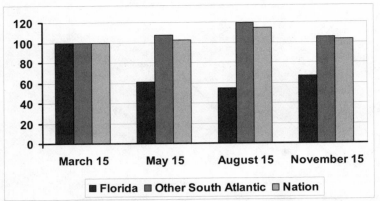

Chart 9–13. Weekly Payroll in Hotels in Florida, Other South Atlantic States, and the United States by Quarter, 1954 (Index March 15=100)

mature destination by the 1950s. Many of the characteristics of tourists in 1958 remained true for the ensuing half-century.

In 1958, before the introduction of jet aircraft, most tourists came to Florida by automobile. The average size of the traveling party was lower in the winter (2.3 persons) than in the summer (3.1 persons), reflecting the fact that retired couples tended to visit the state in the winter and families tended to visit in the summer. Tourists spent a longer time in the winter; the average traveling party stayed 29 days in the winter and 12 days in the summer. More than 30 percent of winter tourists were visiting friends and relatives, compared to 24 percent in the summer. Reflecting the high inflow of retirees (and supporting workers) in the 1950s, more than 10 percent of survey respondents indicated that the purpose of their visit was to purchase or look for a Florida home or property.

The dominance of the northern states (and Canada) in the state's winter tourism was particularly evident in the survey; more than three-quarters of all the tourists came from those origins. In the summer, on the other hand, the other southern states accounted for 45 percent of tourists, compared to 53 percent from "up north." The southern half of the peninsula attracted more than 75 percent of the winter tourists and more than 60 percent of the summer tourists. The tourist season was in the winter months in central and southern Florida; the tourist season in the northern part of the state was in the summer months.[29]

The survey asked tourists what they most looked forward to during their visit to Florida. The atmosphere of relaxation and fun and the state's beaches were the two responses tourists gave most often. More than one in four tourists

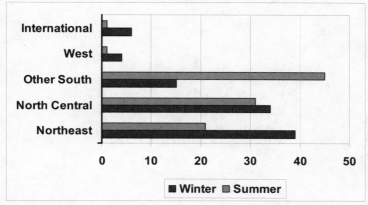

Chart 9–14. Geographic Origin of Florida Tourist Parties as a Percent of Total Number of Tourist Parties, Winter and Summer 1958

said that fishing was their goal, in both the summer and winter seasons. Among the commercial attractions tourists mentioned were Cypress Gardens and Silver Springs. Outgoing tourist parties indicated that they had spent an average of $606 during their trip to the state in the winter and $298 in the summer. Much of the difference is attributable to the longer stay of winter tourists. On a per-person-day basis, winter tourists spent 10 more in Florida than summer tourists.[30]

Changes in national economic conditions significantly slowed the Florida boom in 1957. There was a sharp increase in the national rate of inflation in 1957, when it rose above 3 percent.[31] This was the peak rate it reached in the 1950s, except for 1951, when a consumer panic at the outbreak of the Korean War led to a temporary increase in prices as people attempted to stock up on goods that had been in short supply during World War II.

The Federal Reserve reacted to the increase in inflation by tightening monetary policy. Short-term interest rates, as measured by the one-year treasury bill rate, rose from about 1 percent in 1954 (a recession year) to 4 percent in the third quarter of 1957.[32] As the recession deepened, the Federal Reserve relaxed its policy, and interest rates fell almost to 1 percent in the second quarter of 1958. However, as inflation picked up again in 1960, the Federal Reserve again tightened its policy, and a very mild recession occurred in 1960–1961.

The tight money episodes slowed the national economy and the movement of retirees and tourists to Florida. U.S. per capita personal income fell from an annual rate of 4 percent growth in 1956 to 0 percent in 1957 and -2 percent in 1958 as the tight money policy squeezed the economy. Although there was a recovery in 1959, it proved to be short lived. Growth fell again in

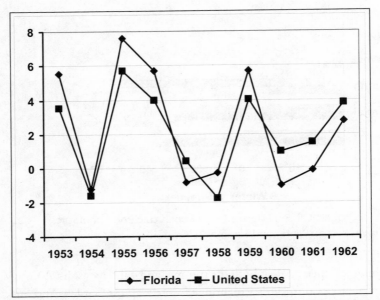

Chart 9–15. Annual Percentage Growth in per Capita Income, Florida and the United States, 1953–1962, Adjusted for Inflation

1960 and remained low in 1961. Per capita income in Florida closely followed the national trend with the exception of a sharper decline in 1960. In the five-year period 1957–1961, Florida experienced four years of negative growth in inflation-adjusted per capita income. The 1950s boom had truly ended.

Chapter 10

1960

The Rise of the Sunshine Economy

By 1960, Florida's population of 5 million made it the tenth most populated state in the country. Since 1930, the population of the state had more than tripled; most of the growth occurred in the 1950s. The state not only was much more populous than its nearest neighbors, Georgia and Alabama, but it had more people than any of the other states in the South except for Texas. It was closing in on Massachusetts, the only New England state with a larger population. Among its neighbors in the Caribbean, Florida's population was still smaller than Cuba's 7 million and the combined population of Haiti and the Dominican Republic of more than 6 million.

Population density was higher in the state than in the nation, and in this respect the state now resembled its neighbors in the southeast more than the western states it had resembled earlier in the century. Florida was no longer a frontier state, and the industries associated with the frontier declined significantly in importance from 1930 to 1960. The state's population density was still considerably lower than that of the states from Massachusetts west to Illinois, where population densities were more than twice the national average.[1]

Florida experienced a decline in its per capita income relative to the national level in 1951, when it was 83 percent of the national level. From that point, state per capita personal income trended upward during the boom years before closing the 1950s at about 90 percent of the national level.[2]

Six Florida counties had per capita incomes above the national average in 1960.[3] These included Miami-Dade and Monroe counties at the extreme south; Hendry, an agricultural county immediately east of Palm Beach, which had major cattle and sugar industries; Brevard and Orange counties in the east central part of the peninsula; and Duval County in the northeast. Three additional counties had per capita incomes above the state average—Palm Beach, Collier, and Sarasota counties. Per capita income was low in the Tampa-St. Petersburg area.

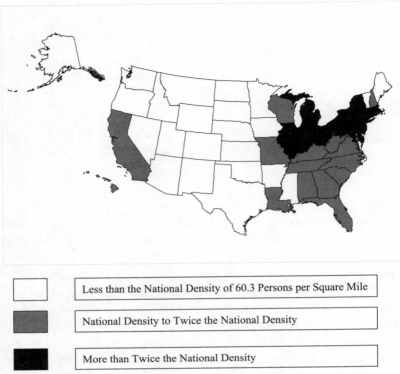

U.S. Map 10–1. Population per Square Mile by State Compared to National
Level, United States, 1960

As we saw in the last chapter, the 65 and older age group accounted for a
larger share of the population of Florida (11 percent) than it did nationally (9
percent). This was the result of the in-migration of retired persons who were
attracted by the state's mild winter climate. The higher percentage of retirees in
Florida than in the nation made earnings a smaller proportion of per capita income in the state (78 percent) than in the nation (84 percent). Florida residents
received a higher proportion of their income as "unearned" (property) income
and net personal transfers (including net Social Security receipts).

The importance of the state's tourism-retirement sector showed up in the
relatively large proportion of earnings in transportation, trade, and services.
These industries accounted for 47 percent of earnings in the state, compared to
39 percent nationally. The share of earnings accounted for by manufacturing in
Florida was half that of the national figure. The high level of in-migration and
the resulting job creation resulted in a relatively large construction industry in
Florida.

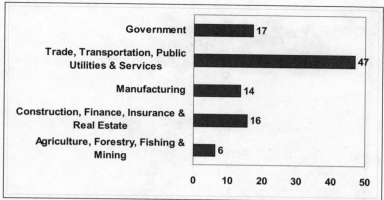

Chart 10–1. Earnings of Florida's Industries, 1960 (by Percent of Total Earnings)

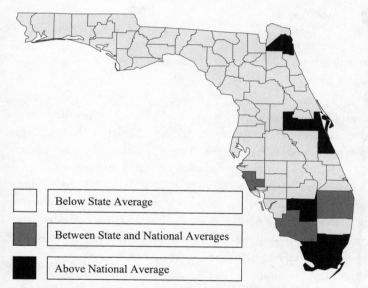

Florida Map 10–1. Per Capita Income in Florida by County Compared to State Average, 1960

Agriculture was the largest contributor to labor earnings in eighteen of the state's sixty-seven county economies in 1960. Most of the county economies where agriculture was most important were found along the backbone of the peninsula, but agriculture was also the largest industry in the northernmost tier of counties, where the eastern panhandle and northern peninsula meet.

Counties for which manufacturing was the largest industry were located in northern Florida. Forest products had typically dominated these county economies for a century, and in many counties a new and large paper industry had

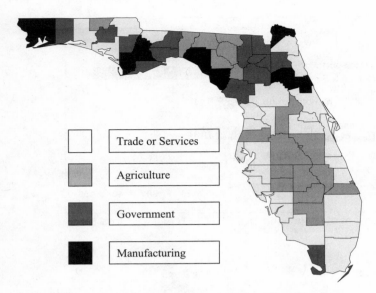

Florida Map 10–2. Leading Industries in Florida's Counties, 1960

developed since 1930 and gum naval stores had experienced a rapid decline. Government employment was important in another group of northern counties. One of these, Okaloosa County, had a military installation that employed relatively large numbers of civilians (Eglin Air Force Base). The large government payroll in Monroe County also reflected military employment of civilians. Other counties that had large government payrolls included Leon County, home to Tallahassee, the state capital; Alachua County, home to the University of Florida; and Union County, between Gainesville and Jacksonville, home to the state's largest prison. In some small rural counties, the local school district and county government together had the largest payroll.

The largest employer in almost all the remaining counties was trade or services. This was true of the state's largest metropolitan areas, Miami to West Palm Beach, Tampa–St. Petersburg, Orlando, and Jacksonville. It was also true of some smaller counties with large retired and tourist populations such as St. Johns and Volusia counties in the northeast and Manatee, Sarasota, Lee, and Collier counties in the southwest.

In 1950, the state's sunshine sector, which included tourism-retirement, citrus, and vegetables, accounted for more than 50 percent of the economic base for the first time. Although it slipped back a little in 1960 as the maritime sector increased its share, the sunshine industries remained close to the 50 percent level and dominated the state's economic base for the remainder of the century. The state's frontier industries—lumber and naval stores, cattle, and phosphate

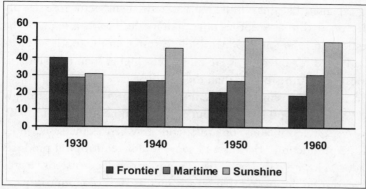

Chart 10–2. Share of Florida's Frontier, Maritime, and Sunshine Industries in the State's Economic Base by Decade, 1930–1960 (by Percent of Total Production)

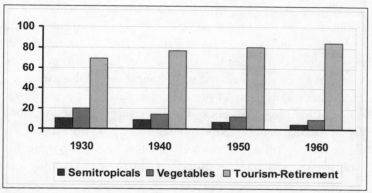

Chart 10–3. Share of Semitropical, Vegetable, and Tourism-Retirement Industries in Production of Florida's Sunshine Sector by Decade, 1930–1960 (by Percent of Total Production)

mining—fell to third place behind the maritime sector, which was dominated by the federal military payroll. By 1960, Florida had truly become the Sunshine State and left its frontier characteristics behind.

Tourism-retirement accounted for more than 80 percent of the state's sunshine sector in 1960. The state's tourist industry recovered strongly from the economic contraction in the early 1930s and finished the decade more than 50 percent higher than its pre-Depression 1929 level.[4] The war largely cut off the flow of tourists to the state, although military trainees used many hotels. At the war's end, pent-up demand led to a sharp increase in earnings from tourism followed by a decline during the national recession of 1949. The wave of in-migration of retirees in the 1950s impacted most of the state's tourist industries, since retirees have similar expenditure patterns to tourists, aside from their housing expenses. Earnings in the tourism-retirement sector rose sharply during the decade, with the exception of temporary declines as a result of the national recessions in 1954 and 1958. In 1960, earnings in the tourism-retirement sector, adjusted for inflation, were 80 percent higher than their level in 1950 and almost seven times higher than their 1929 level.

Production in Florida's sunshine agriculture sector also increased strongly from 1930 to 1960. The 1960 level was four and a half times the level in 1930. Production of vegetables, melons, potatoes, and strawberries increased more rapidly than the production of citrus and some minor semitropical products such as avocados.[5] However, the state's citrus industry developed extensive processing facilities during this period that greatly increased its economic impact.

South Florida's vegetable industry expanded substantially in the 1930s, especially in Dade, Broward, and Palm Beach counties. This expansion was made possible by several discoveries by agricultural scientists and development of vegetable varieties. In 1925, after nailhead rust seriously affected tomatoes, a Dania grower developed the Grothen Globe variety.[6] Discoveries about adding minerals to farmland also helped boost production during this period. In 1926, USDA scientists had experimented with manganese sulphate in an effort to protect tomatoes from nailhead rust. The year after these experiments, a farmer who had planted tomatoes noticed higher yields in the soil that had been treated with the manganese.[7] Shortly thereafter it was shown that the chemical could be used as an inexpensive substitute for the stable manure that farmers normally planted with their tomatoes in the marl soil of Dade County.

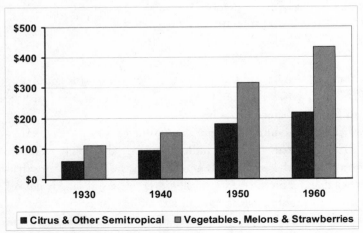

Chart 10–4. Value of Citrus and Other Semitropical Products and Vegetables, Melons, and Strawberries in Florida's Sunshine Agricultural Production by Decade, 1930–1960 (in Millions of 2000 Dollars)

In 1927, scientists at the Everglades Experiment Station discovered that adding copper sulphate to sawgrass muck made it possible to grow crops there.[8]

By 1939, Palm Beach County, with 68,229 acres, had the largest acreage in vegetables in the state.[9] This was more than three times the acreage of Broward County, which had the second largest acreage, and Miami-Dade County, which was ranked fourth in the state. For example, Palm Beach County had more than 38,000 acres in beans; Broward County had more than 13,000. In the late 1930s, production of Irish potatoes was expanded in Miami-Dade County, and by 1949 the value of potatoes produced in the county was more than one-third larger than the value of production in St. Johns County, whose industry centered at Hastings was the traditional center of production in the state. In the late 1940s, the introduction of hybrid corn varieties adapted to south Florida's climate and day length stimulated production in the Everglades area.[10]

An important innovation in vegetable marketing was the introduction of state farmer's markets in 1935. The state had attempted to assist farmers with marketing ever since establishing a marketing bureau in the department of agriculture in 1917.[11] The bureau was financed by a tax on fertilizer. Although the bureau made considerable progress in the 1920s by introducing grading standards and inspections at shipping points, many farmers were still shipping on consignment and failing to obtain established prices for freight on board. An Agricultural Marketing Board was established by an act of the legislature in 1929 to promote and assist in the development of marketing cooperatives. Vegetable farmers were slow to join cooperatives, however, perhaps because they were too independent and would not obey the rules of cooperatives and perhaps because they were too geographically dispersed. In 1933, the act was broadened to permit the creation and operation of state farmers' markets. The first state farmers' market was opened in Sanford in January 1935, and by the mid-1940s, twenty-seven such markets were in operation around the state. Half the markets sold vegetables, which accounted for about 25 percent of the total shipping value of vegetables by 1946. The farmers' markets retained this share of total vegetable shipping value throughout the 1950s.

The growth in Florida's vegetable acreage in the ten years after the end of World War II was not matched nationally.[12] National acreage in vegetables raised for sale trended slowly downward during the 1950s after reaching a peak in 1950. The decline in the national acreage was a response to a 10 percent decline in national per capita consumption from 1946 to 1960.[13] From 1946 to 1960, fresh vegetable consumption declined by 18 percent and consumption of canned vegetables declined by 4 percent. There was a substantial increase in frozen vegetables per capita, although it remained a small part of consumption.

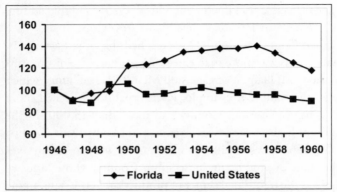

Chart 10–5. Acreage in Vegetables, Florida and the United States, 1946–1960 (Annual Data, Index 1946=100)

National vegetable prices, measured as the unit value of farm production adjusted for inflation, declined slowly in the postwar period, and this may have been another factor that caused the gradual decline in acreage. Florida's prices declined as well, but they remained above the national level during the decade. The excess of Florida over national vegetable prices narrowed in the 1950s, which may have been the result of increased production as vegetable acreage expanded in the state.

Tomatoes accounted for more than 25 percent of the value of vegetable production in Florida in 1959. Snap beans, corn, and potatoes each accounted for 10 percent, and peppers, watermelons, cucumbers, and celery each accounted for 8 percent. Acreage in the production of three vegetable crops declined between 1929 and 1959. There was a very large decline in the acreage planted in sweet potatoes during this period, from about 20,000 acres to less than 1,500. This probably reflected a shift in tastes among American, especially southern, consumers away from the traditional sweet potato to "Irish" potatoes. There was also a decline in strawberry acreage because summer crops in the North could be preserved after the quick-freeze process was invented.[14] Acreage in peas also declined as the fresh market declined in favor of the processed product.

Florida's advantage in vegetables was in fresh products. The largest increases in acreage were in sweet corn, which increased by more than 28,000 acres, and radishes, which increased by more than 20,000 acres. Acreage in lettuce more than doubled to almost 3,000 acres. Florida had been a major lettuce producer in the early 1920s, but its market had been virtually wiped out by the development of crisphead iceberg lettuce in California and Arizona.[15] Iceberg quickly replaced Florida's butterhead Big Boston lettuce. Attempts to grow iceberg lettuce in Florida were not successful because it tended to go to seed prematurely in Florida's climate. However, in the 1939–1940 season, new strains of iceberg lettuce were successfully grown in several sections of the state and a new fertilizing regime was introduced.

Palm Beach County, with more than 90,000 acres, had by far the largest acreage in vegetables in the state in 1959. The county had 24,000 acres in sweet corn, 19,000 in snap beans, and 15,000 in radishes. The county also had about 8,000 acres each in celery and escarole. Miami-Dade County, with over 40,000 acres, had the second largest acreage. Tomatoes were the county's largest crop with about 20,000 acres, followed by 8,000 acres in beans and 5,000 acres in potatoes.

Six counties had between 10,000 and 20,000 acres in vegetable production. The neighboring counties of Alachua and Marion each had large crops of watermelons. St. Johns County continued to have a large potato industry, and Seminole County continued to have a large celery industry. Orange County had about 5,000 acres in radishes and 4,000 acres in sweet corn. The vegetable industry of Hillsborough County was relatively diversified.

In 1945, Florida's production of oranges overtook California levels for the first time since the disastrous freezes of the 1890s.[16] By 1960, Florida's production of oranges was almost three times as large as production in California. The big growth in Florida production was made possible by the invention of orange juice concentrate in 1944. California continued to lead Florida in the production of oranges for the fresh market, as it continued to do for the rest of the twentieth century, but Florida quickly became dominant in orange juice. California's oranges are grown in an arid climate and thus tend to have a

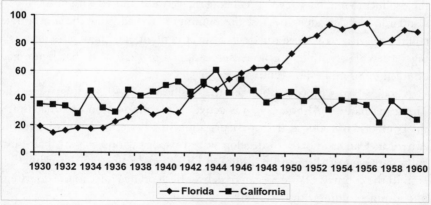

Chart 10–6. Orange Production, Florida and California, 1930–1960, in Millions of Boxes (Annual Data)

relatively low juice content and a relatively thick skin. Florida's oranges have a thinner skin and more juice. Many consumers find it easier to peel California oranges and find them less "messy," and Florida's oranges have less appeal in the fresh market. The exception is the Florida tangerine.

The liabilities that Florida oranges have in the fresh market are their strengths in the juice market. During World War II, the greatly increased demand of the U.S. military for juice led to a substantial expansion of canned orange juice. Canned juice continued to have an appeal after the war ended, but many consumers squeezed their own orange juice at that time. It became clear that if a technology for preserving a tasty orange juice could be developed, a large market could be created. Part of the challenge was finding a means of extracting water from the juice—a method of developing a concentrate. The traditional method boiled the water out of the juice, but that method resulted in a loss of flavor.[17] An alternative technology, which froze orange juice and achieved concentration by separating ice crystals from the juice, encountered technical and economic difficulties that prevented its commercial success.

High-vacuum evaporation of orange juice was part of the solution. One of the first firms to employ the technology was the National Research Corporation of Boston, which had developed the technology for dehydrating and prolonging the life of penicillin, blood plasma, and streptomycin.[18] In response to a 500,000-pound order from the U.S. military for powdered orange juice in 1945, the firm opened a plant near Orlando. The order was later canceled because of the war's end, but the company began to ship frozen concentrate instead of powder under the Minute Maid brand in 1946.

At about the same time, Florida researchers began the practice of adding orange juice back into orange concentrate before freezing. The result enabled the product to retain its flavor after being thawed and diluted with water. It also standardized the product, because the amount of juice added to the concentrate could be varied to achieve the desired sugar content. The new product was a big success. Forty million gallons were shipped in 1950, and that figure had doubled to 80 million by 1960.

A major citrus processor entered the business in 1949, trading under the Tropicana name.[19] Although it was active in the production of concentrate, the company introduced flash pasteurization in 1954 and commissioned the American Can Company to develop waxed-paper cartons in pint, half-pint, and quart sizes. It shipped fresh juice in refrigerated trucks and distributed it around the country. Dairies began to deliver fresh orange juice to the doorsteps of consumers along with fresh milk.

The growth in the market for processed oranges enabled growers to avoid costly procedures designed to enhance the appearance of fruit. Other desirable results of the development of orange processing was the ability to extract juice from freeze-damaged fruit and the ability to use fruit that would formerly have been culled as unacceptable to the fresh market. Processing the fruit also led to the development of orange by-products, including citrus-peel oil and animal feed developed from the residue after juice is extracted.[20]

In December 1957 and January–February 1958, Florida experienced the coldest three-month period ever recorded.[21] There were six significant freezes, although none was as severe as the freezes in the 1890s. The Florida Citrus Commission set standards for the extent to which freeze-damaged fruit could be used for orange juice concentrate.

Grapefruit production followed the pattern of orange production during the early 1930s as it recovered from the damage inflicted by the 1929 infestation of the Mediterranean fruit fly. By 1934, production had again reached the 1929 level, and it continued to expand until the end of World War II. Military demand during the war also affected the demand for canned grapefruit juice. During the war years, more of the crop was devoted to juice and less to sections. The situation reversed after the war ended. The volume of grapefruit sections remained the same, aside from the wartime interruption, from the mid-1930s to 1960.

Beginning in the late 1930s, Texas became an important competitor in the grapefruit market. Indeed, in 1944, production in Texas equaled the level in Florida because of an October hurricane and end-of-season drought in Florida.

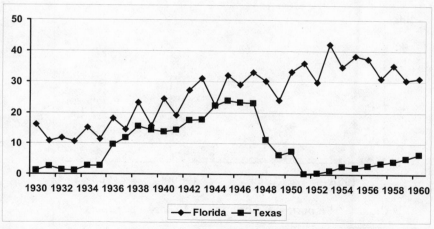

Chart 10–7. Grapefruit Production, Florida and Texas, 1930–1960, in Millions of Boxes (Annual Data)

In 1948–1949 and 1949–1950, Texas experienced back-to-back freezes that reduced the acreage in trees from 122,500 to 35,600 in 1951–1952.[22] Although acreage increased in the 1950s, it was still less than two-thirds of the pre-freeze level in 1960–1961. Production fell drastically, amounting to 36 percent of the 1947–1948 level in 1960–1961.

Florida's maritime industries had emerged as the second largest sector in the state's economic base by 1960. The sector was dominated by the military payroll in the state, which accounted for over 80 percent of total production. The sector had lost one industry since 1930, the state's sponge fishery, but it was in the process of gaining the new industry of cruising in 1960.

Florida's share of the national military payroll reached a high of 5.3 percent in 1942 and 1943 but it trended downward after World War II, reaching a low of 3 percent in 1951. Thereafter, the share rose relatively sharply, approaching 5 percent by the end of the 1950s. Almost all the military installations in Florida were facilities for naval or air force personnel. The federal military payroll was concentrated in nine Florida counties in 1958.[23] These included Escambia, Okaloosa, and Bay counties in the northwest; Duval County in the northeast; Orange and Hillsborough counties in central Florida; and Palm Beach, Miami-Dade, and Monroe counties in the south. The Palm Beach Air Force Base in Boca Raton was closed in the early 1960s. Counties adjacent to military installations had some military payrolls because of commuting.

Florida's fishing industry was the second largest of the state's maritime

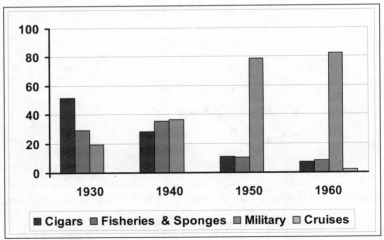

Chart 10–8. Share of Cigar, Fishery and Sponge, Military, and Cruise Industries in the Value of Production of Florida's Maritime Sector by Decade, 1930–1960 (by Percent)

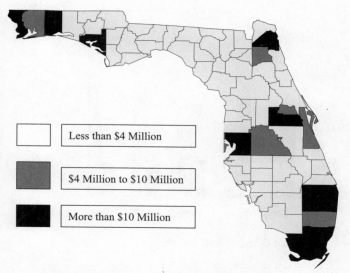

Florida Map 10–3. Value of Military Payrolls in Florida's Counties, 1958

sectors in 1960. The catch had grown significantly during World War II, particularly on the state's east coast. After the war, the east coast catch dropped sharply, but production on the Gulf coast expanded.[24] Most of Florida's fish were classified as food fish, with the exception of menhaden, which was processed into fish oil and meal.[25] The ranking of Florida's food fish remained similar between 1923 and 1960.[26] Black mullet and red snapper were the two largest fisheries, even though both were smaller in 1960 than they had been in 1923. Pompano fishing, which did not become significant until after 1940, was the third largest fishery in 1960. King mackerel, sea trout, and grouper were ranked fourth through sixth in 1960; all three were larger in 1960 than they had been in 1923. Shrimp was by far the biggest shellfish fishery in Florida in 1960. Indeed, the value of shrimp landings was 64 percent larger than the value of black mullet, the largest of the food-fish fisheries. In 1960, Florida's shrimp fishery had recently enjoyed a renaissance. Shrimp production had declined after 1923, particularly in the 1940s. During that period, the fishery was located primarily along the northeast coast, centered at St. Augustine. When catches declined there, shrimp fishermen explored the state's Gulf coast, seeking new grounds. In 1950, a shrimp fisherman discovered the Key West grounds, and during the first full season of fishing on Florida's Gulf coast (1950–1951), 300 ships produced 15 million pounds.[27] At about the same time, new grounds in the Bay of Campeche, east of the Yucatan Peninsula in Mexico, were also discovered.

The relatively long distance between the home ports of the shrimp fleets and

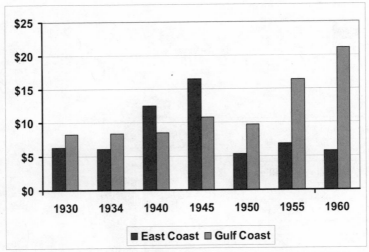

Chart 10–9. Fish Catch on Florida's East and Gulf Coasts, 1930–1960, in Millions of 1960 Dollars (Selected Years)

the shrimping grounds, especially the Campeche grounds, made it necessary for producers to use larger shrimp boats than they had used in the near-shore fishery of northeast Florida. In addition, the size of the ships, which were larger than the ones used for near-shore fishing, meant that the possible home bases for the fleets were limited to ports capable of handling boats with relatively deep drafts. In the early years, the shrimp fleets were based in Key West and the twin ports of Fort Myers and Fort Myers Beach. Two factors stimulated the demand for shrimp: the relative ease with which shrimp could be frozen and the development of the trucking industry, which made it possible to ship the product quickly to distant and widely dispersed markets.[28]

Blue crabs constituted the second largest shellfish fishery. They were found on both coasts, with the largest production in the Big Bend area of the state stretching from Franklin County south to Citrus County, although there was very limited production in one of the counties (Taylor) in that sequence. In addition, more than 1 million blue shell crabs were landed in each of these counties: Lee on the west coast and Indian River and Nassau on the east coast.

The Ten Thousand Islands area south of Naples on the southwest corner of the peninsula featured a clam fishery. In 1945, however, a devastating red tide killed the clam beds, and by 1960 no production was reported for Collier and Monroe counties in the annual edition of *Fishery Statistics of the United States*.

An 1955 economic study of the fisheries noted that they were characterized by low wages but had a high labor cost per pound of fish caught. Employment was seasonal in a number of fisheries, and more than 15 percent consisted of casual fishermen: "those whose principal business was something other than fishing and who received less than one-half their annual compensation from fishing."[29] The study noted that barriers to entry, such as setup costs, were relatively low in many fisheries, especially when grounds were located near ports, and that large economies of scale were not a feature of most fishing operations. More than 50 percent of oystermen and fishermen were self-employed.

Florida's historic sponge industry had disappeared by 1960. Production peaked in 1936 at a little more than 600,000 pounds, but it had fallen to about 200,000 pounds by the beginning of World War II.[30] Production remained stable during the war at about this level, but it declined sharply after the war ended. An outbreak of red tide destroyed many of the beds in the late 1940s. Although the beds had recovered by the late 1950s, synthetic sponges had replaced natural products on the market.

Cigar manufacturing in Florida declined in the 1930s and 1940s before experiencing a revival in the postwar years. The industry, which was the second largest manufacturer in the state in 1929, had fallen to tenth place by 1958. The decline in cigar manufacturing was partly explained by a shift in consumer demand from cigars to cigarettes that had occurred in the first half of the twentieth century. Mechanization also gradually reduced state production, which relied on hand methods to produce premium cigars using highly skilled Cuban workers who commanded high wages.

Within Florida, the location of production shifted in the 1920s. Swisher and Son had purchased rolling machines for making tobacco in 1923, and in 1927 they moved their corporate headquarters from Tampa to Jacksonville.[31] By the end of the 1930s, the company was producing 100 million cigars a year at its Jacksonville factory. By 1940, the company was producing the King Edward, the world's most popular cigar, and the Jacksonville factory was the largest cigar-manufacturing operation in the world under one roof.

Between the censuses of 1947 and 1958, labor productivity almost doubled in Florida's cigar industry.[32] One of the fruits of the increased labor productivity was an increase in the wages of production workers by one-third during the eleven-year period.

Like the maritime sector, Florida's frontier sector had lost an industry and gained an industry during the 1930–1960 period. The gum naval stores industry came to an end during these decades, but the new industry, paper manufacturing, was the largest industry in the sector in 1960.

During the decade of the 1930s, lumber production fell by almost 40 per-

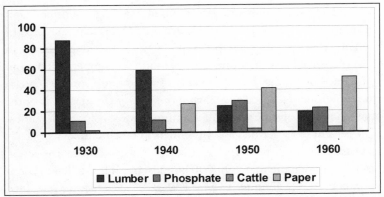

Chart 10–10. Share of Lumber, Phosphate, Cattle, and Paper Industries in Value of Production of Florida's Frontier Industries by Decade, 1930–1960 (by Percent)

cent.[33] It declined further in the 1940s before production stabilized. The decline in the industry was partly the result of the Depression of the 1930s, but it was also attributable to the exhaustion of the forests of long-leaf pine trees, particularly in the state's panhandle. As a result of the decline in the lumber industry, gum naval stores declined sharply in the 1930s.[34] Employment in the industry fell from about 14,000 in 1929 to 500 in 1939. The collapse of the industry came about when a method was developed to distill wood as a by-product of the state's new paper industry. This was one of many examples where chemistry created manmade substitutes for "natural" products. Instead of paying a labor force to go into the forests to tap the resin from the trees, the trees were cut down and brought to be turned into pulp at a mill; the resin was extracted chemically rather than by hand. By 1939, wood distillation accounted for 64 percent of the production of turpentine and rosin in the state.

Florida's paper-manufacturing industry began in 1931 with the opening of a pulp mill at Panama City in the panhandle region of the state. The mill was constructed by the Southern Kraft Division of International Paper Company.[35] Research by Dr. Charles Herty had proved that younger pines produced pulp for kraft paper whose quality matched that of the traditional spruce pine from the northern states.[36] Kraft paper was a heavy brown paper used to make corrugated boxes and grocery bags. A big boost for the new industry occurred when the St. Joe Company opened a plant in Port St. Joe east of Panama City in 1938.[37] The plant was a joint venture between Almours Securities and Mead Company, an Ohio firm that had been in the paper business for 100 years. Almour Securities was the holding company for the Florida interests of Alfred I. du Pont, who had begun to amass vast holdings of forest land in the severely depressed panhandle area of the state in the latter half of the 1920s. A member of the family that owned the chemical company DuPont, he had lost his management position with the company as a result of a feud with the rest of the family. When one of the latter became tax commissioner of Delaware in 1925, du Pont transferred his business interests to Florida and made the state his official residence. He avoided purchasing land in the areas experiencing the boom and began to purchase land in the panhandle area. Such land was cheap because much of its timber had been cut, and it became cheaper after the on-set of the Depression. Although du Pont died in 1935, his holdings remained intact and were managed by his brother-in-law Ed Ball, primarily on behalf of a charitable foundation to aid children and the elderly. Almour Holdings took full control of St. Joe Paper in 1940, and the company ultimately accumulated 1 million acres of land in North Florida.

Because pulpwood was produced from 20– and 30–year-old trees (lumber trees were not cut until they were fifty years old), it provided a much faster cash return for owners of forested land. Additionally, the pulpwood indus-try used worked-out turpentine trees and forest thinnings as well as crooked and injured trees that sawmills refused.[38] Finally, because pulpwood factories were located at seaports that were well served by rail and road transportation, Florida's factories processed trees from Georgia and Alabama. Paper and allied products increased their share of the state's manufacturing production as the share of lumber products and gum naval stores declined. Production doubled in the seven years between 1947 and 1954 before stabilizing at the end of the decade.

The remaining frontier industries, cattle-herding and phosphate mining, experienced increased production between 1930 and 1960. The state's cattle in-dustry completed the transition from open-range herding of unimproved stock to cattle ranching in fenced areas with pedigreed stock and planted pastures be-tween 1930 and 1950. A highlight was the widespread introduction of Brahman cattle to the state in the 1930s. U.S. Sugar helped pioneer the cross-breeding of English breeds, such as Angus, Herefords, and Shorthorns, with Brahmans.[39] In the late 1940s, breeding experiments revealed that the Braford breed was well adapted to south Florida's climate and topography.[40] Florida cattle production doubled in the 1950s.[41] The modernized cattle industry required less land per cow. Land requirements fell, perhaps from as many as forty acres per cow to three acres, permitting a substantial expansion of herd sizes and encouraging the growth of pasture land.[42] Land in pasture peaked in the state in 1954, twenty years before the peak in the state's inventory of cattle and calves.

In 1959, the larger urban counties had substantial dairying industries. Brow-ard, Palm Beach, Hillsborough, and Duval counties had more than 10,000 milk cows, and Miami-Dade and Orange had more than 5,000.[43] Four other counties close to large urban areas, Okeechobee, Manatee, Polk, and Clay, also had more than 5,000 dairy cows. Most Florida cattle, however, were raised for beef.

The heart of Florida's beef-cattle industry remained in the counties east of Tampa. The three counties with the largest herds in 1959 were Polk (79,570), Hillsborough (77,064), and Osceola (76,022). Four other counties had more than 50,000 head: Palm Beach (64,574), Hendry (62,630), Okeechobee (56,316), and Marion (53,453).

The remaining frontier industry was phosphate mining. This industry was sensitive to the business cycle, and production fell by 50 percent from 1930 to 1932. Production recovered to the 1930 level by 1941, and it remained close to this level until the end of World War II.[44] The industry enjoyed strong growth after World War II, although there were pauses in 1949, 1955, and 1958 as a result of the national recessions. Production in 1960 was almost three times the level in 1945.

Florida's southern industries—composed of cotton, tobacco, sugar, and a small amount of rice—accounted for no more than 1 percent of the production of the state's economic base in 1960, a share maintained by this group of industries throughout the twentieth century. Production of cotton sank to insignificance during the 1930s, and by 1960 the state's southern sector was largely composed of tobacco and sugar.[45]

The largest center of tobacco production remained in Gadsden County on the east bank of the Apalachicola River, where over 4,000 acres were planted to tobacco.[46] A second center was in Suwannee County in the northern penin-

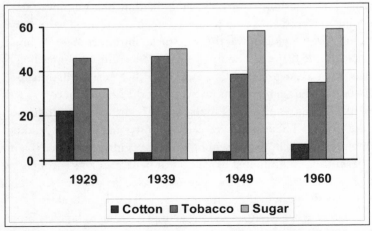

Chart 10–11. Share of Cotton, Tobacco, and Sugar Industries in Value of Production of Florida's Southern Industries by Decade, 1929–1960 (by Percent)

sula, which had more than 3,500 acres in tobacco. The counties surrounding Suwannee had an additional 8,000 acres.

The sugar industry expanded fivefold between 1930 and 1960. The industry doubled during the 1930s, fell during the early years of World War II, and then doubled again between 1942 and 1952. The industry remained relatively stable throughout the 1950s. By 1960, sugarcane was primarily grown in the counties around the southern half of Lake Okeechobee, but there was also a small industry at Fellsmere in Indian River County. Fellsmere Sugar Company was established in 1932 at the bottom of the depression by the salesmanship of Frank Heiser.[47] Its first challenge was to ensure proper drainage. An existing drainage tax district where the company was located was in serious financial difficulties, and Heiser took over maintenance of the ditches and canals on the sugar lands. By 1934, Heiser had planted 1,800 acres in sugarcane. The company added facilities for refining sugar in 1935 and began to market refined sugar in the state under the Florida Crystals brand name in 1936. In 1937, Heiser formed a cooperative of eleven cane growers called the Fellsmere Sugar Producers Association (FSPA) and sold the Fellsmere properties to the cooperative. In 1938, the refinery successfully marketed more than 6 million pounds. Soon after the outbreak of World War II, quotas and the uncertain outlook for labor led Heiser and his fellow investors to sell out to a group of Puerto Rican sugar producers. In 1959, Okeelanta Sugar, based south of Lake Okeechobee, purchased the FSPA operations and transferred its sugar quota to Okeelanta in 1963.

Production around Lake Okeechobee was dominated by the United States Sugar Corporation, which had been established in 1931. U.S. Sugar was a much larger operation than the Fellsmere Sugar Company. In the 1930s, U.S. Sugar had about 25,000 acres in sugarcane, and this increased further in 1945 when Florida's sugar quota was expanded.[48] Just as it was for the Fellsmere Sugar Company, water management was a high priority for U.S. Sugar. Its lands were in several drainage tax districts, all of which were in serious financial difficulties. U.S. Sugar "helped put the districts back in operation, in some cases guaranteeing loans to the district from the Reconstruction Finance Corporation."[49]

Although the USDA had opened a cane-breeding station at Canal Point on the eastern side of Lake Okeechobee in 1920, U.S. Sugar established a research program to find suitable varieties of cane. It also expanded the sugar mill in Clewiston, reputedly making it the largest mill in the world. The mill was fueled by bagasse, the remains of cane from which sugar syrup has been extracted. Another by-product, blackstrap molasses, was used as a material for "the manufacture of ethyl alcohol, acetone, butanol and in the production of high quality silage and cattle feeds."[50]

When faced with a shortage of cane cutters at the outbreak of the war, the industry imported farm workers from the British West Indies under an intergovernmental agreement in 1943. The agreement became part of the temporary H-2 visa program established by the 1952 Immigration and Nationality Act.[51] By 1949, the industry had planted 36,000 acres in sugarcane in the three counties around the southern shores of Lake Okeechobee (Glades, Hendry, and Palm Beach), and a second mill had opened at Okeelanta. The acreage had grown to more than 46,000 ten years later.

By 1960, the sunshine sector, composed of semitropical agriculture, winter vegetables, tourism, and retirement had become the dominant part of the state's economic base. The frontier sector, composed of lumber, naval stores, paper, cattle, and phosphate mining, lost its dominant position by 1940 and continued its relative decline in the 1940s and 1950s. Florida had become the Sunshine State and was no longer part of the country's frontier.

Chapter 11

The 1960s and 1970s

Slowdown, Boom, and Recession

Florida's population growth rate fell sharply as the 1950s ended, dropping from a high of 8 percent in 1956 and 1957 to 6 percent in 1958 and 4 percent in 1959 and 1960.[1] A slight strengthening in 1961 and 1962 was followed by another slowing, and the annual rate of population growth reached a low of just over 2 percent in 1967.

Several unusual events may have slowed in-migration to the state. One was the Cuban missile crisis in 1962. It is not possible to estimate the impact of the crisis, although its relatively swift resolution suggests that the impact was probably transitory. Another event was a public controversy about the sales practices of land installment sales operations in the state. In January 1963, the president of the National Better Business Bureau testified before the Senate Special Committee on Aging about shady practices in Florida: "Swamp merchants in Florida have accumulated many hard-earned dollars from the elderly. They tout land in or near the Everglades or Big Cypress Swamp as 'America's last frontier,' 'Today's best investment' and other glowing terms. The ads do not disclose that the land may be under water all or part of the year."[2] The industry responded by shifting its sales techniques "from a mail order to a personal salesman approach."[3] Both the federal government and the state imposed regulations on developers offering fifty or more lots for sale on the installment plan, "generally requiring full disclosure, pre-approval of all [out-of-state] advertising, the issuance of a prospectus and the customer's right of contract recision within 48 hours."[4]

It is likely that the major reason for the slowdown in the period 1960–1967, however, was a decline in the rate of growth of the national pool of retirees. In both the 1940s and the 1950s, the population aged 65 and over grew by about 35 percent, and this age group grew by more than 30 percent in the 1970s. But, during the 1960s, the population aged 65 and over grew at 17 percent, a reduction of 50 percent in the rate of the previous two decades.[5]

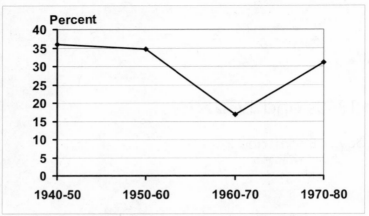

Chart 11–1. Rate of Growth of Population Aged 65 and Older in the
United States, 1940–1950 to 1970–1980

Those who reached the age of 65 during the 1960s were born in the 1895–
1905 period. The limited and somewhat unreliable birth information for this
period shows a decline in the birth rate between 1880 and 1909, but the decline
is continuous both before and after these years.[6] It is likely that the birthrate
underwent a cyclical decline during the 1895–1905 period in addition to the
long-run downward trend because there was a severe economic recession in
1893 and generally depressed economic conditions at least until 1900.

Another factor that may have reduced the size of the over-65 age cohort
in 1960 was the sharp decline in immigration at the outbreak of World War I
in 1914. Immigration peaked at about 1 million in 1910, but during the years
1914–1918 it averaged only 250,000 annually.[7] Most immigrants who were in
their early twenties during World War I would have reached 65 around 1960.

The relatively slow population growth in Florida in the 1960s resulted in a
less vigorous construction industry than had been the case during the boom
time of the 1950s. During the 1960s, the per capita earnings in the state's construction industry lagged behind the national level until the final year of the
decade. Other industries related to construction were also affected by the slowdown. Earnings in real estate services lagged behind the national industry until
the final year of the decade. A similar pattern was evident in earnings in the
manufactures of stone, clay, and glass.

The state's tourist industry was also weak in the first half of the 1960s. Earnings in hotels and other lodging places, part of the more detailed data on personal income that became available beginning in 1958, confirms the weakness
of Florida's tourism sector in the early years of the 1960s. Not until 1965 did
per capita earnings in hotels, adjusted for inflation, exceed their 1960 level.

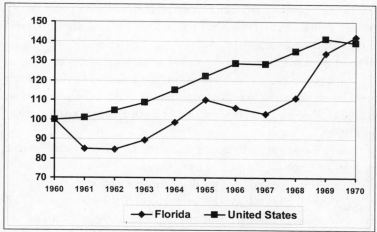

Chart 11–2. Real per Capita Construction Earnings in Florida, 1960–1970 (Index 1960=100)

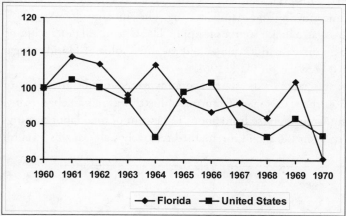

Chart 11–3. Real per Capita Farm Earnings in Florida and the United States, 1960–1970 (Index 1960=100)

The fact that Florida hotel earnings remained weak even after the recession ended in 1961 may be attributable to the same factors as the slowdown in the rate of population in-migration discussed above. That is, the decline in the growth of the national pool of retirees may have had a negative impact on the state's tourism industry in the 1960s because many winter tourists are retirees. A reduction in winter tourism by this group would impact hotel earnings negatively.

The farm sector also struggled in the 1960s. The decade began with Hurricane Donna in 1960. It was called "the most destructive hurricane ever to strike the Florida citrus industry" in 1999.[8] The recovery was interrupted by the largest arctic air mass to date that had ever hit the Florida peninsula in December 1962.[9] A brief recovery in 1964 was followed by a downward trend in farm earnings for the rest of the decade.

The 1959 revolution in Cuba led to an influx of a large number of refugees to Florida, and this group had a major impact on the economy during the rest of the century. The most immediate economic consequence of the revolution, however, was the U.S. embargo on trade with Cuba, which impacted a number of Florida industries.

Much of Tampa's cigar-manufacturing industry had traditionally made hand-rolled cigars with tobacco imported from Cuba. By 1960, however, most of this industry had disappeared as a result of mechanization and a shift in consumer tastes. When Cuban tobacco became subject to the embargo in 1962, what was left of Tampa's traditional industry disappeared. By July 1965, fewer than 100 workers were making cigars by hand in the city. One independent Tampa cigar company survived, Hav-a-Tampa, because it had its own distribution organization.[10] However, another industry gained as a result of the Cuban embargo: sugarcane growing and manufacturing. The embargo closed the U.S. market to Cuban sugar, a major source of supply. The U.S. mainland, including Florida, received an increase in its quota, and the gross value of Florida's sugar production tripled between 1960 and 1964.

Although several sectors of the state's economy experienced difficulties for much of the 1960s, the state's manufacturing industry was remarkably strong. The share of manufacturing rose from about 12 percent of total labor earnings in 1958 to 14 percent in 1962, and it remained relatively stable at this level for

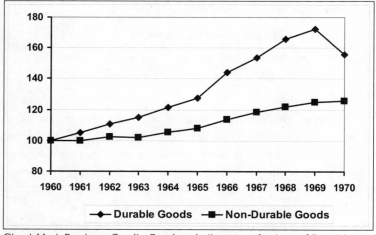

Chart 11–4. Real per Capita Earnings in the Manufacture of Durable and Nondurable Goods in Florida, Indexes 1960=100

three years. A further rise took the share to 15 percent by 1968, the highest share ever recorded by manufacturing in the 1929–2000 period.[11] The increase in Florida's manufacturing sector in the 1960s was in durable goods rather than nondurable goods. Many of the state's traditional manufacturing industries produced nondurable goods such as processed food, cigars, chemicals, paper, and printed matter.

Traditionally, the state had been relatively weak in durables manufacturing except for lumber and stone and clay and glass products. During the 1960s, however, the growth in Florida's manufacture of durable goods took place in other industries, especially the production of machinery and equipment and ordnance (defense manufacturing). These were called technological industries at that time. The business magazine *Florida Trend* observed in 1969 that the manufacture of instruments and electrical machinery did not require industries to be located close to raw materials, fuel supplies, or markets. Instead, they needed "highly-skilled technical and scientific people—the type of worker who can be most easily attracted to Florida by the lure of a more pleasant climate, healthier surroundings, and a better way of life."[12] Engineers responded enthusiastically to the new opportunities in Florida. Charles D. Roelke, the first general manager of Pratt & Whitney's large aircraft engine manufacturing plant that had opened near West Palm Beach in 1958, noted that "before deciding to come here we ran blind ads in a New York newspaper asking for engineering employees for a Florida plant and a New England plant. The response to these ads favored Florida by 30–1. By actual experience, since we have been established here, we have an average of 18 applicants for every job available."[13] Martin Corporation, a defense firm that opened in Orlando in 1957, was one of the largest manufacturing facilities in the state by 1963. A top engineering executive at the firm credited the growth of the facility to its ability to attract excellent technical employees because of "a favorable climate and proximity to recreational areas."[14] Similarly, the general manager of GE's Command Systems Division, which opened in Daytona Beach in 1962 to work on NASA's Apollo moon shot program, noted that the area's climate and recreational advantages made the problem of recruiting high-caliber professional people less difficult.[15] *Florida Trend* noted in 1965 that "the state's new economic development is based primarily on the same God-given attribute which makes citrus and tourism important—the climate."[16] Florida's new technological industry was joining the state's sunshine economic sector. Like the other sunshine industries, it thrived because of Florida's climate.

The warm winter climate benefited manufacturers moving to the state in other ways. *Florida Trend* noted in 1963 that the climate "reduces worker absenteeism from respiratory ailments."[17] The mild winter also reduced the cost of constructing plants. The president of Dynatronics, a defense firm founded in Orlando in 1958, noted that "facilities and plant space are less expensive than in most of the highly industrialized states, partly because of lower costs in the area but largely because the type of construction required for the mild climate is much less expensive than would be required in a more severe climate. The low cost of living, mild climate and abundance of outdoor recreation create desirable living conditions for our employees and contribute to high morale with its attendant high productivity."[18]

Florida's growth in technology manufacturing began in the mid-1950s.[19] This was a time when the end of the Korean War, which permitted a reduction in troop strength, and the perception that the Soviet Union was producing high-technology weaponry led to increased budgets for new weapons systems in the United States. The nation's military-oriented technology industries needed to expand, and many chose to open in Florida because of the relative ease in recruiting engineering talent. Florida also benefited from President Kennedy's decision to send men to the moon in 1961. In 1968, *Florida Trend* noted that "among the top 25 firms receiving NASA contracts, 18 have installations here in Florida at Cape Kennedy."[20]

The state had advantages other than its climate that it used to attract the new industries. These included relatively light business taxes. At the time, for example, there was no corporate income tax. *Florida Trend* claimed in 1963 that the business share of Florida's state taxes was less than half the national average, although it did not explain where it got its data.[21] Unions were not strong in Florida, and *Florida Trend* also claimed that the state lost relatively few days to

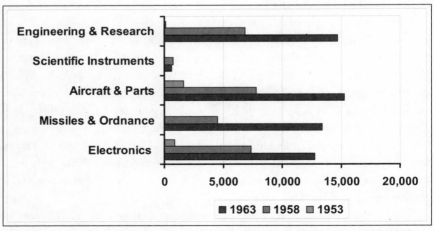

Chart 11–5. Employment Growth in Florida's Technological Industries, 1953, 1958, and 1963

strikes compared to the national average. The state's relatively good transportation system, particularly its many airports with relatively easy connections to the nation's largest cities, constituted another advantage.

In 1969, Florida's technology industries had their largest payrolls in Brevard and Orange counties, near Cape Kennedy, and Miami-Dade, Broward, Pinellas, and Duval counties. The technology industries in Palm Beach, Sarasota, Hillsborough, and Seminole counties also had significant payrolls.

In spite of the strength of durables manufacturing, the weakness of earnings due to the slowdown in population and tourism resulted in slow growth in labor earnings in the state relative to the nation until about 1964. The weakness in labor earnings caused Florida's per capita income, adjusted for inflation, to grow relatively slowly compared to the national growth rate. Beginning about 1964, the growth in Florida real per capita income reached the national rate, and in 1968 the state surpassed the national level.

Beginning in 1964, Florida's construction industry began to recover from its decline earlier in the decade, as Chart 11–2 above illustrates. Although growth was interrupted as a result of a credit crunch in 1966 and the resulting national slowdown in 1967, Florida's construction industry resumed strong growth in 1968 and 1969. The industry continued to grow even during the national economic recession of 1970. By 1970, Florida per capita construction earnings, adjusted for inflation, had risen by 40 percent over their 1967 level. By 1973, the peak year of the boom in Florida, per capita labor earnings in construction were double their 1967 level.

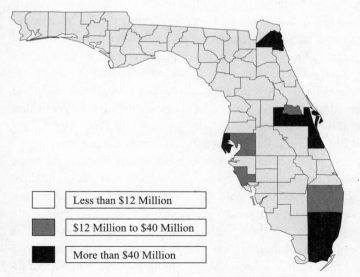

Less than $12 Million

$12 Million to $40 Million

More than $40 Million

Florida Map 11–1. Technology Industry Earnings in Florida by County, 1969

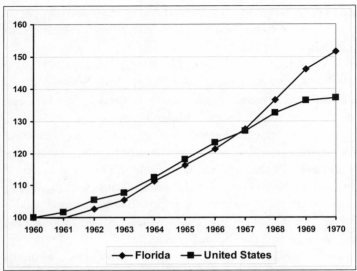

Chart 11–6. Real per Capita Income in Florida and the United States, 1960–1970 (Index 1960=100)

A number of structural changes had occurred in Florida's development industry in the years before 1967. The industry had consolidated to facilitate the development of large tracts of land. In the 1950s, developers constructed new developments that were relatively remote from existing urban areas.[22] Examples of these tract (or city) developments were Lehigh Acres, located twelve miles east of Fort Myers; Cape Coral, west of Fort Myers; and Port Charlotte, located on the north shore of Charlotte Harbor across from Punta Gorda. Such developments required large amounts of capital to finance construction and national marketing campaigns. Three large Florida development companies were floated on the stock market by the end of the 1960s, including General Development, GAC Properties, and Deltona Corporation. Large companies that already had access to the capital markets purchased other large Florida developers in that decade; Westinghouse Corporation purchased Coral Ridge Properties in Fort Lauderdale, and Penn Central Railroad purchased Arvida Corporation.[23]

In addition, new products had been developed for the Florida real estate market. One was the development of cheap housing communities in the form of trailer parks. One observer notes that "trailer living became dignified by park design and the development of modular prefabricated units that changed the name to mobile homes."[24] By 1967, mobile home production accounted for about 7 percent of the total dwelling units built nationally, and more than 2 percent of the population lived in such units.[25] Mobile homes accounted for 33 percent of all housing priced under $10,000 that year. Florida ranked fourth in the nation in the production of mobile homes, behind California, Indiana, and Michigan. Alfred A. Ring, chairman of the University of Florida's Department of Real Estate and Urban Land Studies, noticed its particular appeal to retirees living in Florida: "To large numbers of retirees it is a new Eden. Mobile parks offer a community spirit, a feeling of belonging, a friendly atmosphere engendered by like minded neighbors, which is unmatched by any area containing a similar size and number of conventional homes."[26]

Even more important than mobile home communities was the development of the condominium, a new form of real estate. As explained in 1962 by Brown L. Whatley, president of Arvida, a leader in the introduction of condominiums to Florida's real estate market, "The basic theory of condominium ownership is that different parts of a building, together with joint rights of co-ownership in other parts of the building and facilities[,] may be separately owned, sold, mortgaged, leased and taxed."[27] Interest in condominiums began in the United States when the Commonwealth of Puerto Rico enacted its Horizontal Property Act in 1958. The motivation in Puerto Rico was to spur the development of multifamily housing on an island constrained by a lack of space. Whatley saw that condominiums would attract more retirees to Florida: "Retirees are a large and still growing segment of Florida's population. Via condominium ownership, these senior citizens will be able to enjoy all the advantages of simple fee ownership, while at the same time living close to urban centers (where high land values often prohibit construction of single family dwellings) and enjoy the social and cultural advantages—and the convenience—which urban living brings."[28]

The condominium form of ownership received a strong endorsement when Congress passed the Housing Act in 1961, which authorized the FHA to insure mortgages on individually owned units in multifamily structures. This was followed by enabling legislation passed by the Florida legislature in 1963 which set out the rules and conditions governing the establishment of condominiums in the state. The legislature extended the homestead exemption to owner-occupied condominium units in 1967.

The advantages of simple fee ownership included the fact that owners could deduct mortgage interest against income taxes and take advantage of the homestead exemption against property taxes if they chose to make the unit their primary residence. Urban areas offered more medical facilities and a broader range of cultural activities than did the remote tract developments. Condominiums also enabled retirees to live on the beach—an option that was much more expensive in a single-family dwelling.

The social advantages of condominium developments were much the same as those of mobile home communities. Because condominium dwellers interacted with each other in clubhouses and recreational facilities, they got to know their neighbors. A Florida high-rise developer, Stanton D. Sanson, noted that condominium developments defeated loneliness. "There's always something to do. . . . You can always get up a bridge game, or go visiting in someone else's apartment."[29] The condominium also appealed to those who wanted the advantages of ownership without the headaches of maintaining their property.[30] Associations of condominium owners provided central services such as yard and building maintenance and security. This was particularly appealing to owners who wanted to occupy their units seasonally. They could return to their northern residences during the summer months confident that their Florida condominiums were secure and maintained.

Condominium units also appealed to individuals close to retirement age. As inflation rose, it appeared to many that condominium prices would rise and that units should be purchased sooner rather than later. In many condominium complexes, it was possible to rent out units on a seasonal basis.[31] The purchase of a unit that would be rented out would lock in the lower current prices, provide rental income that would cover at least part of the mortgage payments on the unit, provide a tax deduction to workers while their incomes were high (prior to retirement), and possibly provide a tax-deductible trip to Florida in connection with the management of the unit. The condominium association or a local real estate agent could handle the marketing of the rental unit and collecting the rent.

Over time, investors who did not intend to occupy their units entered the market, as did Florida residents of working age interested in first and second homes. A survey of 1,000 buyers by the developer of the Palm Aire golfing condominium complex in Pompano Beach between 1966 and 1970 found that only 20 to 25 percent of owners were retired. A third of the owners in the complex occupied their units year-round, another third occupied the units seasonally, and the remainder occupied their units "for short intervals at various times of the year."[32]

Many condominium units involved large tracts of land. The major land development companies required to bring these developments to market had architectural and planning staffs similar to the development team Richard Merrick assembled to develop Coral Gables earlier in the century. These companies constructed more than condominium units—they constructed roads, water and sewage systems, and, of course, recreational facilities. Local governments adapted to these circumstances by upgrading their own planning capabilities. This trend accelerated in the early 1970s as planned unit developments became popular, permitting developers of large tracts to shift density around within their tracts so as to preserve environmental resources such as wetlands. Golf courses, for example, could be located in parts of a large tract where housing was undesirable.

The state also became interested in urban planning to preserve the environment. This was partly a reaction to the Clean Air Act (1970) and the Clean Water Act (1977). It was also stimulated by the major drought in south Florida in 1971. The state legislature passed the Local Government Comprehensive Planning Act in 1975, which required local governments to project the population within their jurisdictions and develop a feasible plan for providing infrastructure and preserving the local environment.[33]

The boom in construction in 1968 coincided with a return to population growth greater than 3 percent for the first time since 1963. The growth rate did not quicken in 1969 or 1970, however, because income taxes were temporarily raised in 1969 in an effort to reduce the federal budget deficit and the national economy experienced a recession in 1970. In 1971, the state's population growth rate approached 5 percent, and it remained at this very high rate through 1974. Rates of population growth at 5 percent or more were not repeated in the remainder of the twentieth century.

As it had in the 1950s, the new wave of in-migrants to Florida included a large number of retired persons. The decennial census, the only source of accurate information on the age distribution of the population, showed a jump in the 65+ age group in Florida between 1960 and 1970 (much of this presumably came in the final years of the decade) and another jump between 1970 and 1980 (much of this presumably occurred in the early years of the decade).

Data on condominium units did not become available in the U.S. census until 1980. An indication of the growth of these units is available from the growth of high-rise multifamily (five or more in a structure) units between

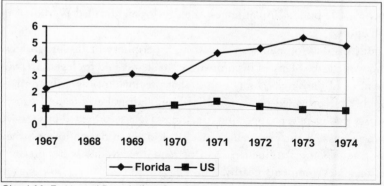

Chart 11-7. Annual Population Growth Rate in Florida and the United States, 1967–1974 (by Percent)

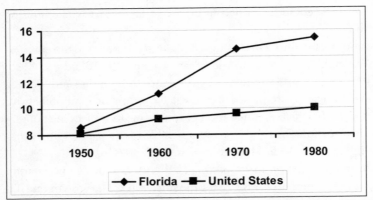

Chart 11–8. Population Ages 65 and Older, Florida and the United States by Decade, 1950–1980 (by Percent of Total Population)

1960 and 1980.[34] By the end of the 1970s, almost one in four housing units in Florida was a high-rise multifamily unit.

A large part of the growth in condominiums occurred in the state's southeast counties. The biggest growth in high-rise housing was in Broward and Miami-Dade counties, each of which constructed about 130,000 high-rise units during the 1970s. Palm Beach County constructed more than 60,000 units. Pinellas County, which also constructed around 60,000 high-rise units, was the only other county in the state to construct more than 30,000 high-rise units during the 1970s.

One of the more successful condominium developers in the southeast part of the state was H. Irwin Levy, who developed four Century Village developments, two in Palm Beach County and two in Broward County. He began his first development in 1968 in West Palm Beach and had sold almost 8,000 units by 1974.[35] These four developments contained enough housing for more than 50,000 people. He built a similar large-scale development called Wynmoor in Broward County.

Levy built his developments on the western periphery of the urban area, where land was cheap. Many of his units were small and sold for less than two-thirds the price of the single-family homes that previous in-migrating retirees had favored.[36] He provided recreational facilities, cultural events, and educational courses that were very appealing to retirees. He also provided bus service to shopping areas. As the population increased in these developments, they gained enormous political influence, securing road improvements and preventing undesirable developments nearby.

Retiree-oriented condominium developments were also built on or near the beach. In the community of Hallandale, the southernmost beachfront city in

Broward County (population over 36,000 in 1980), most of the housing was high-rise units—71.3 percent of the city's housing. The appeal of this housing to retired persons is evident from the fact that 50.1 percent of the city's residents were aged 65 years and over.

In addition to the creation of vertical multistory condominiums, the condominium concept was also applied horizontally to low-rise single-family developments that were often surrounded by walls and accessed through gates protected by security guards. These gated communities often had golf courses and were particularly appropriate to the parts of Florida where there was a mix of wetlands and uplands. Density could be concentrated on the upland portion of the development and the wetlands could be used for golf courses or other recreational uses.

The focus of condominiums and gated communities on recreational facilities had an unexpected unpleasant consequence when high rates of inflation persisted into the middle 1970s. Condominium dwellers had agreed to escalator clauses in their leases with the condominium developers that allowed for monthly maintenance fees to rise with inflation. Although this seemed reasonable at the end of the 1960s when inflation rates were relatively low, it was regarded as a major burden in the mid-1970s when inflation rose above 10 percent.

Florida's tourism also increased in from 1965 to 1973. Earnings in the tourism-retirement sector increased by more than 50 percent between 1965 and 1973. The growth in the number of condominium units that could be occupied by tourists

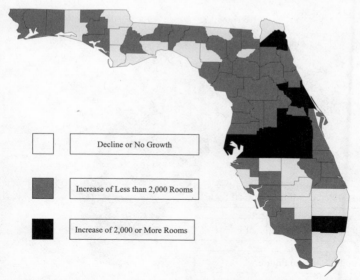

Florida Map 11–2. Development of Hotel and Motel Units in Florida by County, 1970–1975

on short-term rentals had a negative impact on traditional hotel and motel capacity in the state. After an increase in 1968, the number of hotel and motel units remained relatively stable in the state until 1972. However, the number increased by more than 25 percent between 1971–1972 and 1975–1976.[37]

The increase in capacity in 1972 was related to the opening of Disney World near Orlando. Most of the growth in hotel units occurred in Central Florida, especially in Orange County, where the number of units increased by 10,261, and Osceola County, where the number of units increased by 4,520. Nearby Volusia and Seminole counties also experienced large increases in the number of units (2,440 and 1,320 respectively). There was also significant growth in the Tampa–St. Petersburg area (4,627 and 1,620 respectively).

In only one county in the southeast part of the state, Monroe, did the number of new hotel units exceed 1,000. Two counties in the region had large declines in the number of hotel units, namely Miami-Dade, which experienced a decline of 3,737 units, and Palm Beach County, which experienced a decline of 1,007 units. No other county in the state experienced a decline of more than 200 units except Sarasota, where the number of units declined by 216.

The boom in Florida pushed the state's recorded per capita income to the national level in 1973 for the first time since 1929, the year that official estimates of the state's personal income became available. The parity of incomes was only transitory, however, as the economic difficulties that began in 1973 pushed the Florida level below the national level beginning in 1974.

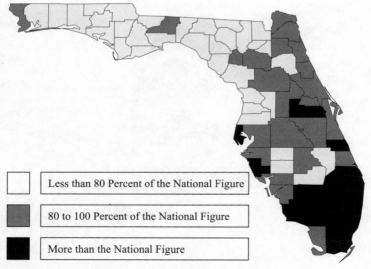

Florida Map 11–3. Per Capita Income in Florida by County Compared to the National per Capita Income, 1973

With the exception of Orange County, the region of Florida where per capita incomes exceeded the national level was in the southern half of the peninsula. South of a line drawn southwest from Martin County to Collier County, the only county with a per capita income below the national level was Monroe. North of this imaginary line, the only counties with per capita incomes above the national level were Sarasota, Pinellas, and Indian River (with the exception of Orange County). Per capita incomes were more than 20 percent below the national level in north Florida between Escambia and Duval counties, except for Leon County, where the state capital was located.

The economic boom in the early 1970s was accompanied by a high rate of inflation.[38] Inflation reached 5 percent in 1969, an unusually high level during peacetime. In 1971, President Nixon instituted price controls that temporarily suppressed inflation in 1972, but it returned to 6 percent in 1973. The federal government tightened monetary and fiscal policies in 1973; it reduced the federal budget deficit from 2 percent to 1 percent in 1973 and to less than half of one percent in 1974 and increased the treasury bill rate from an average of 5 percent to 7 percent in 1973 and 8 percent in 1974.[39] The result was a recession that began at the end of 1973.

In 1973, Arab exporters imposed an oil embargo in connection with the Yom Kippur War, which added to the recessionary pressures. It became clear that oil exporters as a group could raise prices, at least in the short run, by limiting production. The Organization of Petroleum Exporting Countries (OPEC) instituted production quotas, resulting in a doubling of oil prices in 1974.[40] This price increase acted as a tax on U.S. consumers, adding to the pressures of the recession. The embargo led to oil shortages and distortions in the economy caused by controls the federal government instituted. The U.S. economy went into its most severe recession since the 1930s. Real per capita income fell by 3 percent between the peak year of 1973 and the low year of 1975.

The recession was more severe in Florida than in other parts of the country. Florida's per capita income fell by 7 percent between the 1973 high and the 1975 low. In addition, the state's economy remained depressed for two additional years after the U.S. economy had recovered to its 1973 level in 1976. Florida did not return to its 1973 peak per capita income until 1978.

One reason for the severity of the recession in Florida was a dramatic slowdown in population growth. The annual rate of population growth fell from more than 5 percent in 1973 to less than 2 percent in 1976. The population slowdown may have partly reflected difficulties retirees experienced who were attempting to sell their homes up north when mortgage rates were high. The slowdown in population growth, together with the tight monetary conditions, led to a sharp drop in construction earnings. Nationally, construction earnings

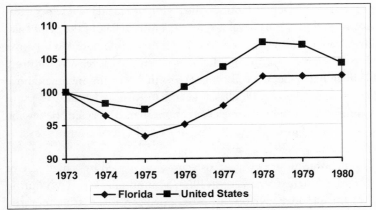

Chart 11-9. Personal Income per Capita in Florida and the United States, 1974–1980, Adjusted for Inflation (Index 1973=100)

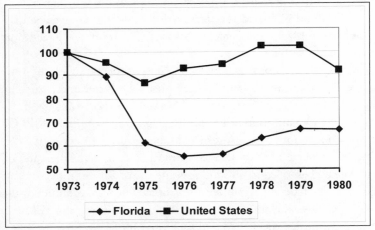

Chart 11-10. Construction Earnings per Capita, Florida and the United States, 1973–1980, Adjusted for Inflation (Index 1973=100)

declined by 12 percent. The decline in Florida was 45 percent. The slowdown in population growth, aggravated by overspeculation in the condominium market, explains the greater decline in the state. The counties that had experienced the greatest increases in condominium construction during the boom, such as Miami-Dade, Broward, Palm Beach, Sarasota, and Pinellas, all experienced greater declines in construction earnings, adjusted for population and inflation, during the 1973–1976 contraction.[41]

The tourist industry was also hit hard by the 1974–1975 recession. We have

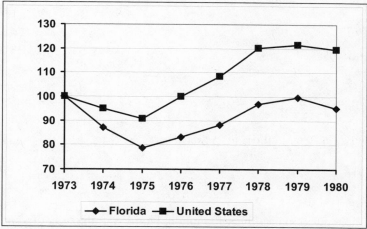

Chart 11–11. Hotel Earnings per Capita, Florida and the United States, 1973–1980, Adjusted for Inflation (Index 1973=100)

seen repeatedly that the state's tourist industry is cyclical—it declines during national recessions and expands during national expansions. The decline during the 1974–1975 national recession was reinforced by an oil shortage and resulting sharp increases in prices for gasoline and jet fuel. The central Florida counties that had experienced a boom in tourism, especially Orange and Osceola counties, also experienced a large decrease in hotel earnings when the state's tourism industry declined. It is possible that too many hotels and lodging places had been built in the central part of the state, as had occurred in condominiums farther south. Hotel earnings at the national level recovered by 1976, and by 1978, national hotel earnings per capita adjusted for inflation were 20 percent above their peak in 1973. The industry in Florida did not recover to the 1973 level until 1979.

Chapter 12

1980

A Northern Population in a Southern Setting

In 1980, with a population just under 10 million, Florida was the seventh most populated state in the nation. The population had almost doubled since 1960. The state had added 2 million people during the 1960s and almost 3 million more in the 1970s. The density of people per square mile in Florida was 180.7, more than twice the density of the continental United States of 76.1.[1] Florida had a higher population density than all the states west of the Mississippi, and it was higher than the other southern states. Its population density was in the range of the densities of the northern states between Chicago and Boston, although it was considerably lower than most of them.

In 1980, half of the state's population had been born in the southern states, including Florida, and half had been born outside the South.[2] More Floridians had been born in northern states than in Florida. As a result of in-migration, Florida had a northern population in a southern setting.

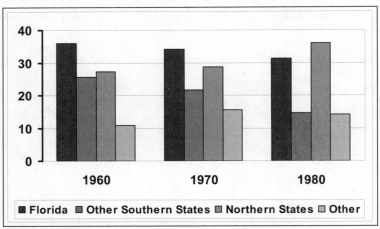

Chart 12–1. Region of Birth of Florida's Residents by Percent of Florida Population

Since the 1950s, a disproportionate number of in-migrating northerners had been retirees, and this had caused the share of the state's population who were aged 65 and over to rise above the national average from that decade. By 1980, about one in six Floridians was in this age group, compared to about one in nine for the nation as a whole.[3] As the population became less southern, the black percentage of the population declined because the northern in-migrants were predominantly white. Indeed, by 1980, the percentage of Florida's population that was black (14 percent) was similar to the black percentage in some of the large northern states (Illinois 15 percent, New York 14 percent, Michigan and New Jersey each 13 percent). The black percentage in Florida, however, was still slightly greater than the national average (14 percent compared to 12 percent).

Blacks in Florida, and elsewhere in the nation, faced discrimination in 1960 that had serious negative impacts on their incomes. The median income of nonwhite households in Florida in 1960 was 50 percent of that of white households.[4] One factor leading to the disparity in income was inequality of educational opportunity. A series of federal court decisions in the late 1960s and early 1970s ruled that the education the state provided for blacks in the state's segregated public K-12 schools was inferior to the education it provided to the white population. Black enrollment rates in education in 1960 were less than the rates for equivalently aged white population.[5] Two percent fewer blacks in the 5–to-13 age group, 5 percent fewer blacks in the 14–to-18 age group, and 4 percent fewer blacks in the 19–to-24 age group were enrolled in the public and private educational systems. At the college level, opportunities for the black population were very limited. Prior to a court decision that took effect in 1962, blacks were unable to enroll in any of the state's universities except for Florida Agricultural and Mechanical University in Tallahassee, where the range of programs available was much smaller than at the University of Florida in Gainesville. In addition, the fact that most public colleges and universities were not open to blacks in Florida's urban areas (where the majority of the black population lived in 1960) made a college education relatively expensive for this less-affluent part of the population

By 1980, participation rates in the educational system had increased for all age groups and for both races. The most dramatic increase had occurred at the postsecondary ages. In addition black participation had substantially increased at the high school ages. Indeed, by 1980, the participation rate of blacks for the high school ages was the same as the rate for whites. The improved educational opportunities for blacks and other factors significantly improved the relative income position of blacks. Black household and family median incomes rose to about 60 percent of the white levels by 1980, an increase from the 50 percent

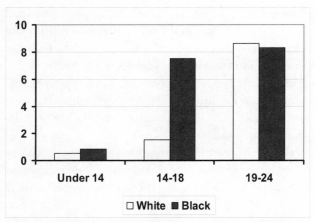

Chart 12–2. Increase in Enrollment in Florida's Public and Private Schools from 1950 to 1980 by Age Group and Race

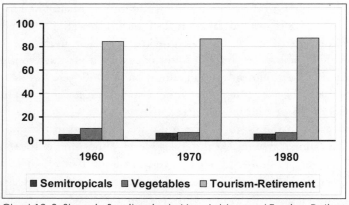

Chart 12–3. Share in Semitropicals, Vegetables, and Tourism-Retirement in Value of Production of Florida's Sunshine Industries, 1960, 1970, and 1980 (by Percent)

level of 1960. Factors such as improved education, however, affect the younger population and it is some time before their full benefits are realized.

The relative importance of the four parts of the state's economic base in 1980 was similar to their relative importance in 1960. The biggest change was a further increase in the importance of the sunshine industries from the 1960 level of 49 percent in 1960 to 58 percent of the total. The sunshine sector was dominated by tourism-retirement in 1980, as it had been in 1960; in 1980, tourism-retirement accounted for more than 50 percent of the state's economic base. The share of the citrus industry in the state's economy had increased slightly, and the share of vegetable production had decreased.

An important development that affected tourism in the 1960–1980 period was the introduction of jet aircraft at the end of the 1950s and the ensuing rise in air travel. In the 1960s, the number of air passengers nationally tripled; the increase in Florida was just slightly lower than that level.[6] During the 1970s, the number of airline passengers in the nation increased another 80 percent. The increase in Florida was much more rapid—more than 150 percent.

Data on the distribution of Florida tourists by travel mode show that the share of airline tourists increased from about 11 to 18 percent during the 1960s, while the share of automobile, rail, and bus tourists decreased.[7] By 1977, the last year before a major change in statistical methodology, the market share of airline tourists had increased to 28 percent.

Surveys of Florida's tourists began to distinguish travelers by mode of travel in 1958, and distinct differences soon became evident. One difference that emerged was that air travelers stayed for shorter periods at their destinations. Between 1960 and 1970, the average length of stay in Florida declined from twenty days to twelve days. In 1970, auto tourists spent about thirteen days in the state and air tourists spent nine. The reduction in travel time (by air) from the northern states to Florida made it possible for more northerners to make a quick visit to Florida. Air tourists traveled in smaller parties than did automobile tourists. This observation, like the observation on length of stay, would hold true for the remainder of the century. It reflected the economies of scale furnished by automobile travel. A higher proportion of air tourists tended to come from the Northeast states, and a higher proportion of automobile tourists tended to come from the Midwest. Air tourists tended to visit the southern half of the peninsula and automobile tourists tended to visit the northern half of the peninsula. The exception was the Walt Disney World area, which was a top-three destination for both groups by 1980. It replaced St. Petersburg as a top three destination for air tourists and it replaced Miami-Dade for automobile tourists.[8]

Although the share of the production of the sunshine sector accounted for by citrus remained relatively stable while the share accounted for by vegetables declined between 1960 and 1980, the actual production of citrus doubled and production of vegetables increased by more than 60 percent. Oranges continued to dominate the Florida citrus industry in 1980, accounting for almost 80 percent of production. Virtually all of the rest was accounted for by grapefruit. Citrus production expanded by more than 50 percent during the 1960s in spite of two freezes, especially the severe freeze in December 1962.[9] As a result of the freeze, the orange crop production was 33.3 percent lower than the production of the previous year and the grapefruit crop was 13.7 percent lower.[10] Because there was extensive damage to trees, production declined again

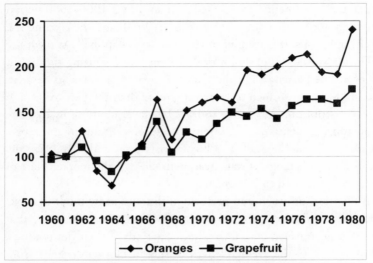

Chart 12–4. Gross Output of Orange and Grapefruit Industries in Florida, 1960–1980, Adjusted for Inflation (Index 1960=100)

in the 1963–1964 year. The freeze was much more severe in north-central than in south-central Florida. It also had a negative impact beyond the year of the freeze itself because it destroyed a large number of trees. In fact, production in 1963–1964 was lower than in 1962–1963. A second freeze in 1967–1968 reduced production by 27 percent from the 1966–1967 record level.[11]

Citrus production expanded by another 50 percent during the 1970s in spite of another freeze in the 1976–1977 crop year. January 1977 was remarkable in the southern half of Florida as the month when snow fell.[12] Orange production had been projected to reach a record 213 million boxes before the cold weather, but actual production was 187 million—a 12 percent decline. There was a similar decline in grapefruit production. Although the number of trees lost was modest because most were dormant at the time of the freeze because of cool weather in November and December, the productivity of the trees was reduced. It remained low until record production was achieved in the 1979–1980 crop year.

The difficulties the Florida industry faced in the last years of the 1970s took place while there was a rapid rise in Brazilian production of citrus products, which was closing in on the U.S. level in 1980.[13] From 1975–1976 to 1979–1980, Brazilian production more than doubled, while U.S. production increased by about 10 percent. Brazil was clearly emerging as a major competitor for the U.S. citrus industry.

Production of Florida vegetables increased by more than 60 percent in real

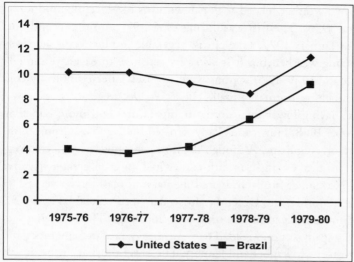

Chart 12–5. Production of Oranges, United States and Brazil, 1975–1976 through 1979–1980, in Millions of Metric Tons

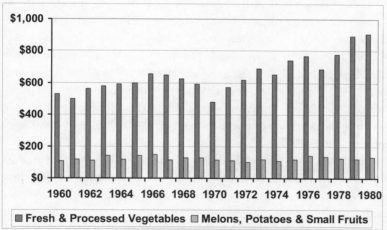

Chart 12–6. Gross Output of Vegetable Crops in Florida 1960-1980 in Millions of 1982–1983 Dollars

terms between 1960 and 1980, although the share of the industry in the production of the sunshine sector declined.[14] Vegetables, as conventionally defined, accounted for the bulk of production, followed by watermelons and potatoes, each of which had production valued at about 7 percent of the grand total. Production of small fruits (strawberries) was a negligible part of the total in this period.

There were two weather-related major downturns in vegetable production in the 1960s and 1970s. The first was during 1968–1970 and the second during the freeze of January 1977. Like citrus, vegetable production is adversely affected by freezing weather, but it is also very sensitive to excessive rainfall. The 1968–1969 and 1969–1970 seasons were adversely affected both by cold temperatures and above-normal rainfall. The 1968–1969 vegetable season was characterized as having lower-than-normal temperatures and more rain than usual.[15] In October 1968, Hurricane Gladys crossed the peninsula from southwest of Ocala to St. Augustine. Although the hurricane adversely affected vegetable production, heavy rains a month earlier had an even greater negative impact. A mid-November frost terminated the harvesting of tender vegetables in north and west Florida, and December frosts damaged vegetables in the Everglades. March rains delayed the planting of spring crops. The following year (1969–1970) was again wet and cold. There was heavy rain in September and October and frosts in November and January. The lower third of the peninsula experienced heavy rains in March. Production of tomatoes, the state's most important vegetable crop, was down by 22 percent from the previous year's level.

The impact of a freeze in early 1977 showed up most significantly in the difference between acreage planted in vegetables, including watermelons, potatoes, and strawberries, and the corresponding acreage that was harvested. Crops damaged from freezes were often abandoned in the fields, causing the acreage harvested to be significantly less than the acreage planted. The harvested acreage in the 1976–1977 crop year amounted to only 84 percent of the total planted, down from 91 percent in the preceding year. Over 89 percent of planted acreage was harvested in each of the years from 1969–1970 to 1979–1980, with the exception of 1976–1977.

During the 1960–1980 period, Florida ranked second in vegetable production nationally.[16] In 1960, California, Florida, and Idaho were the top three states in production of vegetables, melons, and strawberries. Florida was ranked second both in the aggregate of vegetables, potatoes, and strawberries and in vegetables alone. Florida was also ranked second at the end of the period, both in the aggregate and in vegetables alone.

Florida sold virtually all of its vegetables on the fresh market, as did other states capable of production early or very late in the year.[17] Tomatoes dominated the state's vegetable production. This dominance increased from 1960, when it accounted for 30 percent of production, to 1980, when it accounted for 34 percent. Production of sweet corn and peppers also increased substantially during the period, but production of snap beans and celery declined. By 1980, production of snap beans was less than the production of lettuce, which had increased rapidly during the period.

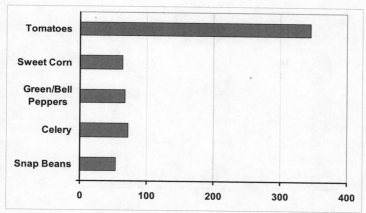

Chart 12–7. Gross Output of Principal Vegetable Crops in Florida in 1980, in Millions of 1982–1983 Dollars

In 1960, Florida ranked first among the states that produced snap beans, sweet corn, cucumbers, eggplant, escarole, peppers, tomatoes, and watermelons for the market. It ranked second in production of cabbage and celery. Two decades later, in 1980, the state retained the same rankings among the states.[18]

The geography of vegetable production changed in the state during these two decades. The acreage in southwest Florida and Palm Beach County increased. In Broward and Miami-Dade counties, acreage in vegetables declined, probably due to urbanization. Acreage also declined in Alachua and Marion counties, but acreage in the surrounding counties increased, particularly to the south. A decline in Seminole County was the result of the loss of the celery industry. Larger farms were needed to produce celery efficiently than were available in Seminole, and this was the reason for the decline of the local industry.[19]

Watermelons accounted for the largest acreage among the state's vegetables. The data show a transfer of production from Alachua and Marion counties and their neighbors in central to southwest Florida, especially De Soto and Hendry counties. As a result, production per acre in this crop more than doubled between 1958–1963 and 1978–1983.[20] Florida's most valuable vegetable crop was tomatoes. During the 1960–1980 period, there was a transfer of acreage in tomatoes from Miami-Dade County and Alachua County to southwest Florida, especially Collier and Lee counties. The statewide yield in tomatoes more than tripled from 1960 to 1980. Palm Beach County substantially increased its production of celery, sweet corn, and radishes. However, there was a reduction in its large bean industry. There was also a reduction in potatoes and cabbages. Yields per acre in these three crops gained little between 1960 and 1980.

Florida's maritime industry constituted the second largest component of

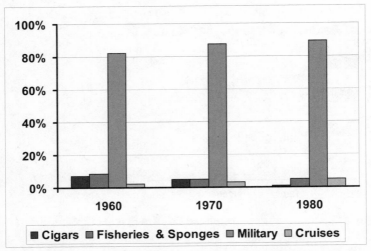

Chart 12–8. Share of Cigars, Fisheries and Sponges, Military Contracts, and Cruises in Value of Production of Florida's Maritime Industries, 1960, 1970, and 1980 (by Percent)

the state's economic base in 1980, the same ranking as in 1960. The sector was dominated by military payrolls, which accounted for just under 90 percent of the total. As it had been in 1960, Florida's maritime sector in 1980 was dominated by expenditures at military bases. Fishing retained a 5 percent share of the sector total, but the share of cigar manufacturing declined to almost zero. The share of earnings from the cruise industry, while accounting for only 5 percent, had doubled since 1960.

Earnings of military personnel in Florida increased substantially between 1960 and 1980, rising by more than 80 percent above the rate of inflation. The increase occurred from 1963 to 1972 as the military budget was expanded during the Vietnam War. Earnings remained flat between 1972 and 1978, and there were small declines in 1979 and 1980.

Earnings data from the U.S. Bureau of Economic Analysis became available for Florida counties for the first time in 1969. Four counties had military earnings of more than $200 million (in 1982–1984 dollars): Duval, Okaloosa, Escambia, and Miami-Dade. Three counties had earnings between $100 million and $200 million: Orange, Hillsborough, and Monroe. Okaloosa, Miami-Dade, and Hillsborough counties all had important air force bases; the other counties listed had naval facilities. There were no major army facilities in the state. By 1980, the military payroll in Miami-Dade and Monroe counties had fallen sharply, but there had been substantial growth in Orange, Brevard, and Bay counties.

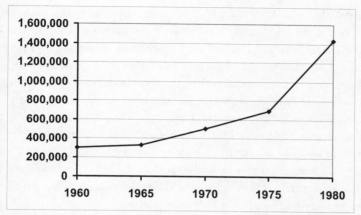

Chart 12–9. Number of North American Cruise Passengers, 1960–1980

The cruise industry, which carried passengers primarily from Miami and Fort Lauderdale to destinations in the Caribbean, became important, especially in the last half of the 1970s. The number of cruise passengers from North American ports increased from 300,000 in 1960 to 1.4 million in 1980.[21] Most of these passengers originated in Miami. The second largest cruise port was Port Everglades in Fort Lauderdale.

Carnival Cruise Lines, the largest cruise company operating out of Florida by the end of the twentieth century, got its start in 1966. At that time, two Israeli-owned car ferries, the Bilu and the Nilu, were operating under charter as cruise ships out of the port of Miami. The business was struggling and an Israeli national, Ted Arison, persuaded the owners to transfer the charter to him.[22] He instituted a successful marketing program, but the Israeli owners went bankrupt as a result of business difficulties in Europe and the mortgage holder required the ships to be returned to Israeli waters. As a result, Arison had cruise passengers and their deposits but no ships. He read of Knut Kloster, a Norwegian who had commissioned a new car ferry, the *Sunward*, to run between Britain and Gibralter. Kloster had failed to obtain permission to land at Gibralter—he had a cruise ship with no passengers, the reverse of Arison's situation. Kloster agreed to reassign the ship to Miami and operate it under the name of Norwegian Caribbean Lines. Arison's organization was responsible for marketing the ship. The joint venture was very successful and three more ships were added between 1968 and 1971. The enlarged capacity caused Arison to extend his marketing campaign beyond the state.

Competitors soon appeared. Among the most important was Ed Stephan, a Miami Beach hotelier, who obtained financing from Norwegian investors and formed Royal Caribbean Cruise Line to undertake Miami cruises. He put three ships in service between 1970 and 1972.[23] Because the ships were designed specifically for cruises, they departed from the design of previous ships, which were modeled on ocean liners, and helped develop the new cruise ship design. Modern cruise ships are built for passenger comfort rather than speed and contain large public spaces. In many respects they are reminiscent of the Victorian grand hotels: their scale is large, they emphasize public rather than private spaces, and they provide entertainment and activities for the passengers (guests) on a daily basis. Stephan added a Viking Crown Lounge that completely encircled the funnel of his *Song of America*, which he launched in 1982.

Stephan's original marketing plan was also unique.[24] He concentrated on two major out-of-state markets, Los Angeles and San Francisco, and reduced costs by chartering wide-bodied aircraft for passengers from those cities to Miami. Stephan's marketing strategy demonstrated the strong connection between jet aircraft and the cruise industry. The introduction of jets facilitated the development of the cruise industry by enabling passengers to travel rapidly to and from the cruise ports in Florida and elsewhere, making it possible to spend a week cruising without using up too many of the relatively limited vacation days available to most American workers.

In 1971, Knut Kloster canceled the marketing contract with Arison, created his own marketing organization, and continued to expand his operations.[25] In 1979, he purchased the transatlantic liner *France*, which had been built in 1961, and refurbished her as the cruise ship *Norway*. The *Norway* was more than twice the size of other cruise ships being introduced around 1980, and it began the trend toward much larger cruise ships that characterized the remainder of the century.

In 1972, Ted Arison found himself in the same position he had been in 1967—he had cruise passengers and a marketing organization but no ship. He turned to Meshulam Riklis, another Israeli, and persuaded him to put up the capital needed to buy the Canadian Pacific Liner *Empress of Canada*.[26] Riklis was the majority shareholder in American International Travel Service, a travel tour operator that operated under the Carnival name. Riklis established a subsidiary Carnival Cruise Lines to own and operate the *Empress of Canada*, which was sailing under the name *Mardi Gras*. After entering service in 1972, the *Mardi Gras* operated at a loss for a year and a half because only the top two decks were available for passengers. The ship sailed with construction workers busy upgrading the two lower decks to make them suitable for cruise-ship passengers. Carnival marketed the *Mardi Gras* as a "fun ship" and began the shift within the cruise industry from destination-driven trips to trips that emphasized the pleasure of the journey itself. The Carnival marketing program broadened the market for cruises and changed its emphasis.

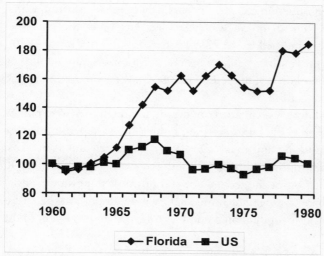

Chart 12–10. Real Earnings per Capita in Water Transportation, Florida and the United States, 1960–1970 (Adjusted for Inflation, Index 1960=100)

The development of the cruise industry expanded the scope of Florida's maritime sector. In the late 1960s, per capita earnings from water transportation (which includes goods as well as passenger transportation) in Florida, adjusted for inflation, increased by 60 percent at a time when national earnings grew by 20 percent. In the first half of the 1970s, earnings remained high in Florida while they declined nationally. The Florida industry shrank temporarily during the 1974–1976 recession, but by the end of the decade, Florida real per capita earnings in water transportation were 80 percent higher than they had been in the mid-1960s.[27] During the same period, the corresponding earnings had stagnated at the national level.

Between 1960 and 1980, the share of fisheries declined from 8 percent to 5 percent of the production of the state's maritime sector. Landings of fish declined during the 1960s, falling about 10 percent from 1960 to 1971, in spite of some growth in the middle of the decade (1965–1967).[28] In the 1970s, production again trended downward in real terms, falling another 10 percent between 1971 and 1979, although there was a sharp uptick in 1980. The unit value per pound of fish increased, rising from 43 cents in 1967 to $1.05 in 1979.[29] (The price fell temporarily in 1980 as supply increased sharply.) Downward production and rising prices indicate a rising cost of production. The rising cost of production in the 1970s was presumably related to the high rate of inflation in the early years of the decade and the sharp increase in fuel prices in 1973–1974.

Most of Florida's production consisted of shellfish, especially shrimp, which accounted for 70 percent of production. Detailed data by county and species, which were first published in the *Florida Statistical Abstract* in the 1970s, showed that the largest landings of shrimp were in Monroe County, followed by Lee County and Franklin County.[30] The Tampa–St. Petersburg area also had significant landings of shrimp.

Florida's frontier industries remained important, although they were ranked third in the size of their contribution to the production of the economic base in 1980, after the sunshine and maritime sectors. Paper remained the most important of Florida's frontier industries in 1980, accounting for more than 40 percent of the production of the sector. The second most important frontier industry was phosphate mining, which was slightly more important than lumber manufacturing. Cattle production accounted for less than 10 percent of the sector.

The paper industry expanded strongly between 1958 and 1977 in response to a big increase in the demand for the industry's products.[31] New uses were found for paper in the 1960s. Consumers greatly increased their use of paper plates, paper towels, and paper garbage bags, and hospitals began to use paper linens and operating-room uniforms that could be disposed of after each use.[32] Florida's industry expanded capacity to meet the growing demand. Although, the state's industry produced a range of paper products, much of the industry's output went into the production of kraft paper. To some extent, the industry replaced the gum naval stores industry that had been so important in the beginning of the century. Sulfate turpentine and tall oil were produced as by-products of the paper pulping process. In fact, the Glidden Paint Company Division in Jacksonville—which used to process turpentine from the gum turpentine

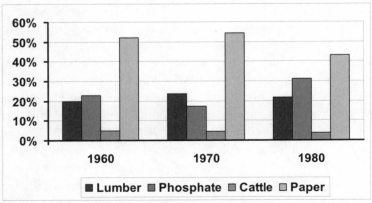

Chart 12–11. Share of Lumber, Phosphate, Cattle, and Paper Products in Value of Production of Florida's Frontier Industries, 1960, 1970, and 1980 (by Percent)

industry, which obtained turpentine by processing resin obtained manually in the pine forests—switched its source of supply to the state's papermills in 1957.

The capital of the paper industry doubled between the census years of 1963 and 1972, and it tripled between 1972 and 1982. This massive increase in capital resulted in a big increase in labor productivity, which doubled between the census years of 1963 and 1977. A decline between 1977 and 1982 was caused by the back-to-back recessions in 1980 and 1981–1982, when the industry retained its labor force although production fell. This phenomenon, which economists call labor hoarding, takes place when an industry decides to retain skilled labor because of the cost of replacing laid-off workers during an economic recovery.

Florida's lumber industry increased production by 50 percent between the census years of 1958 and 1967, but this growth was overshadowed by a boom during the next five years, when output increased by more than 75 percent. The boom in production was caused by an increase in prices of over 60 percent from the recession low in 1970 to 1973. The increase in prices, in turn, was caused by the national housing boom. The inflation-adjusted value of new housing units rose by more than 50 percent between 1967 and 1972. The recession of 1974–1975 was accompanied by a sharp downturn in residential construction. The sector made a partial recovery in 1977 and 1978 before collapsing a second time as a result of the tight monetary policy the federal government instituted in 1979. By 1980, residential construction had returned to its 1960 level.

Florida phosphate production more than tripled from 1960 to 1980.[33] Production doubled between 1960 and 1966 as the worldwide demand for fertilizer increased sharply. The capacity of the industry was expanded as oil companies

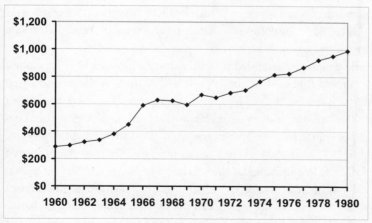

Chart 12–12. Production of Phosphate in Florida, 1960–1980, in Millions of 1980 Dollars (Adjusted for Inflation, Annual Data)

entered the industry.[34] Production fell slightly during the national recession in 1970 but continued to increase during the more severe recession of 1974–1975. The continued growth was partly due to the fact that a new market opened in the Soviet Union after the United States initiated a foreign policy of détente in 1972.

Phosphate prices remained very stable during the 1960s and early 1970s. The "overburden," the land above the phosphate deposits, was very unstable and required strip mining instead of mining by the use of tunnels. The massive electric-powered draglines that were used to strip away the overburden consumed huge amounts of electricity when in operation (as much electricity as a city of 10,000), and the large increase in the price of oil in the mid-1970s led to a sharp increase in phosphate prices.

Growing public concern about environmental issues also impacted the phosphate industry in the 1970s. Phosphate mining polluted the land and had the potential to create water pollution. Fertilizer manufacturing plants, which used phosphate as an input, that were located near the mines created air pollution. The industry faced increasingly tougher environmental regulation during the decade.

Phosphate mining created deep trenches filled with water, and land reclamation was expensive. Rebates on the state's severance tax on phosphate ore and the increase in land values in the early 1970s generated efforts to reclaim land in the state that had potential urban uses, especially mined land. But reclaiming the land was a difficult process. The phosphate mills to which the ore was transported separated the phosphate rock from clay and gravel by immersing it in water. The watery residue was pumped into ponds, and it took years before the liquid evaporated and land reclamation could begin. In the interim, dikes around the ponds had a tendency to break. In December 1971, a breach near Fort Meade poured $1 billion of mud-saturated water into the Peace River. The mud choked the river's oxygen supply, killing plants and wildlife.

Florida cattle production trended upward between 1960 and 1972, peaking at almost 50 percent higher than the 1960 level.[35] This was the period when fast-food restaurant chains, such as McDonald's, greatly expanded their share of the consumer's dollar. Many of these restaurants served hamburgers, and beef consumption per capita rose by 36 percent from 1960 to 1972. Beef production declined in 1973 and 1974 as corn prices increased sharply. A number of factors led to the rise in corn prices. One was bad weather in the United States, which reduced production sharply in 1974.[36] Another was the devaluation of the U.S. dollar in the wake of the collapse of the Bretton Woods fixed exchange rate regime in 1971. The dollar's decline lowered the foreign currency price of U.S. corn exports. Finally, demand also increased because of large purchases by

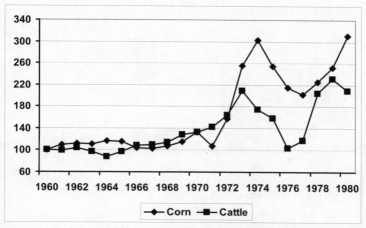

Chart 12–13. Cattle and Corn Prices National Data, 1960-80 (Index 1960=100)

the Soviet Union under an agreement signed by the Nixon administration. The Soviet Union experienced a weather-induced harvest failure in 1972.[36]

Corn was an important feed for cattle in feed lot operations and, although cattle prices rose, they did not rise as much as corn prices. The result was a squeeze on feed-lot operators, who increased their sales of cattle and reduced their purchases. In 1974, cattle prices fell as the corn price continued its upward climb. Florida's grass-fed beef were insulated from the rise in corn prices, but they shared in the cattle price declines as feed-lot demand fell beginning in 1974. Florida cattle production fell in 1974 and slowly trended back upward for the remainder of the decade.

Sugarcane production dominated Florida's southern sector in 1980, account-ing for 88 percent of the estimated value added in the sector. Cotton had be-come virtually insignificant.

Sugarcane production increased significantly during the first half of the 1960s after the U.S. market was closed to Cuban sugar exports as a result of the Castro revolution.[37] Florida's sugar quota was increased and the state's sugarcane production quadrupled from 1960 to 1964. Production increased sharply again in the early 1970s. In the words of a contemporary observer, "Beginning in the 1970s, the energy crisis, inflation, and global commodity shortages struck at the basic foundation of the [sugar] program. The supply management system's assumption of a world surplus of sugar was challenged, as world consumption outstripped production in 4 of the 5 years from 1970 through 1974. The result was a dramatic swelling of sugar prices, which the Sugar Act's provisions were unable to stem."[38] The price of U.S. sugar more than quadrupled from 1972 to 1974. The federal government made changes to the Sugar Act, eliminating

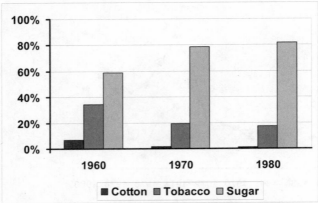

Chart 12–14. Share of Cotton, Tobacco, and Sugar in Value of Production of Florida's Southern Industries, 1960, 1970, and 1980 (by Percent)

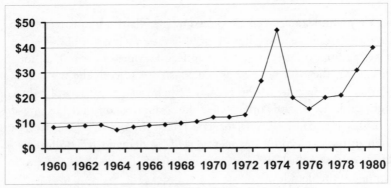

Chart 12–15. Price of Sugarcane, 1960–1980, in Dollars per Ton

domestic quotas and removing import restrictions on refined sugar. Soon after, the problem of surpluses reappeared and a new system of protection was instituted that allowed growers to obtain loans against their crops and forfeit the crop if the price was low.

Tobacco production declined in Florida between 1960 and 1980.[39] This was largely because the state's shade-tobacco industry came to an end in the first half of the 1970s. Consumer demand for cigars had declined, especially large cigars that used the shade-grown wrapper leaf.[40] The decline was also attributable to increases in labor costs as workers left Gadsden County in search of better opportunities elsewhere.

Chapter 13

The 1980s and 1990s

Economic Strength and Slowdown

After the first increase in oil prices in 1973–1974, tight monetary policy and the resulting recession brought the inflation rate down, but only to 6 percent, a high rate by historical standards. As the recession deepened, the Federal Reserve relaxed its tight interest policy, but it resumed that policy as soon as the economy began to recover. The interest rate on treasury bills doubled from the fourth quarter of 1976 to the first quarter of 1979.[1]

Another shock to the economy occurred in 1979. The inflation rate jumped sharply as the price of oil increased in the wake of the Iranian revolution. The price of oil more than doubled in real terms from March 1979 to March 1980, and the national rate of inflation jumped to 11 percent in 1979 and 13 percent in 1980.[2] The Federal Reserve responded by tightening monetary policy again, pushing the interest rate on treasury bills from 10 percent to 14 percent. As a new recession began in 1980, the Federal Reserve relaxed its policy, but as inflation remained unacceptably high, it tightened its money policy once again at the end of 1980. The interest rate on treasury bills reached 16 percent in late 1981. The result was a second national recession in 1982. The tight monetary policy achieved its objective—the rate of inflation declined from 13 percent in 1980 to 3 percent in 1983.

The back-to-back recessions had a severe impact on the national economy. In 1980, national per capita income, adjusted for inflation, dropped by 3 percent and remained lower than its 1979 level until 1983. However, Florida's per capita income grew in 1981 and decreased in 1982 before enjoying a strong recovery in 1983.[3]

Normally, we would expect Florida's economy to dip downward during a national recession because of a decline in tourism. This would be especially true in a recession accompanied by a sharp increase in oil prices, as occurred in 1980–1982. These expectations are confirmed by the data for the period of the

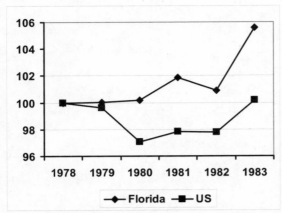

Chart 13–1. Per Capita Personal Income, Florida and the United States, 1978–1983, Adjusted for Inflation (Index 1978=100)

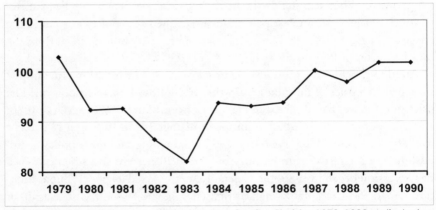

Chart 13–2. Tourism-Retirement Earnings per Capita, Florida, 1979–1990, Adjusted for Inflation (Index 1978=100)

recessions of the early 1980s. Earnings in Florida's tourism-retirement sector declined by about 20 percent from a high in 1979 to a low in 1983.

Other sectors of the economy expanded to counteract the depressing effect of the decline in tourism. One positive factor was a sharp growth in property income, especially in Florida. High interest rates undoubtedly contributed to the strength of this income source. Another positive factor was a high rate of in-migration, a portion of which must have been comprised of retirees. Population growth exceeded 3 percent in 1979–1981, a rate the state had not seen since the boom year of 1974 and would not see for the remainder of the century.

The growth in Florida's property income compensated for a decline in the state's labor earnings during 1980–1982, enabling the state to maintain its total

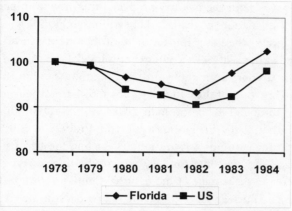

Chart 13–3. Per Capita Labor Earnings in Florida and the
United States, Adjusted for Inflation (Indexes 1978=100)

per capita income. However, the recession in Florida's labor earnings was not as severe in the state as in the nation. The decline in the state was 7 percent between 1978 and 1982; the decline in the nation was 9 percent during that period.

One reason for the smaller decline in labor earnings was the better performance of the state's construction industry. The strong rate of in-migration was a major source of the state's construction growth. In contrast to the national situation, per capita construction earnings in Florida grew in 1979 and remained above the 1978 level until 1982. That year, per capita construction earnings in Florida declined by about 10 percent, which was half the national decline. In 1984, Florida's construction earnings were about 10 percent above the 1978 level; nationally, construction earnings were 10 percent below the 1978 level.

Once the recession period ended in 1982, the remainder of the decade of the 1980s was characterized by a period of unprecedented economic strength in Florida's economy (that is, unprecedented since data on personal income became available for the state in 1929). Florida's per capita income began the decade about 2 percent below the national level, but it reached the national level in 1983. With the exception of a slight decline in 1983, the state remained at or above the national level of personal income per capita for the remainder of the decade. There were only two other occasions when Florida's real per capita income reached the national level during the 1929–2000 period, the boom years of 1972 and 1973. Florida's per capita income matched or exceeded the national level as a result of faster growth in earnings per capita in the state. The strength in the local economy rather than increased property income or personal transfers from elsewhere in the country propelled this growth in per capita income. Part of the explanation for the fact that earnings in Florida were higher than the national level is the lesser impact there of the severe national recessions of the beginning of the 1980s. A second major source of the strength of the state's economy was a boom in manufacturing. Per capita earnings in manufacturing rose from 41 percent of the national value in 1978 to 49 percent in 1985, where it remained through 1987 before falling back in 1988–1990. This was the highest share of the national value Florida achieved from 1929 to 2000. The strength in manufacturing earnings was in durables, such as lumber; furniture; stone, clay, and glass; and machinery and equipment. Florida's earnings in durables manufacturing as a percentage of the national figure rose from 41 percent in 1980 to a peak of 51 percent in 1987 before falling back at the end of the decade.

Durables manufacturing was strong across all the industries, but especially in machinery and equipment. Per capita earnings in machinery and equipment, including industrial equipment, electric and electronic equipment, transportation equipment, and instruments, rose from 44 percent of the national figure to a peak of 54 percent in 1987. Other durables, including lumber; furniture; stone, clay, and glass; and metal industries products, rose from 37 percent of the national figure to a peak of 45 percent.

A sharp increase in the national defense budget partly explains the growth of Florida's manufacturing in the 1980s. Government outlays for national defense, adjusted for inflation, grew by more than 50 percent from 1980 to 1989.[4] In addition to increased spending on personnel, the military also increased its purchases of equipment, much of which is sold by manufacturing companies. The value of defense contracts whose prime contractor was in Florida doubled

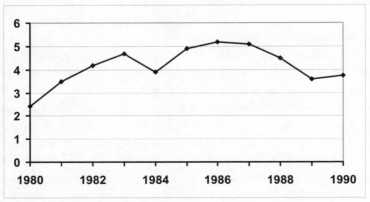

Chart 13–4. Value of Defense Contracts in Florida, 1980–1990, in Billions of 1982–1984 Dollars (Selected Years)

in real terms from 1980 to 1985.[5] It remained at about $5 billion (in 1982–1984 dollars) before declining at the end of the decade.

During the 1980s, manufacturing employment grew by 15 percent in Florida. During the same decade, manufacturing employment nationally remained stable in the southern states and fell by about 12 percent in the northern states.[6] The decline in the northern states overwhelmed a small increase in the western states during the 1980s, leading to a decline in manufacturing nationally. Although manufacturing employment fell nationally, output actually increased.[7] National labor productivity in manufacturing grew strongly during the 1980s, rising by 70 percent during the decade. This occurred because labor productivity rose, which enabled the national economy to produce more output with fewer workers. The increase in Florida was similar, although most of Florida's increase occurred in the first half of the decade.

In spite of rapid growth in the state, the level of earnings per worker remained lower in Florida, however. Although this is partly explained by a lower skill level in the work force, it is also explained by the relative weakness of unions in the southern states, where union shops were less prevalent. In addition, workers in southern states were willing to accept lower wages because the climate was more desirable or, perhaps, because living costs were cheaper.[8]

Earnings in high-technology manufacturing, defined to include industrial machinery, electric and electronic equipment, and transportation equipment other than motor vehicles, were largely found in the large urban centers of the state, especially Palm Beach, Broward, Miami-Dade, Hillsborough, and Orange counties. There was also a large industry in Brevard County, the location of the Kennedy Space Center.

A particularly noteworthy example of new high-tech manufacturing in Florida is IBM's entry in the 1980s to Palm Beach County. In 1980, IBM, the leading computer company in the world at the time, recognized the need to enter the new personal computer market, and it established a new division in Boca Raton to bring an IBM personal computer to market in one year.[9] The short time frame meant that the machine would have to be built with existing technology.[10] A computer chip from Intel Corporation was selected as well as an operating system from Microsoft. The specifications of the system were made available to other companies, which quickly developed peripheral hardware and software applications for the new machine. The openness of the system's architecture, however, encouraged the development of clones, equivalent machines called IBM compatibles, that eventually pushed IBM out of the production of personal computers altogether. In the 1980s, however, IBM's presence in Florida was part of the state's economic growth; manufacturing and design of its personal computer employed 10,000 at the Boca Raton facility.

Palm Beach County hosted a number of other large high-technology establishments in the 1980s, including branches of Pratt & Whitney and Motorola
Corporation. Siemens Corporation, the large German industrial conglomerate,
also located a large facility in the county.

Not all sectors of the state economy were as strong as manufacturing in
the 1980s. We have seen that tourism-retirement, as measured by the excess of
state earnings in transportation, trade, and services over the national share, was
particularly hard hit by the recessions at the beginning of the decade. By 1990,
per capita earnings in this sector were only 2 percent above their 1978 level.
Agriculture also had difficulties in the 1980s. Nationally, per capita farm earnings fell by 40 percent from 1978 to 1980. After a further decline in 1983, national farm earnings recovered by 1988. In Florida, weakness in farm earnings
stemmed from seven freezes from 1981 to 1990—only the 1983–1984 harvest
year escaped a freeze.

The freezes of the 1980s drastically reduced Florida's orange production.[11]
At the end of the 1970s, Florida was producing more than 200 million boxes
of oranges. By 1981–1982 production had fallen to 126 million boxes, and,
with one exception, it remained below 150 million boxes during the remaining
years of the decade. The state's citrus production did not return to the level of
200 million boxes until 1994–1995. The 1980s freezes caused a disruption in
production that lasted about as long as the impact of the catastrophic freezes
of 1894–1895. Because the freezes were spread out over a nine-year period,
production could continue at a low level and the industry avoided the total
destruction of the late 1890s, but the freezes set back the industry and had far-
reaching consequences.

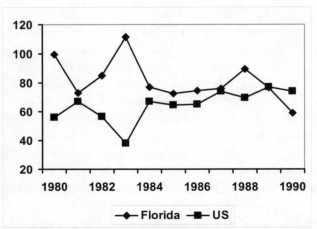

Chart 13–5. Farm Earnings per Capita, Florida and the United States,
1980–1990, Adjusted for Inflation (Index 1978=100)

The freezes cost Florida orange growers about $1.5 billion (in 1980 dollars) in the value of oranges on the tree during the decade.[12] The largest losses were in 1981–1982 and 1985–1986, when the loss exceeded 33 percent of the value of the crop (in 1980 dollars). There were also large losses in 1989–1990 and 1986–1987, when the losses exceeded 20 percent. In addition to annual production losses, the state's acreage in citrus-bearing trees fell from about 775,000 in 1980 to about 535,000 in 1990, a decline of about 30 percent.[13] This loss of capital exceeded $2 billion (in 1980 dollars).

Before the freezes of the 1980s, Florida's largest orange-producing region was a northern tier of counties running west from Orange County and a southern tier consisting of Polk County and its neighbors to the west and south. Martin and St. Lucie counties on the east coast were another center of orange production. Indian River County to the immediate north was a large producer of grapefruit. As a result of the freezes, the northern tier of counties stretching westward from Orange County stopped producing major crops of oranges. Orange production shifted to the south, as it had after the catastrophic freezes in 1894–1995. The three counties immediately south of Polk—Hardee, Highlands, and De Soto—each produced more than 1 billion pounds of oranges, as did Hendry County.

By 1979–1980, Florida supplied a large market for frozen concentrated orange juice in the United States. However, during the 1980s, the shortfall in Florida orange production created a shortage of orange juice concentrate that was made up by imports. Orange juice imports jumped from under $200 million in 1980–1981 to almost $500 million in 1988–1989. The freeze in the final year of the decade caused the value of imports to reach $650 million.[14] In addition, domestic producers in the United States and Florida were unable to retain export markets during the decade. In 1985–1986, exports of frozen

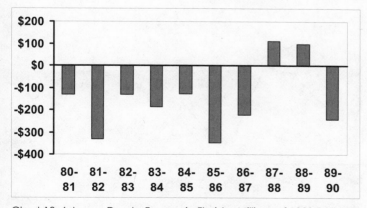

Chart 13–6. Losses Due to Freezes in Florida, Millions of 1980 Dollars

concentrated orange juice were about half their 1980–1981 level, the year before the freezes began.

Brazil was the major beneficiary of Florida's difficulties. In 1981–1982, Brazil's production of oranges exceeded U.S. production for the first time, and the gap widened as the 1980s progressed. Even after Florida's industry returned to its previous production levels in the mid-1990s, Brazilian production remained substantially larger. The United States and Florida were pushed into a permanent position in second place as a result of the freezes of the 1980s.

Florida's phosphate industry also had a difficult time in the 1980s. Phosphate production fell by 30 percent in 1982 and remained low in 1983 in reaction to the national recession that had affected agriculture.[15] A reduction in crop prices and high costs due to gasoline prices and interest rates squeezed farmers nationwide and reduced the demand for phosphate fertilizer. The value of the U.S. dollar rose sharply in the first half of the 1980s, and the resulting decline in demand for exports led to a second sharp drop in demand for phosphate in 1986 and 1987. This downturn was exacerbated by a downturn in farm crop prices. The downturns in the phosphate industry led to a substantial decline in employment of about 33 percent during the 1980s.

In the 1980s, Florida's state government increased its main source of tax revenue, the general sales tax, by raising the rate to 5 percent in 1982 and 6 percent in 1987. These increases were a result of the failure of state tax revenues to grow as quickly as the population and the rate of inflation. Prior to the national recession of 1974–1975, state taxes per capita exceeded $700, measured in 1982–1984 dollars.[16] By 1982, the figure had trended downward to less than $600. During this same time period, population growth increased the demand for government services and rising inflation raised the cost of providing such services. Once the sales tax rate was increased in 1982, the

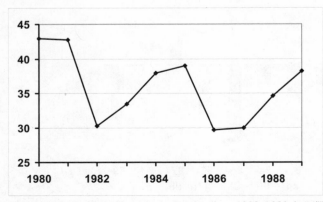

Chart 13–7. Florida's Phosphate Production, 1980–1988, in Millions of Metric Tons

trend began to reverse and inflation-adjusted sales tax revenues per capita began to rise.

One of the problems with the state's tax base was that some taxes did not tend to rise with the general level of inflation. One of these was the tax on gasoline, which was levied based on the number of gallons purchased rather than the value of those gallons. This tax, which was levied to pay for road construction and maintenance, did not rise with inflation, although the cost of constructing new roads did. In 1983, the tax on gasoline was changed to a sales tax instead of a levy based on the number of gallons.[17]

However, although inflation-adjusted per capita state taxes increased in the 1980s, they were still below the 1973 level in 1987.[18] Revenues had risen almost enough to cover the increase in population and prices, but they had not expanded with the growth of the real economy. Put more simply, state taxes were 6 percent of personal income in 1973 and they were 5 percent of personal income in 1987—they were a declining share of the state's economy.

One problem with Florida's general sales tax was that it applied to goods more than to services. Sales in retail stores were subject to the tax with the exception of food at the grocery store and pharmaceuticals. These items were exempted in order to reduce the regressivity of the tax—that is, the tendency of the tax to fall more heavily on lower-income groups. However, goods were a declining proportion of consumer spending; in the period 1970 to 1990, national consumer spending on goods declined from 55 percent to 45 percent. Hence in Florida there was a push to broaden the base of the sales tax.

In 1987, the new governor, Bob Martinez, pushed broadening of the general sales tax through the legislature to cover many services that had previously been exempted, such as professional fees and advertising.[19] After protests from the public, the governor agreed to repeal the broader tax and the legislature increased the sales tax rate to 6 percent. The increase in the rate ensured that

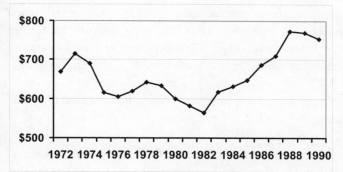

Chart 13–8. State Taxes per Capita, Florida and the United States, 1989–1997, in 1982–1984 Dollars

inflation adjusted sales tax revenues per capita ended the 1980s at a higher level than their previous peak in 1973.

If the sales tax had been broadened to include professional fees, it would have introduced an element of a personal income tax into Florida's tax system since the tax base would have been composed of the incomes of the professionals subject to the tax. The tax would have fallen on the earnings of one group of professionals and it would have excluded the earnings of professionals paid by salary. There was an element of unfairness in this strategy that suggested that a personal income tax might have achieved the objective of broadening the tax base in a more equitable fashion.

During the 1980s there were calls to introduce a personal income tax in Florida, one of the few states that did not have one.[20] The tax was prohibited by a constitutional amendment passed in 1924, and polls since then have consistently suggested that any proposal to reinstate the tax continues to lack public support. However, in the 1990s state tax revenues grew as a share of the state economy because the growth industry of tourism has added to the state's tax base. Out-of-state consumers add dollars to the base of the sales tax by spending on food, drink, and shopping and the base includes some services such as lodging and many personal services that attract the tourist dollar. Additionally, the low rate of inflation in the 1990s may have reduced the demand for increased state revenues and reduced the need for tax reform in the state.

The 1990s opened with a national recession largely brought about by the tight monetary policy the Federal Reserve pursued in the late 1980s. Inflation fell below 2 percent in 1986, in part because of a collapse of oil prices—the reverse of the sharp increases that had occurred in 1974 and 1979. Between October 1985 and October 1986, prices of oil imports fell from $25.74 to $11.98 per barrel, a decline of more than 50 percent.[21] As oil prices trended back upward, the rate of inflation increased—doubling from 2 percent in 1986 to 4 percent in 1987.

The Federal Reserve became concerned about rising inflation and tightened its monetary policy. The one-year interest rate for treasury bills increased from 5.99 percent in the third quarter of 1986 to 7.13 percent in the third quarter of 1987.[22] In the fourth quarter, however, there was a big decline in the stock market and the Federal Reserve temporarily abandoned its tightening to prevent a financial crisis. Once the crisis had passed, the Federal Reserve returned to its tight monetary policy, and the interest rate for treasury bills peaked at over 9 percent in the first quarter of 1989.

The national economy went into recession in July 1990 and began its recovery in March 1991. Florida's economy went down with the national economy. Nationally, the decline in per capita income, adjusted for inflation, was about

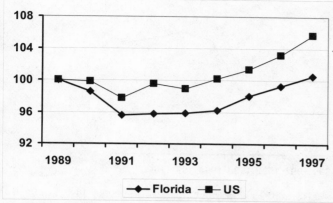

Chart 13–9. Personal Income per Capita, Florida and the United States, 1989–1999, Adjusted for Inflation Index 1989=100)

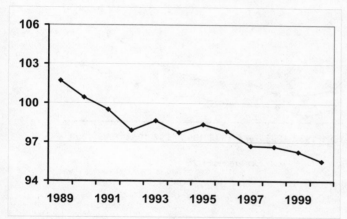

Chart 13–10. Florida per Capita Income as a Percent of National per Capita Income, 1988–2000 (Annual Data)

2 percent. The Florida decline was more severe at almost 5 percent. Although the nation recovered in 1992, Florida remained below its 1989 level until 1996. Earnings in Florida, per capita and adjusted for inflation, followed a similar pattern during the recession as did personal income as a whole. The decline was more severe in the state, where recovery took longer than in the nation.

The severity of the recession created fiscal problems for the state. Between 1990 and 1992, revenues from the general sales tax, per capita and adjusted for inflation, declined by 10 percent.[23] The decline forced cutbacks in state spending because the state constitution required the state budget to be balanced.

Having reached the national level of per capita income in the last half of the 1980s, the 1990s proved a disappointment as Florida's per capita income fell

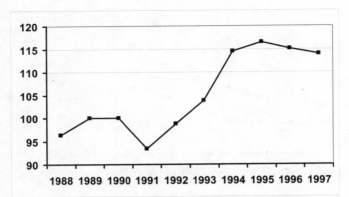

Chart 13–11. Tourism-Retirement Earnings per Capita, Florida, 1988–1997, Adjusted for Inflation (Index 1989=100)

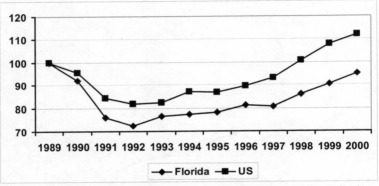

Chart 13–12. Construction Earnings per Capita, Florida and the United States, 1989–2000, Adjusted for Inflation (Index 1989=100)

back below the national level. This was a decade when the growth of Florida's economy slowed down. The biggest decline took place at the beginning of the decade, but another decline occurred in the last half of the decade.

Tourism has historically been the primary transmitter of national economic recessions to Florida, and the 1990–1991 recession was no exception. Earnings in the state's tourism-retirement sector declined by 7 percent in 1991 but it had returned to its prerecession level by 1993. The lingering weakness of the state economy after the national recession ended was not due to a weakness in tourism.

Florida's construction sector experienced a sharp decline with the onset of the national recession, and it continued to be depressed for the rest of the decade. Earnings in construction declined more sharply than earnings in general, both nationally and in the state. The biggest decline in construction earnings took place in 1992, one year after the general national recovery had begun. Nationally, construction earnings returned to their pre-recession level by 1998, but in Florida, they were still below the pre-recession level at the end of the decade.

Construction earnings in Florida have historically been linked to the state's population growth—faster population growth has been accompanied by faster construction earnings and vice versa. Population growth in Florida was slower in the 1990s than in any other decade since 1930.[24] The growth rate fell from 3 percent in 1990 to 2 percent in 1992, and it ended the decade below 2 percent.

In the last half of the twentieth century, Florida's population growth was dominated by the net in-migration of retirees. For example, in the 1950s and 1970s, Florida had exceptionally rapid population growth as large waves of retirees moved to the state, while in the 1960s a slowdown in retiree in-migration was accompanied by a relatively slow rate of population growth.[25] A similar situation occurred in the 1990s—Florida's population aged 65 and older grew by 20 percent in this decade, about half the rate of growth during the 1980s and substantially slower than the 70 percent growth in the 1970s.

The slow growth of Florida's 65+ age group in the 1990s was caused by a slowdown of the growth of the corresponding national population. In the 1970s, the national population aged 65 and older grew by more than 30 percent; in the 1980s, the national population aged 65 years and over grew by more than 20 percent; but in the 1990s it grew by just over 10 percent. Indeed, the 1990s was the only decade in the twentieth century when the age group under 65 years grew more rapidly than the 65+ age group.

The relatively slow growth of the 65+ population in the 1990s is attributable to low birth rates in the United States in the 1930s. The U.S. birth rate declined from over 21 births per 1,000 population in 1930 to fewer than 19 per 1,000 population by 1933, a rate at which it remained for the rest of the decade.[26]

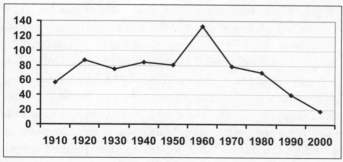

Chart 13–13. Percent Growth in Florida's Population, Ages 65 Years and Older by Decade, 1910–2000

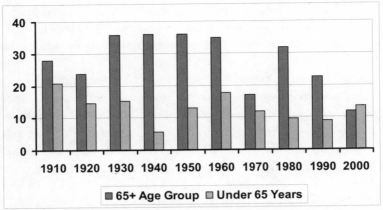

Chart 13–14. Percent Growth in Population per Decade by Age Group, United States, 1910–2000

The reduced birth rate of this generation decreased the national pool of retirees sixty years later. Added to the slowing in the growth of the number of new retirees is evidence that Florida was losing its attractiveness for this group. The state's share of the national population aged 65 and older nearly leveled off in the 1990s at 8 percent of the national total after rising consistently since 1950. Reasons for this probably included the willingness of an increasing number of active retirees to remain in the cold northern winters and the cost-of-living advantages of nearby states such as Alabama and Georgia, which had lower land costs than the southern half of the Florida peninsula. Although at first glance the decline in "market share" among retirees might be regarded as threatening to the Florida economy, the enormous size of the Baby Boom generation will more than compensate for the reduced share in the first two decades of the twenty-first century.

In the 1990s, a growing rate of international migration to the state partly mitigated the decline in population growth due to the smaller number of retirees who moved to the state.[27] In 1960, about 5 percent of the state's population was foreign born, both in Florida and the United States. The share of the foreign born in Florida grew in the 1960s as a result of the influx of Cuban refugees, although the foreign-born population remained a stable share of the national total. Strong growth continued in Florida's share of the national foreign-born population for the remainder of the century, although not until the 1980s did the foreign-born population increase its share of the national total significantly. In the 1990s, the share of foreign-born residents jumped in both Florida and the nation; by 2000, the foreign born accounted for one-sixth of Florida's population and one-ninth of the national total. This large immigrant

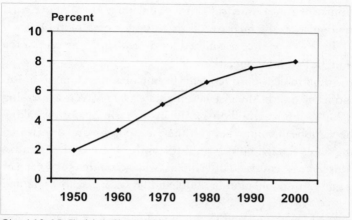

Chart 13–15. Florida's Share of U.S. Population, Ages 65 Years and Older by Decade, 1950–2000 (by Percent)

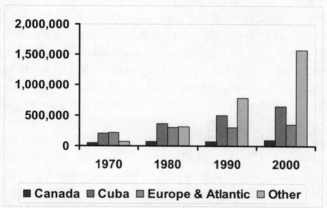

■ Canada ■ Cuba ■ Europe & Atlantic □ Other

Chart 13–16. Number of Foreign-Born Residents of Florida by Place of Origin by Decade, 1970–2000

population internationalized the state and positioned it to serve as a gateway to South and Central America for American and European companies and a gateway for companies from that area to the United States.

In 1970, three parts of the world accounted for close to 90 percent of the total foreign-born population in Florida: Europe (41 percent), Cuba (38 percent), and Canada (8 percent). This percentage declined in each of the following three decades. By 2000, Europe, Cuba, and Canada accounted for just over 40 percent of the state's total foreign-born population. In the last three decades of the century, the fastest growth in Florida occurred in the South American–born population, which increased its share from 6 percent in 1980 to 15 percent in 2000. Colombia, with 6 percent of the state's foreign born, was the largest source of South American–born population. The state's Central American–born population also increased its share, from 3 percent in 1980 to 9 percent in 2000. By 2000, Mexico accounted for more than 75 percent of the state's Central American–born population.

The large growth in foreign-born residents from Cuba, the Dominican Republic, and Central and South America gave the state a large Spanish-speaking population. In 2000, almost 1 million Floridians lived in Spanish-speaking households. The Caribbean countries (with the exception of Cuba) increased their share of the state's foreign born from 7 percent in 1980 to 17 percent in 2000. Most of this increase consisted of Haitians, who accounted for 7 percent of the state's foreign-born population in 2000, and Jamaicans, who accounted for 5 percent.

The large foreign-born population in the state illustrated its role as an immigration gateway as well as its attractiveness to immigrants who may have entered the United States at other locations. At the end of the twentieth century, California attracted the largest number of legal immigrants (more than 200,000 in 2000), followed by New York and Florida (each of which received about 100,000 in 2000). No other state attracted more than 70,000. The fourth most popular state was Texas, with 63,000. In 2000, the largest foreign-born populations lived in the large urban counties, namely, Miami-Dade with more than 1.1 million, Broward with more than 400,000, and Hillsborough, Orange, and Palm Beach, each with more than 100,000. Together these counties accounted for slightly less than 2 million of Florida's foreign-born population—75 percent of the total.

Relative to the size of the resident population, Miami-Dade and Broward counties had more than 200 foreign born per 1,000 residents in 2000. Indeed a majority of Miami-Dade's population was foreign born, the only one of the more than 4,000 counties in the United States for which this was true.[28] A third county, Hendry, an agricultural area, also had more than 200 foreign born per 1,000 residents. The counties with the largest number of foreign born per 1,000 residents were all in the southern half of the peninsula. They included the large urban areas of Palm Beach, Hillsborough, and Orange counties and other counties with large agricultural industries, including Okeechobee, St. Lucie, Hardee, De Soto, and Collier.

Cuba was the largest source of the foreign-born population in Miami-Dade County, as it was for the state as a whole. Cuba was also the largest source of foreign born in Monroe County and Hillsborough County.[29] Mexico, the second largest source, was the largest source of the foreign-born population in thirty of the state's sixty-seven counties; this is attributable to the tendency

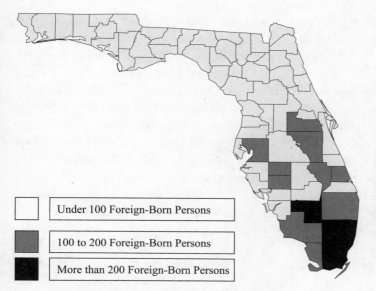

Florida Map 13–1. Foreign-Born Population by County per 1,000 Residents, Florida, 2000

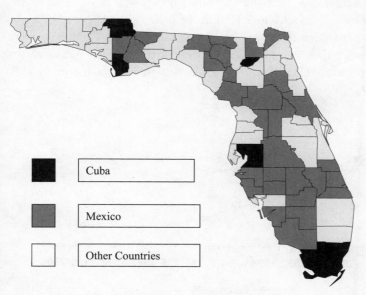

Florida Map 13–2. Largest Source of Foreign-Born Residents in Florida by County, 2000

for the Mexican-born population to work in agriculture. Among the other countries that contributed population to the state were Jamaica, which was the largest source of the foreign-born population in Broward County; Haiti, the largest source in Palm Beach and Orange counties; Canada, the largest source in Pinellas County; and the Philippines, the largest source in Duval County.

Although most of the story of Florida's economy in the 1990s is about a reduction in the rate of population growth, other parts of the economy also experienced adverse shocks. Chief among these was the manufacturing sector that had grown so spectacularly in the previous decade. Much of the gain in the 1980s was lost in the 1990s. While manufacturing earnings in both the nation and the state fell during the 1990–1991 recession, their paths diverged during the rest of the decade. The U.S. manufacturing sector bumped along at the level it had reached at the bottom of the recession, while Florida's sector kept declining until the middle of the decade, when it stabilized at a new low level.

The decline in manufacturing was not concentrated in one or two industries—it was spread across most of the sector and included both durables and nondurables. Earnings in durables declined more rapidly than earnings in nondurables at the beginning of the decade, but both sectors ended the decade at 20 percent below their 1989 levels.

One factor that led to a decline in manufacturing, both in the state and in the nation, was increased international competition. The U.S. trade balance in manufactures turned negative in 1982 and the deficit grew larger until about 1988, at least in part due to a very high dollar exchange rate. Companies were forced to improve their competitiveness, and the trade deficit decreased between 1988 and 1992. Thereafter, the trade deficit grew larger and many U.S.

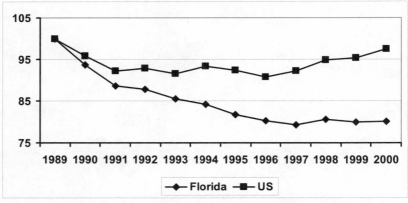

Chart 13–17. Manufacturing Earnings per Capita, Florida and the United States, 1989–2000, Adjusted for Inflation (Index 1989=100)

companies continually restructured under the pressure of international competition. Some of Florida's largest manufacturing facilities closed, including IBM in Boca Raton and Pratt & Whitney in West Palm Beach.

A second negative factor for manufacturing was the decline in the military budget after the breakup of the Soviet Union at the beginning of the 1990s. National defense outlays, adjusted for inflation, fell by 33 percent between 1990 and the low point of 1998. The value of defense contracts awarded to prime contractors located in Florida actually began falling at the end of the 1980s. They fell by about 30 percent between 1987 and 1989 and they stabilized at the new low level for the rest of the decade.

Chapter 14

2000

A Tourism-Retirement Economy

By 2000, Florida was a major economy: it had the fourth largest gross state product in the country, behind California, New York, and Texas. If Florida was a separate country, it would have had the thirteenth largest economy in the world. Sixteen million Floridians had a larger level of national production than 1 billion Indians.[1]

In 2000, Florida had the fourth largest population in the country after California, Texas, and New York, and it was growing at a much faster rate than New York. Florida's population density resembled the densities in the northeast states rather than the other states in the South; it was more than three times the national average.[2] It ranked eighth among the fifty states, higher than Ohio and Pennsylvania, the states that rounded out the top ten.

Florida continued to have a different age pattern than the nation, with relatively fewer young people and relatively more senior citizens. In both Florida and nation, a little over 50 percent of the population was aged between 25 and 64. However, the percentage of the population aged 65 and over was about 5 percent higher in Florida than in the nation, and the percentage aged under 25 was lower by a similar percentage. The state's age structure had clearly been influenced by the in-migration of retirees in the previous decades of the century.[3]

The percentage of the population aged 65 years and over exceeded the national percentage by 15 percent or more in nine Florida counties in 2000. These included Citrus, Hernando, and Sumter counties north of Tampa; Sarasota and Charlotte counties south of Tampa; Highlands County northeast of Charlotte; and three east coast counties, Flagler, Indian River, and Martin.

The greater number of retirees in the state led to a lower labor force participation rate—that is, a lower percentage of the population aged 16 and over who were in the labor force. However, the Florida labor force participation rate was only 2 percent below the national rate. This fact plus the fact that the state's

65+ population is 5 percentage points higher than the national rate suggests that more of Florida's residents in this age group participate in the labor force than the same age group does in the nation.[4]

The composition of personal income is another evidence of the influence of the relatively large retired population in the state.[5] In 2000, labor earnings accounted for a much smaller proportion of personal income in Florida (66 percent) than in the nation (77 percent). Dividends, interest, rental income, and net personal transfers were much more important in the state.[6] Dividends, interest, and rental income are evidence of the relatively large retired population because they represent earnings on savings accumulated to provide retirement income.

The largest personal transfers were receipts under old age and survivor's insurance; that is, receipts from the Social Security program. These transfers amounted to 44 percent of the total in Florida and 39 percent nationally. The second largest item in Florida was receipts under the Medicare program, another program that benefits the retired population. Together, Social Security and Medicare accounted for about 70 percent of the state's personal transfer receipts, compared to 60 percent nationally.

The relatively large number of senior citizens in the population may also have influenced the composition of government expenditures. Florida's state and local governments devoted a smaller share of their budgets to education than did state and local governments across the nation as a whole. In 2000, Florida's governments expended 45 percent of their public service budgets on education compared to the national share of 49 percent.[7] Since Florida has relatively fewer people in the lower age groups, a lower share of education in

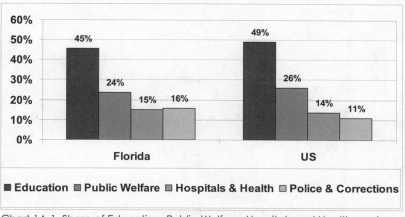

Chart 14–1. Share of Education, Public Welfare, Hospitals and Health, and Police and Corrections in Florida's Budget by Percent (Average of the 1997 and 2002 State Censuses)

the public service budget is to be expected. But it is instructive to see which category of expenditures had a higher share in Florida than in the United States. Spending for police protection and corrections (prisons) accounted for 16 percent in the state, compared to 11 percent in the United States.

The relatively short planning horizon of senior citizens would tilt their preferences in favor of public expenditures that yield immediate benefits and away from expenditures where the benefits are delayed. The state's senior citizens might be expected to be more supportive of police protection and less supportive of public education than their national counterparts, in part because many senior citizens may see themselves as benefiting more directly from police protection than from education, especially if their grandchildren live outside the state. Additionally expenditures on police and corrections yield immediate benefits by deterring crime and removing offenders from the population at large. In contrast, the benefits of educational expenditures are delayed to the future, when schoolchildren reach adulthood. Furthermore the short planning horizon of senior citizens makes them more likely to favor public projects that are paid for over an extended period of time, especially if benefits are realized relatively quickly. Expenditures to acquire parks and beaches, for example, have these characterisitics.

We saw in the last chapter that per capita personal income in Florida was less than the national level in 2000. The state's figure of $28,500 was almost 95 percent of the national figure of $30,000. One result of the lower per capita income was a lower level of state and local government taxes and charges, such

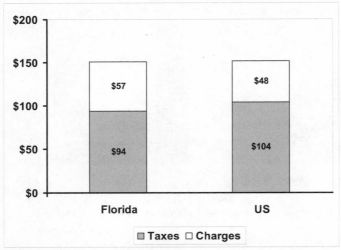

Chart 14–2. State and Local Taxes and Charges in Florida per $1,000 of Personal Income, 2002

as user fees, per capita in Florida compared to the aggregate of the other states in the nation.[8] Taxes and charges were 4 percent higher nationally than in the state. On the other hand, taxes and charges relative to personal income were the same in the state as in the nation. Florida's low per capita taxes were in line with the state's lower per capita income.

The 1997 and 2002 *Census of Governments* showed that Florida relied more on charges and less on taxes than other states did. Florida also continued to collect more in taxes and charges at the local level than at the state level. Florida's local governments collected a larger share of their budgets in charges and a smaller share in the form of taxes than was true at the state level or in other states.

In twelve of Florida's sixty-seven counties, per capita personal incomes exceeded the national level. These included Nassau and St Johns in the northeast; Seminole in the east central peninsula; Indian River, Martin, Palm Beach, Broward, and Monroe counties in the southeast; Collier, Sarasota, and Manatee in the southwest; and Pinellas in the west-central part of the peninsula.

Per capita incomes were lower in the counties that contain the central cities of major metropolitan areas than they were in the nearby suburban counties. For example, Miami-Dade County had a lower per capita income than Broward and Palm Beach counties to the north. Similarly, per capita income was lower in Hillsborough County than in Manatee County to the south or Pinellas County to the west. Seminole County had a higher per capita income than Orange County, and Duval County had a lower per capita income than Nassau County to the north or St. Johns County to the south.

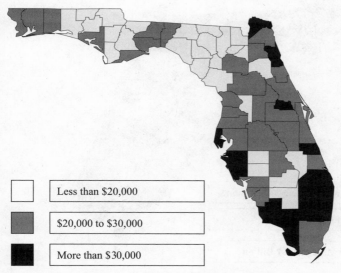

Florida Map 14–1. Per Capita Income in Florida by County, 2000

Per capita income is usually reported on a place of residence basis. As a result, suburban counties on the outskirts of large metropolitan counties often have relatively high per capita income, especially when higher wage workers in the metropolitan counties choose to live in the suburban counties. Government statisticians apply an adjustment for "net commuter income" that has the effect of reducing income in the metropolitan counties and increasing it in the adjacent suburban counties. Six counties in the state had a positive adjustment of more than $1 billion because of net commuter income. These included Broward County north of Miami, Seminole County north of Orlando, Clay and St. Johns counties south of Jacksonville, Pasco County north of Tampa, and Santa Rosa County east of Pensacola. Four counties had a negative adjustment of more than $3.6 billion—Miami-Dade, Hillsborough (Tampa), Orange (Orlando), and Duval (Jacksonville). Some smaller northern counties also had negative commuter income, including Escambia (Pensacola), Okaloosa (Destin), Bay (Panama City), Leon (Tallahassee), and Alachua (Gainesville).

Property income (dividends, interest, and rent) was relatively high in most of the counties that had a high concentration of people aged 65 years and over. This was especially true of Indian River and Martin Counties on the east coast and Sarasota on the west coast. Earnings per employee were highest in the state's major metropolitan counties. These included Miami-Dade, Broward, Palm Beach, Hillsborough, Pinellas, Orange, and Duval. Earnings per worker were also high in Brevard County, a traditional manufacturing center; Leon

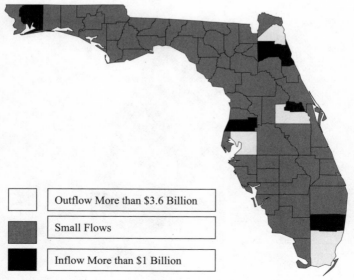

Outflow More than $3.6 Billion

Small Flows

Inflow More than $1 Billion

Florida Map 14–2. Net Commuter Income in Florida by County, 2000

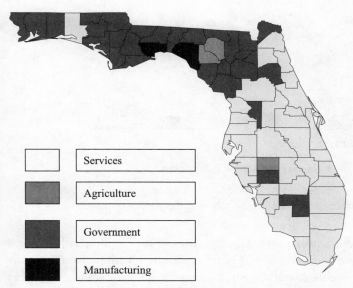

Florida Map 14–3. Leading Earnings Source in Florida Counties by Industry, 2000

County, the seat of state government; and Hamilton County, a small county where government is the largest employer. Collier County on the southwest and Nassau County on the northeast also had high earnings per employee.

Government was the leading source of labor earnings in north Florida, and services were the leading source of labor earnings in central and south Florida in 2000. Agriculture was the leading industry in Hardee, Lafayette, and Suwannee counties. Manufacturing was the leading source in Wakulla and Taylor counties.[9]

Florida's sunshine industries accounted for more than 70 percent of the state's economic base in 2000. This was considerably higher than the 58 percent share recorded in 1980. The share of each of the other sectors in the economic base declined in the period 1980 to 2000. The largest declines were in the maritime sector (from 25 percent to 17 percent) and the frontier sector (from 16 percent to 10 percent). The southern industries were a relatively insignificant part of the state's economic base, as they had been since the twentieth century began.

Tourism-retirement accounted for more than 90 percent of the production of the state's sunshine industries as the twentieth century drew to a close. Citrus and vegetables accounted for a similar small share, in both cases below 5 percent.

Earnings in the tourism-retirement sector accounted for about two-thirds of the state's economic base in 2000. Florida's tourism-retirement industry became increasingly specialized over the last half of the twentieth century. In 2000, the

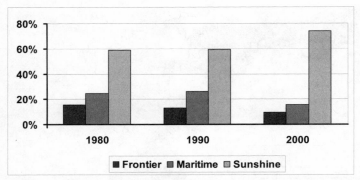

Chart 14-3. Share Frontier, Maritime, and Sunshine Economies as a Percent of the Value of Production of Florida's Economy, 1980, 1990, and 2000

tourism-retirement sector was the largest portion of the economies of Broward, Miami-Dade, and Monroe counties in the southeast; Charlotte County in the southwest; and Hillsborough, Pinellas, Orange, and Citrus counties north of Tampa. The retirement portion of earnings in the tourism-retirement sector presumably dominated in Citrus and Charlotte counties, where at least 30 percent of the population was 65 and older; and the tourism portion presumably dominated in Hillsborough, Miami-Dade, Monroe, and Orange counties, where the 65 and older population accounted for less than 15 percent of the total.[10]

Production of sunshine agricultural products was relatively evenly divided between citrus and vegetables in 2000. Gross output of citrus products amounted to 44 percent and gross output of vegetables, broadly defined, amounted to 56 percent of the state's sunshine agricultural sector.[11] The experience of the two sectors had been different during the previous twenty years. The freezes of the 1980s reduced citrus production, and the industry had been in a recovery mode during much of the 1990s. In contrast, Florida's production of vegetables, potatoes, melons, and strawberries had risen by more than 40 percent in the twelve years after 1980. Production fell by about 8 percent in 1993 and remained stable for the remainder of the decade.

Most Florida orange production is processed into juice, and during the freezes of the 1980s, imports rose sharply in order to maintain a relatively constant level of orange juice per capita.[12] As production recovered in 1990s, prices fell, per capita consumption rose, and the share of imports declined. Yet imports provided 20 percent of the juice consumers purchased in 2000, compared to 10 percent in 1980.

The recovery of Florida orange production and the continuing supply from overseas put downward pressure on the price of Florida oranges. In the harvest

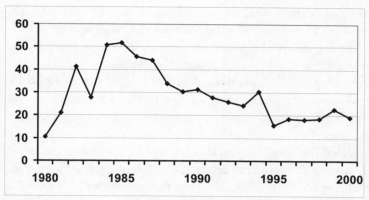

Chart 14–4. Share of Imported Orange Juice in U.S. Consumption, 1980–2000, by Percent (Selected Years)

year of 1999–2000, the on-tree price, expressed in 1982–1984 dollars, was little more than 50 percent of the 1979–1980 level.[13] However, in the 1990s, consumer preferences for orange juice shifted away from juice reconstituted from concentrate toward not-from-concentrate (NFC) juice. Although such juice had been available for many years, it was relatively expensive. In the 1990s, however, consumers, perhaps seeking fresher or more natural products, switched to NFC, which accounted for a majority of grocery store sales in 1998.[14] NFC juice was more expensive to transport, which deterred foreign producers from entering the industry and provided some relief to Florida processors.

Beginning in 1992, Brazilian-based orange juice processors began to purchase production facilities in Florida, perhaps partly in response to the growing popularity of NFC. But the Florida location also provided them with tariff-free access to the U.S. market. Additionally, the combination of orange juice from two widely separated regions (Florida and Brazil) diversified their operations and made their incomes less sensitive to conditions affecting either region.

Toward the end of the 1990s, the tariff protection that U.S. orange juice processors enjoyed came under attack. This tariff had originally been adopted as part of the Smoot-Hawley Tariff Act of 1930, which raised the tariff on over 20,000 imported goods. President George H. W. Bush proposed a Free Trade Area of the Americas (FTAA) in 1990, and negotiations began after the Summit of the Americas meeting in Miami in 1994. Toward the end of the decade, negotiations began to stall due to significant differences in the policy positions of the United States and Brazil. The latter, in particular, pressed to remove protection to U.S. agricultural products, including orange juice and sugar, both commodities of high interest to Florida. This raised a concern in Florida, especially since the precedent-setting North American Free Trade Area (NAFTA) had already reduced the tariff on orange juice from Mexico. Developing countries also pressed the United States (and the European Union) to remove trade barriers against their agricultural exports as part of the Doha Trade Round under the auspices of the World Trade Organization. Although negotiations for both the FTAA and the Doha Trade Round remained stalled in the first decade of the twenty-first century, it appears likely that tariff protection for Florida citrus and sugar will be reduced, if not eliminated, when further liberalization of world trade takes place.

Florida remained the dominant world producer of grapefruit at the end of the twentieth century. However, per capita consumption declined during the 1980s before leveling off in the 1990s.[15] Some of the decline may have been due to medical advice that individuals on a widely used cholesterol-lowering drug stop consuming grapefruit. Additionally, working consumers displayed increasing reluctance to take the time to section fresh grapefruit at breakfast time. And the retired consumers, who have more time, were more likely to be taking the cholesterol-lowering drug.[16]

Exports did not provide much compensation for the static nature of domestic consumption of grapefruit during the 1990s. Although there were some successes in opening foreign markets to exports of fresh grapefruit from Florida, including Japan in 1989 and China, India, and the Philippines in 1999, the share of fresh grapefruit exported during the 1990s remained at the same level as in the 1980s.[17]

Gross output of Florida's vegetables, broadly defined to include melons, potatoes, and strawberries, increased by over 40 percent in the twelve years

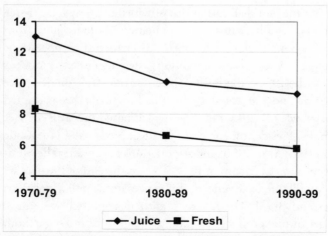

Chart 14–5. Averages of Pounds of Grapefruit Juice and Fresh Grapefruit Consumed per Capita in the United States by Decade, 1970s, 1980s, and 1990s

after 1979–1980.[18] After that, Florida's vegetable production declined, ending the 1990s about 8 percent below the 1991–1992 peak. The average level of vegetable prices in the 1990s, relative to the general level of consumer prices, was 20 percent less than the average level of prices in the 1980s, and the 1980s average was almost 20 percent below the 1970s value.

Vegetable prices declined in the United States in the 1990s as the domestic market for fresh vegetables was opened to more foreign competition.[19] The Uruguay Trade Round reduced the U.S. tariff on vegetables by 16 percent over a six-year period that ended in 2001. The tariff on Canadian imports was phased out in January 1998 and tariffs on Mexican imports were phased out over nine years beginning in 1994.

Winter tomato production in Mexico competes directly with the winter production of Florida growers and was subject to a tariff rate quota during the phase-in period. Such a quota was subject to the part of the tariff remaining during the phasing-out period; exports above the quota were subject to the general tariff non-NAFTA members paid. During the period 1994–2000, Mexican tomato exports to the United States increased by 80 percent over their before-NAFTA level in 1989–1993.

Mexican growers use different practices to produce fruits and vegetables for the export and domestic markets. Mexico's export industries grow products to meet consumer demand in foreign markets, retail preferences, and governmental restrictions (limits on chemical and pesticide residues, programs to deal with quarantined pests, etc.). The technology is quite similar to that used in the United States because U.S. firms are active in the Mexican export industries. Producers for Mexico's domestic market tend to use more labor than producers

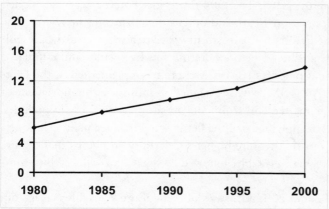

Chart 14–6. Imported Fresh and Frozen Vegetables as a Percent of U.S. Consumption, 1980–2000 (Selected Years)

in the United States and they use more traditional methods of cultivation and harvesting.[20]

In 1996, when Florida tomato producers charged Mexican producers with selling at a price below fair-market value, the United States and Mexico reached an agreement that suspended retaliatory tariffs. The agreement contained a minimum price for Mexican imports sold on the U.S. market. Although the agreement has held into the twenty-first century, Florida's tomato industry is clearly under pressure from Mexico.

One area of Florida's vegetable production was largely lost in the 1990s due to environmental issues. Lake Apopka in northwest Orange and southeast Lake counties is in the Ocklawaha chain of lakes that includes Dora, Eustis, and Griffin lakes and, ultimately, the Ocklawaha and St. Johns Rivers.[21] The lake was considered to be Florida's largest polluted lake as a result of the loss of 20,000 acres of wetlands along its northern shore in the 1940s and discharges from citrus-processing plants and shoreline communities, both of which had ceased by the 1980s.

The Lake Apopka Restoration Act was passed in 1985 with the goal of reducing the amount of phosphorous entering the lake, removing phosphorous and other sediment by filtration, eliminating gizzard shad, and restoring the north shore farmlands to wetlands. When the Water Management District warned vegetable growers to limit pesticide usage, the growers obtained special legislation that enabled them to sell their land to the state.[22] As of 2004, the Water Management District had purchased more than 19,000 acres, mostly farmland that had been used for vegetable production.

Environmentalists also targeted of the Everglades region south and west of Lake Okeechobee, where agricultural practicies were seen as sources of phosphorous pollution in the 1990s. The 1994 Everglades Forever Act was designed to restore Everglades National Park and other public lands in the region. The act provided for the development of storm-water treatment areas where polluted water would be filtered before entering the Everglades and stipulated that best management practices (BMPs) were to be implemented in the Everglades Agricultural Area. BMPs were designed to minimize the movement of nutrients, particulate matter, and sediments off site.[23] Typical BMPs included changes in methods of applying fertilizer, better water management techniques, rotations among crops that require higher soil fertility and crops that require lower soil fertility, such as vegetables followed by sugarcane followed by a summer rice crop.[24]

Between the 1982 and 2002 Censuses of Agriculture vegetable acreage declined in St. Johns, Flagler, and Seminole counties as consumer preferences shifted away from cabbage; acreage in cabbage in Florida declined by more than

7,000 acres. Acreage in radishes also declined because of an adverse movement in consumer tastes. This affected Palm Beach County, where there was some growth in the production of peppers and sweet corn. The number of acres devoted to watermelon production in the state declined by more than 13,000, following a decline of more than 15,000 acres between 1959 and 1982. This may be partly attributable to a shift in consumer preferences, but it is also due to the relative inefficiency of this vegetable as a land use. Declines of more than 1,000 acres were recorded in north central Florida, especially Marion, Sumter, Levy, and Gilchrist counties. Tomato production declined by more than 7,000 acres in Miami-Dade County. However, this decline was more than compensated by a growth in snap beans of almost 8,000 acres.

In addition to snap beans, there were large increases in cucumber and potato production, both of which increased by around 4,000 acres between 1982 and 2002, and strawberries, which increased by more than 2,500 acres. Manatee County had a large increase in cucumbers (4,150 acres), Collier County had a large increase in potatoes (2,280 acres) and Hillsborough County had a large increase in strawberries (2,639 acres).

Defense constituted almost 90 percent of Florida's maritime sector at the end of the 1990s.[25] Post–Cold War cutbacks had cut the share of defense in this sector of the state's economy. The relative share of fisheries had also declined since 1980, but there had been a large increase in the cruise industry, measured as earnings in water transportation.[26]

Earnings of military personnel in Florida increased substantially between

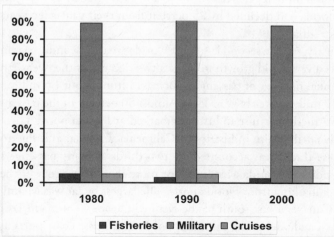

Chart 14–7. Share of Fisheries, Military Contracts, and Cruises in the Value of Production of Florida's Maritime Industries, 1980, 1990, and 2000 (by Percent)

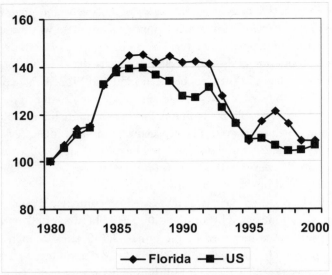

Chart 14–8. Real Military Earnings, Florida and the United States, 1980–2000 (Index 1980=100)

1980 and 1987 as the Reagan administration increased military spending.[27] National expenditures declined after 1987, but earnings in Florida's military facilities continued to rise. In 1992, military earnings in Florida declined as the pace of national defense cutbacks increased, partly as a result of the breakup of the Soviet Union and partly as a result of the efforts to balance the federal budget. There was a temporary increase in 1996 and 1997, but by 1999, military earnings in Florida had declined by 25 percent from their values ten years earlier (adjusted for inflation).

The cruise industry was the second largest of Florida's maritime industries in 2000. It experienced very rapid growth in the last two decades of the twentieth century.[28] The annual number of passengers increased from about 1.5 million in 1980 to almost 7 million twenty years later. Almost 50 percent of the passengers in the North American cruise industry embarked at Florida ports. There were also relatively small cruise industries in California, Canada, and Puerto Rico; together these three areas accounted for two-thirds as many passengers as Florida. Three ports in Florida accounted for more than 90 percent of the cruise passengers embarking from Florida ports. The largest by far was Miami, followed by Port Canaveral just south of the Kennedy Space Center and Port Everglades in Fort Lauderdale. The popularity of Florida's east coast ports as points of departure stemmed from their closeness to the Caribbean, the number-one cruising destination in the world. Forty-five percent of the capacity of

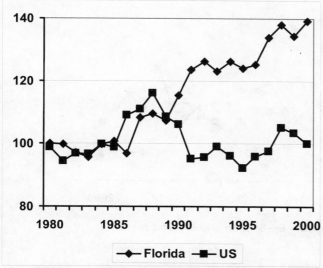

Chart 14–9. Per Capita Earnings in Water Transportation, Florida and the United States, 1980–2000, Adjusted for Inflation (Index 1980=100)

the worldwide cruise industry was located in the Caribbean in 2000. Although the South Atlantic states, including Florida, were the origin of the largest group of passengers for the North American cruise fleet, the industry drew passengers from throughout the United States.[29] The industry also drew passengers from Canada, Europe, and other parts of the world.

The rapid growth of the cruise industry appeared in the state's economy as a sharp increase in earnings from water transportation. While per capita earnings, adjusted for inflation, declined by more than 20 percent for the nation as a whole from 1980 to 2000, they grew by about 40 percent in Florida. Since cruise ships are essentially large hotel resorts that happen to float on the sea, they have similar impacts on the state economy. They purchase food and supplies within the state and pay port fees and property taxes. Florida received more than a third of all expenditures the cruise industry made in the United States in 2000. Additionally, the state was the home of corporate or administrative offices for fifteen cruise lines.[30]

Production of Florida's fisheries contracted from 1980 to 2000, with most of the decline occurring in the 1990s.[31] The decline in the production of fin fish exceeded 50 percent between 1980 and 2000, with most of the decline taking place in the first half of the 1990s. Landings of shrimp and invertebrates fluctuated around their 1980 production level during the 20-year period before declining at the end of the 1990s.

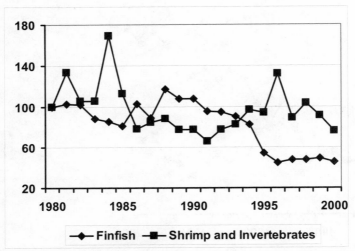

Chart 14–10. Landings of Fin Fish and Shrimp and Other Invertebrates in Florida, 1980–2000, in Millions of 2003 Dollars (Index 1980=100)

The decline in production of the state's fisheries in the 1980–2000 period occurred when per capita consumption of fish was rising, particularly in the early part of the period. Although production declined in the 1990s, the price per pound of the fish landed at Florida ports increased sharply. Much of the price increase occurred after 1993 and may have been related to increased competition from recreational fishers and regulation that limited commercial catches from state waters.[32]

Since both demand and prices were rising between 1980 and 2000, the reductions in output must have reflected restrictions on supply and increased production costs. National fisheries experienced a similar trend, which resulted in a sharp increase in the share of imports of fish consumed in the United States. In 1980, imports of fresh and frozen fish accounted for 56.8 percent of consumption. By 2000, imports accounted for over 80 percent of consumption.[33]

Florida's paper industry remained the most important of the state's frontier industries in 2000, accounting for 53 percent of the production of the sector.[34] The second most important frontier industry was the manufacture of wood products. Phosphate mining had fallen to about 10 percent of the sector, and the cattle industry was at 3 percent.

At the end of the twentieth century, 47 percent of Florida's land area was forested and more than 80 percent of the forest land was located in the northern part of the state.[35] Paper manufacturing accounted for more than half the output of the forest products manufacturing sector, and wood products accounted

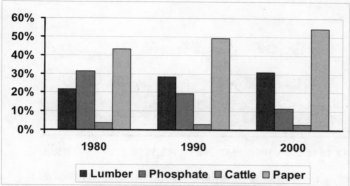

Chart 14–11. Share of Lumber, Phosphate, Cattle, and Paper Industries in Value of Production of Florida's Frontier Industries, 1980, 1990, and 2000 (by Percent)

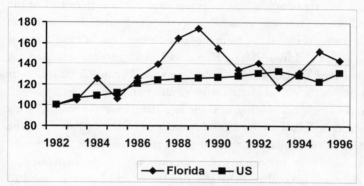

Chart 14–12. Value of Production of Paper and Allied Products in Florida, 1982–1996, Adjusted for Inflation (Annual Data; Index 1982=100)

for almost 30 percent.[36] Florida's three pulp mills accounted for about 25 percent of the production of the paper industry, and the state's four paperboard mills accounted for another 20 percent. Converted paper products, primarily corrugated and solid-fiber boxes, accounted for about a third of the industry's production. Production by the state's paper manufacturing industry expanded by over 60 percent from 1985 to 1989, a time when the national industry grew by 12 percent.[37]

In the late 1980s, prices for paperboard expanded rapidly. As supply increased, prices leveled off, and they began to fall in 1990. Florida's production of paper fell, and the industry suffered a severe recession.

A dramatic change occurred in one of Florida's leading firms in the industry, St. Joe Paper Company. This company was founded in the 1930s to manage the forestry assets that Alfred I. du Pont had accumulated. The company oper-

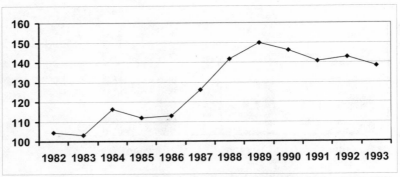

Chart 14–13. Paperboard Producer Price Index, 1982–1993 (Index 1982=100)

ated a large pulp mill in Port St. Joe east of Panama City and provided lumber to the mill from its extensive holdings of forest land in the eastern half of the state's panhandle. Du Pont had created the Nemours Foundation to receive the net income from his Florida investments and distribute it "for the care and treatment of crippled children."[38] The Nemours Foundation also received net income from du Pont's other Florida holdings, which included Florida East Coast Industries, which owned Henry Flagler's railroad.

After du Pont's death, his holdings and the foundation were managed by his brother-in-law, Ed Ball. Ball used the funds generated by St. Joe Paper and the other companies to accumulate additional assets and avoid debt. As a result, the foundation had a large amount of assets but only a relatively small income. In 1974, the attorneys-general of the states of Florida and Delaware sued to change the trustees of the Nemours Foundation, which was annually disbursing only about 1 percent of its assets, compared to the standard disbursement of 5 percent. The settlement of the case required the foundation to disburse 3 percent annually.[39]

In 1981, after the death of Ed Ball, trustees accounting for a minority of the votes in the trust sued to force divestiture of assets to ensure that the 3 percent was disbursed. The trustees wanted to sell St. Joe Paper and other assets and invest the proceeds in a portfolio of financial assets that would yield a larger annual income. Such a portfolio would also diversify the assets of the trust and make its income less subject to the volatility of the paper industry. Although the Florida Supreme Court allowed the foundation to keep the companies, it was clear that a restructuring was needed to ensure that the 3 percent disbursement rate was achieved each year. The new CEO of St. Joe Paper initiated an initial public offering to sell 14 percent of the company in the mid-1980s and established a real estate division to develop some of its undeveloped land.[40] The funds raised in the stock offering provided the company with a cushion that could be used to supplement the dividends it paid to the foundation if they were below the 3 percent minimum.

When the paper industry entered a recession in the early 1990s, St. Joe's forest products division made losses, and management considered further restructuring. It sold the pulp mill in Port St. Joe to Florida Coast Paper, a joint venture backed equally by Smurfit Stone Container Corporation and Four M Corporation, the parent company of Box USA.[41] Four M took over the box plants and Smurfit-Stone took over the pulp mill. The company's lumber could be used by the new owners of the mill and by other pulp mills nearby. Florida Coast Paper had difficulty operating the mill profitably, and it shut it down temporarily in 1996 and 1997. The company declared bankruptcy in 1999 and announced the permanent closing of the mill in 2000.[42]

An even more radical restructuring of St. Joe Paper came in 1997 when the company recast itself as a land development company, took over Arvida Corporation, one of the most successful south Florida land development companies, and turned the management of St. Joe over to the chief executive of Arvida. As the century ended, St. Joe was still providing lumber to the local pulp mills, but it was expanding its real estate division to build new communities on its extensive lands.

About half the production of Florida's lumber manufacturing industry in 1997 was accounted for by a residual "other" category in the industry's statistics. The major products in this category were wooden windows and doors, wood containers and pallets, and mobile homes. Veneer, plywood, and engineered wood products (whose main product was roof trusses) accounted for another third of the industry's production.

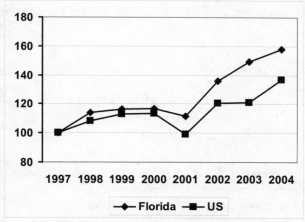

Chart 14–14. Value of Production of Lumber, Florida and the United States, 1997–2004, Indexes 1997=100

Lumber production expanded by more than 60 percent both in Florida and in the nation as a whole in the five years after the recession low of 1982.[43] Although Florida's lumber industry began a downward trend after that year, the national industry continued to expand for two years before following the state industry downward. The state and national industries hit bottom in 1994 before trending upward until 1996, the last year before the U.S. Census Bureau radically changed the industrial classification of economic statistics as part of the 1997 economic census.

The price of southern pine, the major product of Florida's lumber industry, was relatively stagnant in the decade after the recession hit its low in 1982 and the expansion of the industry absorbed excess capacity.[44] By 1991, however, a shortage of capacity had developed, and the price of southern pine rose by over 60 percent in the following three years. The increase in prices stimulated production in 1995 and 1996. After 1997, the newly defined wood-product manufacturing industry followed a moderate upward trend both in the state and the nation. In 2001, the recession led to a larger decline nationally, but the state industry recovered strongly in 2002, 2003, and 2004.

Production of Florida phosphate trended downward during 1980–2000 from a record high level at the beginning of the period. Several substantial downturns occurred during the downward trend. Downturns took place in the 1980s, and another downturn occurred in 1993 as international demand softened.[45]

The major phosphate reserves in southern Polk and western Hillsborough counties began to be mined out in the 1990s, and production began to move southward. Stricter environmental controls raised the cost of opening new mines and shutting old ones and constituted one reason for the consolidation of the industry.[46] Larger-scale enterprises were needed to pay for the cost of moving the industry.

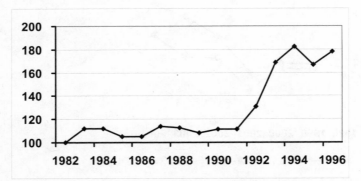

Chart 14–15. Value of Production of Paper and Allied Products in Florida, 1982–1996, Adjusted for Inflation (Annual Data)

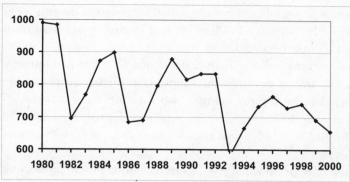

Chart 14–16. Value of Production of Phosphate in Florida, 1980–2000, in Millions of 1980 Dollars

One concern was the impact of the industry on the quality of the regional water supply. The phosphate-bearing matrix that is excavated contains sand and clay and is slurried with water in field wells before being pumped to the beneficiation (processing) plant. The phosphate is separated from the sand and clay after fuel oil, fatty acids, and sulphuric acid has been added. Clay waste from the ore washing is sent to settling areas so water can be recovered for reuse and the clays can be consolidated to a largely dewatered composition.[47] Environmental permits require plants to be close to or at zero water discharge. In addition, some mines obtain treated sewage water from the local government to use in the plant. The treatment and management of water in the mining complex adds to the cost of operation. Additionally, the clay areas have limited economic value when mines are closed because they cannot support structures, such as houses, without pilings.[48]

There was also concern about the reclamation of mined areas. Beginning in 1975, the state required phosphate mines to reclaim land that had been strip-mined. Later in the century, phosphate companies not only had to present detailed plans for reclaiming the land, but they had to submit a reclamation plan during the permitting process to show how reclamation would occur as production proceeded.

Finally, there were concerns about phosphogypsum stacks created at the mines. Phosphogypsum is a by-product of the process of creating phosphoric acid, an essential component of modern fertilizers. For every ton of acid created, five tons of phosphogypsum was created.[49] The by-product is stored in stacks, and because there is very little use for the material, companies are required to manage the stacks for a long period of time. This is an additional cost of production for the industry.

In 2001, a high level of rainfall led to an overfilling of a phosphate stack at Piney Point, and a spill occurred into Tampa Bay. Since then, the industry has incurred the costs of impounding the stacks with lined covers to prevent water recharge. Additionally, the water has been treated by lime neutralization to make it suitable for discharge into Tampa Bay.

The phosphate mining industry is an example of a Florida-based industry that was affected by stricter environmental controls in the last quarter of the twentieth century. Another frontier industry, paper manufactures, was also affected. A number of agricultural industries were also affected, including the dairy industry in the Okeechobee area and the sugar and vegetable industries in the Everglades area.

The tightening of environmental regulations in Florida in the last decades of the twentieth century is consistent with the view that environmental degradation is high when countries or regions are at a low level of economic development as measured by per capita income. As development takes place, environmental degradation increases. But after it reaches a "tipping point," environmental regulations are tightened and the extent of environmental degradation declines. This view can be explained by a benefit-cost analysis. At low levels of economic development, the benefits of economic activity that has negative consequences for the environment are seen as greater than the costs imposed on society, but at higher levels of development, the costs become more important than the benefits. Benefits to the local community include jobs and incomes, and costs include out-of-pocket expenses (for health care, for example) and lost wages. As the economy develops, wages increase, and this raises the costs of environmental damage. If economic development provides alternative job opportunities, the benefits may also be less appreciated. Finally, economic development increases the ability to pay for environmental regulation and improvements.

This theory may also help explain the growth in public concern about traffic congestion created by the intensive housing development of the last quarter of the twentieth century. Traffic congestion may be the negative social consequence that is most widely felt by the neighbors of a new development. Congested schools, parks, beaches, and even restaurants and malls may also generate increasing public concern. The time individuals spend in congested traffic reduces the time available to them for work or leisure. As economic development occurs, the value of time increases, raising the cost of traffic congestion. This makes public opposition to new developments more likely.

Cattle production also trended downward during the 1980s from a very high level at the end of the 1970s before stabilizing in the 1990s.[50] The downward trend in production reflected a downward trend in cattle prices, especially in the period before 1986. Although prices recovered in the last years of the 1980s, production continued to decline.

Chart 14–17. Value of Production of Cattle in Florida, 1980–2000, in Millions of 1982–1984 Dollars

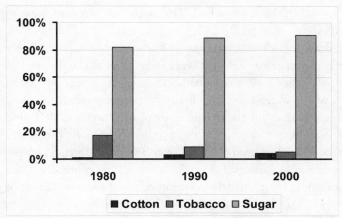

Chart 14–18. Share of Cotton, Tobacco, and Sugar in Value of Production of Florida's Southern Industries, 1980, 1990, and 2000 (by Percent)

The decline in relative prices reflected a decline in consumer demand for beef. In 1980, Americans consumed 72 pounds of beef per capita.[51] By 2000, consumption had declined by 10 percent to 65 pounds. Consumption of chicken rose from 33 pounds to 54 pounds over the same period. By 2000, chicken had displaced much of the beef consumption that was typical of earlier generations, and Florida had developed a significant broiler industry in response to the change in consumer preferences.

Sugarcane production continued to dominate Florida's southern sector throughout the 1980–2000 period. The other two crops in this sector accounted for less than 10 percent of its production in 2000: there was a modest increase in cotton production in the 1990s, but this was counterbalanced by a decline in the production of tobacco.

Sugarcane production expanded strongly in the 1980–2000 period, increasing by 50 percent.[52] Sugar prices completed their downward trend. The price of sugar fell to close to $30 per ton in 1981, and it remained at about this level for the remainder of the century. The stability of the price presumably reflected the support the Agriculture and Food Act of 1981 gave to the market; this act was renewed in 1985, 1990, and 1996.[53] It renewed the loan or purchase program that had been introduced in 1977 when the exceptionally high prices of 1974–1975 were seen as an aberration and the United States had returned to its longtime practice of controlling imports and protecting domestic production.

U.S. sugar consumption declined from 84 to 66 pounds per capita from 1980 to 2000, and the reduction was presumably borne by foreign suppliers.[54] The share of sugar in total U.S. consumption of caloric sweeteners declined from 60 percent to less than 40 percent. Consumption of high-fructose corn syrup more than tripled in the same period. This sweetener replaced sugar in carbonated beverages.

As the century drew to a close, the situation Florida agriculture faced was significantly different from conditions 100 years earlier. Production in most of the state's agriculture was not lower than it had been a century earlier, but it had declined as a share of the state's overall economy. Vegetable production relied on protection from imports, but the extent of this protection was declining because of NAFTA. Orange juice, the primary product of the state's signature agricultural industry, also relied on significant protection from foreign competition. Sugar, the state's most valuable field crop, also relied on protection from foreign competition. Brazil was the primary competitor in the production of both orange juice and sugar.

Florida's agriculture was subject to tight environmental controls that were

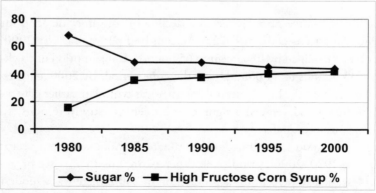

Chart 14–19. Consumption of Sugar and High-Fructose Corn Syrup in the United States as Percent of Total Consumption of Caloric Sweeteners, 1980–2000

gradually imposed in the last decades of the twentieth century, as were its phosphate mining and paper-manufacturing industries. There were also conflicts between the state's very large urban population and the relatively small population that depended on agriculture. These conflicts were particularly acute where matters of water quality were involved, but they also showed up in the unwillingness of a large section of the urban population to allow their citrus trees to be cut in order to protect the state's commercial citrus industry from citrus canker and even in conflicts over the fishery resources, especially in areas near the shore.

By 2000, most of Florida's population derived its livelihood from urban pursuits, and this contrasted with the population in the state a century earlier. The state's population in 2000 was much less supportive of the nonurban parts of the economic base than had been true in 1900. But it would be foolish to imagine that the fundamental structural change that is characteristic of economic development will cease in the twenty-first century. Floridians in 2100 will have a different set of economic interests than those in the state did in 2000.

Chapter 15

The Future Economic Development of Florida

This book has traced the remarkable economic development of Florida since the end of the Civil War in 1865. Florida was one of the nation's most sparsely populated states at the end of that war, with fewer than 200,000 persons, but by the beginning of the twenty-first century it was on its way to becoming the third most populated state in the nation. At the end of the nineteenth century, Florida was a small economy on the periphery of the national economy; by the end of the twentieth century, it had developed into one of the major economies of the nation.

Florida's advantage at the end of the Civil War was its access to wealthy growing economies in the northern United States. The state needed to exploit this access by developing goods and services for which there would be a strong and growing demand in the northern states and to attract labor and capital from elsewhere in the country to develop the industries that would produce these goods and services. The industries that sell large amounts of goods and services to other parts of the country (and the rest of the world) are referred to collectively as the state's economic base. During the past century the state's economic base has grown substantially and its composition has changed. An important part of the explanation for the changes has been the dramatic decline in unit transportation costs, which enabled a peripheral state like Florida to export perishable products to the nation's economic core stretching from Boston to Chicago and to import tourists, seasonal residents, and retirees, who would purchase goods and services within the state.

As the twentieth century began, the dominant sector of the state's economic base consisted of the state's frontier industries—industries engaged in exploiting the natural resources of its abundant forests and self-renewing grasslands. The state also had a small phosphate mining industry. These industries sold their products to the more developed parts of the United States and to Cuba and Western Europe.

The northern part of Florida had participated in the antebellum southern economy that had been dominated by the export of cotton, tobacco, cane sugar, and rice. The end of the shameful practice of slavery had changed the structure of the southern economy but not the dependence of millions of southerners on these exports. The southern economy was under severe economic pressure in the last decades of the nineteenth century. Increased competition from the countries of the British empire had developed during the North's blockade against southern exports to Europe during the Civil War. Additionally, the location of the cotton economy was moving westward, and from this new location western cotton producers were capturing market share from the antebellum cotton producers in the southeast. The southern sector of the state's economic base had shrunk significantly by 1900. Cotton growing in Florida had come to be dominated by a specialty product, the long staple sea-island cotton, until the boll weevil and changing market conditions virtually eliminated the industry in the 1920s. Florida also had developed a small specialty industry in shade tobacco that survived through the first half of the twentieth century until it was eliminated (at least in part) because of a change in consumer tastes. By the end of the twentieth century, only cane sugar remained as a significant remnant of the state's antebellum past.

National defense, the cruise industry, and the state's fisheries constitute the third collection of Florida industries that enabled the state to produce and sell goods and services to the rest of the United States and, in some cases, other parts of the world. We have called these industries Florida's maritime economy. Prior to the nineteenth century, Spain had valued Florida for its strategic geographic position at the cross roads between Central and South America and Western Europe. The United States also valued the state for its strategic geographic position when it took control of it in the early decades of the nineteenth century. By the end of that century, the United States had a significant naval presence in the state, and as the twentieth century progressed, this presence expanded and was joined by major air force facilities. Florida's warm winter also made the state attractive for military training programs. Finally, in the last decades of the century, private capital developed the cruise industry at the state's ports.

The fourth component of the state's economic base in 1900 was the sunshine sector, composed of the industries developed as a result of Florida's warm winter climate relative to the rest of the country. This sector included citrus and winter vegetable production and winter tourism. During the twentieth century, the state would also gain from the in-migration of retired persons, who share many of the characteristics of tourists.

As the twentieth century opened, the remnant of Florida's southern economy accounted for less than 1 percent of the production of the state's economic

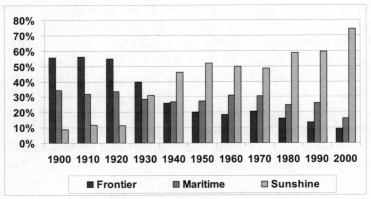

Chart 15–1. Share of Frontier, Maritime, and Sunshine Industries in Value of Production of Florida's Economic Base by Decade, 1900–2000 (by Percent)

base. The dominant part of the base in 1900, accounting for almost two-thirds, was the state's frontier sector, which included lumber, naval stores, cattle, and phosphate mining. The state's maritime industries were in second place, accounting for one quarter of basic production. The sunshine industries, which were temporarily depressed by the great freezes in 1894–1895 and the lesser freeze of 1899, accounted for less than 10 percent.

During the twentieth century, the sunshine industries increased their share of the economic base and the frontier industries declined in relative importance. The big expansion of the share of the sunshine industries began in the 1920s as the state's tourist industry expanded its market beyond the affluent to middle-income consumers. A key part of this expansion occurred as the cheap affordable automobile enabled consumers to significantly reduce the cost of a trip to Florida during the winter. By 1930, the sunshine industries constituted the second largest component of the base, having doubled their share to 25 percent during the preceding decade.

The images of the poverty and suffering of the Great Depression at the beginning of the 1930s make it easy to overlook the substantial positive changes in the state's economy that occurred during the decade. The long-term secular decline in the state's frontier industries was halted by the development of the paper industry, and the southern sector even received a small boost from the development of the sugarcane industry around Lake Okeechobee. By the end of this decade, the sunshine sector accounted for 45 percent of the state's economic base. Much of this growth was due to a growth in tourism, particularly in the last half of the decade. In the twenty-first century we can still see the evidence of this earlier growth in the art deco hotels that have survived in south Miami Beach.

The sunshine sector reached 50 percent of the state's economic base in 1950 as tourism recovered from wartime disruption and the citrus industry expanded after the invention of frozen concentrated orange juice. In the 1950s, the first great wave of retirees came to the state. Many factors stimulated this population inflow, including Social Security and the growth of private pensions, the widespread adoption of air conditioning, and the growth of federal mortgage programs that made it possible for retirees to own second homes and year-round homes in the state.

A strong expansion of the state's maritime industries kept the share of the sunshine industry in the state's economic base relatively stable in the 1950s and 1960s. Military earnings in Florida remained high after World War II ended as wartime installations in the state were made permanent. There was further expansion in the 1950s when military payrolls in the state more than doubled. The state's fisheries also experienced a considerable expansion in the 1950s, and the new cruise industry began to develop in the 1960s

The share of the sunshine industries jumped in the 1970s as the second great wave of retiree in-migration impacted the state's economy. A growing national pool of retirees was one factor that stimulated this second large inflow, but the development of condominium housing, often in gated communities with attractive recreational facilities, was probably the main stimulant. The state's tourist industry expanded with the opening of Disney World at the beginning of the decade.

By 2000, the sunshine industries accounted for more than 70 percent of the production of the state's economic base, the maritime industries accounted for 17 percent, and the frontier industries accounted for about 10 percent. The tourism-retirement sector alone accounted for almost 66 percent. Florida's economic base had become increasingly specialized, a hallmark of an open trading system.

The focus on the economic base, however, obscures the fact that Florida's economy had grown less dependent on the exports of goods and services by the end of the twentieth century. The four sectors of the economic base together accounted for less than 10 percent of the state's personal income in 2000, a decline from about 20 percent fifty years earlier and from about 30 percent at the beginning of the century. This is a normal feature of a large economy—workers in large economies primarily produce goods and services for their neighbors rather than for people living in other regions.

Florida's future economic development will be more like development in what economists call a "closed" economy—an economy with limited relations with the rest of the world, rather than the "open" economy that characterized the state during the twentieth century. A closed economy experiences develop-

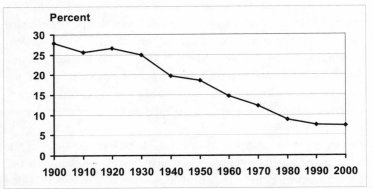

Percent

Chart 15–2. Florida Economic Base, Share of Personal Income by Decade, 1900–2000

ment because of an increase in the productivity of its labor force, whereas an open economy develops by exploiting its access to growing external markets. Factors that increase labor productivity include improved skills of the work force, obtained through education and on the job training, and technological advances, broadly defined to include the development of new products and improved production techniques. Improvements in education and training as well as technological advances come about as a result of government leadership and private intiative.

The twentieth century illustrated the dynamic nature of the state's economy; industries came and went and some industries expanded faster than others. Changes in technology and consumer tastes are important parts of these developments in an open trading system. Perhaps the most important technological developments for Florida's economy in the late nineteenth and the twentieth centuries occurred in the transportation sector. Railroads were followed by automobiles which in turn were followed by aircraft, and technological improvements in these forms of transportation, and also in shipping, brought Florida goods and services to customers more cheaply and facilitated a great expansion in the state's export-oriented industries. But technological developments also led to the loss of two of Florida's basic industries, gum naval stores and sponge fisheries. The products of both of these industries were obtained using different technologies at the end of the century compared to the beginning: sponges were produced synthetically and turpentine was produced as a by-product of paper manufacturing. Technological improvements also led to the development of the new basic industries of paper manufacturing and the production of orange juice concentrate.

Changes in consumer preferences also impacted the state economy. The state's cigar manufacturing was almost completely eliminated in part because of a decline in consumer preferences due to concerns about the health effects of smoking, and this was also a factor in the loss of the shade-tobacco industry. Consumer tastes for beef were greatly stimulated by the development of the fast-food industry in the 1960s; the reverse happened in the 1980s as chicken was increasingly substituted for beef on health grounds. A new cruise industry was developed in the 1960s in response to new consumer demands, stimulated by imaginative entrepreneurs, many of whom were based in Florida.

Florida's industries were subject to increasing environmental regulation in the last quarter of the twentieth century. As I noted earlier in this book, I believe an important part of the explanation for this development is the rising incomes of the population that increase the economic losses from adverse industrial health impacts on the environment. Among the industries so impacted were Florida agriculture and the state's phosphate-mining industry.

The dynamic nature of Florida's economy can be illustrated by comparing the three largest industries in the economic base in 1900 to the three largest in 2000. In 1900, lumber manufacturing, cigar manufacturing, and fisheries were the three largest components of the economic base. These industries accounted for 71 percent of the basic sector. In 2000, the three largest components of the base were tourism-retirement, military payrolls, and paper manufacturing. These accounted for 91 percent of the economic base. Not one of the three largest sectors in 1900 was still one of the three largest in 2000. Additionally, the economic base had become less diversified in 2000 compared to 1900, a manifestation of the greater specialization noted above.

During the twentieth century Florida experienced a huge increase in its

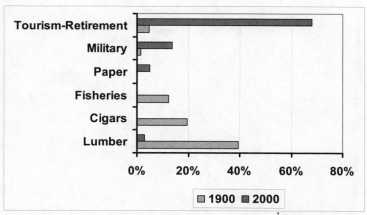

Chart 15–3. Three Largest Industries in the Economic Base, 1900 and 2000 (Percent of the Total Production of the Economic Base)

tourism-retirement industry. It is likely that there will be one more wave of in-migrating retirees in the early decades of the twenty-first century as the huge post–World War II generation of Baby Boomers retires. Thereafter, however, the only external source of substantial additional in-migration that is likely to grow will probably be international immigration, since future national cohorts of retirees will grow smaller. As the impact of the retirement of the Baby Boomers fades, the economic development of the state will increasingly depend on the actions of Floridians rather than on the willingness of people elsewhere in the country to buy a group of products reflective of Florida's unique geographical location. The ability of Florida to improve the skills of its workforce and to develop new technology will determine the extent to which the population will experience further increases in its standard of living. The future will not be the same as the past.

Notes

Preface

1. Mormino, "Sunbelt Dreams and Altered States," 3.

Chapter 1. 1900: A Western Economy in a Southern Setting

1. U.S. Bureau of the Census, *Twelfth Census of the United States Taken in the Year 1900*, Vol. 1, *Population: Part 1*, xix. This source also contains aggregate figures from census data for Puerto Rico and Cuba collected by the U.S. War Department in late 1899. Population figures for Florida counties and towns were published in U.S. Bureau of the Census, "Population of Florida by Counties and Minor Civil Divisions." The estimated population of the native peoples of Florida in 1513 is from Milanich, "Original Inhabitants," 14. Estimates of the population of Haiti and the Dominican Republic are from Stearns, "Dominican Republic, 1882–1899." A figure of 748,530 is given for the population of Jamaica in 1900 in Bulmer-Thomas, "The Wider Caribbean in the Twentieth Century," 31.

2. For a history of sea-island cotton, see U.S. Bureau of the Census, *Twelfth Census of the United States Taken in the Year 1900*, Vol. 6, *Agriculture*, Part 2, *Crops and Irrigation*, 416–417. For a history of the industry in Florida, see Paisley, "Madison County's Sea Island Cotton Industry."

3. Siebert, "The Early Sugar Industry in Florida"; Martin, *Florida during the Territorial Days*, 114; Dodd, "Florida in 1845," 9; Tebeau, *A History of Florida*, 182–183; Dillon, "South Florida in 1860," 449. For the decline in cotton prices, see Williams, "Florida in the Union," 221.

4. Dodd, "Florida in 1845," 9, gives the reference for St. Augustine tobacco production. See also DuPont, "History of the Introduction and Culture of Cuba Tobacco in Florida"; Avant, *J. Randall Stanley's History of Gadsden County*, Chapters 8 and 16; and U.S. Bureau of the Census, "Agriculture: Florida," 12. The story in Avant conflicts somewhat with the information in U.S. Bureau of the Census, *Twelfth Census of the United States Taken in the Year 1900*, Vol. 6, *Agriculture*, Part 2, *Crops and Irrigation*, 501, which reverses the order of the introduction of the two types of tobacco.

5. Johnson, *Florida's Mineral Industry*, 12; production data from Blakey, *The Florida Phosphate Industry*, 154; Brown, *Fort Meade, 1849–1900*, chapter 8; U.S. Bureau of the

Census, Special reports, *Mines and Quarries: 1902, Census Bulletin* 9, 194–196,917–930.

6. U.S. Bureau of the Census, "Manufactures: The Lumber Industry," 34; U.S. Bureau of the Census, *Tenth Census of the United States, 1880*, vol. 3, *Report of the Productions of Agriculture*, 147–149; Rerick, *Memoirs of Florida*, 1:289; Akerman, *Florida Cowman*, 100–125 and 107. The road on the Florida mainland to the Sanibel Causeway is called Summerlin Avenue after Jacob Summerlin, who owned the facilities at Punta Rassa and was Florida's most famous cattle dealer in the 1870s and 1880s. The statement that range cattle were undercounted in 1890 is in U.S. Bureau of the Census, *Twelfth Census of the United States Taken in the Year 1900*, Vol. 5, *Agriculture*, Part 1, *Farms, Live Stock, and Animal Products*, cxlvi. The statement that citrus land was converted to cattle-raising is in U.S. Bureau of the Census, "Agriculture: Florida," 2.

7. Campbell and Unkrich, *The Lumber Industry*, 12–13. For data on board feet see U.S. Bureau of the Census, "Manufactures: The Lumber Industry" 74, 76–78. See also Bennett, "The Historical Development of the Lumber Industry in Florida," 49–55.

8. U.S. Bureau of the Census, "Manufactures: Turpentine and Rosin," 6.

9. The correct measure of the value of production is value added. This is calculated by subtracting the value of goods and services purchased from other industries from the value of sales or shipments, including inventory changes, in order to avoid double counting. The value of sales or shipments, including inventory changes, is called gross output. Statistics for value added were available for manufacturing and mining industries in 1900, but only gross output was available for other industries, especially agriculture. I made estimates of value added for the missing cases that are at best very approximate. The value of cattle sold or slaughtered was available in the census, as was the value of the livestock inventory. I calculated the ratio of the value of cattle not kept for milk plus steers two years old and older to this value (and the value of the sheep and lambs and hog inventory) at 79.5 percent. I assumed this to be the share of cattle in the value of animals sold or slaughtered. Finally, I assumed that 90 percent of gross cattle production was value added. A number of the statistics in the 1900 census refer to the preceding year (1899).

10. I assumed the value added by fisheries and sponges to be 65 percent of gross output. Labor costs alone amounted to 55 percent of revenue in mullet and Spanish mackerel operations and to a similar percent of the revenue of snapper and grouper operations in 1955, as reported in Osterbind and Jones, "A Short Report on Florida's Commercial Fisheries." I computed the military payroll by multiplying the number of U.S. soldiers, sailors, and marines residing in the state by the average manufacturing wage. The Florida manufacturing wage was higher than the national wage in 1900.

11. The main provisions of the tariff acts as they related to cigars are presented in Baer, *The Economic Development of the Cigar Industry in the United States*, 108–111. Baer notes that Cuba was the main source of cigar imports after 1860 (49). Poyo, "The Cuban Experience in the United States," 20, suggests that the increased U.S. tariffs may have resulted from Cuban manufacturers expanding exports to the United States as exports to Western Europe fell in the face of rising European tariff pressures in the

1850s. Additionally, the relatively favorable tariff treatment of Cuban cigar tobacco encouraged Cuban manufacturers to establish factories inside the U.S. tariff wall. See also Mormino and Pozzetta, *The Immigrant World of Ybor City*, 64.

12. Baer, *The Economic Development of the Cigar Industry in the United States*, 107.

13. For basic data on fisheries, see U.S. Bureau of the Census, *Statistical Abstract of the United States: 1950*, 680–681. Florida Department of Agriculture, *Report of the Commissioner of Agriculture of the State of Florida: 1899–1900* provides data on the sponge fishery from the *Report of Sponge Fisheries for 1900 by the U.S. Commissioner of Fish and Fisheries*. See also Jahoda, *River of the Golden Ibis*, Chapter 22; and Straub, *History of Pinellas County*, Chapter 17.

14. Dodd, "The Wrecking Business on the Florida Reef," 199. Multiply by 20 to convert these numbers to 2000 dollars.

15. Data on tourist expenditures around 1900 are not available and there is not much that can be used as a basis for estimation. For Chart 1–8, I derived an estimate from an estimate of earnings in the Florida tourist industry in 1930 based on state personal income data from the U.S. Bureau of Economic Analysis. I computed labor earnings in Florida's tourist industry as the excess of the percentage share of Florida labor earnings in transportation, trade, and services over the corresponding U.S. percentage share times total Florida labor earnings. I ascribed the difference in these two numbers to tourism. I deflated the result by the consumer price index. I then backed this estimate to 1920 using the growth in licensed lodging units in the state between 1919 and 1928 (obtained from the annual reports of the Florida Hotel Commission). I backed the 1920 estimate to 1910 and 1900 using the decadal growth in rail passenger receipts (obtained from annual reports of the Florida Railroad Commission).

16. The U.S. census provided estimates of production of the individual semitropical products, but only a total for their value. I derived the figures for Chart 1–8 by valuing production using the statewide average unit values for the individual products given in the *Report of the Commissioner of Agriculture of the State of Florida—1899*. This report presented grapefruit production in terms of barrels rather than the boxes the U.S. census used. I assumed that a box of grapefruit had the same unit value as a box of oranges. I assumed that value added was 53 percent of the value of gross output. This was the average value added percentage across thirteen vegetables grown for sale in 1955, the earliest date that data on value added percentages was available (prepared by the Florida Agricultural Experiment Station and published in Florida Department of Agriculture, *Florida Vegetable Summary: 1955*). The U.S. census also included figs as a semitropical product, but production was much larger in Georgia and the Carolinas than in Florida. Olive production was insignificant in Florida. Florida had some additional products, such as sugar apples and sapodillas, whose production was insignificant. Data on pineapples are from U.S. Bureau of the Census, "Agriculture: Florida," 12.

17. The basic data come from the reports of the Florida Commissioner of Agriculture. There is an inconsistency between the U.S. census and the state source; the U.S. census records larger production of limes than grapefruit in 1899, whereas the state reports consistently show larger grapefruit production values.

18. U.S. Bureau of the Census, *Twelfth Census of the United States Taken in the Year 1900*, Vol. 6, *Agriculture*, Part 2, *Crops and Irrigation*, 294–295.

19. The data in Chart 1–09 are from the biennial reports of the Florida Commissioner of Agriculture. The data include the crops common to all reports: beets, beans, cabbage, cucumbers, eggplants, peas, potatoes, squash, tomatoes, watermelons, and strawberries. Data were missing for Dade, Monroe, Nassau and Volusia counties. I used U.S. census acreage data where available and data from adjacent biennial reports otherwise. I used data on production per acre and unit values from adjacent biennial reports to construct the data for missing values.

Chapter 2. The Transfer of Public Lands

1. In 1860, the provisions of the Swamp Land Act were extended to Minnesota and Oregon. The acreage transferred to Florida is given in Shaw and Fredine, *Wetlands of the United States*, Table 1.

2. The Swamp Land Act is quoted in DeGrove, "The Administration of Internal Improvement Problems in Florida, 1845–69," 32; see page 33 for a discussion of the "greater part" language. See also the discussion in Knetsch, "Hamilton Disston and the Development of Florida," 13. Using the lands to develop a modern transportation network could be justified by arguing that the network would stimulate development that would bring about the desired drainage.

3. DeGrove, "The Administration of Internal Improvement Problems in Florida, 1845–69," 48.

4. Governor Perry quoted in Cash, *The Story of Florida*, 387.

5. Abbey, "The Union Bank of Tallahassee," 226; Paisley, *The Red Hills of Florida*, 99–100 .

6. The following paragraphs draw upon DeGrove, "The Administration of Internal Improvement Problems in Florida, 1845–69," especially 40–88 and 120. There is also a useful discussion in Brown, "The Florida Atlantic and Gulf Central Railroad, 1851–68," especially 417 and 427–428.

7. *Journal of the Proceedings of the House of Representatives 1852*, quoted in DeGrove, "The Administration of Internal Improvement Problems in Florida, 1845–69," 42.

8. Johns, *Florida during the Civil War*, 136.

9. The experience of Florida's railroads during the Civil War and its aftermath is described in Shofner, *Nor Is It Over Yet*, 111; Pettengill, *The Story of the Florida Railroads*, 28–31; and Johns, *Florida during the Civil War*, 137.

10. Shofner and Rogers, "Confederate Railroad Construction," 219–220.

11. Shofner, *Nor Is It Over Yet*, 115; Pettengill, *The Story of the Florida Railroads*, 33.

12. Brown, "The Florida Atlantic and Gulf Central Railroad," 427–428; Pettengill, *The Story of the Florida Railroads*, 36. The purchaser, William E. Jackson, is listed as one of the recipients of IIF lands in the table in Shofner, *Nor Is It Over Yet*, 113.

13. Blake, *Land into Water—Water into Land*, 42–61.

14. Shofner, *Nor Is It Over Yet*, 115, 251.

15. See Rerick, *Memoirs of Florida*, 1:349–350; Sharp, "Samuel A. Swann and the Development of Florida."

16. Details on Hamilton Disston and his purchases are found in Knetsch, "Hamilton Disston and the Development of Florida"; Hanna and Hanna, *Lake Okeechobee*, 204; and Davis, "The Disston Land Purchase."

17. Hanna and Hanna, *Lake Okeechobee*, 95.

18. Tischendorf, "Florida and the British Investor," 122–123. Reed's fellowship in the Royal Society is noted in *Leading Men of London*, 354.

19. Pettengill, *The Story of the Florida Railroads*, 36.

20. Hanna and Hanna, *Lake Okeechobee: Wellspring of the Everglades*, 97; Grismer, *The Story of St. Petersburg*, 48–57; Orser, "'Florida and the British Investor' Revisited," 184; Dayton, "A Short History of the San Antonio Area"; Brown, *In the Midst of All*, 133; Tischendorf, "Florida and the British Investor," 123; Matthews, "'He Has Carried His Life in His Hands,'" 7–8.

21. Dodson, "Hamilton Disston's St. Cloud Sugar Plantation," 357–358.

22. The mouth of the Caloosahatchee River is actually at Punta Rassa, beside where the Sanibel Causeway existed a century later.

23. Dodson, "Hamilton Disston's St. Cloud Sugar Plantation," 358.

24. Blake, *Land into Water—Water into Land*, 51. Blake cites an article in the *New York Times*.

25. Grismer, *The Story of St. Petersburg*, 50.

26. See the discussion of the Golden Crescent in the history section of the city's web site. http://www.ci.tarpon-springs.fl.us/historicalindex.html.

27. Grismer, *The Story of St. Petersburg*, 51–57, 61–68.

28. Knetsch, "Hamilton Disston and the Development of Florida."

29. Ibid., 58; Pettengill, *The Story of the Florida Railroads*, 87.

30. IIF Minutes, VII, 532, quoted in Dovell, "The Railroads and the Public Lands of Florida," 256.

31. Eliot, "The Everglades," 206; Smith, *Report on Reconnaissance of the Everglades, Made to the Secretary of the Treasury, June 1848*; Dovell, "The Everglades before Reclamation," 30–33.

32. McCally, *The Everglades*, 91.

33. Long, "Florida's First Railroad Commission, 1887–1891," 255.

34. See Blake, *Land into Water—Water into Land*, 93–104.

35. More detail is given in Dovell, *Florida: Historic, Dramatic, Contemporary*, 2:718–720, 751–752.

36. Knetsch, "The Impact of Drainage on the Development of Early Broward County," 30–38; English, "Davie: First Reclaimed Land in the Everglades," 29–32.

37. Tebeau, *A History of Florida*, 349; Hanna and Hanna, *Lake Okeechobee*, 137–149; Blake, *Land into Water—Water into Land*, 116, quoting an article from the *Jeffersonian Magazine*; Weidling and Burghard, *Checkered Sunshine*, 41.

38. The 1910 census counted 336 persons in Fort Lauderdale, 283 in Dania, 246 in Hallandale, 256 in Deerfield, and 350 in Pompano, making a total of 1,471; U.S. Bureau of the Census, *Thirteenth Census of the United States: 1910*, Vol. 2, *Population: Reports by States, Alabama– Montana*, 304, 308.

39. Hanna and Hanna, *Lake Okeechobee*, 262. The death toll from the 1900 Galves-

ton hurricane was more than 8,000, according to the U.S. National Oceanic and Aeronautical Administration.

40. Urban population was defined by the U.S. Census of Population as persons living in places with a population of 2,500 or more, except for 1880, when it was defined as places with a population of 4,000 or more.

Chapter 3. Developing the Rail Network

1. Pettengill, *The Story of the Florida Railroads*, 30.
2. Smyth, *The Life of Henry Bradley Plant*, 45; Covington, *Henry B. Plant*, 43.
3. Grossman, *American Express*, 38. See also the letter of former governor R. B. Bullock of Georgia, who noted that in Plant's early days developing the express business out of Augusta, bank officials were the chief patrons of the business. The letter is quoted in Smyth, *The Life of Henry Bradley Plant*, 99–101.
4. Smyth, *The Life of Henry Bradley Plant*, 52.
5. The decline began in October 1873 and continued until March 1879, according to the National Bureau of Economic Research. This economic contraction is the longest ever recorded in U.S. history.
6. Johnson, "Henry Bradley Plant," 119.
7. Mueller, *Steamships of the Two Henrys*, 19.
8. Florida Department of Agriculture, *Report of the Commissioner of Agriculture of the State of Florida: 1901/1902*, 203.
9. Martin, "Henry Morrison Flagler"; Akin, *Flagler: Rockefeller Partner and Florida Baron*, 3–10.
10. "John D. Rockefeller."
11. Stephen Harkness made a fortune from his investment in Rockefeller, Andrews and Flagler. After his death, his wife founded the Commonwealth Fund in New York, a philanthropic organization that still exists a century later.
12. Martin, "Henry Morrison Flagler," 262.
13. Henry Morrison Flagler Museum.
14. Akin, *Flagler: Rockefeller Partner and Florida Baron*, 72–74.
15. Martin, *Florida's Flagler*, 78–79.
16. Flagler quoted in Martin, *Florida's Flagler*, 95.
17. "William Backhouse Astor Jr." Astor's son and heir was John Jacob Astor IV, who perished when the ocean liner *Titanic* sank in 1912.
18. Martin, *Florida's Flagler*, 131.
19. Quoted from a letter written by Henry Flagler by Akin, *Flagler: Rockefeller Partner and Florida Baron*, 135–136.
20. Bramson, *Speedway to Sunshine*, 20.
21. "Jupiter Ridge History"
22. Quote from J. E. Ingraham in Marchman, "The Ingraham Everglades Exploring Expedition," 41.
23. Akin, *Flagler: Rockefeller Partner and Florida Baron*, 162.
24. Crawford, "Sam Maddox and the Florida Waterway," 9.

25. Mueller, *Steamships of the Two Henrys*, 34.

26. Akin, *Flagler: Rockefeller Partner and Florida Baron*, 213.

27. Bramson, *Speedway to Sunshine*, 69.

28. Martin, *Florida's Flagler*, 208–222.

29. Akin, *Flagler: Rockefeller Partner and Florida Baron*, 215–220; Knetsch, "The Peonage Controversy," 23.

30. Williamson, "William D. Chipley."

31. Pettengill, *The Story of the Florida Railroads*, 114–121.

32. Johnson, "The Florida Railroad," 306–309.

33. The classic statement of the importance of railroads is Jencks, "Railroad as an Economic Force in American Development." The view that the importance of railroads should be reduced is associated with Fogel, "A Quantitative Approach to the Study of Railroads on American Economic Growth." In "Transport Innovation and Economic Growth," David argues that Fogel went too far in his criticism.

Chapter 4. Sunshine Agriculture before 1900

1. Jackson and Davies, *Citrus Growing in Florida*, 1–4.

2. Robinson, "Some Aspects of the History of Citrus in Florida," 59–60.

3. Davis, "Early Orange Culture," 232.

4. Hanna and Hanna, *Florida's Golden Sands*, 232–235.

5. Williams, *A View of West Florida*, 67–68.

6. Robinson, "Count Odette Phillippi," 91; Jackson and Davies, *Citrus Growing in Florida*, 30–31; Robinson, "Some Aspects of the History of Citrus in Florida," 62–63; Weeks, "Florida Gold," 6–7. Robinson's spelling, which he quotes from a tombstone and a tablet at the grave, is usually replaced with "Philippe" by more modern writers such as Jackson and Davies; see *Citrus Growing in Florida*, 1–4. These gravesite markers use the title "Dr." rather than "Count." The Kingsley Plantation at Fort George became a national park in the twentieth century.

7. Weeks, "Florida Gold," 6–8.

8. Bass, "Historical Sketch of the D. D. Dummitt Grove at Allenhurst," 234–235; Robinson, "Some Aspects of the History of Citrus in Florida," 61.

9. Davis, "Early Orange Culture," 235.

10. Quote attributed to Warren O. Johnson, meteorologist in charge, Federal State Warning Service, Lakeland, Florida. Quoted in Attaway, *A History of Florida Citrus Freezes*, 13.

11. Williams, "Florida in the Union," 247.

12. Taylor, "The Fruit Industry," 320.

13. Carse and Foss, *Florida: Its Climate, Soil, and Productions*, 92.

14. Amundson, "The American Life of Henry Shelton Sanford," 153–157.

15. Fry, *Henry S. Sanford*, 4.

16. McMakin, *General Henry Shelton Sanford and His Influence on Florida*, 72.

17. Hume, *Citrus Fruits*, 43, 50–57.

18. Amundson, "The American Life of Henry Shelton Sanford," 235.

19. Attaway, *A History of Florida Citrus Freezes*, 22–27.

20. Amundson, "The American Life of Henry Shelton Sanford," 259–262.

21. Chase and Company survives at the beginning of the twenty-first century as Sunniland Corporation. See "The History of Sunniland Corporation" and the Chase Papers in the Florida History Collection at the University of Florida.

22. Attwood, "The Fruits of Florida," 140.

23. The basic data for Florida Map 4–2 are from Carse and Foss, *Florida: Its Climate, Soil and Productions*, 92. The data were collected in connection with the tenth census of the United States by A. A. Knight, the census supervisor in Florida. Data were not available for fourteen counties, most of which are located in the panhandle area where there was little production and were reported on the map in the lowest category. I converted the data originally reported in number of oranges to boxes by simple division. I assumed 150 oranges per box following Clark, "The Development of the Florida Citrus Industry before 1895."

24. Harris, "History of the Orange Industry in Florida," 205–215; Sampson, "Pioneering in Orange and Lemon Culture in Florida," 193–197; Kells, "Early Days at Citra, Florida," 128–130; Stevens, "Reminiscences of a Pioneer Orange Grower," 130–140.

25. Russell, *Classic Crates from Florida*, 10; Weeks, "Florida Gold," 81.

26. These prices are unit values per equivalent box from the 1880 census data, as reported in U.S. Department of Agriculture, *Florida, Its Climate, Soil, Productions, 1882*, 91–92, and from the U.S. Bureau of the Census, *Eleventh Census of the United States: 1890*, Vol. 5, *Report on the Statistics of Agriculture*, 588.

27. Weeks, "Florida Gold," 102.

28. Quoted from the Articles of Incorporation in the files of the Florida Secretary of State in Clark, "The Development of the Florida Citrus Industry before 1895," 108.

29. Warner, "Development of Marketing Citrus Fruits in Florida," 198–200.

30. Weeks, "Florida Gold," 190.

31. Clark, "The Development of the Florida Citrus Industry before 1895," 81.

32. *Florida Times-Union*, quoted in Clark, "The Development of the Florida Citrus Industry before 1895," 97.

33. Webber, "The Two Freezes of 1894–95 in Florida," 162.

34. The sources of the information in this paragraph and in Chart 4–1 are "Census of the State of Florida, 1885," 14; "Census of the State of Florida, 1895," 13; U.S. Bureau of the Census, *Eleventh Census of the United States: 1890*, Vol. 1, *Report on Population*, Part 1, 3; U.S. Bureau of the Census, *Twelfth Census of the United States Taken in the Year 1900*, Vol. 1, *Population*, Part 1, 2.

35. U.S. Bureau of the Census, *Twelfth Census of the United States Taken in the Year 1900*, Vol. 5, *Agriculture*, Part 1, *Farms, Live Stock, and Animal Products*, cxxxi.

36. Other counties experienced losses, but some counties experienced gains. As a result, the net loss to the state as a whole was the same as the gross loss to the five counties enumerated as the northern Orange Belt.

37. Lippincott, "Market Products of West New Jersey," 249–295.

38. Corbett, "Truck Farming in the Atlantic Coast States," 426.

39. The description of the flooding and the Alachua sink comes from Taylor, "Romance of Payne's Prairie"; and Rosenberger, "A History of the Florida Vegetable Industry," 17.

40. The source of the information in this paragraph and in Florida Map 4–6 is U.S. Bureau of the Census, *Twelfth Census of the United States Taken in the Year 1900*, Vol. 6, *Agriculture*, Part 2, *Crops and Irrigation*, 309.

41. Paisley, *From Cotton to Quail*, 44–45.

42. Florida Map 4–07 is drawn using the 1880 configuration of counties in order to make it possible to compare with Florida Map 4–06 above. Lake County, which was formed from Orange and Sumter counties, existed in 1890 but not in 1880. I added the production of Lake County and that of Orange County to draw Florida Map 4–07.

43. The state's 1889 census contained no report for Manatee County. I estimated values for this county's production by using the acreages and quantities in the state's 1890 census for Manatee and valuing the production using Hillsborough County 1889 unit values. The state census totals were larger than those in the U.S. census because some of the state's data were not included in the category "produce of market gardens" in the U.S. census.

44. I follow the Florida convention of treating the strawberry as a vegetable since its cultivation is so similar to that of vegetables in general.

45. Rerick, *Memoirs of Florida*, 2:255.

46. Rolfs, "Founders and Foundations of Florida Agriculture," 139.

47. Bruton and Bailey, *Plant City*, 136–150.

48. Technically, watermelons are not a vegetable, but they are normally grouped with vegetables in the Florida context. The same is true of potatoes.

49. U.S. Bureau of the Census, *Twelfth Census of the United States Taken in the Year 1900*, Vol. 6, *Agriculture*, Part 2, *Crops and Irrigation*, 318.

50. Shofner, *History of Jefferson County*, 379.

51. Florida Department of Agriculture, *Florida, a Pamphlet Descriptive of Its History*, 553–554. New York investor S. V. White extended the railroad to Daytona, almost to the Atlantic coast.

52. Rosenberger, "A History of the Florida Vegetable Industry," 28.

53. Sanford Historical Society, *Images of America*, 67–72.

54. Rosenberger, "A History of the Florida Vegetable Industry," 29.

55. Penny, "Shipping and Growing of Vegetables," 184.

56. Persons quoted in Rerick, *Memoirs of Florida*, 2:237.

Chapter 5. Tourism before 1930

1. Walvin, *Beside the Seaside*, 13–20.

2. Richmond, "Emerson in Florida," 75–83.

3. Brinton, *A Guide-Book of Florida and the South*, 115–130.

4. Olney, *A Guide to Florida*, 25.

5. Logan quoted in Barbour, *Florida for Tourists, Invalids and Settlers*, 189.

6. Stowe, *Palmetto Leaves*, 130.

7. Tyler, *Where to Go in Florida*, 30.

8. New England Emigrant Aid Company, *Florida: The Advantages and Inducements Which It Offers to Immigrants*, 3–4.

9. I have observed this in a number of datasets over the years. It is most obvious in international travel, particularly transoceanic travel. Longer stays spread the fixed transportation cost, thereby reducing daily total expenditures.

10. Cabell and Hanna, *The St. Johns: A Parade of Diversities*, 221–234.

11. Davis, *History of Jacksonville*, 363.

12. See the three one-page articles by Frederick H. Kent III, "From the Commodore," in *FYC Newswaves,* the newsletter of the Florida Yacht Club, June–August 2007, 2. See also Lee, *The Tourist's Guide of Florida*, 148.

13. The figure for the early 1870s is from Ward, *Old Hickory's Town: An Illustrated History of Jacksonville*, 128. In 1882–1883, 39,810 winter visitors were entered in the registers of the hotels and large transient boarding houses; Davis, *History of Jacksonville*, 491.

14. Brown, *Inventing New England*, 15–16; Aron, *Working at Play*, 131.

15. Stowe, *Palmetto Leaves*, 247.

16. The attraction's web site notes that the waters are up to eighty feet deep, http://www.silversprings.com.

17. Martin, *Eternal Springs*, 113.

18. Graham, "The Flagler Era," 186–209.

19. Brinton, *A Guide-Book of Florida and the South*, 66–69.

20. Lee, *The Tourist's Guide of Florida*, 174–175.

21. Ibid., 200.

22. Florida East Coast Hotel Company, *East Coast of Florida*.

23. U.S. Bureau of the Census, *Abstract of the Twelfth Census of the United States, 1900*, 300. I computed average wages by dividing total wages by the number of wage earners.   24. Limerick, Ferguson, and Oliver, *America's Grand Resort Hotels*, 37.

25. Sterngrass, *First Resorts*, 132–137, and elsewhere under "flirting" in the index.

26. Davis, *History of Jacksonville*, 152–154.

27. Martin, *Florida's Flagler*, 103–116.

28. Hanna and Hanna, *Florida's Golden Sands*, 205–206; Ormond Beach Historical Trust, *Ormond Beach*, Chapter 8.

29. Gold, *History of Volusia County, Florida*, 137–156; Ormond Beach Historical Trust, *Ormond Beach*, Chapter 7.

30. Martin, *Florida's Flagler*, 141–145.

31. Lenfestey, *"An Elegant Frontier,"* 11.

32. Ibid., 9–10; Covington, *Henry B. Plant and the Tampa Bay Hotel*, 58.

33. Quoted from an advertising brochure by Lenfestey, *"An Elegant Frontier,"* 4–5.

34. Covington, *Henry B. Plant and the Tampa Bay Hotel*, 58–74.

35. Ibid., 74.

36. Lenfestey, *"An Elegant Frontier,"* 4, 6. The letterhead is quoted on page 6.

37. The data are from Florida Railroad Commission, *Annual Report of the Railroad Commission of the State of Florida.* Data up to 1917 were for the July–June fiscal year; in 1918, the data were changed to a calendar-year basis.

38. Broward County was not officially established as a county until 1915.

39. I obtained the price of a touring Model T from the Web site of the Model T Ford Club International Inc. at http://www.modelt.org/tprices.html. For the information in this paragraph and in Chart 5–3, I divided the data from this source by the consumer price index to compute the price of the Model T in year 2000 dollars.

40. The average annual wage of a manufacturing worker in 1921 was $1,180; *U.S. Census of Manufactures Taken in 1921.* I computed the wage as total wages divided by the average annual number of workers from the census table reproduced in the U.S. Bureau of the Census, *Statistical Abstract of the United States: 1922*, 200.

41. The data are from the United States, Department of Commerce, Bureau of the Census, *Historical Statistics of the United States: Colonial Times to 1970*, part 2, series Q 148–162, 716.

42. The data are in the U.S. Bureau of the Census, *Statistical Abstract of the United States: 1929*, 376.

43. Fisher, *The Pacesetter*, 78–80. Florida established its state road-building program in 1915.

44. Redford, *Billion Dollar Sandbar*, 47–53; Fisher, *The Pacesetter*, 12–38.

45. Fisher to Henry Ford, September 1912, quoted in Fisher, *The Pacesetter*, 78–80.

46. Eyrich, "Old Dixie Highway"; "Whatever Happened to the Dixie Highway?"

47. Arsenault, *St. Petersburg and the Florida Dream*, 189, Dunn, *Yesterday's St. Petersburg*, 30; Weidling and Burghard, *Checkered Sunshine*, 91; "Broward County Florida, Reprint," 41; Jahoda, *River of the Golden Ibis*, 282–284; Grismer, *The Story of Sarasota*, 192–193.

48. Davis, *History of Jacksonville*, 176–177.

49. George, "Passage to the New Eden," 441–464.

50. Arsenault, *St. Petersburg and the Florida Dream*, 86, 193, 204; Dunn, *Yesterday's St. Petersburg*, 31.

51. "Spring Training History"; Keller, "Pitching for St. Petersburg"; Covington, "The Chicago Cubs Come to Tampa." A history of early spring training is found in Holmes, "From Cooperstown."

52. Holmes, "From Cooperstown."

53. Cox, "David Sholtz," 142.

54. Kerber, "William Edwards and the Historic University of Florida Campus," 333–334.

55. Grismer, *The Story of Sarasota*, 231; and Huebner, "The Cleveland Indians and Spring Training in Lakeland," 19.

56. The basic data for the information in this paragraph and in Florida Map 5–1 are from Florida Hotel Commissioner, *Report of the Hotel Commissioner of the State of Florida* for 1927–1928, 11–12.

57. For both 1919 and 1929, I ascribed the difference between state and national figures for jobs in transportation, trade, and domestic and personal service to tourism in Florida. In 1919, jobs in these fields amounted to 30.4 percent of the total in Florida and 25.8 percent of the national total; U.S. Bureau of the Census, *Fourteenth Census of the United States Taken in the Year 1920*, Vol. 4, *Occupations*, 48. In 1929, jobs in these

fields amounted to 37.9 percent of the total in Florida and 30.5 percent of the national total; U.S. Bureau of the Census, *Fifteenth Census of the United States: 1930, Population*, Vol. 5, *General Report on Occupations*, 54. The number of Florida tourist jobs in 1920 was 17,724 and the number in 1930 was 44,321.

Chapter 6. The 1920s: Urbanization, Boom, and Collapse

1. Vanderblue, "The Florida Land Boom," 120–121.

2. In 1930, the U.S. census defined the urban population as those living in places with a population of at least 2,500. U.S. Bureau of the Census, *Fifteenth Census of the United States: 1930, Population*, Vol. 2, *General Report: Statistics by Subject*, 7.

3. Urban population by county in 1920 is from U.S. Bureau of the Census, *Fourteenth Census of the United States Taken in the Year 1920*, vol. 1, *Population 1920: Number and Distribution of Inhabitants*, 158. Urban population for 1930 is from U.S. Bureau of the Census, *Fifteenth Census of the United States: 1930, Population*, Vol. 3, Part 1, *Alabama–Missouri*, 412.

3. Daytona Beach absorbed two neighboring towns in 1925, so much of its growth was due to a boundary change.

4. The population of towns in 1930 is in U.S. Bureau of the Census, *Fifteenth Census of the United States: 1930, Population*, Vol. 3, Part 1, *Alabama–Missouri*, 421. The population of towns in 1920 is in U.S. Bureau of the Census, *Fourteenth Census of the United States Taken in the Year 1920*, vol. 3, *Population 1920: Composition and Characteristics of the Population by State*, 195–196.

5. Arsenault, *St. Petersburg and the Florida Dream, 1888–1950*, 187–198.

6. Redford, *Billion Dollar Sandbar*, 21–61.

7. Ibid., 65.

8. Ibid., 71.

9. Ibid., 67. The Lummus brothers were both presidents of Miami banks.

10. Harner, *Florida's Promoters*, 51–53.

11. Grismer, *The Story of Sarasota*, 208–213.

12. Weidling and Burghard, *Checkered Sunshine*, 101.

13. Redford, *Billion Dollar Sandbar*, 98.

14. The first automobiles were driven to the beach on the new causeway on January 1, 1920. Muir, *Miami, U.S.A.*, 137.

15. Armbruster, *The Life and Times of Miami Beach*, 16.

16. U.S. Bureau of the Census, *Fifteenth Census of the United States: 1930, Population*, Vol. 1, *Number and Distribution of Inhabitants*, 216–218.

17. Hanna and Hanna, *Florida's Golden Sands*, 336.

18. Steig, "A Look into the Past."

19. The city beautiful movement grew out of the 1893 Chicago Exhibition. See Hines, "Architecture: The City Beautiful Movement."

20. Construction of new buildings for the new university had not begun when the real estate boom ended in 1926.

21. Sisto, "Miami's Land Gambling Fever of 1925," 61.

22. From Walter C. Hill in an inspection report published by the Retail Credit Company of Atlanta, September 1925, quoted in Vanderblue, "The Florida Land Boom," 118.

23. Ibid., 119.

24. The basic data come from Kuznets, *National Income and Its Composition*. I divided Kuznet's data by the Consumer Price Index. I obtained the annual population series from the U.S. Bureau of the Census Web site.

25. These data are from U.S. Bureau of the Census, *Statistical Abstract of the United States*, annual issues for 1924–1926. The number of cities was 272 in 1924–1926, an increase from the 1923 figure of 269.

26. For the information in this paragraph and for Chart 6–2, the data for Jacksonville and Tampa are from U.S. Bureau of the Census, *Statistical Abstract of the United States*. I obtained data for Miami for the years 1922–1925 from city records reproduced in Sessa, "Real Estate Expansion in Miami and Its Environs during the 1920s," 223. The 1926 data for Miami are from U.S. Bureau of the Census, *Statistical Abstract of the United States*.

27. Data on all reporting banks are in U.S. Bureau of the Census, *Statistical Abstract of the United States*. Issues consulted were 1924–1928.

28. Vanderblue, "The Florida Land Boom," 116.

29. Data are from the Commissioner of Internal Revenue, U.S. Treasury, as reported in U.S. Bureau of the Census, *Statistical Abstract of the United States*. Issues consulted were 1925–1929. The data refer to individual income tax returns. I obtained labor income from the tax revenue data by totaling wages, salaries, and income from businesses and partnerships. Property income includes rent and royalties, dividends, interest and investment income, and interest from government obligations. In 1925, personal taxable income in Florida was based on tax returns with incomes of $1,500 or higher rather than $1,000 or higher, as in previous years. U.S. Bureau of the Census, *Statistical Abstract of the United States: 1926*.

30. The assessed values include real estate, personal property, and railroad and telegraph property. Assessed values are established at the beginning of the fiscal year. The data are from Florida State Comptroller, *Florida Comprehensive Annual Financial Report*. State law required assessed values to be set at 50 percent of market value. There were problems in enforcing this law, and analyses suggest that the ratio of assessed values to market values was lower in more wealthy counties and more urban counties. See Eldridge and Durrance, *The Assessment of Real Estate for Purposes of Taxation*, 10–11.

31. Sessa, "Real Estate Expansion in Miami and Its Environs during the 1920s," 258–297. This is the main source for the material in the next few paragraphs.

32. Hanna and Hanna, *Florida's Golden Sands*, 342.

33. Curl, "Boca Raton and the Florida Land Boom," 29.

34. See Semes, "From Rising Sun to Daunting Storm," 100–106.

35. Weidling and Burghard, *Checkered Sunshine*, 127.

36. Sessa, "Real Estate Expansion in Miami and Its Environs during the 1920s," 332.

37. The national data for the information in this paragraph and in Chart 6–4 come

from Kuznets, *National Income and Its Composition*; U.S. Bureau of Labor Statistics web site, consumer price index data set; and the U.S. Bureau of the Census web site, population data set. I developed the data on Florida personal income before 1929. I derived estimates for 1920–1928 using the debits to bank accounts series published in U.S. Bureau of the Census, *Statistical Abstract of the United States* for Tampa and Jacksonville. The data for 1921–1929 are in *Statistical Abstract of the United States: 1930*, Table 303, 289, and the data for 1920 are in *Statistical Abstract of the United States: 1928*, Table 293, 284. I computed the percentage change in the sum of the two debit values from the 1929 value for each year from 1920 to 1928 and applied this information to the 1929 personal income value. I computed intercensal population estimates assuming a constant annual percentage growth rate from 1920 to 1925 and constant annual increases between 1925 and 1930. The methodology resulted in increasing annual increases between 1920 and 1925 and constant annual increases between 1925 and 1930. I deflated the per capita income estimates by the consumer price index and expressed them as index values.

38. Hill quoted in Vanderblue, "The Florida Land Boom," 119.

39. See Arsenault, *St. Petersburg and the Florida Dream,* 253, where he notes that the strength of the national economy kept the tourist industry in Florida's west coast resort cities strong. Also, Curl cites the *New York Times* article "Boca Raton and the Florida Land Boom," which reported that 1927 was the best winter season in Palm Beach up to that time.

40. Florida State Comptroller, *Annual Report 1932,*

41. Ibid., 7–9. The figures for 1928–1929 were not available to the author.

42. The data in this paragraph and in Chart 6–6 are from U.S. Bureau of the Census, *Statistical Abstract of the United States.* No data were available for Tampa in 1928; I used the 1927 net debt figure for 1927. To obtain a capital outlays figure, I applied the percentage decline from 1927 to 1928 in Miami to the 1927 figure for Tampa.

43. This was the period before branch banking was permitted. Most banks had a single office.

Chapter 7. 1930: A Frontier Economy with a Sunshine Sector

1. Data on the population of Cuba, the Dominican Republic, Haiti, and Puerto Rico in 1930 are available at http://www.populstat.info/.

2. Five-year growth rates are not available for 1860–1870 and 1830–1840.

3. For immigration data, see U.S. Bureau of the Census, *Historical Statistics,* Part 1, Table C89–119. For data about the U.S. Army, see U.S. Bureau of the Census, *Statistical Abstract of the United States: 1921,* Table 461, 809.

4. U.S. Bureau of the Census, *Fourth Census of the State of Florida Taken in the Year 1915,* 19; U.S. Bureau of the Census, *Fourteenth Census of the United States Taken in the Year 1920,* vol. 3, *Composition and Characteristics of the Population by States,* 184.

5. For a discussion of the controversies created by the migration of Florida black workers to northern cities during World War I, see Shofner, "Florida and the Black Migration," 268–289. Census data do not support Shofner's statement that there was

a decline in the black population of Jacksonville. The population actually rose slightly between 1915 and 1920 from 36,035 to 41,520, after a strong increase from the 1910 population of 29,293. U.S. Bureau of the Census, *Thirteenth Census of the United States: 1910*, Vol. 2, *Population: Reports by States, Alabama–Montana*, 195; *The Fourth Census of the State of Florida Taken in the Year 1915*, 32; U.S. Bureau of the Census, *Fourteenth Census of the United States Taken in the Year 1920*, vol. 3, *Composition and Characteristics of the Population by States*, 195. Many Florida blacks undoubtedly passed through Jacksonville, the major rail hub for Florida. The Florida headquarters of several affected businesses were probably also in the city.

6. U.S. Bureau of the Census, *Fifteenth Census of the United States: 1930, Population*, Vol. 2, *General Report: Statistics by Subject*, 146. I obtained land areas in 1950 from U.S. Bureau of the Census, *Statistical Abstract of the United States: 1955*, 9.

7. U.S. Bureau of the Census, *Fifteenth Census of the United States: 1930, Population*, Vol. 1, *Number and Distribution of Inhabitants*, 199–215.

8. Campbell and Unkrich, *The Lumber Industry*, 57.

9. U.S. Bureau of the Census, *Fifteenth Census of the United States, Manufactures: 1929*, Vol. III, *Reports by States*, 120.

10. The basic data in Chart 7–2 come from Campbell, *The Naval Stores Industry*, 43–44. I used prices for 1905–1906 to aggregate the production figures and converted the constant price series to an index for graphic presentation.

11. Butcher, "Florida's Phosphate," 215–220.

12. The annual data in Chart 7–3 come from Blakey, *The Florida Phosphate Industry*, 154–155.

13. In 1902, Florida had 61 phosphate mines; in 1929, it had 18. U.S. Bureau of the Census, *Abstract of the Twelfth Census of the United States, 1900*, 431, and U.S. Bureau of the Census, *Fifteenth Census of the United States, Mines and Quarries: 1929*, 98.

14. *The Third Census of the State of Florida Taken in the Year 1905*, 188–253; Florida Department of Agriculture, *Report of the Commissioner of Agriculture of the State of Florida*, Part 2, *1915–1916*, 321–329.

15. Mealor and Prunty, "Open-Range Ranching in Southern Florida," 367–368.

16. Ibid., 374.

17. Dawson, "Cattle Tick Eradication," 176.

18. Akerman, *Florida Cowman*, 234–243.

19. Ibid., 234. The Florida cattleman quoted was John Cone (308).

20. Florida Department of Agriculture, *Report of the Commissioner of Agriculture of the State of Florida, 1923–24*, 28–29; *Nineteenth Census of Crops and Manufactures 1926/27*, 32–33; *Twentieth Census of Crops and Manufactures 1931/32*, 31–32. A small number of counties did not provide data for the report in each of the years, but the omissions do not obscure the trends.

21. No estimates of tourism expenditures are available for 1930. I estimated tourism from state-level personal income data available from the U.S. Bureau of Economic Analysis. First, I computed the excess of the Florida share over the U.S. share of private nonfarm labor earnings for transportation and communication (1 percent), trade (3 percent), and services (10 percent). Second, I adjusted this difference upward by the

ratio of U.S. per capita income to Florida per capita income (1.35). I multiplied the result by total Florida labor earnings in each of the three industries and totaled this figure to give an estimate of the labor earnings of the tourist industry of $20 million. Third, I converted labor earnings to total value added using the ratio of rent, interest, and profit income to labor earnings for the nation (1.276). The estimated value added by tourism was $26.2 million. This number is smaller than the value added by the lumber industry and about the same as the value added by the cigar industry. The figure for tourism is an underestimate since it assumes that all expenditures by Florida residents (excluding visitors) on hotels, trade, and services take place within the state. Later in the twentieth century, the state tourism agency measured the industry using the estimated in-state expenditures of tourists. This method obtained data from surveys and, unfortunately, made several major changes in methodology. I measured the size of the sunshine agricultural industries by converting their gross output measures to value added using the ratio of value added for all crop industries to gross output as obtained from the U.S. census taken in 1929. Value added was obtained as the value of production less expenditures for fertilizer, interest, electricity, gas, and fuel. The interest and gas and fuel components were very approximate. The estimates implied that value added was 70 percent of gross output. I made an additional adjustment to citrus based on the number of nursery trees reported in the 1926–1927 state census.

22. U.S. Bureau of the Census, *Thirteenth Census of the United States: 1910*, Vol. 5, *Agriculture: General Report and Analysis*, 719; U.S. Bureau of the Census, *Fourteenth Census of the United States Taken in the Year 1920*, Vol. 5, *Agriculture: General Report and Analytical Tables*, 873.

23. Hardee, "Pineapples," 12–18; McLendon, "The Pineapple Industry in Florida and Its Future," 93.

24. Dorn, "The Avocado Today in Dade County," 161–170.

25. Florida Department of Agriculture, *Florida Citrus Summary: 1948*, 9, 31. Data for 1920 and 1930 from *Florida Citrus Summary: 1948*, 9, 31; data for 1909 from U.S. Bureau of the Census, *Thirteenth Census of the United States: 1910*, Vol. 5, *Agriculture: General Report and Analysis*, 718; U.S. Bureau of the Census, *Twelfth Census of the United States Taken in the Year 1900*, Vol. 6, *Agriculture*, Part 2, *Crops and Irrigation*, 612–613 for production measured in boxes. I obtained unit values from Florida Department of Agriculture, *Report of the Commissioner of Agriculture of the State of Florida, 1899/1900*, 101–104.

26. Walker, "The Canning of Grapefruit," 84.

27. U.S. National Agricultural Statistics Service, *Agricultural Statistics, 1936*, 133.

28. U.S. Bureau of the Census, *Fourteenth Census of the United States. State Compendium, Florida*, 75–79; U.S. Bureau of the Census, *Fifteenth Census of the United States: 1930, Agriculture*, Vol. 2, Part 2, *The Southern States*, 720–725.

29. Florida Map 7–2 uses the 1919 configuration of counties.

30. U.S. Departyment of Agriculture, *Agricultural Statistics, 1944*, 195–195.

31. Webber, "Whence and Whither the Citrus Industry?" 10.

32. The data underlying Chart 7–6 come from the Commissioner of Agriculture re-

ports for 1900/01, 1909/10 and 1919/20 and Florida Department of Agriculture, *Florida Vegetable Summary: 1940*. I deflated the data by backdating the vegetable price index using citrus prices before 1930. The mixture of data sources introduces errors. This is why I reported the changes in vegetable acreages in the text, since they confirm the strong expansion of the industry in the 1920s, not only nationally but also in Florida.

33. U.S. Bureau of the Census, *Fourteenth Census of the United States Taken in the Year 1920*, V, *Agriculture*, 819; U.S. Bureau of the Census, *Fifteenth Census of the United States: 1930, Agriculture*, Vol. 2, Part 2, *The Southern States*, 702.

34. McKay et al., "Marketing Fruits and Vegetables," 621.

35. Ibid., 705–709.

36. Florida Department of Agriculture, *Census of Crops and Manufactures: 1926/1927*, 36.

37. U.S. Bureau of the Census, *Fifteenth Census of the United States, Manufactures: 1929*, Vol. 2, *Reports by Industries*, 1376–1381.

38. U.S. Bureau of the Census, "Manufactures: Florida," 4; *Census of Manufactures: 1914, Florida*, 258; U.S. Bureau of the Census, *Fourteenth Census of the United States, State Compendium: Florida*, 99; U.S. Bureau of the Census, *Fifteenth Census of the United States, Manufactures: 1929*, Vol. 3, *Reports by States*, 120.

39. Jahoda, *River of the Golden Ibis*, 221.

40. Quoted in Long, "The Open-Closed Shop Battle," 106.

41. Wilfredo Rodriguez quoted in Ingalls and Perez, *Tampa Cigar Workers*, 178.

42. I obtained data on the value and weight of fish that were landed on the Atlantic and Gulf coasts of Florida from U.S. Bureau of the Census, *Statistical Abstract of the United States: 1950*, 680–681. I computed unit values from these data to calculate constant values. I assumed value added to be 65 percent of gross output, based on Osterbind and Jones, "A Short Report on Florida's Commercial Fisheries."

43. Radcliffe, "Fisheries of Florida," 229.

44. Ibid., 228–229.

45. Cato and Sweat, "Fishing: Florida's First Industry," 33.

46. U.S. Bureau of the Census, *Historical Statistics of the United States: Colonial Times to 1970*, part 1, series L 319–320, 560.

47. Jahoda, *River of the Golden Ibis*, 264–268.

48. Dau, *Florida Old and New*, 329.

49. Radcliffe, "Fisheries of Florida," 231.

50. For Chart 7–9, I obtained 1899 gross output and unit values from U.S. Bureau of the Census, "Agriculture: Florida," 10; 1909 gross output and unit values from U.S. Bureau of the Census, *Thirteenth Census of the United States: 1910*, Vol. 5, *Agriculture: General Report and Analysis*, 621, 676, 681, 685; 1919 gross output and unit values from U.S. Bureau of the Census, *Fourteenth Census of the United States, State Compendium: Florida*, 60; 1929 gross output and unit values from U.S. Bureau of the Census, *Fifteenth Census of the United States: 1930, Agriculture*, Vol. 4, *General Report: Statistics by Subjects*, 764, 813, 817, 819.

51. The acreage data are from the U.S. censuses of 1900 and 1909 and state censuses

for 1919–1920 and 1931–1932. I estimated data for missing counties from the state reports using total acreages allocated between upland and sea-island cotton using a state census for an adjacent year.

52. Paisley, "Madison County's Sea Island Cotton Industry," 285–305. The data in Chart 7–10 are from the state agricultural censuses (except for 1899) and represent unit values. The sizes of bales and bags may have changed somewhat over the period but probably not enough to affect the trend in prices.

53. For Chart 7–11, 1905 was the first year the Florida Commissioner of Agriculture's report distinguished shade from open-field tobacco. 1926–1927 and 1931–1932 are the closest years to 1929 for which the commissioner compiled agricultural statistics.

54. The prices are unit values calculated from the state agricultural censuses.

55. Avant, *J. Randall Stanley's History of Gadsden County*, 155.

56. Ibid., 170–171.

57. Retail price data from U.S. Bureau of the Census, *Statistical Abstract of the United States: 1922*, 506; *1929*, 332; *1933*, 288.

58. Sitterson, *Sugar Country*, 346, 353–355.

59. Ibid., 365–370.

60. Sitterson, *Sugar Country*, 357.

61. Heitmann, "The Beginnings of Big Sugar in Florida," 39–61.

62. Sitterson, *Sugar Country*, 365

63. Data on personal income, a direct measure of the aggregate Florida economy, are available from the U.S. Bureau of Economic Analysis for 1929 forward. The state personal income estimates became available in the 1950s, although estimates were prepared for years back to 1929. Schwartz and Graham, "Personal Income by States, 1929–54." See the brief history of the data in U.S. Bureau of Economic Analysis, *State Personal Income: 1929–87*. The data presented in this chapter reflect recent revisions that include employer contributions to social insurance and unemployment compensation. They were available at the Bureau of Economic Analysis Web site.

64. Labor earnings exclude net personal transfers. These were a small component in 1929, before federal social security, unemployment compensation, and most welfare programs were established.

65. The data in Chart 7–12 are from the census of occupations as reported in volume 4 of the *Census of Population: 1930*, as published by the U.S. Bureau of the Census. I computed services as the total of employment in transportation, trade, public services, professional services, domestic and personal services, and clerical occupations.

Chapter 8. 1930–1945: Depression, Recovery, and War

1. Calculations are based on U.S. Bureau of Economic Analysis state personal income data, available at http://www.bea.gov. Midyear population estimates are available from the U.S. Census Bureau at the same site. I deflated the data using the U.S. Bureau of Labor Statistics Consumer Price Index.

2. For an overview of the Depression, the economic theories that have been advanced to explain its severity, and the personal recollections and views of a group of

economists who were graduate students in the 1930s and were major leaders in the economics profession in the postwar world, see Parker, *Reflections on the Great Depression*.

3. Hall and Ferguson, *The Great Depression*, 63–66.

4. Temin, *Did Monetary Forces Cause the Great Depression?* 170–72.

5. A history of the development of the state personal income estimates is found in U.S. Bureau of Economic Analysis, *State Personal Income: 1929–87*, M1–M4.

6. Per capita property income adjusted for price changes fell more rapidly in Florida than in the nation.

7. U.S. House of Representatives, *Review [of] Mediterranean Fruit Fly Claims in Florida*, 6–21.

8. For Chart 8–4, I computed frontier-maritime earnings as the sum of earnings in agricultural services, forestry, fishing, mining, and manufacturing as found in the U.S Bureau of Economic Analysis personal income data. I did not include military earnings, part of the maritime sector, because they are not driven by the interplay of the national and state economies. Per capita military earnings adjusted for price changes declined in the state and rose in the nation during 1929–1933.

9. Data from U.S. Bureau of the Census, *Statistical Abstract of the United States: 1930*, 263; and U.S. Bureau of the Census, *Statistical Abstract of the United States: 1934*, 236.

10. Rogers, "The Great Depression," 304

11. The data were gathered by the U.S. Bureau of the Census and published in the *Statistical Abstract of the United States*, issues 1928, 1931, 1935 and 1936. Chart 8–6 used 1933 data for Jacksonville and 1934 data for Miami and Tampa. Data for the latter two cities were not published for 1933.

12. The data for most state and local governments were for 1932. Florida was one of a small number of states for which data relevant to 1931 were collected. I obtained the Florida data from U.S. Bureau of the Census, *Financial Statistics of State and Local Governments: 1932*, 268–307. Data for the other states were published in U.S. Bureau of the Census, *Statistical Abstract of the United States: 1937*, 208–223.

13. Fort Lauderdale cut city operating expenses from $685,000 in 1926 to $142,000 in 1929, as reported in Weidling and Burghard, *Checkered Sunshine*, 146, 178. Schools began to charge tuition, enlarge elementary classes, shorten the school year, cut out nonessential subjects, and cut teacher salaries. See Bauer, "Sarasota: Hardship and Tourism in the 1930s," 141–142; and Rogers, "The Great Depression," 312–313.

14. Joubert, "Local Public Debt Policy in Florida: Part I," 1–2.

15. The exception was Bay County in the Panhandle.

16. Florida State Comptroller, *Report of the Comptroller of the State of Florida, 1934–35*, 127.

17. I calculated this estimate by assuming that county government debts were on a fixed payment schedule over twenty years with an interest rate of 5 percent. I expressed the resulting annual payment as a percentage of countywide assessed property values. In "Local Public Debt Policy in Florida: Part I," Joubert notes that Florida's local public debt bore an interest rate close to 6 percent in 1938.

18. Much of the discussion of the debt problems of local governments below fol-

lows Joubert, "Local Public Debt Policy in Florida: Part I," and "Local Public Debt Policy in Florida: Part II." The Municipal Bankruptcy Act, introduced in the Senate by Senator Fletcher of Florida and in the House by Rep. J. Mark Wilcox of West Palm Beach, enabled insolvent local governments to compel 75 percent of their bondholders to negotiate a restructuring of their debt, but it was probably feasible only for special taxing districts, where the number of bondholders was small.

19. The underlying data in Chart 8–7 are from U.S. Bureau of the Census, *Statistical Abstract of the United States: 1941*, 247–249. The debt is gross; that is, it does not subtract sinking-fund balances. It does not include the debt of public enterprises.

20. The underlying data in Chart 8–8 come from the *Florida Superintendent of Public Instruction, Report of the Superintendent of Public Instruction of the State of Florida, 1936/38*, Part 1, *Educational Progress in Florida,* , 244–247.

21. Tebeau discusses the racing tax in *A History of Florida*, 396–397.

22. Bordo, Golden, and White, *The Defining Moment*, 10.

23. Donovan, "A Decade of Federal Expenditures in Florida."

24. Rainard, "Ready Cash on Easy Terms," 293; Arsenault, *St. Petersburg and the Florida Dream*, 259.

25. Weinberger, "Economic Aspects of Recreation," 459.

26. The data in Chart 8–13 are a tabulation of a list in Breslauer, *Roadside Paradise*, 32–34.

27. Florida Hotel Commissioner, *Report of the Hotel Commissioner of the State of Florida, 1931/32*, 13; *1933/34*, 15; *1935/36*, 10; *1937/38*, 20; *1939/40*, 11.

28. Armbruster, *The Life and Times of Miami Beach*, 21–24.

29. Eutsler, "The Social Security Program in Florida," 1.

30. Ibid.

31. Hall and Ferguson, *The Great Depression*, 144–147.

32. David M. Ramsey, "Military Installations in Florida," unpublished manuscript in P. K. Yonge Library of Florida History, University of Florida.

33. Rogers, "Florida in World War II," 41; Mormino, "World War II," 329.

34. Diettrich, "Florida's War Economy, II," 1–2.

35. Diettrich, "Florida's War Economy, I," 1.

36. Mormino, "World War II," 331.

37. Schumann, "Compensation from World War II through the Great Society," 23–27.

38. U.S. Bureau of the Census, *Statistical Abstract of the United States: 1964*, 228. I obtained the data from a survey that excluded railroads, government institutions, construction, and extractive industries. It also excluded administrative, executive, and professional employees.

Chapter 9. 1945–1960: Postwar Readjustment and Boom

1. Attaway, *Hurricanes and Florida Agriculture*, 171–180. Attaway labels the storm a Category 4–5, but the data he provides about sustained winds are consistent with a Category 2 storm.

2. Dovell, *Florida: Historic, Dramatic, Contemporary*, 844. Fifty-nine million 1947 dollars converts to over half a billion 2000 dollars.

3. Mathews, "Water: Friend and Foe," 283

4. Blake, *Land into Water—Water into Land*, 176–184.

5. Carter, *The Florida Experience*, 94.

6. Tebeau, *A History of Florida*, 424–426.

7. Colburn, "Florida Politics in the Twentieth Century," 359. See also Colburn and deHaven-Smith, *Government in the Sunshine State*, 37.

8. Dovell, *Florida: Historic, Dramatic, Contemporary*, 887.

9. The data on taxes come from the U.S. Bureau of the Census, *Compendium of State Government Finances in 1947, State Finances 1947*, No. 2, 7–10. More detail on Florida's taxes before 1949 can be found in Donovan, "Sources of Florida's Tax Revenues."

10. *Compendium of State Government Finances in 1947, State Finances 1947*, No.2, 11.

11. Ibid., 12.

12. Donovan, "How to Balance Florida's Budget," 1; Donovan, "Florida's 1949 Revenue Program," 1.

13. The basic data are from U.S. Bureau of the Census, *Sources of Tax Revenue*, as reproduced in Donovan, "Florida's 1949 Revenue Program."

14. The source for the data in Chart 9–6 is U.S. Bureau of the Census, *1957 Census of Governments*, Vol. 6, no. 5, 66; *1957 Census of Governments*, Vol. 6, no. 8, *Florida*, 7.

15. U.S. Bureau of Economic Analysis, *Personal Income and Outlays, 1929–2004*, available at http://www.bea.gov.

16. I obtained the birthrate information in this paragraph and in Chart 9–7 from U.S. National Center for Health Statistics, *Vital Statistics of the United States 1984*, I, *Natality*, 1.

17. U.S. Bureau of the Census, *Statistical Abstract of the United States: 1964*, 754; *1944*, 735; *2004*, 605.

18. Data on the assets of FHLB and FNMA are in the annual editions of the *Statistical Abstract of the United States* issues for 1948 through 1956. The series stops in 1955 because of a shift from net to gross assets.

19. Data for the number of people by age group in Florida in 1950 and 1960 is published in U.S. Bureau of the Census, *Census of Population: 1960*, Vol. 1, *Characteristics of the Population*, Part 11, *Florida*, page 11–33. Florida is the eleventh volume in the alphabetical listing of states listed as parts of volume one for the nation as a whole, which is the reason it is part 11 and the single page is numbered 11–33.

20. The sources for U.S. data in this paragraph are in the following U.S. Bureau of the Census publications: *Sixteenth Census of the United States: 1940*, Vol. 2, *Characteristics of the Population*, Part 2, *Florida–Iowa*, 56 (for 1940 data); *Statistical Abstract of the United States: 1955*, 29 (for 1950 data); *United States Census of Population: 1960*, Vol. 1, *Characteristics of the Population*, Part 1, *United States Summary*, page 1–167 (for 1960 data).

21. See the following publications of U.S. Bureau of the Census: *Sixteenth Census of the United States: 1940, Population: State of Birth of the Native Population*, Table 13;

United States Census of Population: 1950, Special Reports: Nonwhite Population by Race, Table 25; *United States Census of Population: 1950*, Vol. 2, *Characteristics of Population*; *United States Census of Population: 1960*, Vol. 1, *Characteristics of the Population*, Part 1, *United States Summary*, 109; *United States Census of Population: 1960, Subject Reports*, *Nativity and Parentage*, 115, 123, 131, 139, 147; *United States Census of Population: 1960, Subject Reports, State of Birth*, page 19–23.

22. The Florida data for this paragraph and Chart 9–10 are drawn from U.S. Bureau of the Census, *United States Census of Population: 1950*, Vol. 2, *Characteristics of the Population*, Part 10, *Florida*, page 10–32 (for 1940); and U.S. Bureau of the Census, *United States Census of Population: 1960*, Vol. 1, *Characteristics of the Population*, Part 2, *Florida*, page 11–3 (for 1950 and 1960).

23. The material in this paragraph is a summary of the extensive discussion in Arsenault, "The End of the Long Hot Summer," 597–628.

24. Colburn and deHaven-Smith, *Government in the Sunshine State*, 34.

25. The data in Chart 9–11 come from the state personal income dataset available on the U.S. Bureau of Economic Analaysis web site. I netted employer and employee contributions to Social Security out of personal transfer payments. There is also a small statewide residence adjustment included in the personal transfer figures. This is an estimate of the incomes of out-of-state commuters.

26. I obtained the 1950 and 1960 data on the age distribution of the population by county for the discussion in this paragraph and for Florida Map 9–1 from U.S. Bureau of the Census, *Census of Population: 1960*, Vol. 1, *Characteristics of the Population*, Part 11, Florida, Table 27.

27. U.S. Bureau of the Census, *Census of Business 1948, Service Trades, Hotels*, Bulletin 2–S-10, Table 10A; US Bureau of the Census, *Census of Business 1954, V, Selected Service Trades—Summary Statistics*, 6–2 to 6–5; US Bureau of the Census, *Census of Business 1958, Selected Services Hotels, Motels and Tourist Courts*, 6–2:6–4; U.S. Bureau of the Census, *Census of Business 1963, Six, Selected Services, Summary Statistics*, 6–1:6–7. The data come from the *Census of Selective Services*. The 1948 figures include all hotels and tourist courts. The 1954 figures include all hotels, and motels and tourist courts with payrolls. The 1958 and 1963 figures include hotels and motels but not trailer parks and camps.

28. George Evans Company and Grant Advertising, *Tourist Studies in Florida*. A total of 32,285 questionnaires were collected including 19,348 from incoming tourists (many at Florida welcome stations) and 12,937 from exiting tourists (many by air, bus, and train common carriers). Data on winter tourists referred to the period December 1957 through March 1958 and data on summer tourists referred to the period June 1958 through September 1958. Those traveling solely on business were excluded from the survey.

29. The survey included two other destination regions: North Florida, which extended east from the Apalachicola River but excluded the coastal counties in the northeast, and the Everglades, which consisted of the interior counties in the south end of the peninsula. None of the tourists who completed the survey were traveling to the

Everglades Region, and 1 percent of the respondents in the winter and the summer seasons indicated that their primary destination was North Florida. Respondents could indicate that they kept on the move during their visit (14 percent so indicated in the winter and 21 percent in the summer).

30. Although this difference might appear small, it should be remembered that a high proportion of winter tourists stayed with friends or relatives. Additionally, the large summer traveling parties presumably took advantage of economies of scale in hotel rooms and automobile transportation.

31. I calculated inflation using the Consumer Price Index.

32. The interest rate is a three-month average of monthly data downloaded from the Federal Reserve Bank of St. Louis, FRED database.

Chapter 10. 1960: The Rise of the Sunshine Economy

1. National density excludes Alaska and Hawaii. Florida's density of 91.8 persons per square miles exceeded the national rate of 60.3. I used land areas from the 2000 census to compute density.

2. The per capita income figures for the state and nation come from the personal income dataset produced by the U.S. Bureau of Economic Analysis.

3. The U.S. Bureau of Economic Analysis dataset does not have personal income data for Florida counties before 1969. The figures used in this paragraph and in Florida Map 10–1 were developed by the Bureau of Business and Economic Research at the University of Florida and published in Kafoglis, "Personal Income Received in Florida Counties: 1960," 9–13.

4. Earnings in Florida tourism are computed by the excess share of transportation, trade, and services in total earnings in the state relative to the nation.

5. For the information in this paragraph and for Chart 10–4, I obtained gross output of vegetables for 1940–1960; I obtained the unit values from the annual editions of Florida Department of Agriculture, *Florida Vegetable Summary*. I assumed value added to be 56 percent of gross output.

6. Mounts, "A History of Tomato Development in Florida," 183.

7. Rue and Mazzuchelli, "Manganese Sulphate," 155.

8. Jamison, "A Brief History of the Commercial Vegetable Industry," 234.

9. Data from the U.S. Bureau of the Census, *Sixteenth Census of the United States: 1940, Agriculture*, Vol. 1, *Statistics for Counties*, Part 3, *South Atlantic States*, County Tables VII and XIII; U.S. Bureau of the Census, *United States Census of Agriculture: 1950*, vol. 1, no. 18, *Florida*, County Table 5 and County Table 11.

10. Speer, "The Vegetable Deal in the Muck Lands of Palm Beach County," 124.

11. LaGodna, "Greens, Grist, and Guernseys"; Rosenberger, "A History of the Florida Vegetable Industry," 2–7.

12. U.S. National Agricultural Statistics Service, *Agricultural Statistics, 1948*, Table 282; *1949*, Table 288; *1950*, 291; *1951*, Table 281; *1954*, Table 286; *1959*, Table 307. I interpolated data for 1954–1955.

13. U.S. Bureau of the Census, *Historical Statistics of the United States*, Part 1, 331.

14. Bruton and Bailey, *Plant City*, 141–143.

15. Writers' Program, *Iceberg Lettuce*.

16. U.S. National Agricultural Statistics Service, *Agricultural Statistics, 1939*, Table 252; *1942*, Table 293; *1944*, Table 205; *1945*, Table 211; *1946*, Table 230; *1949*, Table 234; *1951*, Table 229; *1953*, Table 239; *1954*, Table 230; *1959*, Table 249. Data obtained by interpolation for 1954 and 1955.

17. Matthews, "Frozen Concentrated Orange Juice from Florida Oranges"; Wenzel, Atkins, and Moore, "Frozen Concentrated Orange Juice," 180. Research at the University of Florida in 1942 showed that frozen concentrate stored for twenty-two months retained its taste and color and could not be distinguished from fresh juice.

18. "The History of Minute Maid," available at http://www.minutemaid.com/about/History.jsp.

19. "Historical Timeline," available at http://www.tropicana.com/TRP_Tropicana-History/CompanyHistory.cfm.

20. Gohl, "Citrus By-Products for Animal Feed."

21. Attaway, *A History of Florida Citrus Freezes*, 85–136.

22. Florida Department of Agriculture, *Florida Citrus Summary: 1964*, 5; *Florida Citrus Summary: 1980*, 5.

23. The data in this paragraph and in Florida Map 10–3 come from the county-level personal income data prepared by the Bureau of Business and Economic Research of the University of Florida. Although the bureau's reports indicate that military earnings can be obtained by subtracting civilian income from total labor income, the resulting series seems to include adjustments for commuting income that overwhelm the military earnings component after 1958. The source does not give sufficient information to resolve the issue. The 1958 data are in Kirkpatrick, "Personal Income Received in Florida Counties: 1958."

24. U.S. Bureau of the Census, *Statistical Abstract of the United States: 1953*, Table 837; *Statistical Abstract of the United States: 1963*, Table 982.

25. Marcus, "A Brief Summary of Florida's Fisheries," classified menhaden as the only nonfood fish in the 1960 landings data (3). In the 1940 data, there were significant landings of some fish not normally eaten in the United States, such as sharks and sunfish. These fish are eaten in Asia.

26. The 1940 and 1960 data are from U.S. Fish and Wildlife Service, *Fishery Statistics of the United States*, as reproduced in U.S. Bureau of the Census, *Statistical Abstract of the United States: 1963*, 702–703. The data for 1923 are from Radcliffe, "Fisheries of Florida." The 1923 reference had no data for pompano and clams and insufficient data for freshwater fishing. The *Fishery Statistics of the United States* publications contain some differences in nomenclature that might indicate differences in coverage, such as "mullet" versus "black mullet," "cero and kingfish" versus "kingfish or king mackerel," and "king whiting" versus "kingfish."

27. Cato and Sweat, "Fishing: Florida's First Industry," 35.

28. Diettrich and Hamilton, "Florida's Shrimp Industry."

29. Osterbind and Jones, "A Short Report on Florida's Commercial Fisheries," 2.

30. U.S. Bureau of the Census, *Historical Statistics of the United States: Colonial Times to 1970*, Part 1, Series L 319–320, 560.

31. "Corporate History of Swisher International," available at http://www.swisher.com/main/history.cfm.

32. The productivity chart is based on the manufacturing censuses: U.S. Bureau of the Census, *Fifteenth Census of the United States, Manufactures: 1929*, Vol. 3, *Reports by States*, 1376–1381; U.S. Bureau of the Census, *Biennial Census of Manufactures: 1935*, 1264; U.S. Bureau of the Census, *Sixteenth Census of the United States, Manufactures: 1939*, Vol. 2, *Reports by Industries*, Part 1, *Groups 1 to 10*, 272; U.S. Bureau of the Census, *Census of Manufactures: 1947*, Vol. 3, *Statistics by States*, Table 3; U.S. Bureau of the Census, *Census of Manufactures: 1954*, Vol. 3, *Area Statistics*, Table 4; U.S. Bureau of the Census, *Census of Manufactures: 1958*, Vol. 3, *Area Statistics*, Table 4. There was a small change in the definition of the industry between 1947 and 1958, and earlier censuses calculated productivity using production workers (wage earners).

33. I obtained value added for lumber, gum, naval stores, and paper from the U.S. Census of Manufactures publications cited in the previous note. I deflated lumber production using the wholesale price index for southern dressed pine obtained from the U.S. Bureau of Labor Statistics Web site for 1947 forward. I rearcasted this price index back to 1929 using the wholesale price index for lumber and wood products from U.S. Bureau of the Census, *Historical Statistics of the United States: Colonial Times to 1970*, 199. I obtained the values for 1919 and 1899 using the yellow pine price series (04085) available on the National Bureau of Economic Research Web site.

34. I deflated the value added of naval stores value using the wholesale price for turpentine in U.S. Census Bureau, *Historical Statistics of the United States: Colonial Times to 1970*, Part 1, Series E 123–134, 207–208.

35. Bell, *Glimpses of the Panhandle*, 182–183.

36. Shofner, "Alfred I. Du Pont: His Impact on Florida," 344.

37. Ziewitz and Wiaz, *Green Empire*, 50–57; Shofner, "Alfred I. Du Pont: His Impact on Florida," 343–344.

38. Ziegler, "Florida's Forest Land and Forest Industry," 2.

39. Akerman, *Florida Cowman*, 250.

40. United Braford Breeders, "History of the Braford Breed," available at http://www.brafords.org/history.html.

41. I obtained cash receipts from cattle and calves from Florida Department of Agriculture, *Florida Livestock Summary: 1963*, 5. I also used this source to deflate receipts by the average annual price per 100 pounds of cattle Florida farmers received. I assumed value added to be 48 percent of marketing based on data available for 1962.

42. Akerman, *Florida Cowman*, 247.

43. U.S. Bureau of the Census, *United States Census of Agriculture: 1959*, vol. 1, no. 29, *Florida*, County Table 8.

44. For annual data on phosphate production, see Blakey, *The Florida Phosphate Industry*, 154–155.

45. For Chart 10–11, 1929 gross output and unit values are from U.S. Bureau of the

Census, *Fifteenth Census of the United States: 1930, Agriculture*, Vol. 4, *General Report, Statistics by Subjects*, 764, 813, 817, 819; U.S. Bureau of the Census, *United States Census of Agriculture: 1945*, vol. 1, Part 18, *Florida*, State Table 2; U.S. Bureau of the Census, *United States Census of Agriculture: 1950*, vol. 1, no. 18, *Florida*, State Table 12; U.S. Bureau of the Census, *United States Census of Agriculture: 1959*, vol. 1, no. 29, *Florida*, State Table 8.

46. U.S. Bureau of the Census, *United States Census of Agriculture: 1959*, vol. 1, no. 29, *Florida*, County Table 11.

47. Patterson, "Raising Cane and Refining Sugar," 408–428; Sitterson, *Sugar Country*, 371.

48. Heitmann, "The Beginnings of Big Sugar in Florida," 58, notes that the sugar quota for Florida was 30,000 acres in 1934 and 79,000 acres in 1945. Sitterson, *Sugar Country*, 372, notes that U.S. Sugar accounted for about 90 percent of the state's sugar output in the early 1950s. According to McGovern, *The First Fifty Years*, 5, Southern Sugar, which was the predecessor of U.S. Sugar, controlled 100,000 acres in 1930.

49. McGovern, *The First Fifty Years*, 6.

50. Federal Writers' Project, *Florida's Sugar Bowl*, 31.

51. Heitmann, "The Beginnings of Big Sugar in Florida," 60.

Chapter 11. The 1960s and 1970s: Slowdown, Boom, and Recession

1. Annual midyear population estimates are included in the U.S. Bureau of Economic Analysis personal income dataset.

2. Quoted in Darragh, "Shakeout in Land Development!" 21

3. "Florida's Land Development Giants," 16.

4. Ibid., 16, 18; "What's Happening in Florida's Real Estate?" 25.

5. The data in this paragraph and in Chart 11–1 are in the following U.S. Bureau of the Census publications: *Fifteenth Census of the United States: 1930, Population*, Vol. 2, *General Report: Statistics by Subjects*, Table 24; *Sixteenth Census of the United States: 1940*, Vol. 2, *Characteristics of the Population*, Part 2, *Florida–Iowa*, Table 7; *Statistical Abstract of the United States: 1955*, Table 22; *United States Census of Population: 1960*, Vol. 1, *Characteristics of the Population*, Part 1, *United States Summary*, Table 65; *1970 Census of Population*, Vol. 1, *Characteristics of the Population*, Part A, *Number of Inhabitants*, Section 1, *United States, Alabama–Mississippi*, 263–264; *1980 Census of Population*, Vol. 1, *Characteristics of the Population*, Chapter C, *General Social and Economic Characteristics*, Part 1, *United States Summary*, Table 67.

6. U.S. Bureau of the Census, *Historical Statistics of the United States: Colonial Times to 1970*, Part 1, Series B 1–4, 49. The reference notes that accurate measures of birth registration completeness on a nationwide basis were obtained for the first time in 1940 and showed the registration to be 92.5 percent complete. The problem of underregistration was more severe forty years earlier.

7. U.S. Bureau of the Census, *Historical Statistics of the United States: Colonial Times to 1970*, Part 1, Series C 89–119, 105.

8. Attaway, *Hurricanes and Florida Agriculture*, 226.

9. Attaway, *A History of Florida Citrus Freezes*, 97.

10. See "New Look for an Old Industry."

11. The peak share for 1968 was matched in 1943 and 1944.

12. "Florida's Economy," 36.

13. Quoted in "Big Push for Florida Industries," 29.

14. Quoted in ibid., 30.

15. Ibid., 33

16. "What National Defense Means to Florida's Economy," 18

17. Quoted in "Big Push for Florida Industries," 28.

18. Quoted in ibid.

19. The data in Chart 11–5 on technology employment came from the Florida Development Commission Electronics Directory 1963 and were reproduced in "Florida Technological Industries," 25.

20. "What Would Peace Do to the Florida Economy?" 14.

21. "Big Push for Florida Industries," 29.

22. "What's Happening In Florida Real Estate?" 22.

23. "Land Development Changes," 90–91 and "Florida's Land Developing Giants," 20–30.

24. "Land Development," 100.

25. "The Real Estate Industry," 29–30. It is likely that the data in the article came from a University of Florida report written by Alfred A. Ring, chairman of the university's Department of Real Estate and Urban Land Studies. See "'Trailer-Way' of Life Shows Growth," 38.

26. "The Real Estate Industry," 30.

27. "Condominium in Florida," 20–22. See "Florida's Land Developing Giants," 26, on Arvida's role in introducing condominiums to the Florida real estate market.

28. "Condominium in Florida," 20–22.

29. "What's Happening in Florida Real Estate?" 30.

30. "Land Development," 100.

31. "The Condominium: A New Lifestyle in Florida," 46.

32. Ibid., 54.

33. A brief summary of the comprehensive planning (also called growth management) legislation is to be found in Florida Legislative Committee on Intergovernmental Relations, *Report on the Development of a State Urban Policy*, 32–49.

34. *Census of Housing 1960*, I, Part 3, Table 28; *Census of Housing, 1970, Detailed Housing Characteristics*, Table 62; *Census of Housing, 1980, Detailed Housing Characteristics*, Table 93.

35. Dale Koppel, "H. Irwin Levy, b. 1926, Developer," *St. Petersburg Times*, November 28, 1999.

36. For example, an 814–square-foot housing unit built in 1973 in Century Village at West Palm Beach with 2 bedrooms, 1.5 baths sold for $22,500. The following year, a 1–bedroom sold for $16,500. These were the first parcels I came across in the database of the Palm Beach Property Appraiser, which recorded sales from the initial year of construction. This database is available from the Palm Beach County Property Appraiser in West Palm Beach.

37. The hotel and motel unit figures for 1971–1972 refer to July 1, 1971; University

of Florida, Bureau of Economic and Business Research, *Florida Statistical Abstract: 1972*, 579. The figures for 1975–1976 refer to January 1976; University of Florida, Bureau of Economic and Business Research, *Florida Statistical Abstract 1975*, 460.

38. Consumer price index data from the U.S. Bureau of Labor Statistics Web site.

39. The budget deficit as a percent of GDP is in *The Budget and Economic Outlook: Fiscal Years 2008 to 2017*, table E-13, available at the Congressional Budget Office web site, http://www.cbo.gov.

40. Crude oil prices are from the *Monthly Energy Review*, available at the U.S. Energy Information Administration Web site.

41. Data on county-level personal income are available at the Web site of the U.S. Bureau of Economic Analysis from 1969.

Chapter 12. 1980: A Northern Population in a Southern Setting

1. I obtained the land areas for states from the U.S. Census of Population 2000, GCT-PH1–R, downloaded from the census bureau Web site. On the home page http://www.census.gocv, select American Factfinder, then Datasets, then Geographic Comparison Tables, and then United States and Puerto Rico.

2. The data in this paragraph and in Chart 12–1 come from U.S. Bureau of the Census, *1980 Census of Population: Florida*, Vol. 1, *Characteristics of the Population*, Chapter D, *Detailed Population Characteristics*, Section 1, Table 194.

3. U.S. Bureau of the Census, *1980 Census of Population: Florida*, Vol. 1, *Characteristics of the Population*, Chapter C, *General Social and Economic Characteristics*, Table 62; U.S. Bureau of the Census, *1980 Census of Population*, Vol. 1, *Characteristics of the Population*, Chapter C, *General Social and Economic Characteristics*, Part 1, *United States Summary*, Table 98.

4. U.S. Bureau of the Census, *1980 Census of Population: Florida*, Vol. 1, *Characteristics of the Population*, Chapter C, *General Social and Economic Characteristics*, Table 65.

5. U.S. Bureau of the Census, *United States Census of Population: 1960*. Vol. 1. *Characteristics of the Population*, Part 2, *Florida*, Table 94, 101; U.S. Bureau of the Census, *1980 Census of Population: Florida*, Vol. 1, *Characteristics of the Population*, Chapter C, *General Social and Economic Characteristics*, Tables 18 and 76.

6. The basic data source on enplanements is from the U.S. Federal Aviation Administration, *FAA Statistical Handbook of Aviation*. Data were also obtained from University of Florida, Bureau of Economic and Business Research, *Florida Statistical Abstract* and U.S. Bureau of the Census, *Statistical Abstract of the United States*. The earliest figure for Florida that I found was for 1963. I extrapolated the number back to 1960 using its relationship to the national figure

7. Florida Division of Tourism, *Florida Tourism Report 1960*, 3; *Florida Tourist Study 1970*, 3; 1977 *Florida Tourist Study 1977, An Executive Summary*, 3; and University of Florida, Bureau of Economic and Business Research, *Florida Statistical Abstract: 1978*, 419. These data from the Division of Tourism of the Florida Department of Commerce tend to be unreliable because of the division's tendency to periodically make significant changes in its methodology. The annual personal interview surveys of tourists by travel

mode are very accurate, in my experience, but errors tend to occur when the methodology combines travel modes.

8. Miami-Dade and Broward counties were the top two destinations for air tourists in 1965, 1970, and 1980; Volusia (Daytona Beach) and Pinellas (St. Petersburg) were in the top three destinations in 1965 and 1980. Broward County was in the top three auto destinations in 1970.

9. Florida Department of Agriculture, *Florida Citrus Summary: 1980*, contains twenty years of data by type of citrus on production (in boxes) and on tree prices per box. I valued production at 1980 prices and expressed it as an index for Chart 12–4.

10. Ibid., 4. See also Attaway, *A History of Florida Citrus Freezes*, 102–107.

11. Florida Department of Agriculture, *Florida Citrus Summary: 1968*, 1.

12. Attaway, *A History of Florida Citrus Freezes*, 139–149. See also the weather summaries in Florida Department of Agriculture, *Florida Citrus Summary: 1976–1977*, *Florida Citrus Summary: 1977–1978*, and *Florida Citrus Summary: 1978–1979*.

13. Data on U.S. and Brazilian production in this paragraph and in Chart 12–4 are from U.S. National Agricultural Statistics Service, *Agricultural Statistics: 1977*, Table 307; *1979*, Table 322; *1980*, Table 321; *1981*, Table 320; *1982*; Table 286.

14. Florida Department of Agriculture, *Florida Vegetable Summary: 1961*, 2–5; *1963*, 2; *1965*, 2; *1967*, 3; *1969*, 3; *1971*, 3; *1973*, 12; *1975*, 12; *1976*, 12; *1978*, 12; *1979*, 12; *1981*, 12.

15. Summaries of the weather and other events of the vegetable seasons are given in Florida Department of Agriculture, *Florida Vegetable Summary: 1969* and *Florida Vegetable Summary: 1970*. See also Attaway, *Hurricanes and Florida Agriculture*, 277.

16. Vegetable production by state for 1960 is available in U.S. National Agricultural Statistics Service, *Agricultural Statistics: 1963*. The end-of-period ranking is for 1978, obtained from *Agricultural Statistics: 1979*, Table 215. The data are for 1978 because the *Agricultural Statistics* publication reduced its coverage of vegetable statistics in 1980.

17. Processing accounted for 2 percent of Florida's vegetable production in 1978, in contrast to 22 percent for California. Texas and Arizona, ranked third and fourth, also had little processed production (5 percent and less than 1 percent, respectively). New York and Michigan, ranked fourth and fifth, had more significant processing (26 percent and 24 percent, respectively).

18. The rankings refer to 1961 and 1978; the data are in U.S. National Agricultural Statistics Service: *Agricultural Statistics: 1963*; and *Agricultural Statistics: 1979*.

19. Sanford Historical Society, *Images of America*.

20. Yield per acre in hundredweight as computed from the data in Florida Department of Agriculture, *Florida Vegetable Summary*.

21. Data in this paragraph and in Chart 12–9 from Cudahy, *The Cruise Ship Phenomenon in North America*, xvi; and Dickinson and Vladimir, *Selling the Sea*, 133.

22. Dickinson and Vladimir, *Selling the Sea*, 23–36.

23. Cudahy, *The Cruise Ship Phenomenon in North America*, 60–64.

24. Dickinson and Vladimir, *Selling the Sea*, 26.

25. Cudahy, *The Cruise Ship Phenomenon in North America*, 98–105.

26. Dickinson and Vladimir, *Selling the Sea*, 30–34.

27. Earnings in water transportation also include a contribution from goods traffic through the state's sea ports. I believe that by far the greatest source of growth during the 1965–1980 period was the cruise industry.

28. I deflated the data from the *Statistical Abstract of the United States* using 1982–1983 unit values. The decline to 1970, a year with a substantial uptick, was about 3 percent.

29. I deflated the nominal unit values using the price index with a base of 1982–1983.

30. University of Florida, Bureau of Economic and Business Research, *Florida Statistical Abstract: 1972*, Table 11.042; *1973*, Table 11.042; *1974*, Table 11.04; *1975*, Table 10.4.

31. U.S. Bureau of the Census, *Census of Manufactures: 1958*, Vol. 3, *Area Statistics*, Table 4; U.S. Bureau of the Census, *Census of Manufactures: 1963*, Vol. 3, *Area Statistics*, Table 5; U.S. Bureau of the Census, *Census of Manufactures: 1967*, Vol. 3, *Area Statistics*, Part 1, *Alabama–Montana*, Table 5; University of Florida, Bureau of Economic and Business Research, *Florida Statistical Abstract: 1974*, Table 12.09; *Census of Manufactures: 1977*, Vol. 3, *Area Statistics*, Part 1 *Alabama–Montana*, Table 5; *Census of Manufactures: 1982*, *Geographic Area Series, Florida*, Table 5. The *Annual Survey of Manufactures* became available in the 1960s for the intercensal years. Some of the data from this source was reproduced in University of Florida, Bureau of Economic and Business Research, *Florida Statistical Abstract*, which commenced publication in 1967.

32. "Paper: The Florida Product You Throw Away," 16–49. The article called Palatka, southwest of St. Augustine, the toilet paper center of the United States and noted that the state produced 30 million envelopes per week.

33. For the information in this paragraph and in Chart 12–12, I obtained Florida production data for 1960–1970 from Blakey, *The Florida Phosphate Industry*; and Florida production data for 1980–1989 from Moore, *Mining Activity*, 266. I estimated Florida production data for 1971–1979 using the average share of Florida in U.S. production 1980–1982. I obtained U.S. production data from U.S. Bureau of the Census, *Statistical Abstract of the United States: 1974*, Table 1150; *1976*, Table 1225; *1979*, Table 1342; *1982*, Table 1310; *1987*, Table 1237. Blakey, *The Florida Phosphate Industry*, contains unit values for Florida from 1960 to 1970. I used U.S. unit values for 1971–1980.

34. "Phosphate's Expansion Boom," 36–38; "Phosphate Spruces Up, Courts the World," 289–295.

35. Cattle production data from Florida Department of Agriculture, *Florida Livestock Summary: 1963*, 5; *1973*, 3; *1978*, 3. Mark Tripson, a longtime cattleman from Vero Beach, pointed out the influence of the expansion of the fast-food restaurant chains to me. I obtained per capita beef consumption from U.S. Bureau of the Census, *Statistical Abstract of the United States*.

36. "Questions on Feed Cost." See also Schertz, "The Year of Economics"; Luttrell, "Food Production and Prices."

37. Sugarcane production and values from Florida Department of Agriculture, *Florida Field Crops Summary: 1919–1967*, 15; *1972*, 3; *1977*, 4; *1981*, 5.

38. Crawford, "Sam Maddox and the Florida Waterway," 17; quoted in Alvarez and Palopolous, "The History of U.S. Sugar Protection."

39. Tobacco production and values from Florida Department of Agriculture, *Florida Field Crops Summary: 1919–1967*, 17–20; *1972*, 3; *1977*, 5; *1981*, 6.

40. Pando, "Shrouded in Cheesecloth," Chapters 4–6, has a detailed discussion of the end of the shade-tobacco industry.

Chapter 13. The 1980s and 1990s: Economic Strength and Slowdown

1. The interest is the constant maturity rate for the one-year treasury bill (Series GS1), downloaded from the FRED database at the Federal Reserve Bank of St. Louis Web site, available at http://research.stlouisfed.org/fred2/data/GS1.txt. I calculated inflation using the consumer price index, base 1982–1984, available on the U.S. Bureau of Labor Statistics Web site.

2. Oil-price data from Energy Information Administration, *January 2005 Energy Information Review*, Table 9.1. This publication is available at their web site, http://www. eia.doe.gov. Click on "more" under "Publications and reports" and then on "Monthly Energy Review." Under related links, click on previous editions of MER and select 2005 and January.

3. The next several pages are derived from my analysis of the personal income data for Florida and the United States produced by the U.S. Bureau of Labor Statistics.

4. For U.S. defense budget outlays, see U.S. Bureau of the Census, *Statistical Abstract of the United States: 1992*, Table 52.

5. For prime contracts awarded to Florida, see U.S. Bureau of the Census, *Statistical Abstract of the United States: 1984*, Table 562; *1985*, Table 548; *1986*, Table 551; *1987*, Table 529; *1990*, Table 541; *1991*, Table 547. Data since 1996 are available from the Department of Defense Web site at siadapp.dmdc.osd.mil/procurement/Procurement. html. Click on Historical Reports, then Geographic. Prime contracts are contracts where the prime (lead) contractor is located in Florida. Subcontractors may be located outside the state.

6. Employment by standard industrial classification by state downloaded from the web site of the U.S. Bureau of Economic Analysis.

7. Manufacturing output is part of the gross state product series available from the U.S. Bureau of Economic Analysis Web site.

8. Kenny, "The Labor Market," 93–108. Kenny found similar results when he updated his study in Scoggins and Pierce, *The Economy of Florida*. I believe the significance of the climatic variable represents the lower local cost of the bundle of consumption goods desired by Floridians. Workers are willing to accept lower wage rates because the cost of the goods and services they wish to buy are lower in the state.

9. In what may have been its first entry into the personal computer market, IBM developed the short-lived IBM 5100 Portable Computer in 1975, but its price tag of around $10,000 made it a nonstarter in the new market that developed in the late 1970s. See Bellis, "Inventors of the Modern Computer."

10. See Spector, "PC History."

11. Orange production data from Florida Department of Agriculture, *Florida Citrus Summary: 1991–1992*, 4; *Florida Citrus Summary: 1997–1998*, 4.

12. The figures in Chart 13–7 come from Attaway, *A History of Florida Citrus Freezes,*. 240. The data were provided by Ron Muraro, Agricultural Economist, Citrus Research and Education Center, Lake Alfred, Florida. I computed losses using the assumption that the production level of 1979–1980 was sustained throughout the decade.

13. Attaway, *A History of Florida Citrus Freezes*, 237.

14. Florida Department of Citrus, Economic and Market Research, *Citrus Reference Book: 2003*, Table 49.

15. The data in this paragraph were produced by the Florida Phosphate Council and reproduced in Moore, "Mining," 153–158. The data refer to "crop" years ending on June 30. The article is also the source of the commentary on the industry's experience in the 1980s.

16. University of Florida, Bureau of Economic and Business Research, *Florida Statistical Abstract: 1975*, Table 23.39; Florida State Comptroller, *Comprehensive Annual Financial Report: 1987*, 130.

17. Cain and Francis, "Financing State Government," 147.

18. Florida State Comptroller, *Comprehensive Annual Financial Report: 1992*, 130.

19. Tash, "The Services Tax," 78.

20. Koenig, "Putting off the Inevitable."

21. Data are from the United States Department of Energy, Energy Information Administration, *January 2005 Energy Information Review*, Table 9.1.

22. The one-year constant maturity treasury rate is cited in note 1 above.

23. Florida State Comptroller, *Comprehensive Annual Financial Report*: 1992, 133; *1993*, 5; *1994*, 5; *1995*, 5.

24. I computed population growth rates from the decennial totals of the Florida population. *2000 Census of Population and Housing, Population and Housing Unit Counts, Florida,* PHC-3–11(RV), Table 1, Population: Earliest Census to 2000, and Housing Unit Counts 1950 to 2000

25. I obtained data for this paragraph and for Chart 13–13 on population over 65 for Florida and the United States from the following U.S. Census Bureau publications: *1970 Census of Population*, Vol. 1, *Characteristics of the Population*, Part A, *Number of Inhabitants*, Section 1, *United States, Alabama–Mississippi*, Table 51; *1980 Census of Population*, Vol. 1, *Characteristics of the Population*, Chapter C, *General Social and Economic Characteristics*, Part 1, *United States Summary*, Table 98; *1990 Census of Population, General Population Characteristics: United States*, Table 1; *2000 Census of Population and Housing*, Part 1, *Summary Population and Housing Characteristics: United States*, Table 1; *1970 Census of Population*, Vol. 1, *Characteristics of the Population*, Part A, *Number of Inhabitants*, Section 1, *United States, Alabama–Mississippi*, Section 1, Chapter B, Table 21; *1980 Census of Population: Florida*, Vol. 1. *Characteristics of the Population*, Chapter C, *General Social and Economic Characteristics*, Table 14; *1990 Census of Population, General Population Characteristics: Florida*, Section 1, Table 1; *2000 Census of Population and Housing, Population and Housing Counts: Florida*, Table 1.

26. For this paragraph and Chart 13–15, I downloaded birthrates per 1,000 population from the National Center for Health Statistics, Centers for Disease Control, *Vital Statistics of the United States: 1984*, Vol. 1, *Natality*, Table 1–1, available at http://www.cdc.gov/nchs/data/vsus/nat84_1.pdf.

27. U.S. Bureau of the Census: *United States Census of Population: 1960*, Vol. 1, *Characteristics of the Population*, Part 2, *Florida*, Tables 98 and 99; *1970 Census of Population*, Vol. 1, *Characteristics of the Population*, Part 11, *Florida*, Section 2, Chapter D, Tables 140 and 141; *1980 Census of Population: Florida*, Vol. 1, *Characteristics of the Population*, Chapter C, *General Social and Economic Characteristics*, Tables 61, 63, and 65; *1990 Census of Population, General Population Characteristics: Florida*, Tables 19 and 23; U.S. Bureau of the Census, American Factfinder, 2000 Census of Population, Tables P21 and PCT19 downloaded from the census web site at http://www.census.gov. Click on Your Gateway to Census 2000, then American Factfinder, then datasets. Choose Census 2000 Summary File Three and click on List All Tables. Tables P21 and PCT19 give details on the foreign-born population for 2000. Select Florida and the U.S. under the Select Geography drop-down menu. Selecting county-Florida-All Counties yields the data underlying Florida Maps 13–1 and 13–2; *United States Census of Population: 1960*, Vol. 1, *Characteristics of the Population*, Part 1, *United States Summary*, Tables 98 and 99; *1970 Census of Population, I, Characteristics of the Population*, Part 1, *United States*, Section 2, Chapter D, Tables 140 and 141; *1980 Census of Population*, Vol. 1, *Characteristics of the Population*, Chapter C, *General Social and Economic Characteristics*, Part 1, *United States Summary*, Tables 61, 63, and 65; *1990 Census of Population, General Population Characteristics: United States*, Tables 19 and 23. For 2000 data see the earlier part of this end note; Gibson and Lennon, "Historical Census Statistics on the Foreign-Born Population of the United States: 1850–1990," Table 1; Malone, Baluja, Costanzo, and Davis, "The Foreign-Born Population: 2000," Table 1.

28. Malone, Baluja, Costanzo, and Davis, "The Foreign-Born Population: 2000," show that in 2000, Los Angeles County's foreign-born population of 3.4 million was larger than Miami-Dade's foreign-born population of 1.1 million. Cook County in Illinois had a foreign-born population of the same size as Miami-Dade's, and Queens County in New York had a slightly smaller population of 1.0 million (page 9).

29. It is not surprising that Cuba was the largest source of foreign-born residents in Union County between Gainesville and Jacksonville (where the state's prison complex is located). Not only was Cuba the largest source of the general foreign-born population, it was also the largest source of foreign-born residents of the prison facilities.

Chapter 14. 2000: A Tourism-Retirement Economy

1. The state's gross state product was $470 billion for the period 2000–2005, compared to India's $461 billion, as reported in the *World Development Indicators* database (available at devdata.worldbank.org/data-query). The statement in the text represents a degree of exaggeration since it fails to take into account differences in purchasing power parity.

2. Density obtained from Table GCT-PH1. "Population, Housing Units, Area, and

Density, United States and Puerto Rico, 2000," available at the U.S. Bureau of the Census American Factfinder Web site. The national population density of 79.6 includes Alaska and Hawaii but excludes Puerto Rico. In addition to the seven states with higher densities than Florida, the District of Columbia had the highest density in the nation. Florida's density was 296.4 persons. The national density excluding Alaska and Hawaii is 94.5.

3. Age pattern obtained from Table GCT-P15, Selected Age Groups: 2000," available at the U.S. Bureau of the Census American Factfinder Web site. The information is also available in Table GCT-P5, Age and Sex 2000, United States—States; and Puerto Rico.

4. Labor force participation obtained from Table QT-P24, "Employment Status by Sex, United States and Florida, 2000," available at U.S. Bureau of the Census American Factfinder Web site.

5. The personal income and earning data in this chapter come from the U.S. Bureau of Economic Analysis Web site.

6. Personal transfers are the net of employer and employee contributions to social insurance (Social Security).

7. I obtained these data from U.S. Census Bureau, Table 1, "State and Local Government Finances by Level of Government and by State," of the 1997 and 2002 census of governments, available at http://www.census.gov/govs/www/estimate02.html. I computed the budget shares for the census years 1992, 1997, and 2002 and found that the pattern to the shares was the same in each of the three censuses. It was possible to exclude capital outlays from the figures for 2002 since a rapidly growing state such as Florida can be expected to have higher capital expenditures. The "shares" in Chart 14–1 are the shares in the total of the four categories (education, public welfare, hospitals and health, and police and correction), not the shares in the total of all expenditures by state and local governments. The 2000 census of population showed Florida with 23 percent under 18 years of age compared to 26 percent nationally. It also showed that Florida had 8 percent aged between 18 and 24 compared to 10 percent nationally.

8. These data are in Table 1 "State and Local Government Finances by Level of Government and by State," part of the 1997 and 2002 census of governments, available at http://www.census.gov/govs/www/estimate02.html.

9. The largest employer listed on Taylor County's Web site is a paper mill; see http://www.taylorcountychamber.com/demographics.ivnu. The largest employer listed on Wakulla County's Web site is a defense manufacturing firm; see http://www.wakulla county.org/edc/major_employers.htm.

10. A small amount of data had to be estimated using ratios derived from nearby counties because the original source withheld the information under disclosure rules. It was necessary to make interpolations in two large counties, Sarasota and Manatee, because of disclosure restrictions. I made the interpolations using Pinellas County data.

11. Florida Department of Agriculture, *Florida Citrus Summary: 1999–2000*, 1; Florida Department of Agriculture, *Florida Vegetable Summary: 1999–2000*, 12.

12. Consumption and import data from the U.S. Department of Agriculture, Economic Research Service web site, http://www.ers.usda.gov/data/foodconsumption/. Under Data, click on the spreadsheets link. From the list of Excel spreadsheets click on Selected Fruit Juices, Per capita Availability. Go to the Orange tab to get imports and consumption (disappearance).

13. U.S. National Agricultural Statistics Service, *Agricultural Statistics, 1983*, Table 283; *1984*, Table 278; *1985*, Table 277; *1987*, Table 276; *1989*, Table 278; *1991*, Table 278; *1993*, Table 269; *1995–1996*, Table 269; *1997*, Table 5–24; *1999*, Table 5–25; *2001*, Table 5–29. I deflated the on-tree price using the Consumer Price Index.

14. Hart, "The U.S. Orange Juice Tariff and the 'Brazilian Invasion' of Florida," 9–10.

15. Per capita consumption data are available at the U.S. Department of Agriculture, Economic Research Service web site, http://www.ers.usda.gov/data/foodconsumption/ spreadsheets.

16. Personal interview with citrus processor Randy Sexton of Vero Beach.

17. Thornsbury, Brown, and Spreen, "U.S. Fresh Citrus and Global Markets," 1.

18. Florida Department of Agriculture, *Florida Vegetable Summary: 1981*, 12; *1983*, 12; *1984*, 12; *1985*, 12; *1986*, 12; *1987*, 12; *1988*, 12; *1990*, 12; *1991*, 12; *1992*, 12; *1993*, 12; *1995*, 12; *1996*, 14; *1998*, 12; *1999*, 12; *2000*, 12.

19. Zahniser and Link, "Effects of North American Free Trade Agreement on Agriculture and the Rural Economy," 95.

20. Huang, "Global Trade Patterns in Fruits and Vegetables," 41.

21. See the article "Lake Apopka, Cleaning up Florida's most polluted large lake" on the web site of the St. Johns River Water Management District, http://www.sjrwmd.com. The publication appears to have been superseded by the Lake Apopka General Fact Sheet in 2007.

22. McNutt, "Florida Grower Diversifies in Spite of Water, Development Pressures."

23. South Florida Water Management District, *Everglades Program Best Management Practices Annual Report, Water Year 2003*, 10, web site http://www.sfwmd.gov. The easiest way to locate the report is to enter the partial title *Everglades Program Best Management Practices 2003* into the search box on the site. Click on Water Year 2003.

24. Water Resources Group, Everglades Research and Education Center, Institute of Food and Agricultural Sciences, University of Florida, *Sustainable Agriculture: Best Management Practices— What Are They?* poster presented at the South Florida Restoration Science Forum, May 1999, available at sofia.usgs.gov/sfrsf/rooms/sustain/management; Executive Committee, Florida Division, American Society of Sugar Cane Technologists, "Sugarcane and the Everglades: A Good Relationship Science Can Improve," available at http://www.assct.org/florida/flenviron.htm.

25. Data for the tobacco manufacturing industry are not included in the maritime sector for 2000. The new industry classification (NAICS) adopted in the census of 1997 drastically changed the definition of the tobacco manufacturing industry from the old Standard Industrial Classification (SIC). Production on an SIC basis (value added) in the annual survey of manufactures for 1996 was $133.2 million. One year later,

the bureau of the census put production on an NAICS basis at $436.9 million. U.S. Bureau of the Census: *Annual Survey of Manufactures, 1996, Geographic Area Statistics,* 3–34; *Census of Manufacturing, 1997, Geographic Area Series, Florida,* 8. The omission of tobacco manufactures underestimates the contribution of the sector, but the inclusion of the entire water transportation earnings (see next note) provides an offsetting overestimate.

26. Water transportation earnings also included earnings connected with the transfer of goods through the state's ports, not just cruise passengers.

27. A discussion of the trends and impact of Florida's defense industry for most of the 1980–2000 period can be found in Lenze, "Military Bases and Defense Manufacturing."

28. Data came from Dickinson and Vladimir, *Selling the Sea,* 133. See also Business Research & Economic Advisors, *The Contribution of the North American Cruise Industry to the U.S. Economy in 2000.*

29. The Central and Mountain Region includes all states between Georgia and California and between Texas and Michigan.

30. Business Research and Economic Advisors, *The Contribution of the North American Cruise Industry to the U.S. Economy in 2000,* 7.

31. The data for this paragraph and Chart 14–10 come from the United States National Marine Fisheries Service. I obtained the data from the University of Florida, Bureau of Economic and Business Research, *Florida Statistical Abstract: 1983,* Table 10.40; *1984,* Table 10.40; *1985,* Table 10.40; *1986,* Table 10.40; *1987,* Table 10.40; *1988,* Table 10.40; *1989,* Table 10.40; *1990,* Table 10.40; *1991,* Table 10.40; *1992,* Table 10.40; *1993,* Table 10.40; *1994,* Table 10.40; *1995,* Table 10.40;. *1996,* Table 10.40; *1997,* Table 10.40; *1998,* Table 10.40; *1999,* Table 10.40; *2000,* Table 10.40; *2001,* Table 10.40; *2002,* Table 10.40. I interpolated the 1993 data using state data provided by the Florida Fish and Wildlife Conservation Commission. The commission also provided data that made it possible to compute unit prices for fin fish, invertebrates, and shrimp by county in 2003; I used these prices to value data on annual pounds landed by county.

32. Milon, "Natural Resources and the Environment," 164. The regulation banned the use of nets by commercial fishers in state waters. See also Adams, Jacob, and Smith, "What Happened after the Net Ban?"

33. Jerardo, "Import Share of U.S. Food Consumption Stable at 11 Percent."

34. The data for this paragraph and for Chart 14–11 come from the 1997 Economic Census. This Census reclassified industries from the Standard Industrial Classification (SIC) to the North American Industrial Classification System (NAICS). As a result, the coverage of the paper and lumber industries changed. The changes in the case of these two industries seem to be relatively small at the national level and they are probably even smaller at the state level. Information on the changes in coverage is available at the Bureau of the Census web site, http://www.census.gov/epcd/ec97brdg/.

35. Carter and Jokela, "Florida's Renewable Forest Resources."

36. Hodges, Mulkey, Alavapati, Carter, and Kiker. *Economic Impacts of the Forest Industry in Florida.*

37. The data for Chart 14–12 come from the Annual Survey of Manufactures of the U.S. Bureau of the Census for the period 1882 to 1996.

38. DuPont's will as quoted in Ziewitz and Wiaz, *Green Empire*, 50.

39. Ziewitz and Wiaz, *Green Empire*, 86

40. Ibid., 110.

41. Ibid., 116.

42. Ibid., 118–119.

43. The data come from the *Annual Survey of Manufactures*.

44. The producer price index for dressed southern pine came from the U.S. Bureau of Labor Statistics web site (Series Id: wdu081102), http://www.bls.gov. Click on Producer Price Indexes and then Get Detailed PPI Indexes. Under Create Customized Tables, click on Commodity Data—Discontinued Series. Select Not Seasonally Adjusted, then 08 Lumber and Wood Products and 1102 Southern Pine, Dressed. .

45. Florida phosphate production data for Chart 14–16 are from Moore, "Mining Activity," 263–273. National production and value from U.S. Bureau of the Census, *Statistical Abstract of the United States: 1990*, Table 1208; *1992*, Table 1168; *1994*, Table 1166; *1997*, Table 1153–1154; *1999*, Table 1168–1169; *2001*, Table 869–870. I deflated the Florida data using the national unit values. Data since 1999 are available at U.S. Geological Survey, "Mineral Commodity Summaries: Phosphate Rock," available at minerals.usgs.gov/minerals/pubs/mcs/.

46. "Regulations, Reclamations & Rising Costs," 18–23. I am grateful to Gary Albarelli, librarian at the Florida Institute of Research, for directing my attention to this article and making it available to me.

47. "New Mines Take Shape," 27–30. I am grateful to Gary Albarelli for directing my attention to this article and making it available to me.

48. Author's interview with Mike Lloyd, director of the Florida Institute for Phosphate Research, August 8, 2006.

49. See http://www.stackfree.com for a discussion of phosphogypsum. This site is sponsored by Aleff Group, Dr. Phosphate Inc., Florida Institute of Phosphate Research, and Rothamsted Research of the United Kingdom.

50. Cattle production data for Chart 14–17 are from Florida Department of Agriculture, *Florida Livestock Summary: 1992*, 1, 43; *1999*, 2, 30; *2003*, 1, 28.

51. Beef consumption data from Florida Department of Agriculture, *Florida Livestock Summary: 1992*, 2; *1999*, 2; *2003*, 2. Consumption is on a boneless trimmed equivalent basis.

52. Sugar cane production and values from Florida Department of Agriculture, *Florida Field Crops Summary: 1986*, 4; *1994*, 6; *2002*, A24.

53. Alavrez and Palopolous, "The History of U.S. Sugar Protection," 4.

54. Data on consumption of caloric sweeteners for Chart 14–19 from U.S. Bureau of the Census, *Statistical Abstract of the United States: 2005*, Table 199.

Bibliography

Web Sites Containing Economic and Population Statistics

Federal Reserve Bank of St. Louis: research.stlouisfed.org/fred2/.

This Web site contains the Federal Reserve Economic Data (FRED) database of 3,000 data series. It includes data on interest rates and monetary aggregates. The one-year treasury constant maturity rate is available back to 1953. The M1 money supply is available back to 1975, and the M2 money supply is available back to 1980.

Federal Reserve Archival System for Economic Research (FRASER): fraser.stlouisfed.org/

This site contains scanned published versions of economic data from the last half of the twentieth century, including the *Economic Report of the President*, an annual publication of the Council of Economic Advisors since 1947. This source offers extensive national data series, many of which go back to 1929, in a statistical appendix.

Florida Heritage Collection: palmm.fcla.edu/fh/.

This site is a component of the cooperative project among Florida's public universities to archive materials from archives, libraries, and special collections. Economic and population data can be found using the site's search capability. For example, a search for the word "population" located three state censuses of population reports: *The Fifth Census of the State of Florida Taken in the Year 1925, The Sixth Census of the State of Florida, 1935,* and *The Seventh Census of the State of Florida, 1945.* Most Florida data published at the state level before 1930 came from the State Department of Agriculture. The Florida Heritage Collection contains *Florida, an advancing state, 19099–19179–1927, an industrial survey,* which was prepared by the Commissioner of Agriculture. A search under "advantages" turned up *Florida: a pamphlet descriptive of its history, topography, climate, soil, resources and natural advantages,* published by the Florida Bureau of Immigration in 1882. The Commissioner of Lands and Immigration published *Florida: its climate, soil and productions, with a sketch of its history, natural features and social condition* in 1870 which contained a census of population for 1867 on page 8. The Florida Heritage Collection also contains a number of guidebooks to Florida published in the last third of the nineteenth century.

Florida Historical Quarterly: palmm.fcla.edu/FHQ/.

This is another component of the Florida Heritage Collection Web site. *Florida Historical Quarterly* contains a number of articles with historical data such as population estimates from state censuses. Useful articles include Roland Harper, "Ante-Bellum Census Enumerations in Florida"; Dorothy Dodd, "The Florida Census of 1825"; and Dorothy Dodd, "Florida's Population in 1845."

Florida State Comptroller: http://www.fldfs.com/aadir/statewide_financial_reporting/index.htm.

This web site contains the *Florida Comprehensive Annual Financial Report* from 2002 to the present. Each report contains data for the most recent ten years.

National Bureau of Economic Research: http://www.nber.org.

This nongovernmental organization is the authority on the dates of national economic recessions from December 1854 forward. The dates are found in the data section under Business Cycle Dates. The NBER Collection also contains a Macrohistory Database with some series that go back to the nineteenth century.

U.S. Agricultural Economic Research Service: www.ers.usda.gov.

This Web site, part of the U.S. Department of Agriculture site, contains economic data on Florida agriculture, including value added, since 1949. To access the value added data select the farm economy tab and then the farm income tab. On the page select "see all data files." On the bottom of the datasets page select Microsoft Excel Spreadsheets. Choose Florida and the range of dates on the menus that appear. The web site also contains data on national food consumption and the import share in national food consumption.

U.S. Bureau of the Census: http://www.census.gov.

This Web site contains datasets from the decennial censuses of population and housing and the quinquennial economic censuses since 1980. The site also offers scanned versions of the decennial census publications since 1790. Scanned versions of the annual *Statistical Abstract of the United States*, beginning with the 1878 edition are also available on the site. *Historical Statistics of the United States: Colonial Times to 1970*, Parts 1 and 2, is available in the Statistical Abstract section of this site.

The economic censuses typically included the census of agriculture, census of manufactures, census of minerals, and census of selected services, including transportation and wholesale and retail trade. Prior to 1960, the economic censuses for the years ending in zero (in whole or in part) were included as volumes of the decennial census and are available in the census website. Economic censuses were also conducted in the middle of the decade beginning in 1914 for manufactures and 1925 for agriculture. These mid-decade economic censuses are not currently available on the census web site. The economic censuses have been expanded since a new industrial classification system was introduced in 1997 and are available on the census web site. The *Annual Survey of Manufactures* since 1994 is available in the Business and Industry Section of this site. Many census bulletins and census briefs are also available on this site.

U.S. Bureau of Economic Analysis: http://www.bea.gov.

This Web site contains the national accounts, including gross domestic product, personal consumption expenditure, and various price deflators. Annual data generally go back to 1929. It also contains state and local data, including personal income. State data go back to 1929, and local (county) data go back to 1969. The personal income dataset also includes annual midyear population estimates and employment data.

U.S. Bureau of Labor Statistics: http://www.bls.gov.
This Web site contains monthly data on prices, unemployment, and the labor force. Data on the consumer price index and all commodities producer price indexes go back to 1913. For the consumer price index, select consumer price index from the home page, choose all urban consumers (old series), and then check U.S. All Items, 1967=100. Enter 1913 as the initial year before retrieving the data. Unemployment data by county goes back to 1990.

U.S. Energy Information Administration: http://www.eia.doe.gov/
This Web site contains the *Monthly Energy Review*.

U.S. Geological Survey: minerals.usgs.gov/minerals/pubs.
This Web site has scanned versions of the *Minerals Yearbook* from 1932 to 1993. This is obtained by selecting Minerals Yearbook, followed by Volume I and Phosphate Rock. The section of the yearbook entitled *Minerals Yearbook: The Mineral Industry of Florida* is available from 1994 can be obtained by selecting Minerals Yearbook and then Volume II, Florida..

U.S. National Agricultural Statistics Service: http://www.usda.gov/nass/pubs/agstats.htm.
This Web site contains scanned versions of the publication *Agricultural Statistics* from 1994 through 2005. Printed versions of the annual publication before 1994 are not available on the web site but are available from the Government Printing Office in Washington, D.C. Prior to 1936, the statistical information was published in the statistical section of the *Agricultural Yearbook*, also available from the Government Printing Office. NASS has recently become responsible for conducting the Census of Agriculture which is found at this site.

Florida Office of NASS: http://www.nass.usda.gov/Statistics_by_State/Florida/Publications/index.asp. The site contains scanned versions of the *Citrus Summary*, *Field Crops Summary*. *Livestock and Poultry Summary* and *Vegetable Summary* publications for Florida. Much of the annual Florida data goes back to the 1920s.

U.S. National Center for Health Statistics: http://www.cdc.gov/nchs.
This Web site contains *Vital Statistics of the United States* from 1994. It also contains scanned versions of previous reports. To obtain these, select More Publications from the list of Publications and Reports on the home page and then select Vital Statistics of the United States from the List of Reports.

Printed Serials Containing Population and Economic Statistics

Florida Commissioner of Agriculture. *The Fifth Census of the State of Florida Taken in the Year 1925.* Tallahassee: T. J. Appleyard, 1926.
———. *The Seventh Census of the State of Florida, 1945.* Tallahassee: N. Mayo, Commissioner of Agriculture, 1946.
———. *The Sixth Census of the State of Florida, 1935.* Winter Park, Fla.: Orange Press, 1936.

Florida Commissioner of Lands and Immigration. *Florida: Its Climate, Soil and Productions, with a Sketch of Its History, Natural Features and Social Condition.* Jacksonville, Fla.: Edward M. Cheney, 1869.

Florida Department of Agriculture. *Census of Crops and Manufactures: 1926/1927.* Tallahassee, Fla.: Florida Department of Agriculture.

———. *Census of Crops and Manufactures: 1931/1932.* St. Augustine, Fla.: Florida Department of Agriculture.

———. *Census of Crops and Manufactures: 1936/1937.* Tallahassee: Florida Department of Agriculture.

———. *Census of the State of Florida: 1885.* Tallahassee: Florida Department of Agriculture, 1885.

———. *Census of the State of Florida: 1895.* Tallahassee: Florida Department of Agriculture, 1895.

———. *Census of the State of Florida: 1905.* Tallahassee: Florida Department of Agriculture, 1905.

———. *Census of the State of Florida: 1915.* Tallahassee: Florida Department of Agriculture, 1915.

———. *Florida Citrus Summary: 1948–2000.* Tallahassee: Florida Department of Agriculture, 1961–2000. http://www.nass.usda.gov/Statistics_by_State/Florida/Publications/Citrus/index.asp.

———. *Florida Field Crops Summary: 1919–2002.* Tallahassee: Florida Department of Agriculture, 1919–2002. http://www.nass.usda.gov/Statistics_by_State/Florida/Publications/Field_Crops/index.asp.

———. *Florida Livestock Summary: 1963–2003.* Tallahassee: Florida Department of Agriculture, 1963–2003. http://www.nass.usda.gov/Statistics_by_State/Florida/Publications/Livestock_and_Poultry/index.asp.

———. *Florida Vegetable Summary: 1961–2000.* Tallahassee: Florida Department of Agriculture, 1961–2000. http://www.nass.usda.gov/Statistics_by_State/Florida/Publications/Vegetables/index.asp.

———. *Report of the Commissioner of Agriculture of the State of Florida.* Tallahassee: Florida Department of Agriculture. Annual publication, issues from 1889 to 1923–1924.

Florida Department of Citrus, Economic and Market Research. *Citrus Reference Book.* Gainesville: Florida Department of Citrus, 2003. Issues of the *Citrus Reference Book* since 1964 are the department's web site, http://www. FloridaJuice.com.

Florida Division of Tourism. *Florida Tourism Report.* Tallahassee. Annual publication. Title varies. Early issues were published for the Florida Economic Development Commission.

Florida Hotel Commissioner. *Report of the Hotel Commissioner of the State of Florida. Tallahassee.* Biennial publication. *Issues* 1931–1932: Franklin Press; 1933–1936, 1935–1936, 1937–1938, and 1939–1940: Tikes Press Quincy.

Florida Legislature. *Florida, an Advancing State, 19099–19179–1927: An Industrial Survey.* Tallahassee: Department of Agriculture, 1928. Florida Railroad Commission. *Annual Report of the Railroad Commission of the State of Florida.* Tallahassee. Annual. Issues: fourth (1901): Tallahassee Book and Job Office; fifth 1902): I. B. Hilson, State Printer; sixth (1903): Tallahassee Book and Job Office; seventh (1904): Collins Book and Job Office; ninth (1906): Capital Publishing Company; tenth (1907): Capital Publishing Company; eleventh (1908): Capital Publishing Company; twelfth (1909): Typographical Union Label; thirteenth (1910): Typographical Union Label.

Florida State Comptroller. *Comprehensive Annual Financial Report.* Published by the Florida State Comptroller, Tallahassee. Since 2002 the report has been published by the Chief Financial Officer of Florida. Available online since 2002 at http://www. fldfs.com/aadir/statewide_financial_reporting/index.htm. Printed versions prior to 1993 contain consistent data back to 1980. Data from the report were also published in the section on Government Finance and Employment in *Florida Statistical Abstract.*

———. *Report of the Comptroller of the State of Florida.* Tallahassee. Biennial. Issues for 1932–1933 and 1934–1935: Rose Printing Company.

Florida Superintendent of Public Instruction. *Report of the Superintendent of Public Instruction of the State of Florida.* Tallahassee. Biennial. Issues 1936–1938: State Superintendent of Public Instruction.University of Florida, Bureau of Economic and Business Research. *Florida Statistical Abstract.* Gainesville: Bureau of Economic and Business Research. Issued annually since 1967.

U.S. Bureau of the Census. *Abstract of the Twelfth Census of the United States, 1900.* Washington, D.C.: Government Printing Office, 1902.

———. "Agriculture: Florida." *Census Bulletin* 165 (April 29, 1902).

———. "Annual Survey of Manufactures 1996" M(96)-AS3. Bureau of the Census home page, http://www.census.gov, publications under Business and Industry/Annual Survey of Manufactures/Geographic Area Statistics.

———. *Biennial Census of Manufactures: 1935.* Washington, D.C. Government Printing Office, 1938.

———. *Census of Business 1948, Service Trades, Hotels* Bulletin 2–S-10. Washington, D.C.: Government Printing Office, 1952.

———. *Census of Business 1954, V, Selected Service Trades—Summary Statistics.* Washington, D.C.: Government Printing Office, 1957.

———. *Census of Business 1958, Selected Services Hotels, Motels and Tourist Courts,* BC58–SS5. Washington, D.C.: Government Printing Office, 1961.

———. *Census of Business 1963, Volume Six, Selected Services, Summary Statistics.* Washington, D.C.: Government Printing Office, 1965.

———. *Census of Governments: 1932.* Washington, D.C.: Government Printing Office, 1935.

———. *Census of Governments: 1957.* Vol. 3, no. 5. *Compendium of Government Finances.* Washington, D.C.: Government Printing Office, 1958.

———. *Census of Governments: 1957.* Vol. 6, no. 8. *Florida.* Washington, D.C.: Government Printing Office, 1959.

———. *Census of Manufactures: 1914.* Florida. Washington, D.C.: Government Printing Office, 1917.

———. *Census of Manufactures: 1947.* Vol. 3. *Statistics by States.* Washington, D.C.: Government Printing Office, 1950.

———. *Census of Manufactures: 1954,* Vol. 3. *Area Statistics.* Washington, D.C.: Government Printing Office, 1958

————. *Census of Manufactures: 1958*, Vol. 3, *Area Statistics*. Washington, D.C.: Government Printing Office, 1961.

————. Census of Manufactures 1997, Area Statistics, Florida. http://www.census.gov/prod/ec97/97m31-fl.pdf.

————. *Census of Population: 1960*, Vol. 1, *Characteristics of the Population*, Part 11, Florida. Washington, D.C.: Government Printing Office, 1961.

————. *Compendium of State Government Finances in 1947*. Washington, D.C.: Government Printing Office, 1948.

————. *Eleventh Census of the United States: 1890*. Vol. 1. *Report on Population*. Part I. Washington, D.C.: Government Printing Office, 1895.

————. *Eleventh Census of the United States: 1890*. Vol. 5. *Report on the Statistics of Agriculture*. Washington, D.C.: Government Printing Office, 1895.

————. *Financial Statistics of State and Local Governments: 1932*. Washington, D.C.: Government Printing Office, 1935.

————. *Fifteenth Census of the United States. Manufactures: 1929*, Vol. 1. *Reports by Industries*. Washington, D.C.: Government Printing Office, 1933.

————. *Fifteenth Census of the United States. Manufactures: 1929*. Vol. 2. *Reports by States*. Washington, D.C.: Government Printing Office, 1933.

————. *Fifteenth Census of the United States. Mines and Quarries: 1929*. Washington, D.C.: Government Printing Office, 1933.

————. *Fifteenth Census of the United States: 1930. Agriculture*. Vol. 2, Part 2. *The Southern States*. Washington, D.C.: Government Printing Office, 1932.

————. *Fifteenth Census of the United States: 1930. Agriculture*. Vol. 4. *General Report: Statistics by Subjects*. Washington, D.C.: Government Printing Office, 1932.

————. *Fifteenth Census of the United States: 1930. Population*. Vol. 1. *Number and Distribution of Inhabitants*. Washington, D.C.: Government Printing Office, 1931.

————. *Fifteenth Census of the United States: 1930. Population*. Vol. 2. *General Report: Statistics by Subject*. Washington, D.C.: Government Printing Office, 1933.

————. *Fifteenth Census of the United States: 1930. Population*. Vol. 3, Part 1. *Alabama–Missouri*. Washington, D.C.: Government Printing Office, 1932.

————. *Fifteenth Census of the United States: 1930. Population*. Vol. 5. *General Report on Occupations*. Washington, D.C.: Government Printing Office, 1931.

————. *Fourteenth Census of the United States. State Compendium: Florida*. Washington, D.C.: Government Printing Office, 1924.

————. *Fourteenth Census of the United States Taken in the Year 1920*. Vol. 1. *Population: Number and Distribution of Inhabitants*. Washington, D.C.: Government Printing Office, 1921.

————. *Fourteenth Census of the United States Taken in the Year 1920*. Vol. 3. *Population: Number and Distribution of Inhabitants*. Washington, D.C.: Government Printing Office, 1921.

————. *Fourteenth Census of the United States Taken in the Year 1920*. Vol. 4. *Occupations*. Washington, D.C.: Government Printing Office, 1922.

————. *Fourteenth Census of the United States Taken in the Year 1920*. Vol. 5. *Agriculture: General Report and Analytical Tables*. Washington, D.C.: Government Printing Office, 1922.

————. *Historical Statistics of the United States: Colonial Times to 1970.* Part 1. Washington, D.C.: Government Printing Office, 1975.

————. *Historical Statistics of the United States: Colonial Times to 1970.* Part 2. Washington, D.C.: Government Printing Office, 1975.

————. "Manufactures: Florida." *Census Bulletin* 101 (October 1, 1901).

————. "Manufactures: The Lumber Industry." *Census Bulletin* 203 (June 24, 1902).

————. "Manufactures: Turpentine and Rosin." *Census Bulletin* 126 (January 11, 1902).

————. *1970 Census of Population.* Vol. 1. *Characteristics of the Population.* Part A. *Number of Inhabitants.* Section 1. *United States, Alabama–Mississippi.* Washington, D.C.: Government Printing Office, 1972.

————. *1980 Census of Population.* Vol. 1. *Characteristics of the Population.* Chapter C. *General Social and Economic Characteristics.* Part 1. *United States Summary.* Washington, D.C.: Government Printing Office, 1983.

————. *1980 Census of Population: Florida.* Vol. 1. *Characteristics of the Population.* Chapter C. *General Social and Economic Characteristics.* Washington, D.C.: Government Printing Office, 1983.

————. *1980 Census of Population: Florida.* Vol. 1. *Characteristics of the Population.* Chapter D. *Detailed Population Characteristics.* Washington, D.C.: Government Printing Office, 1983.

————. *1990 Census of Population. General Population Characteristics: Florida.* Washington, D.C.: Government Printing Office, 1992.

————. *1990 Census of Population. General Population Characteristics: United States.* Washington, D.C.: Government Printing Office, 1992.

————. "Population of Florida by Counties and Minor Civil Divisions." *Census Bulletin* 16 (November 20, 1900).

————. *Sixteenth Census of the United States. Manufactures: 1939.* Vol. 2. *Reports by Industries.* Part 1. *Groups 1 to 10.* Washington, D.C.: Government Printing Office, 1942.

————. *Sixteenth Census of the United States: 1940. Agriculture.* Vol. 1. *Statistics for Counties.* Part 3. *South Atlantic States.* Washington, D.C.: Government Printing Office, 1942.

————. *Sixteenth Census of the United States: 1940. Population: State of Birth of the Native Population.* Washington, D.C.: Government Printing Office, 1944.

————. *Sixteenth Census of the United States: 1940. Population.* Vol. 2. *Characteristics of the Population.* Part 2. *Florida–Iowa.* Washington, D.C.: Government Printing Office, 1943.

————. Special Report, Mines and Quarries 1902. Washington, D.C.: Government Printing Office, 1905.

————. *Statistical Abstract of the United States, 1878–.* Washington, D.C.: Government Printing Office, 1878–. http://www.census.gov/prod/www/abs/statab.html.

————. *Tenth Census of the United States.* Vol. 3. *Report of the Productions of Agriculture.* Washington, D.C.: Government Printing Office, 1883.

————. *Thirteenth Census of the United States: 1910.* Vol. 2. *Population: Reports by States, Alabama–Montana.* Washington, D.C.: Government Printing Office, 1910.

————. *Thirteenth Census of the United States: 1910*. Vol. 5. *Agriculture: General Report and Analysis*. Washington, D.C.: Government Printing Office, 1910.

————. *Twelfth Census of the United States Taken in the Year 1900*. Vol. 1. *Population*. Part 1. Washington, D.C.: Government Printing Office, 1901.

————. *Twelfth Census of the United States Taken in the Year 1900*. Vol. 5. *Agriculture*. Part 1. *Farms, Live Stock, and Animal Products*. Washington, D.C.: Government Printing Office, 1902.

————. *Twelfth Census of the United States Taken in the Year 1900*. Vol. 6. *Agriculture*. Part 2. *Crops and Irrigation*. Washington, D.C.: Government Printing Office, 1902.

————. *2000 Census of Population and Housing*. Part 1. *Summary Population and Housing Characteristics: United States*. Washington, D.C.: Government Printing Office, 2002.

————. *2000 Census of Population and Housing*. *Population and Housing Counts: Florida*. Washington, D.C.: Government Printing Office, 2003.

————. *United States Census of Agriculture, 1945*. Vol. 1, no. 18. *Florida*. Washington, D.C.: Government Printing Office, 1948.

————. *United States Census of Agriculture: 1950*. Vol. 1, no. 18. *Florida*. Washington, D.C.: Government Printing Office, 1952.

————. *United States Census of Agriculture: 1959*. Vol. 1, no. 29. *Florida*. Washington, D.C.: Government Printing Office, 1962.

————. *United States Census of Population: 1950*. *Special Reports: Nonwhite Population by Race*. Washington, D.C.: Government Printing Office, 1954.

————. *United States Census of Population: 1950*. Vol. 2. *Characteristics of the Population*. Part 10. *Florida*. Washington, D.C.: Government Printing Office, 1952.

————. *United States Census of Population: 1960*. Vol. 1. *Characteristics of the Population*. Part 1. *United States Summary*. Washington, D.C.: Government Printing Office, 1964.

————. *United States Census of Population: 1960*. Vol. 1. *Characteristics of the Population*. Part 2. *Florida*. Washington, D.C.: Government Printing Office, 1963.

————. *United States Census of Population: 1960*. *Special Reports: Nativity and Parentage*. Washington, D.C.: Government Printing Office, 1965.

————. *United States Census of Population: 1960*. *Special Reports: State of Birth*. Washington, D.C.: Government Printing Office, 1963.

U.S. Bureau of Economic Analysis. *State Personal Income, 1929–87: Estimates and a Statement of Sources and Methods*. Washington, D.C.: Government Printing Office, 1989.

U.S. Department of Health and Human Services. *Vital Statistics of the United States 1984*. Vol. 1. *Natality*. Hyattsville, Md.: U.S. Department of Health and Human Services.

U.S. Federal Aviation Administration. *FAA Statistical Handbook of Aviation*. Washington, D.C.: Government Printing Office. Data reproduced in U.S. Bureau of the Census, *Statistical Abstract of the United States* and University of Florida, Bureau of Economic and Business Research, *Florida Statistical Abstract*.

U.S. Fish and Wildlife Service. *Fishery Statistics of the United States*. Annual Publication. Washington, D.C.: Government Printing Office. Key data reproduced in U.S. Bureau of the Census, *Statistical Abstract of the United States*.

U.S. House of Representatives. *Review [of] Mediterranean Fruit Fly Claims in Florida*, Hearings Before a Subcommittee of the Committee on Agriculture, 73rd Congress, Second Session, pp. 6–21.

U.S. National Agricultural Statistics Service. *Agricultural Statistics*. Published annually. Washington, D.C.: Government Printing Office.

Books and Articles

Abbey, Kathryn T. "The Union Bank of Tallahassee." *Florida Historical Quarterly* 15, no. 4 (April 1937).

Adams, Chuck, Steve Jacob, and Suzanna Smith. "What Happened after the Net Ban?" University of Florida, Institute of Food and Agricultural Science Extension, February 2000. http://www.edis.ifas.ufl.edu/FE123.

Akerman, Joe A., Jr. *Florida Cowman: A History of Florida Cattle Raising*. Kissimmee: Florida Cattlemen's Association, 1976.

Akin, Edward N. *Flagler: Rockefeller Partner and Florida Baron*. Gainesville: University Press of Florida, 1992.

Alvarez, Jose, and Leo C. Palopolous. "The History of U.S. Sugar Protection." University of Florida, Institute of Food and Agricultural Science Extension, June 2002. http://www.edis.ifas.ufl.edu/SC019.

Amundson, Richard J. "The American Life of Henry Shelton Sanford." Ph. D. diss., Florida State University, Tallahassee, 1963.

Armbruster, Ann. *The Life and Times of Miami Beach*. New York: Alfred A. Knopf, 1995.

Aron, Cindy. *Working at Play*. New York: Oxford University Press, 1999.

Arsenault, Raymond. "The End of the Long Hot Summer: The Air Conditioner and Southern Culture." *Journal of Southern History* 50 (February–November 1984): 597–628.

———. *St. Petersburg and the Florida Dream, 1888–1950*. Gainesville: University Press of Florida, 1996.

Attaway, John A. *A History of Florida Citrus Freezes*. Lake Alfred: Florida Science Source, 1997.

———. *Hurricanes and Florida Agriculture*. Lake Alfred: Florida Science Source, Inc., 1999.

Attwood, George W. "The Fruits of Florida." In *Report of the Commissioner of Agriculture for the Year 1867*. Washington, D.C.: Government Printing Office, 186.

Avant, David A., Jr. *J. Randall Stanley's History of Gadsden County*. Tallahassee, Fla.: L'Avant Studios, 1985.

Baer, William N. *The Economic Development of the Cigar Industry in the United States*. Lancaster, Pa.: Art Printing Company, 1933.

Barbour, George M. *Florida for Tourists, Invalids, and Settlers*. New York: D. Appleton & Co., 1884.

Bass, C. A. "Historical Sketch of the D. D. Dummitt Grove at Allenhurst, Which Is

Supposed to Be the Oldest Grove in Florida." In *Proceedings of the Thirty-Ninth Annual Meeting of the Florida State Horticultural Society 1926*. Deland: Florida State Horticultural Society, 1926.

Bauer, Ruthmary. "Sarasota: Hardship and Tourism in the 1930s." *Florida Historical Quarterly* 76, no. 2 (Fall 1997): 135–151.

Bell, Harold W. *Glimpses of the Panhandle*. Chicago, Ill.: Adams Press, 1961.

Bellis, Mary. "Inventors of the Modern Computer: The First Hobby and Home Computers: Scelbi, Mark-8, Altair, IBM 5100." http://inventors.about.com/library/weekly/aa120198.htm.

Bennett, Russell W. "The Historical Development of the Lumber Industry in Florida." In *The Lumber Industry: Studies in Forestry Resources in Florida*, ed. A. Stuart Campbell and Robert C. Unkrich. Gainesville: University of Florida, 1932.

"Big Push for Florida Industries." *Florida Trend* 5, no. 12 (April 1963): 25–33.

Blake, Nelson Manfred. *Land into Water—Water into Land*. Tallahassee: University Presses of Florida, 1980.

Blakey, Arch Frederic. *The Florida Phosphate Industry: A History of the Development and Use of a Vital Mineral*. Cambridge, Mass.: Harvard University Press, 1973.

Bordo, Michael D., Claudia Golden, and Eugene N. White. *The Defining Moment: The Great Depression and the American Economy in the Twentieth Century*. Chicago: University of Chicago Press, 1998.

Bramson, Seth H. *Speedway to Sunshine: The Story of the Florida East Coast Railway*. Ontario, Canada: Boston Mills Press, 1984.

Breslauer, Ken. *Roadside Paradise: The Golden Age of Florida's Tourist Attractions, 1929–71*. St. Petersburg: RetroFlorida Inc., 2000.

Brinton, Daniel Garrison. *A Guide-Book of Florida and the South, for Tourists, Invalids, and Emigrants, with a Map of the St. Johns River*. Jacksonville, Fla.: Columbus Drew, 1869.

Brooks, T. J. *Soils and Fertilizers*. Tallahassee: Florida Department of Agriculture, 1936.

Brown, Dona. *Inventing New England: Regional Tourism in the Nineteenth Century*. Washington, D.C.: Smithsonian Press, 1995.

Brown, Canter, Jr. "The Florida Atlantic and Gulf Central Railroad, 1851–68." *Florida Historical Quarterly* 69, no. 4 (April 1991): 411–429.

———. *Fort Meade, 1849–1900*. Tuscaloosa: University of Alabama Press, 1995.

———. *In the Midst of All That Makes Life Worth Living: Polk County, Florida, to 1940*. Tallahassee, Fla.: Sentry Press, 2001.

"Broward County Florida, Reprint of a 1924 Tourist Brochure." *Broward Legacy* 22 (1999): 3–4.

Bruton, Quintilla Geer, and David E. Bailey, Jr. *Plant City: Its Origins and Its History*. Plant City, Fla.: East Hillsborough Historical Society, 1984.

Bulmer-Thomas, Victor. "The Wider Caribbean in the Twentieth Century: A Long Run Development Perspective." *Integration & Trade Journal* 15 (September–December 2001): 5–56.

Business Research & Economic Advisors. *The Contribution of the North American Cruise Industry to the U.S. Economy in 2000*. Exton, Pa.: Business Research & Economic Advisors for the International Council of Cruise Lines, 2002. http://www. iccl.org/resources/econstudy00.pdf.

Butcher, Harry C. "Florida's Phosphate: A Valuable Resource." In Florida Legislature, *Florida, an Advancing State, 1907–1917–1927: An Industrial Survey*, 215–229. Tallahassee: Florida Department of Agriculture, 1929.

Cabell, James Branch, and Alfred Jackson Hanna. *The St. Johns: A Parade of Diversities*. New York: Farrar and Rinehart, 1943.

Cain, Henry C., and James Francis. "Financing State Government." In *The Florida Handbook, 1985–86*, comp. Allen Morris, 143–151. Tallahassee: Peninsular Publishing Company, 1985.

Campbell, A. Stuart. *The Naval Stores Industry*. Gainesville: Bureau of Economic and Business Research, University of Florida, 1934.

Campbell, A. Stuart, and Robert C. Unkrich, *The Lumber Industry*. Gainesville: Bureau of Economic and Business Research, University of Florida, 1932.

Carse, James B., and James F. Foss. *Florida: Its Climate Soil, Productions, and Agricultural Capabilities*. Washington, D.C.: Government Printing Office, 1882.

Carter, Douglas R., and Erik J. Jokela. "Florida's Renewable Forest Resources." Gainesville; University of Florida, Institute of Food and Agricultural Sciences, 2002. http://www.edis.ifas.ufl.edu/FR143.

Carter, Luther J. *The Florida Experience: Land and Water Policy in a Growth State*. Baltimore, Md.: Johns Hopkins University Press, 1974.

Cash, W. T. *The Story of Florida*. Vol. 1. New York: American Historical Society, 1938.

Cato, James C., and Donald E. Sweat. "Fishing: Florida's First Industry." In *Conference on Florida's Maritime Heritage*, ed. Barbara A. Purdy, 32–36. Gainesville: Florida State Museum 1980.

"The Chase Papers." http://web.uflib.ufl.edu/spec/pkyonge/chase.htm.

Clark, Morita Mason. "The Development of the Florida Citrus Industry before 1895." M.A. Thesis, Florida State University, Tallahassee, 1947.

Colburn, David R. "Florida Politics in the Twentieth Century." In *The New History of Florida*, ed. Michael Gannon, 344–372. Gainesville: University Press of Florida, 1996.

Colburn, David R., and Lance deHaven-Smith. *Government in the Sunshine State*. Gainesville: University Press of Florida, 1999.

Commonwealth Fund. "Foundation History." http://www.cmwf.org.

"The Condominium: A New Lifestyle in Florida." *Florida Trend* 13, no. 6 (October 1970): 24–58.

"Condominium in Florida." *Florida Trend* 5, no. 5 (September 1962): 20–23.

Corbett, L. C. "Truck Farming in the Atlantic Coast States." In *Yearbook of the United States Department of Agriculture 1907*, 425–434. Washington, D.C.: Government Printing Office, 1908.

Covington, James W. "The Chicago Cubs Come to Tampa." *Tampa Bay History* 8, no. 1 (1986) 38–46.

———. *Henry B. Plant and the Tampa Bay Hotel*. Louisville, Ky.: Harmony House Publishers, 1990.

Cox, Marlin G. "David Sholtz: New Deal Governor of Florida." *Florida Historical Quarterly* 43, no. 2 (October 1964): 143–153.

Crawford, H. "Sugar: Many Questions Face Congress." *Food Update* 9 (1978): 16–19.

Crawford, William G., Jr. "Sam Maddox and the Florida Waterway." *Hearsay: The Newsletter of the Washington D.C. Bar Association* 5, no. 5 (November–December 2001): 9–10.

Cudahy, Brian J. *The Cruise Ship Phenomenon in North America.* Centreville, Md.: Cornell Maritime Press, 2001.

Curl, Donald W. "Boca Raton and the Florida Land Boom." *Tequesta* 46 (1986): 20–34.

Darragh, Charles. "Shakeout in Land Development!" *Florida Trend* 5, no. 12 (April 1963): 16–21.

Dau, Frederick W. *Florida Old and New.* New York: G. P. Putnam's Sons, 1934.

David, P. A. "Transport Innovation and Economic Growth: Professor Fogel On and Off the Rails." *Economic History Review* 22 (1969): 506–525.

Davis, T. Frederick. "The Disston Land Purchase." *Florida Historical Quarterly* 17, no. 3 (January 1939): 200–209.

———. "Early Orange Culture in Florida and the Epochal Cold of 1835." *Florida Historical Quarterly* 15, no. 4 (1937): 232–241.

———. *History of Jacksonville, Florida, and Vicinity, 1513 to 1924.* Gainesville, Fla.: University Press of Florida, 1964.

Dawson, Charles F. "Cattle Tick Eradication." In *Thirteenth Biennial Report of the Department of Agriculture of the State of Florida for the Years 1913–1914,* 163–186. Tallahassee, Fla.: T. J. Appleyard, 1915.

Dayton, William G. "A Short History of the San Antonio Area." 2000. http://www.sanantoniofla.com/history.

DeGrove, John Melvin. "The Administration of Internal Improvement Problems in Florida, 1845–69." Master's thesis, Emory University, 1954.

Denslow, David A., Ann C. Pierce, and Anne H. Shermyen, eds. *The Economy of Florida.* Gainesville: Bureau of Economic and Business Research, University of Florida, 1990.

Dickinson, Bob, and Andy Vladimir. *Selling the Sea: An Inside Look at the Cruise Industry.* New York: John Wiley and Sons, 1997.

Diettrich, Sigismond deR. "Florida's War Economy, I: Population Changes." *Economic Leaflets* 4, no. 11 (September 1945).

———. "Florida's War Economy, II: Economic Changes." *Economic Leaflets* 4, no. 11 (October 1945).

———, and Steve F. Hamilton. "Florida's Shrimp Industry." *Economic Leaflets* 10, no. 12 (November 1951).

Dillon, Rodney E., Jr. "South Florida in 1860." *Florida Historical Quarterly* 60, no. 4 (July 1982): 440–454.

Dodd, Dorothy. "The Florida Census of 1825." *Florida Historical Quarterly* 22, no. 1 (July 1943): 34–40.

———. "Florida in 1845." *Florida Historical Quarterly* 24, no. 1 (July 1945): 3–27.

———. "The Wrecking Business on the Florida Reef." *Florida Historical Quarterly* 22, no. 4 (April 1944): 171–199.

Dodson, Pat. "Hamilton Disston's St. Cloud Sugar Plantation, 1887–1901." *Florida Historical Quarterly* 49, no. 4 (April 1971): 356–369.

Donovan, C. H. "A Decade of Federal Expenditures in Florida." *Economic Leaflets* 1, no. 2 (January 1942).

———. "Florida's 1949 Revenue Program." *Economic Leaflets* 10, no. 1 (December 1950).

———. "How to Balance Florida's Budget." *Economic Leaflets* 8, no. 3 (February 1949).

———. "Sources of Florida's Tax Revenues." *Economic Leaflets* 6, no. 3 (February 1947).

Dorn, Harold W. "The Avocado Today in Dade County." In *Proceedings of the Twenty-Sixth Annual Meeting of the Florida State Horticultural Society, 1928*, 161–170 1928. Deland, Florida: Florida State Horticultural Society

Dovell, J. E. "The Everglades before Reclamation." *Florida Historical Quarterly* 26, no. 1 (July 1947): 1–43.

———. *Florida: Historic, Dramatic, Contemporary*. Vol. 2. New York: Lewis Historical Publishing Company, 1952.

———. "The Railroads and the Public Lands of Florida, 1879–1905." *Florida Historical Quarterly* 34, no. 3 (January 1956): 236–258.

Dunn, Hampton. *Yesterday's St. Petersburg*. Miami: E. A. Seemann Publishing, 1973.

DuPont, C. H. "History of the Introduction and Culture of Cuba Tobacco in Florida." *Florida Historical Quarterly* 6, no. 3 (January 1928): 149–155.

Earle, F. S. "Development of the Trucking Interests." In *Yearbook of the United States Department of Agriculture 1900*, 437–452. Washington, D.C.: Government Printing Office, 1901.

Eldridge, John G., and Oscar L. Durrance. *The Assessment of Real Estate for Purposes of Taxation: A Study in Local Government Taxation*. Economic Series 1, no. 1. Gainesville: University of Florida, Bureau of Economic Research, 1930.

Eliot, F. C. "The Everglades." In *Thirteenth Biennial Report of the Department of Agriculture of the State of Florida, 1913/1914*, 205–227. Tallahassee, Fla.: T. J. Appleyard, 1915.

English, Myrtle. "Davie: First Reclaimed Land in the Everglades." *Broward Legacy* 11, nos. 1–2 (1988): 29–32.

Eutsler, Roland B. "The Social Security Program in Florida." *Economic Leaflets* 1, no. 11 (October 1942).

Eyrich, Loren. "Old Dixie Highway." *Two Lane Roads* 32 (Summer 2002).

Federal Writers' Project. Work Projects Administration. *Florida's Sugar Bowl*. Tallahassee: Florida Department of Agriculture, 1939.

Fisher, Jerry M. *The Pacesetter: The Untold Story of Carl G. Fisher*. Fort Bragg, Calif.: Lost Coast Press, 1998.

Florida Bureau of Immigration. *Florida: A Pamphlet Descriptive of Its History, Topography, Climate, Soil, Resources and Natural Advantages*. Tallahassee: Floridian Book and Job Office, 1882.

Florida East Coast Hotel Company. *East Coast of Florida: The New Florida General Information and Hotel List, 1901–1902*. St. Augustine, Fla.: J. D. Rahner, 1901.

Florida Legislative Committee on Intergovernmental Relations. *Report on the Development of a State Urban Policy.* Tallahassee: Florida Legislative Committee on Intergovernmental Relations, 1998. http://www.floridalcir.gov/reports/urban98.pdf.

"Florida Technological Industries." *Florida Trend* 6, no. 8 (December 1963): 24–30.

"Florida's Growth Markets." *Florida Trend* 11, no. 12 (April 1969): 22–43.

"Florida's Land Development Giants." *Florida Trend* 5, no. 12 (August 1970): 16–30.

Fogel, R. W. "A Quantitative Approach to the Study of Railroads on American Economic Growth: A Report of Some Preliminary Findings." *Journal of Economic History* 22 (1962): 163–197.

Fry, Joseph A. *Henry S. Sanford: Diplomacy and Business in Nineteenth-Century America.* Reno: University of Nevada Press, 1982.

Gannon, Michael. *The New History of Florida.* Gainesville: University Press of Florida, 1996.

George Evans Company and Grant Advertising, Inc. *Tourist Studies in Florida, 1958.* Tallahassee: Florida Development Commission, 1959.

George, Paul S. "Passage to the New Eden: Tourism in Miami from Flagler through Everest G. Sewell." *Florida Historical Quarterly* 59, no. 4 (April 1981): 441–464.

Gibson, Campbell J., and Emily Lennon. "Historical Census Statistics on the Foreign-Born Population of the United States: 1850–1900." Population Division Working Paper no. 29. U.S. Bureau of the Census, Washington, D.C., 1999. http://www.census.gov/population/www/documentation/twps0029/twps0029.html.

Gohl, B. I. "Citrus By-Products for Animal Feed." *World Animal Review* 6 (1973): 24–27. http://www.fao.org/DOCREP/004/X6512E/X6512E08.htm.

Gold, Pleasant Daniel. *History of Volusia County, Florida.* Deland, Fla.: E. O. Painter Printing Co., 1927.

Graham, Thomas. "The Flagler Era, 1865–1913." In *The Oldest City: St. Augustine, Saga of Survival,* ed. Jean Parker Waterbury, 181–209. St. Augustine, Fla.: St. Augustine Historical Society, 1983.

Grismer, Karl H. *The Story of Sarasota.* Tampa: Florida Grower Press, 1946.

———. *The Story of St. Petersburg.* St. Petersburg, Fla.: P. K. Smith and Company, 1948.

Grossman, Peter Z. *American Express: The Unofficial History of the People Who Built the Great Financial Empire.* New York: Crown, 1987.

Hall, Thomas E., and J. David Ferguson. *The Great Depression.* Ann Arbor: University of Michigan Press, 1998.

Hanna, Alfred Jackson, and Kathryn Abbey Hanna. *Florida's Golden Sands.* Indianapolis: Bobbs-Merrill, 1950.

———. *Lake Okeechobee: Wellspring of the Everglades.* Indianapolis: Bobbs-Merrill, 1948.

Hardee, W. R. "Pineapples." In *Proceedings of the Twenty-Sixth Annual Meeting of the Florida State Horticultural Society, 1913,* 12–18. Deland: Florida Horticultural Society, 1913.

Harner, Charles E. *Florida's Promoters.* Tampa, Fla.: Trend House, 1973.

Harper, Roland. "Ante-Bellum Census Enumerations in Florida." *Florida Historical Quarterly* 6, no. 1 (July 1927): 42–52.

Harris, James A. "History of the Orange Industry in Florida." In *Proceedings of the*

Thirty-Sixth Annual Meeting of the Florida State Horticultural Society, 1923, 205–215. Deland, Fla: Florida Horticultural Society, 1923.

Hart, Ezequiel. "The U.S. Orange Juice Tariff and the 'Brazilian Invasion' of Florida," Master's Thesis, Fletcher School of Law and Diplomacy, Tufts University, March 2004. http://fletcher.tufts.edu/research/2004/Hart-Ezequiel.pdf.

Heitmann, John A. "The Beginnings of Big Sugar in Florida." *Florida Historical Quarterly* 77, no. 1 (1998): 39–61.

Henry Morrison Flagler Museum. "Henry Morrison Flagler Biography." http://www.flaglermuseum.us/html/flagler_biography.html.

Hines, Thomas S. "Architecture: The City Beautiful Movement." In *Encyclopedia of Chicago History*. http://www.encyclopedia.chicagohistory.org/pages/61.html.

"The History of Sunniland Corporation." http://www.sunniland.com/corporate/sunniland_history_early.php.

Hodges, Alan W., W. David Mulkey, Janaki R. Alavapati, Douglas R. Carter, and Clyde F. Kiker. *Economic Impacts of the Forest Industry in Florida*. Gainesville: Institute of Food & Agricultural Sciences, 2003. http://www.floridaforest.org/pdf/Foresty_Impact_Report.pdf.

Holmes, Dan. "From Cooperstown: A History of Spring Training." February 28, 2002. http://www.thebaseballpage.com/columns/holmes/020228.htm.

Huang, Sophia Wu. "Global Trade Patterns in Fruits and Vegetables." Agriculture and Trade Report No. WRS-04-01. Washington, D.C.: U.S. Department of Agriculture Economic Research Service, 2004.

Huebner, Hal. "The Cleveland Indians and Spring Training in Lakeland, Florida, 1923–27." *Tampa Bay History* 19, no. 1 (Spring/Summer 1997): 19–37.

Hume, H. Harold. *Citrus Fruits*. Rev. ed. New York: Macmillan, 1957.

Ingalls, Robert P., and Louis A. Perez, Jr. *Tampa Cigar Workers: A Pictorial History*. Gainesville: University Press of Florida, 2003.

Jackson, Larry K., and Frederick S. Davies. *Citrus Growing in Florida*. Gainesville: University Press of Florida, 1999.

Jahoda, Gloria. *River of the Golden Ibis*. New York: Holt, Rinehart and Wilson, 1973.

Jamison, F. S. "A Brief History of the Commercial Vegetable Industry." In *Proceedings of the Florida State Horticultural Society 75th Anniversary Meeting*, 75 234–235. Deland: Florida Horticultural Society 1962.

Jencks, L. H. "Railroad as an Economic Force in American Development." *Journal of Economic History* Vol. 4 (1944): 1–20.

Jerardo, Andy. "Import Share of U.S. Food Consumption Stable at 11 Percent." Outlook Report FAU7901. Washington, D.C.: United States Department of Agriculture, Economic Research Service, 2003. http://www.ers.usda.gov/publications/fau/july03/fau7901/.

"John D. Rockefeller, 1839–1937." archive.rockefeller.edu/bio/jdrsr.php.

Johns, John E. *Florida during the Civil War*. Gainesville: University of Florida Press, 1963.

Johnson, Dudley S. "The Florida Railroad after the Civil War." *Florida Historical Quarterly* 47, no. 3 (1969): 292–309.

————. "Henry Bradley Plant and Florida." *Florida Historical Quarterly* 45, no. 2 (October 1966): 118–131.

Johnson, Gwendolyn C. "Florida's Mineral Industry: an Historical Appraisal of a Phase of the Florida Economy." Master's thesis, Florida Agricultural and Mechanical University, 1957.

Joubert, William H. "Local Public Debt Policy in Florida: Part I." *Economic Leaflets* 3, no. 9, nos. 1–4 (August 1944): 1–2.

————. "Local Public Debt Policy in Florida: Part II." *Economic Leaflets* 3, no. 10 (September 1944).

"Jupiter Ridge History." http://www.pbcgov.com/erm/stewardship/jridgehistory.asp.

Kafoglis, Madelyn F. "Personal Income Received in Florida Counties: 1960." In University of Florida, Statistics of Personal Income, Population, Construction and Retail Trade for Florida Counties, State Economic Studies No. 14. Gainesville: Bureau of Economic and Business Research, University of Florida, 1962.B.

Keller, Melissa L. "Pitching for St. Petersburg: Spring Training and Publicity in the Sunshine City, 1914–18." *Tampa Bay History* 15, no. 2 (Fall/Winter 1993): 35–53.

Kells, A. S. "Early Days at Citra, Florida." In P*roceedings of the Thirty-first Annual Meeting of the Florida State Horticultural Society 1918*, 128–130. Deland: Florida Horticultural Society, 1918.

Kenny, Lawrence W. "The Labor Market." In *The Economy of Florida*, ed. David A. Denslow, Ann C. Pierce, Anne H. Shermyen, 93–108. Gainesville: Bureau of Economic and Business Research, University of Florida, 1990.

Kenny, Lawrence W., and J. F. (Dick) Scoggins. "The Labor Market." In *The Economy of Florida*, edited by J. F. (Dick) Scoggins and Ann C. Pierce, 53–70. Gainesville: Bureau of Economic and Business Research, University of Florida, 1995.Kent, Frederick H., III. "From the Commodore." *FYC Newswaves*, vol. 131, June 2007, 2.

————. "From the Commodore." *FYC Newswaves*, vol. 131, July 2007, 2.

————. "From the Commodore." *FYC Newswaves*, vol. 131, August 2007, 2.

Kerber, Stephen. "William Edwards and the Historic University of Florida Campus: A Photographic Essay." *Florida Historical Quarterly* 57, no. 3 (January 1979): 327–336.

Kirkpatrick, Wiley. "Personal Income Received in Florida Counties: 1958." In University of Florida, *Statistics of Personal Income, Population, Construction and Retail Trade for Florida Counties*. State Economic Studies no. 12. Gainesville: Bureau of Economic and Business Research, University of Florida, 1960.

Knetsch, Joe. "Hamilton Disston and the Development of Florida." *Sunland Tribune* 24, no. 1 (1998): 5–19. http://www.lib.usf.edu/ldsu/digitalcollections/S57/journal/v24n1_98/v24n1_98_005.pdf.

————. "The Impact of Drainage on the Development of Early Broward County." *Broward Legacy* 20 (1997): 1–2, 30–38.

————. "The Peonage Controversy and the Florida East Coast Railway." *Tequesta* 59 (1999): 5–29.

Koenig, John. "Putting off the Inevitable." *Florida Trend* (October 1987): 61–66.

Kuznets, Simon. *National Income and Its Composition, 1919–38*. New York: National Bureau of Economic Research, 1941.

LaGodna, Martin M. "Greens, Grist, and Guernseys: Development of the Florida State Agricultural Marketing System." *Florida Historical Quarterly* 53, no. 2 (October 1974): 146–163.

"Land Development." *Florida Trend* 12, no. 12 (April 1970): 100–104.

"Land Development Changes." *Florida Trend* 10, no. 12 (April 1968): 90–91.

Leading Men of London: A Collection of Biographical Sketches. London: British Biographical Company, 1895.

Lee, Henry. *The Tourist's Guide of Florida.* New York: Leve & Alden Printing Company, 1885.

Lenfestey, Hatty. *"An Elegant Frontier": Florida's Plant System Hotels.* Tampa, Fla.: Henry B. Plant Museum, 1999.

Lenze, David G. "Military Bases and Defense Manufacturing." In *The Economy of Florida,* ed. J. F. Scoggins and Ann C. Pierce, 211–227. Gainesville: Bureau of Economic and Business Research, University of Florida, 1995.

Limerick, Jeffrey, Nancy Ferguson, and Richard Oliver. *America's Grand Resort Hotels.* New York: Pantheon Books, 1979.

Lippincott, J. S. "Market Products of West New Jersey." In *Report of the Commissioner of Agriculture for the Year 1865.* Washington, D.C.: Government Printing Office, 1866.

Long, Durward. "Florida's First Railroad Commission 1887–1891." Part 2. *Florida Historical Quarterly* 42, no. 3 (January 1964): 248–257.

———. "The Open-Closed Shop Battle in Tampa's Cigar Industry, 1919–21." *Florida Historical Quarterly* 47, no. 2 (October 1968): 101–121.

Luttrell, Clifton P. "Food Production and Prices—Perspective and Outlook." *Federal Reserve Bank of St. Louis Monthly Review* (January 1976).

Malone, Nolan, Kaari F. Baluja, Joseph M. Costanzo, and Cynthia J. Davis. "The Foreign-Born Population: 2000." *Census 2000 Brief* (December 2003). http://www.census.gov/prod/2003pubs/c2kbr-34.pdf.

Marchman, Watt P. "The Ingraham Everglades Exploring Expedition, 1892." *Tequesta* 7 (1947): 3–43.

Marcus, Robert B. "A Brief Summary of Florida's Fisheries." *Economic Leaflets* 22, no. 12 (December 1963).

Martin, Richard A. *Eternal Springs: Man's 10,000 Years of History at Florida's Silver Springs.* St. Petersburg, Fla.: Great Outdoors Publishing Company, 1966.

Martin, Sidney Walter. *Florida during the Territorial Days.* Athens: University of Georgia Press, 1944.

———. *Florida's Flagler.* Athens: University of Georgia Press, 1949.

———. "Henry Morrison Flagler." *Florida Historical Quarterly* 25, no. 3 (January 1947): 257–276.

———. Matthews, Janet Snyder. "'He Has Carried His Life in His Hands': 'The Sarasota Assassination Society' of 1884." *Florida Historical Quarterly* 58, no. 1 (July 1979): 1–21.

Matthews, R. F. "Frozen Concentrated Orange Juice from Florida Oranges." Gainesville: University of Florida, Institute of Food and Agricultural Sciences, 1994. http://edis.ifas.ufl.edu/CH095.

McCally, David. *The Everglades: An Environmental History*. Gainesville: University Press of Florida, 1999.

McKay, A. W., H.W. Samson, R.R. Pailthrop, L.B. Flohr and L.C. Corbett, L.A. Hawkins, J.R. Maagness, H.P. Gould W. R. Beattie. "Marketing Fruits and Vegetables." In *Agricultural Yearbook, 1925*, 623–710.

McGovern, Joseph J. *The First Fifty Years*. Clewiston, Fla.: U.S. Sugar Corporation, 1982.

McLendon, H. S. "The Pineapple Industry in Florida and Its Future." In *Proceedings of the Twenty-Sixth Annual Meeting of the Florida State Horticultural Society 1920*, 92–97 Deland: Florida Horticultural Society, 1920.

McMakin, Dorothy Primrose. "General Henry Shelton Sanford and His Influence on Florida." Master's thesis, Stetson University, Deland, 1938.

McNutt, Bill. "Florida Grower Diversifies in Spite of Water, Development Pressures." *The Vegetable Growers News* (April 2002). http://www.vegetablegrowersnews.com.

Mealor, W. Theodore, Jr., and Merle C. Prunty. "Open-Range Ranching in Southern Florida." *Annals of the Association of American Geographers*, Vol. 66, No. 3 (Sept. 1976), 360–376.

Milanich, Jerald T. "Original Inhabitants." In *The New History of Florida*, ed. Michael Gannon, 1–15. Gainesville: University Press of Florida, 1996.

Milon, J. Walter. "Natural Resources and the Environment." In *The Economy of Florida*, ed. J. F. Scoggins and Ann C. Pierce, 157–169. Gainesville: Bureau of Economic and Business Research, University of Florida, 1995.

Moore, Thomas. "Mining." In *The Economy of Florida*, ed. David A. Denslow, Ann Pierce, and Anne H. Shermyen, 153–158. Gainesville: University of Florida, Bureau of Business and Economic Research, 1990.

———. "Mining Activity." In *The Economy of Florida*, ed. J. F. Scoggins and Ann C. Pierce, 263–273. Gainesville: University of Florida, Bureau of Business and Economic Research, 1995.

Mormino, Gary R. "Sunbelt Dreams and Altered States: A Social and Cultural History of Florida, 1950–2000." *Florida Historical Quarterly* 81, no. 1 (Summer 2002): 3–21.

———. "World War II." In *The New History of Florida*, ed. Michael Gannon, 323–343. Gainesville: University Press of Florida, 1996.

Mormino, Gary R., and George E. Pozzetta. *The Immigrant World of Ybor City*. Urbana: University of Illinois Press, 1998.

Morris, Allen, comp. *The Florida Handbook, 1949–50*. Tallahassee, Fla.: Peninsular Publishing Company, 1949.

———. *The Florida Handbook, 1985–86*. Tallahassee: Peninsular Publishing Company, 1985.

Mounts, M. U. "A History of Tomato Development in Florida." Seventy-ninth Annual Meeting. *Proceedings of the Florida State Horticultural Society* 79 (1966): 180–184 Deland: Florida Horticultural Society, 1966.

Mueller, Edward A. *Steamships of the Two Henrys*. DeLeon Springs, Fla.: E. O. Painter Printing Co., 1996.

Muir, Helen. *Miami, U.S.A.* New York: Henry Holt and Company, 1953.

New England Emigrant Aid Company. *Florida: The Advantages and Inducements Which It Offers to Immigrants.* Boston: Office of the Company, 1868.

"New Look for an Old Industry." *Florida Trend* 8, no. 3 (July 1965): 21–23.

"New Mines Take Shape." *Phosphorous & Potassium* (September–October 1995): 27–30.

Oemler, A. "Truck Farming." In *Report of the Commissioner of Agriculture, 1885,* 583–627. Washington, D.C.: Government Printing Office, 1885.

Olney, George Washington. *A Guide to Florida.* New York: Cushing, Bardua & Co., 1873. http://www.palmm.fcla.edu/fh/.

Ormond Beach Historical Trust. *Ormond Beach.* Charleston, S.C.: Arcadia Publishing, 1999.

Orser, Frank. "'Florida and the British Investor' Revisited: The William Moore Angas Papers at the University of Florida." *Florida Historical Quarterly* 72, no. 2 (October 1993): 181–189.

Osterbind, Carter C., and Elise C. Jones. "A Short Report on Florida's Commercial Fisheries." *Economic Leaflets* 14, no. 12 (1955).

Paisley, Clifton. *From Cotton to Quail: An Agricultural Chronicle of Leon County, Florida 1860–1967.* Tallahassee: University Press of Florida, 1981.

———. "Madison County's Sea Island Cotton Industry, 1870–1916." *Florida Historical Quarterly* 54, no. 3 (January 1976): 285–306.

———. *The Red Hills of Florida.* Tuscaloosa: University of Alabama Press, 1969.

Pando, Robert T. "Shrouded in Cheesecloth: The Demise of Shade Tobacco in Florida and Georgia." Master's thesis, Florida State University, 2003.

"Paper: The Florida Product You Throw Away." *Florida Trend* (December 1967):16–20, 23.

Parker, Randall E. *Reflections on the Great Depression.* Cheltenham, UK: Edward Elgar, 2002.

Patterson, Gordon. "Raising Cane and Refining Sugar: Florida Crystals and the Fame of Fellsmere." *Florida Historical Quarterly* 75, no. 4 (Spring 1997): 408–428.

Penny, N. O. "Shipping and Growing of Vegetables." In *Proceedings of the Twenty-first Annual Meeting of the Florida State Horticultural Society 1908.* Deland: Florida Horticultural Society, 1908, 183–185.

Pettengill, George W., Jr. *The Story of the Florida Railroads, 1834–1903.* Railway & Locomotive Historical Society Bulletin no. 86. Boston: Railway & Locomotive Historical Society, Baker Library, Harvard Business School, 1952.

"Phosphate Spruces Up, Courts the World." *Florida Trend* (April 1974):289–295

"Phosphate's Expansion Boom." *Florida Trend* (April 1965):36 –38.

Poyo, Gerald A. "The Cuban Experience in the United States, 1865–1940: Migration, Community, Identity." In *Cuban Studies 21,* ed. Louis A. Pérez, 19–36. Pittsburgh: University of Pittsburgh Press, 1991.

"Questions on Feed Cost." *Swine News* 19, no. 6 (July 1996).

Radcliffe, Lewis. "Fisheries of Florida." In Florida Legislature, *Florida, an Advancing State, 19079–19179–1927: An Industrial Survey,* 227–235. Tallahassee: Florida Department of Agriculture, 1929.

Rainard, R. Lyn. "Ready Cash on Easy Terms: Local Responses to the Depression in Lee County." *Florida Historical Quarterly* 64, no. 3 (1986): 284–300.

"The Real Estate Industry." *Florida Trend* 10, no. 3 (July 1967): 20–32.

Redford, Polly. *Billion Dollar Sandbar*. New York: E. P. Dutton, 1970.

"Regulations, Reclamations & Rising Costs." *Phosphorous & Potassium* (July–August 1995): 18–23.

Rerick, Rowland H. *Memoirs of Florida*. 2 vols. Atlanta: Southern Historical Association, 1902.

Richmond, Mrs. Henry L. "Emerson in Florida." *Florida Historical Quarterly* 18, no. 2, (October 1939): 75–83.

Robinson, T. Ralph. "Count Odette Phillippi: A Correction to Florida's Citrus History." In *Proceedings of the Sixtieth Annual Meeting of the Florida State Horticultural Society 1947*, 90–92. Deland: Florida Horticultural Society 1947.

———. "Some Aspects of the History of Citrus in Florida." *Quarterly Journal of the Florida Academy of Sciences* 8, no. 1 (1945): 59–66.

———. Rogers, Ben F. "Florida in World War II: Tourists and Citrus." *Florida Historical Quarterly* 39, no. 1 (July 1960): 34–41.

Rogers, William W. "The Great Depression." In *The New History of Florida*, ed. Michael Gannon, 304–322. Gainesville: University Press of Florida, 1994.

Rolfs, P. H. "Founders and Foundations of Florida Agriculture." In *Proceedings of the Florida State Horticultural Society 1935*, 129–137. Deland: Florida Horticultural Society, 1935.

Rosenberger, Stanley Eugene. "A History of the Florida Vegetable Industry and State Farmers' Markets for Vegetables." Ph. D. diss., University of Florida, 1962.

Rue, Frank B., and Charles A. Mazzuchelli. "Manganese Sulphate." In T. J. Brooks, *Soils and Fertilizers*, 155–159. Tallahassee: Florida Department of Agriculture, 1936.

Russell, Marilyn C. *Classic Crates from Florida*. Winter Haven: Florida Citrus Showcase, 1985.

Sampson, F. G. "Pioneering in Orange and Lemon Culture in Florida." In *Proceedings of the Thirty-Sixth Annual Meeting of the Florida State Horticultural Society 1923*, 193–197. Deland: Florida Horticultural Society, 1923.

Sanford Historical Society. *Images of America*. Charleston, S.C.: Arcadia Publishing, n.d.

Schertz, Lyle P. "The Year of Economics: World Food: Prices and the Poor." *Foreign Affairs*, vol. 52, no. 3: (April 1974), 511–537.

Schumann, Richard E. "Compensation from World War II through the Great Society." *Compensation and Working Conditions* (Fall 2001): 23–27. http://www.bls.gov/opub/cwc/cm20030124ar04p1.htm.

Schwartz, Charles F., and Robert E. Graham, Jr. "Personal Income by States, 1929–54." *Survey of Current Business* 35 (September 1955): 12–22.

Scoggins, J. F., and Ann C. Pierce, eds. *The Economy of Florida*. Gainesville: Bureau of Economic and Business Research, University of Florida, 1995.

Semes, Aretta. "From Rising Sun to Daunting Storm: Miami in Boom and Bust: A Reminiscence." *Tequesta* 58 (1998): 100–106.

Sessa, Frank Bowman. "Real Estate Expansion in Miami and Its Environs during the 1920s." Ph.D. diss., University of Pittsburgh, 1950.

Sharp, Helen R. "Samuel A. Swann and the Development of Florida, 1855–1900." *Florida Historical Quarterly* 20, no. 2 (October 1941): 169–196.

Shaw, Samuel P., and C. Gordon Fredine. *Wetlands of the United States: Their Extent and Their Value to Waterfowl and Other Wildlife*. Department of the Interior Circular 69. Washington, D.C.: U.S. Department of the Interior, 1956. http://www.npwrc.usgs.gov/resource/wetlands/uswetlan/index.htm.

Shofner, Jerrell H. "Alfred I. Du Pont: His Impact on Florida." *Florida Historical Quarterly* 69, no. 3 (1991): 335–347.

———. "Florida and the Black Migration." *Florida Historical Quarterly* 57, no. 3 (1979): 268–289.

———. *History of Jefferson County*. Tallahassee, Fla.: Sentry Press, 1976.

———. *Nor Is It Over Yet: Florida in the Era of Reconstruction, 1863–77*. Gainesville: University Press of Florida, 1974.

Shofner, Jerrell H., and William Warren Rogers. "Confederate Railroad Construction: The Live Oak to Lawton Connector." *Florida Historical Quarterly* 43, no. 3 (January 1965): 218–229.

Siebert, Wilbur. "The Early Sugar Industry in Florida." *Florida Historical Quarterly* 35, no. 4 (April 1957): 312–319.

Sisto, Bénédicte. "Miami's Land Gambling Fever of 1925." *Tequesta*, no. 59 (1999): 52–73.

Sitterson, J. Carlyle. *Sugar Country: The Cane Sugar Industry in the South, 1753–1950*. Lexington: University of Kentucky Press, 1953.

Smith, Thomas Buckingham. *Report on Reconnaissance of the Everglades, Made to the Secretary of the Treasury, June 1848*. Senate Report 242. 30th Congress, 1st Session, August 12, 1848.

Smyth, G. Hutchison. *The Life of Henry Bradley Plant*. New York: G. P. Putnam's Sons, 1898.

Spector, Lincoln. "PC History: The PC at 20." http://pcworld.about.com/magazine/1908p133id52503.htm.

Speer, H. L. "The Vegetable Deal in the Muck Lands of Palm Beach County." In *Proceedings of the Florida State Horticultural Society 1951*, 122–25. Deland: Florida Horticultural Society, 1951.

"Spring Training History." http://www.springtrainingonline.com/features/history_1.htm.

Stearns, Peter N. "Dominican Republic, 1882–1899." In *The Encyclopedia of World History: Ancient, Medieval and Modern*. 6th ed. Boston: Houghton, Mifflin, 2001–2004.

———. "Haiti, 1859–67." In *The Encyclopedia of World History: Ancient, Medieval and Modern*. 6th ed. Boston: Houghton, Mifflin, 2001–2004.

Steig, Stacy. "A Look into the Past." http://www.coralgableschamber.org/discover/index.asp.

Sterngrass, John. *First Resorts*. Baltimore, Md.: Johns Hopkins University Press, 2001.

Stevens, H. B. "Reminiscences of a Pioneer Orange Grower." In *Proceedings of the Thirty-First Annual Meeting of the Florida State Horticultural Society 1918*, 138–140. Deland: Florida Horticultural Society, 1918.

Stowe, Harriet Beecher. *Palmetto Leaves*. 1873; Gainesville: University Press of Florida, 1999.

Straub, W. L. *History of Pinellas County.* St. Augustine, Fla.: The Record Company, 1929.

Swisher International. "Corporate History." http://www.swisher.com.

Tash, Paul. "The Services Tax: We Should Have Quit While We Were Ahead." *Florida Trend* (April 1990): 78.

Taylor, Laura B. "Romance of Payne's Prairie." *Beautiful Florida* 5, no. 8, April 1929.

Taylor, William A. "The Fruit Industry and Substitution of Domestic for Foreign-Grown Fruits." In *Yearbook of the United States Department of Agriculture 1897,* 305–344. Washington, D.C.: Government Printing Office, 1898.

Tebeau, Charlton. *A History of Florida.* Coral Gables: University of Miami Press 1971.

Temin, Peter. *Did Monetary Forces Cause the Great Depression?* New York: W. W. Norton, 1976.

Thornsbury, Suzanne, Mark Brown, and Thomas Spreen. "U.S. Fresh Citrus and Global Markets." EDIS Publication FE 325. Gainesville: University of Florida, Institute of Food and Agricultural Sciences Extension, 2000.

Tischendorf, Alfred P. "Florida and the British Investor, 1880–1914." *Florida Historical Quarterly* 33, no. 2 (October 1954): 120–129.

"Trailer-Way of Life Shows Growth." *Florida Trend* 9, no. 5 (September 1966): 6.

Tyler, Daniel F. *Where to Go in Florida.* New York: Hopcraft, 1881.

Vanderblue, Homer B. "The Florida Land Boom." *Journal of Land and Public Utility Economics* 3, no. 2 (May 1927): 113–131.

Visit Florida. *2002 Florida Visitor Study.* Tallahassee: Visit Florida, 2003.

Walker, Seth S. "The Canning of Grapefruit." In *Proceedings of the Thirty-Sixth Annual Meeting of the Florida State Horticultural Society, 1923,* 84–90. Deland: Florida Horticultural Society, 1923.

Wall, Joseph Frazier, *Alfred I. du Pont: The Man and His Family.* New York: Oxford University Press, 1990.

Walvin, James. *Beside the Seaside.* London: Allen Lane, 1978.

Ward, James Robertson. *Old Hickory's Town: An Illustrated History of Jacksonville.* 2nd ed. Jacksonville: Old Hickory's Town, Inc., 1985.

Warner, S. C. "Development of Marketing Citrus Fruits in Florida." In *Proceedings of the Thirty-Sixth Annual Meeting of the Florida State Horticultural Society 1923,* 198–200. Deland: Florida Horticultural Society, 1923.

Waterbury, Jean Parker, ed. *The Oldest City: St. Augustine, Saga of Survival.* St. Augustine: St. Augustine Historical Society, 1983.

Webber, Herbert J. "The Two Freezes of 1894–95 in Florida and What They Teach." In *Yearbook of the United States Department of Agriculture 1895.* Washington, D.C.: Government Printing Office, 1896. 159–174.

———. "Whence and Whither the Citrus Industry?" *Proceedings of the Fiftieth Annual Meeting of the Florida State Horticultural Society,* 1937, 6–17. Deland: Florida Horticultural Society, 1937.

Weeks, Jerry Woods. "Florida Gold: The Emergence of the Florida Citrus Industry, 1865–95." Ph.D. diss., University of North Carolina, Chapel Hill, 1977.

Weidling, Phillip J., and August Burghard. *Checkered Sunshine: The Story of Fort Lauderdale 1793–1955.* Gainesville: University Press of Florida, 1966.

Weinberger, Julius. "Economic Aspects of Recreation." *Harvard Business Review* 15, no. 4 (Summer 1937): 448–463.

Wenzel, F. W., C. D. Atkins, and Edwin L. Moore. "Frozen Concentrated Orange Juice—Past, Present and Future." In *Proceedings of the Sixty-Second Annual Meeting of the Florida State Horticultural Society, 1949*. Deland: Florida Horticultural Society, 1949. 179–183.

"What National Defense Means to Florida's Economy." *Florida Trend* 8, no. 8 (December 1965): 18–25.

"What Would Peace Do to the Florida Economy?" *Florida Trend* 10, no. 11 (March 1968): 12–16.

"Whatever Happened to the Dixie Highway?" http://www.us-highways.com/dixiehwy.htm.

"What's Happening in Florida's Real Estate?" *Florida Trend* 5, no. 12 (June 1964): 22–33.

Williams, John Lee. *A View of West Florida*. 1827; reprint, Gainesville: University Press of Florida, 1976.

Williams, Edwin D., Jr. "Florida in the Union, 1845–61." Ph.D. diss., University of North Carolina, 1951.

Williamson, Edward C. "William D. Chipley, West Florida's Mr. Railroad." *Florida Historical Quarterly* 25, no. 4 (April 1947): 333–355.

Writers' Program (Fla.). University of Florida. Florida Department of Agriculture. *Iceberg Lettuce: The Story of Florida's Decline and Recovery as a Winter Lettuce Producing State*. Tallahassee: Florida Board of Agriculture, 1941.

Zahniser, Steven, and John Link. "Effects of North American Free Trade Agreement on Agriculture and the Rural Economy." Agriculture and Trade Report WRS0201. Washington, D.C.: U.S. Department of Agriculture Economic Research Service, 2002.

Ziegler, Edwin A. "Florida's Forest Land and Forest Industry." *Economic Leaflets* 5, no. 5 (1946): 1–4.

Ziewitz, Kathryn, and June Wiaz. *Green Empire: The St. Joe Company and the Remaking of the Florida Panhandle*. Gainesville: University Press of Florida, 2004.

Index

332   *Index*

Earnings: compared with personal income, 124; farm 1947, 148–49; Florida and nation 1929, 125; Florida and nation in 1929–1933, 128–30; Florida and nation 1946–49, 147–9; Florida and nation in 1960–1967, 186–9; Florida and nation in 1983–1989, 220–21; industries 1960, 166–67; tourism-retirement earnings defined, 130. *See also* military payroll; tourism

Economic base: 1900–1930 history, 111; 1930–1960 history, 168–69; 1960–1980 history, 204; 1980–2000 history, 243–44; changing composition in 20th century, 263–65; composition in 1900, 20; decline in importance in 20th century, 265–66; defined, 13

Economic recession: in 1938, 143; in 1957–1958, 163; in 1960–1961, 164; in 1973–1975, 199–201; in 1980–1981, 219–20; in 1982, 220–21; in 1990–1991, 228–31

Education finances: 1947 program, 151; impact of depression on, 137–38

Environmental issues: and economic development, 258; and comprehensive planning 1970s, 195; in phosphate industry, 257–58; in Zellwood vegetable production, 248

Everglades: 1948 drainage program, 150; Bolles land sale, 32–33; Broward financing plans, 31–32; early drainage plans, 30; Drainage District reorganized, 34–35

Federal Housing Institutions, 156

Fisher, Carl Graham: and Dixie Highway, 87–88; develops Miami Beach, 128–29; early years, 87, Lincoln Highway, 87

Fishing: 1900–1930 history, 120–21; 1930–1960 history, 176–79; 1960–1980 history, 213–14; 1980–2000 history, 251–52; production in 1900, 15. *See also* sponge fishery

Flagler, Henry Morrison: constructs railroad on East Coast, 49–51; constructs railroad overseas, 52; early years, 45–46; luxury hotels, 81–83; purchases Florida railroads, 48–49; ships, 51; and Standard Oil, 46–47

Florida East Coast and Canal Company, 51

Fort Lauderdale, finger islanding, 95

Freezes: 1835, 57; 1886, 59; 1894–1895, 63–65; 1957–1958, 175; 1962, 187–88, 205; 1977, 208; seven freezes between 1981 and 1989, 224–25

Frontier industries: 1900–1930 history, 111; 1930–1960 history, 179–80; 1960–1980 history, 214; composition 1900, 13; defined, 13

Grapefruit. *See* citrus

Great Depression: causes, 127–28; earnings and income, 128–29; impact on banks, 131–33; impact on local government finances, 133–36; impact on school finances, 136–38; Roosevelt programs and recovery, 176–77; stronger recovery in Florida, 177–78; transmission mechanism, 139–40; turnaround in tourism 1932–1939, 140–41

Hastings, potatoes, 73–74

Hotels. *See* tourism

Hurricanes: 1926 and 1928, 35–36, 102; 1947, 148–49; Donna in 1960, 187

Illiteracy in 1900, 7–8

Ingraham, J. C., employee of Sanford, 43; explores Everglades, 50–51; hired by Flagler, 51–52; and South Florida Railroad, 43

Internal Improvement Fund, activities after Civil War, 25–26; adjustment of railroad claims, 30–32; enabling Act, 23; lands transferred after 1880, 30; pre–Civil War projects, 23

International immigration, 1960–2000, 232–36

Jennings, W. S., 30–31

Lake Worth Drainage District, 34

Land Boom: 1926 hurricane, 102; bad publicity, 101–2; effect of collapse on banks, 105–7; effect of collapse on local government finances, 104–5; effect on per capita income 102–3; effect on state finances, 104; facilitated by speculation, 97–99; stimulated by easy monetary policy, 98; tight money and collapse, 100; transportation bottlenecks, 101

Lawtey strawberries, 71

Levy, H. Irwin, 196

Lincoln Highway. *See* Fisher, Carl Graham

Local Government Finance: impact of Great Depression, 133–36; impact of Land Boom, 104–5

William B. Stronge is professor emeritus of economics at Florida Atlantic University, where he was a member of the Department of Economics for thirty-five years. He is a senior fellow in economics at the university's Catanese Center for Urban and Environmental Solutions and is the author of numerous studies of the Florida economy.